THE INNER CITY

THE INNER CITY

Urban Poverty and Economic Development in the Next Century

Edited by
Thomas D. Boston and
Catherine L. Ross

Transaction Publishers
New Brunswick (U.S.A.) and London (U.K.)

Fourth printing 2001

Library of Congress Catalog Number: 96–50096
ISBN: 1–56000–980–2
Printed in the United States of America

Library of Congress Cataloging-in-Publication Data

The inner city : urban poverty and economic development in the next
    century / edited by Thomas D. Boston and Catherine L. Ross
        p.   cm.
    "Originally published as fall/winter 1996 issue of The review of Black
political economy, vol. 25, no. 2/3"—T.p. verso.
        Includes bibliographical references.
        ISBN 1-56000-980-2 (paper : alk. paper)
        1. Urban poor—United States. 2. Urban policy—United States. 3.
    Inner cities—United States. I. Boston, Thomas D. II. Ross, Catherine
    Laverne, 1948—
HV4045.I58   1997
338.973'009173'2—dc21   96-50096
                                                                CIP

Contents

Co-Editors' Introduction   3
Abstracts of Contributions and Profiles of the Authors   7

PART I: Responses from the Academy   27

1. Economic Development Strategies for the Inner City:
    The Need for Governmental Intervention   29
    Susan S. Fainstein and Mia Gray

2. Entrepreneurship and the Advantages of the Inner City:
    How to Augment the Porter Thesis   39
    John Sibley Butler

3. Business Strategy and Access to Capital in Inner-City
    Revitalization   51
    Gary A. Dymski

4. Rebuilding Inner Cities: Basic Principles   67
    June Manning Thomas

5. Déjà-vu All Over Again: Porter's Model of Inner-City
    Redevelopment   75
    David S. Sawicki and Mitch Moody

6. Taking Back the Inner City: A Review of Recent Proposals   95
    William W. Goldsmith

7. Political Economy of Urban Poverty in the 21st Century:
    How Progress and Public Policy Generate Rising Poverty   111
    Timothy Bates

8. Promoting Economic Development in the Inner City: The
    Importance of Human Resources   123
    Carla J. Robinson-Barnes

9.   The Porter Model of Competitive Advantage for
     Inner-City Development: An Appraisal   131
     C. Michael Henry

10. Michael Porter: New Gilder of Ghettos   161
     Edward J. Blakely and Leslie Small

11. Revitalizing the Inner City: A Holistic Approach   185
     Usha Nair Reichert

12. Reparations and the Competitive Advantage of
     Inner Cities   193
     Richard F. America

13. Potential Welfare Gains from Improving Economic
     Conditions in the Inner City   207
     James Peoples

14. Is the Inner City Competitive?   213
     Margaret C. Simms and Winston J. Allen

PART II: Responses from Community Service Providers   221

15. Overview of the Initiative for a Competitive Inner City 223
     Initiative for a Competitive Inner City

16. Making Comparative Advantage Work for Economic
     Opportunity   233
     *William Schweke, Corporation for Enterprise
     Development*

17. Economic Development or Social Development?
     A Strategy for Rebuilding Inner Cities   251
     Arnold Graf, Industrial Areas Foundation

18. Mr. Porter's "Competitive Advantage" for Inner-City
     Revitalization: Exploitation or Empowerment?   259
     *James H. Johnson, Jr., Walter C. Farrell, Jr.,
     and Geraldine R. Henderson, Urban Investment
     Strategies Center*

19. A Dialogue on The Atlanta Project with Jane Smith,
     Executive Director   291
     Jane Smith, The Atlanta Project

PART III: Responses from Michael Porter and the Editors   301

20. An Economic Strategy for America's Inner Cities:
    Addressing the Controversy   303
    Michael E. Porter

21. Location Preferences of Successful African
    American-Owned Businesses in Atlanta   337
    Thomas D. Boston and Catherine L. Ross

The Inner City

CO-EDITORS' INTRODUCTION

Thomas D. Boston and Catherine L. Ross

We are pleased to present these unique essays that respond to Michael Porter's widely discussed and influential article entitled "The Competitive Advantage of the Inner City."[1] These essays, written by some of the nation's most distinguished urban scholars and practitioners, were originally published as a special issue of *The Review of Black Political Economy*. To make the material accessible to a broad audience, Transaction graciously agreed to publish the special issue in book form. We are particularly grateful to the authors for complying with the solicitation in such a quick fashion. Their response is a measure of the importance and timeliness of inner-city revitalization issues. It is also a measure of the impact that Michael Porter's ideas are having on the nation's urban scholars and practitioners.

Few people who have a genuine interest in the inner city will come away from reading Porter's research feeling the same as they did previously. Some will endorse his prescriptions wholeheartedly. Others will accept his ideas with qualifications. Still, some readers are quite vocal in their opposition to Porter's views. Despite these differing opinions, Porter usually manages to prompt all of his readers to search for new solutions to inner-city distress or to reassess their current approaches. These various opinions are represented in the essays that follow.

We thank each contributor, and we thank Michael Porter for taking time out of his very busy schedule to respond. His research has ignited more discussion and activity on the inner city than perhaps any since the publication of William Julius Wilson's *The Truly Disadvantaged*.[2]

In "The Competitive Advantage of the Inner City," Porter makes the bold assertion that:

> Past efforts have been guided by a social model built around meeting the needs of individuals. Aid to inner cities, then has largely taken the form of relief programs such as income assistance, housing subsidies, and food stamps, all of which address highly visible— and real—social needs.

Programs aimed more directly at economic development have been fragmented and ineffective. These piecemeal approaches have usually taken the form of subsidies, preference programs, or expensive efforts to stimulate economic activity in tangential fields such as housing, real estate, and neighborhood development. Lacking an overall strategy, such programs have treated the inner city as an island isolated from the surrounding economy and subject to its own unique laws of competition. . . .

The time has come to recognize that revitalizing the inner city will require a radically different approach. While social programs will continue to play a critical role in meeting human needs and improving education, they must support—and not undermine—a coherent economic strategy. The question we should be asking is how inner-city-based businesses and nearby employment opportunities for inner city residents can proliferate and grow. A sustainable economic base *can* be created in the inner city, but only as it has been created elsewhere: through private, for-profit, initiatives and investment based on economic self-interest and genuine competitive advantage—not through artificial inducements, charity, or government mandates.

We must stop trying to cure the inner city's problems by perpetually increasing social investment and hoping for economic activity to follow. Instead, an economic model must begin with the premise that inner city businesses should be profitable and positioned to compete on a regional, national, and even international scale. . . .[3]

After surveying past approaches that he considers to be partial or total failures, Porter proposes what he considers to be a radically different approach to revitalizing the inner city. The key, he argues, is that these areas have certain competitive advantages, among which are their strategic location, unmet local demand, capacity to become integrated into regional clusters, and human resources. Porter describes how tapping these advantages, in conjunction with the normal operation of competitive markets, can lead to revitalized inner cities.

As co-editors of this special issue, we will not attempt to summarize or offer judgment on Porter's views or on those of his proponents and opponents. These authors speak clearly for themselves in the following pages. What we have done, however, is to organize a special section of this *Review* that presents the abstract of each contribution along with a profile of the authors. This section precedes the essays.

In assembling this special issue, we were not content to have contributions only from academicians. Instead, we also wanted to hear from practitioners. Therefore, we invited five community service organizations, whose primary focus is the inner city, to present their perspectives on Porter's ideas as well as their organization's strategy for inner-city revitalization. The organizations are: the Initiative for a Competitive Inner City, The Corporation for Enterprise Development, the Urban Investment Strategies Center, and The Atlanta Project. Each brings a unique perspective to the debate.

We asked authors to either respond to Porter's ideas on inner-city revitalization, or to present their own ideas by drawing upon their previous research and experiences. The only qualification was that the contributions should be written in a style that is accessible to a general audience. Hence, they were discouraged from employing the kind of empirical rigor that is usually found in *The Review*. Our hope is that policy analysts, practitioners, scholars and general readers will be able to understand these essays fully.

The idea of organizing this special issue did not originate with the co-editors but rather with Earl Graves and the editors of *Black Enterprise Magazine*. At a recent meeting of the Board of Economists of *Black Enterprise*, Barbara Paige, Executive Director of the Initiative for a Competitive Inner City, was invited to engage in a roundtable discussion on Porter's ideas. Having participated in that discussion, we realized the value that a special issue such as this could make to the overall debate.[4]

We thank those individuals who have helped to make this possible. We thank Donna Kronemeyer of Transaction Publishers for her patience with a process that has taken several months longer than anticipated. We also look forward to this collection of essays being published by Transaction in book form. We thank Whitney Tilson of the Initiative for a Competitive Inner City for his indispensable assistance in coordinating Michael Porter's contribution. We thank Michelle Lopez and Krista Tillery for their research assistance. We also thank the publisher and the editorial board of *The Review* for agreeing to accept our suggestion to redesign the cover of *The Review* by having it feature the work of a prominent African American artist. But above all, we thank Jacob Lawrence, one of the worlds most distinguished artists, for allowing us to use his outstanding print entitled *The Library* to illustrate the journal cover for this special issue. For well over a half century, Lawrence's art has chronicled the history of African Americans, especially their urban experiences. As a result of this, the co-editors wish to dedicate this special issue of *The Review* to Jacob Lawrence and to his wife Gwendolyn Lawrence, whose lifelong devotion has made Jacob's contribution possible. For all that you have done for us, Jacob and Gwendolyn, "this one is for you."

NOTES

1. Michael E. Porter, "The Competitive Advantage of the Inner City" *Harvard Business Review* (May–June, 1995): 55–71.

2. William Julius Wilson, *The Truly Disadvantaged: The Inner City, The Underclass, and Public Policy* (Chicago: University of Chicago Press, 1987).

3. Porter, op. cit., 55–56.

4. Mark Lowery, "Revitalizing Inner Cities," *Black Enterprise* (Board of Economists Report), Vol. 26 (January, 1996): 64–67.

Abstracts of Contributions and Profiles of the Authors*

---

* The arrangement of abstracts corresponds to the table of contents. Each abstract is followed by the author's profile.

Economic Development Strategies for the Inner City: The Need for Governmental Intervention

by Susan S. Fainstein and Mia Gray

inner-cityFederal inner-city programs have always been based on the assumption that the private sector holds the key to urban revitalization. Michael Porter's critique of existing programs, therefore, incorrectly accuses them of failing to nurture private business. Nevertheless, he does provide useful direction in stressing the importance of strategic location, regional clusters, and human resources. The example of Hunts Point Food Distribution Center in the South Bronx is used both to indicate that Porter does identify the comparative advantage of such areas and also to show the need for a much stronger governmental role than Porter describes.

AboutAbout the Authors:**

SusanSusan S. Fainstein is Professor of Urban Planning and Policy Development at Rutgers University. She has written extensively on urban redevelopment and comparative political economy. Her latest book is *The City Builders* (Cambridge, MA, and Oxford, UK: Blackwell, 1994). She recently completed a three-year evaluation of Minneapolis's Neighborhood Revitalization Program, sponsored by the McKnight Foundation. (Urban Planning & Policy Development, Rutgers University, 33 Livingston Ave., New Brunswick, NJ 08901.)

MiaMia Gray is a Ph.D. candidate in the Department of Urban Planning and Policy Development at Rutgers University. She is writing her thesis on the economic role of the medical services and pharmaceutical industry complex in the New York region. (Urban Planning & Policy Development, Rutgers University, 33 Livingston Ave., New Brunswick, NJ 08901.)

Entrepreneurship and the Advantages of the Inner City: How to Augment the Porter Thesis

by John Sibley Butler

Michael Porter's work brings back to the public square the importance of a business, rather than social model, for solving many of the problems of the inner city. His model is grounded in the economic philosophy of Booker T. Washington, which stood at the center of the black community for generations and thus are not new. Porter's ideas, however, do not have a strong enough emphasis on inner-city residents owning enterprises. This article argues that self-employment of inner-city residents is imperative and would allow inner-city residents to become full players in the quest for revitalizing cities in America.

About the Author:
John Sibley Butler is Dallas TACA Centennial Professor in Liberal Arts (sociology) and the Arthur James Douglass Centennial Professor in Entrepreneurship and Small Business in the Graduate School of Business (management) at the University of Texas at Austin. His work is in organizational behavior (military) and entrepreneurship. His latest book is *Entrepreneurship and Self-Help among Black Americans: A Reconsideration of Race and Economics*. (University of Texas, Austin, Department of Sociology/Business, Burdine Hall, Rm 336, Austin, Texas 78712.)

Business Strategy and Access to Capital in Inner-City Revitalization

by Gary A. Dymski

Michael Porter suggests that inner-city economic revitalization depends on making the inner city more open to market forces, and more attractive to large firms, while eliminating inefficient economic-development subsidies. But the inner city has already been open to market forces, and these have devastated its job and wealth structures. Further, large firms cannot be depended on to supply secure inner-city jobs. So mechanisms of capital accumulation—including some community-based institutions that Porter finds inefficient—must be strengthened in the inner city. This essay suggests some policy ideas for enhancing access to capital in the inner city, which Porter admits is in short supply.

About the Author:

Gary Dymski is Associate Professor of Economics at the University of California, Riverside. He is also a Research Associate of the Economic Policy Institute of Washington, DC. He serves on the editorial boards of *The International Review of Applied Economics* and of *Geoforum*. He has co-edited *New Directions in Monetary Macroeconomics: Essays in Honor of Hyman P. Minsky* (Michigan, 1994) with Robert Pollin. He has published articles on banking, post-Keynesian economics, exploitation, and discrimination, including "Discrimination and Redlining in the Credit Market: An Exploratory Model," in Volume 23, Number 3 of *The Review*. (University of California, Riverside, School of Economics, 900 University Avenue, Riverside, CA 92521.)

Rebuilding Inner Cities: Basic Principles

by June Manning Thomas

Michael Porter has offered compelling and useful research explaining how inner-city businesses work. Porter's findings relate more specifically to business development than to general urban revitalization, however. Revitalization must involve whole persons, not simply the business sector. Several basic principles operate in situations of successful urban revitalization: adoption of holistic strategies that combine interrelated social, economic, and physical approaches; active involvement and participation by local residents and institutions; social justice; and paying special attention to creating opportunities and to income distribution.

About the Author

June Manning Thomas is Professor of Urban and Regional Planning, with joint appointment to Urban Affairs Programs, at Michigan State University in East Lansing. She is author of the forthcoming *Redevelopment and Race: Planning a Finer City in Postwar Detroit* (Baltimore: John Hopkins University Press, 1997). Ms. Thomas has collaborated in neighborhood planning with several inner-city Detroit community-based organizations, and while on sabbatical leave served as Strategic Planning

Team Manager for the City of Detroit's successful 1994 application for empowerment zone designation. (Michigan State University, Urban Affairs Programs, Room 126 Owen Hall, East Lansing, MI 48824.)

Déjà-vu All Over Again:
Porter's Model of Inner-City Redevelopment

by David S. Sawicki and Mitch Moody

Michael Porter has advanced a model for the redevelopment of the inner city that ostensibly relies on the private sector, diminishing the role of government. We find little he recommends stands the scrutiny of years of research and practice in inner-city economic redevelopment. We first place his ideas in historic context, then discuss his six major assertions in some detail. In our opinion, Porter contributes to another misformulation of the problem, and therefore a sure loser of a solution. His theory is tailor-made for learning another lesson, true or not, on how the ghetto apparently cannot be redeveloped.

About the Authors:
David S. Sawicki is Professor of Planning and Public Policy at the Georgia Institute of Technology. At present, he also serves as half-time Senior Advisor for Data and Policy Analysis at the Carter Presidential Center's Atlanta Project. In his role as senior advisor at The Atlanta Project (TAP), he directs a team of seven graduate students and professionals who provide policy analysis, policy research, and support for operations and planning to the resource directors in health, housing, economic development, education, children and families, and public safety. Currently his research focuses on two areas. The first is the use of data and information to support grass-roots attempts to solve the problems of persistent poverty. His DAPA group makes extensive use of the latest information processing technology, including geographic information systems. The second surrounds the questions of labor force participation, jobs generation, and economic development planning in areas of impacted poverty. (Georgia Institute of Technology, City Planning Program, Atlanta, GA 30332.)

Mitch Moody is a doctoral candidate in the City Planning Program at Georgia Institute of Technology. He holds a Master's degree in electrical engineering from Georgia Institute of Technology and, after working twelve years in the defense industry, returned to Georgia Institute of Technology for a Master's degree in Public Policy and a Ph.D. in planning. His current interests focus on the regional and local impacts of industrial restructuring and the resulting labor force impacts. Mr. Moody's dissertation research investigates inter- and intra-industry linkages and the effects on inner-city employment, particularly among lesser-skilled workers. (City Planning Program, Georgia Institute of Technology, Atlanta, GA 30332.)

Taking Back the Inner City: A Review of Recent Proposals

by William W. Goldsmith

This essay is a review of several recent proposals for reversing the decline and misery that characterize so many central cities in the United States. Most proposals, the review finds, are too limited to be effective. What is needed, instead, is a thorough attack on the conditions that give rise to inner-city poverty and disability. These conditions include discrimination against people of color and subsidies and other privileges to suburbs.

About the Author:
William W. Goldsmith teaches on urban poverty, national urban policy, and international development at Cornell University. Recent publications include: "The Sustainability of Privilege: Reflections on the Third World City, Poverty, and the Environment," *World Development* (with Porus Olpadwala) and *Separate Societies; Poverty and Inequality in U.S. Cities* (with Edward Blakely), which won the 1993 Paul Davidoff Prize. He holds a B.S. in civil engineering from the University of California, Berkeley, and a Ph.D. in planning from Cornell. (Dept. of City & Regional Planning, 106 West Sibley Hall, Cornell University, Ithaca, NY 14853.)

Political Economy of Urban Poverty in the 21st Century: How Progress and Public Policy Generate Rising Poverty

by Timothy Bates

Living costs in urban areas are held down by the presence of low-wage service industries that draw heavily upon a ghetto labor force. The low wages paid to ghetto residents are embedded in the prices of services the entire community relies on, but the urban labor aristocracy benefits disproportionately. Often lacking time to cook their own meals, raise their children, and clean their households, professionals and managers rely heavily upon services forthcoming from the low-wage sector. Declining wages and increasing deregulation may increase poverty, but they raise living standards among the elite by holding down the cost of the bundle of services that supports their affluent lifestyle. Rebellion from below is called to redress this repressive status quo.

About the Author:
Timothy Bates is Professor of Labor and Urban Affairs at Wayne State University. He also works as a consultant for the U.S. Department of Justice Civil Rights Division, the U.S. General Accounting Office, and the Small Business Administration. He is presently writing a book on small business ownership in the U.S. among Asian immigrants. (Urban and Metropolitan Studies, Wayne State University, 3198 Fab, 656 West Kirby, Detroit, MI 48202.)

Promoting Economic Development in the Inner City: The Importance of Human Resources

by Carla J. Robinson-Barnes

In his 1995 *Harvard Business Review* article entitled "The Competitive Advantage of the Inner City," Michael Porter presents a model for the revitalization of inner cities. The model relies on business development as a strategy for promoting inner-city economic development. This essay begins by providing a brief description of the Porter model. It then suggests that a model for the economic revitalization of inner-city communities must not be limited to the business development strategy. It goes on to outline the role that human resources can play in efforts to foster economic development in these communities.

About the Author:

Carla J. Robinson-Barnes is an assistant professor in the Department of Public Administration and Urban Studies at Georgia State University. Her research interests are in the area of urban economic development planning. In 1993 she served as a neighborhood planning consultant to the Corporation for Olympic Development in Atlanta. (Department of Public Administration & Urban Studies, Georgia State University, University Plaza, Atlanta, GA 30303.)

The Porter Model of Competitive Advantage for Inner-City Development: An Appraisal

by C. Michael Henry

This essay examines the applicability of the Porter model for revitalizing the inner city. A number of important questions are investigated, including the political acceptability and the implications of the model for inner-city residents. In order to fully evaluate its suitability we provide a brief depiction of the forces of inner-city impoverishment followed by a brief rendition of the model and an appraisal of the process of inner-city development it engenders. Finally, we suggest an alternative and assess its likely efficacy relative to the Porter model.

About the Author:

C. Michael Henry is a lecturer in the Department of Economics, Yale University, New Haven, Connecticut. He is the author of numerous articles on economic development and race and economics. (Department of Economics, Yale University, P.O. Box 208268, 28 Hillhouse, New Haven, CT 06511.)

Michael Porter: New Gilder of Ghettos

by Edward J. Blakely and Leslie Small

Michael Porter has provided the first hopeful analysis of the American ghetto economy in thirty years. His perspective is derived from his notion of creating competitive economics. Porter's conceptualization of a competitive ghetto, while inspiring, lacks a strong grounding in ghetto and community economic development. This essay suggests an alternative but complementary paradigm for the economic repositioning of America's most distressed communities.

About the Authors:

Edward J. Blakely is Dean and Lusk Professor of the School of Urban Planning and Development at the University of Southern California. He is the author of *Separate Societies* with William Goldsmith, the 1993 Paul Davidoff Award-winning book. He is also a Guggenheim Fellow. (University of Southern California, School of Urban & Regional Planning, 351 Von KleinSmid Center – Univ. Pk., Los Angeles, CA 90089.)

Leslie Small is a doctoral student in the School of Urban and Regional Development at the University of Southern California at Los Angeles. (University of Southern California, School of Urban Regional Planning, 351 Von KleinSmid Center – Univ. Pk., Los Angeles, CA 90089–0042.)

Revitalizing the Inner City: A Holistic Approach

by Usha Nair Reichert

Michael Porter's "Competitive Advantage of the Inner City" focuses on the key role of private sector businesses in revitalizing and reclaiming the competitiveness of inner-city America. He provides a welcome opportunity to rethink the issue of inner-city revitalization. His views on the role of affirmative action programs and the benefits of private business initiative are valuable contributions to the current debates on these issues. However, if the ultimate objective of inner-city development is sustained revitalization of all positive aspects of the inner-city community, then we need to add a few other dimensions to Porter's model. This essay focuses on a more holistic approach that not only aims to create opportunities, but also to raise the expectations of the people, to forge bonds of community and trust, to improve social justice and equality, and to establish a sense of accountability and ownership within the community. It argues that sustainable, long-term solutions to the complex and wide-ranging problems faced by the inner city can perhaps be best achieved by broad-based community building efforts. This involves the pooling of resources and a commitment by government, community based organizations, local residents, and private businesses.

About the Author:

Usha Nair Reichert is an assistant professor in the School of Economics at the Georgia Institute of Technology in Atlanta, Georgia. Her research interests are in the areas of international economics, economic development, poverty, income distribution, and gender and race-related discrimination. She has also worked with several community outreach projects, focusing on issues such as poverty, healthcare and education. (School of Economics, Georgia Institute of Technology, Atlanta, GA 30332.)

Reparations and the Competitive Advantage of Inner Cities

by Richard F. America

This essay redefines the underlying problem that chronically distressed areas, like inner cities, manifest. It agrees with Porter's analysis of what blocks business formation and job creation. It also embraces the idea of competitive advantage as a basis for public and business strategy for revitalization. But it points to the importance and unavoidable necessity of income and wealth redistribution as part of the remedy. It draws attention to the historic factors—slavery and discrimination—that Porter tends to minimize. These enrich the "Haves," as a class at the expense of the "Have Nots," as a class. They cause black inner-city (and rural) poverty, and they require a redistributive justice budget process—on the Restitution Principle.

About the Author:

Richard F. America is an adjunct lecturer in The School of Business Administration at The Georgetown University, Washington, DC. (1444 Yellow Wood Court, Reston, VA 22090.)

Potential Welfare Gains from Improving Economic Conditions in the Inner City

by James Peoples

This essay reexamines the competitive advantages and disadvantages of the inner city with the objective of uncovering the potential welfare gains that can be realized from encouraging greater participation by the private sector. We begin by categorizing the advantages inherent to the inner city as factor input and product market outcomes. The advantages are then classified as labor and nonlabor production costs and as externalities that flow from these costs. The rationale for making these distinctions is based on the assumption that correcting these problems should attract business. Finally, concluding remarks are made on the possible effectiveness of Porter's approach to improving the economic condition of the inner city.

About the Author:

James Peoples is an associate professor in the Department of Economics, College of Letters and Science at the University of Wisconsin-Milwaukee, Milwaukee, Wisconsin. (Department of Economics, University of Wisconsin-Milwaukee, Milwaukee, WI 53201.)

Is the Inner City Competitive?

by Margaret C. Simms and Winston J. Allen

This essay reports on selected findings from a survey of minority businesses conducted by the Joint Center for Political and Economic Studies. It focuses on the extent to which black-owned businesses contribute to economic development of central cities through employment and recruitment in low-income neighborhoods. The authors find central city firms and those in neighborhoods with high black populations are most likely to have employees from inner-city neighborhoods, but few of these firms are actually located in high poverty areas. This suggests that the focus on inner-city location taken by Porter and some other policy analysts may be too narrow. However, a policy targeted on central cities may be appropriate.

About the Authors:

Margaret C. Simms is Director of Research Programs at the Joint Center for Political and Economic Studies. (1090 Vermont Avenue NW, Suite 1100, Washington, DC 20005–4961.) Dr. Simms is a former editor of *The Review of Black Political Economy* and is the author of numerous books and articles on race and economics.

Winston J. Allen is a research associate at the Joint Center for Political and Economic Studies. (1090 Vermont Avenue NW, Suite 1100, Washington, DC 20005–4961.)

Overview of the Initiative for a Competitive Inner City

by the Initiative for a Competitive Inner City

Responding to the disappointing efforts to revitalize America's inner-city economies, Professor Michael Porter of the Harvard Business School, an internationally recognized authority on competitive strategy, created the Initiative for a Competitive Inner City in 1994. The Initiative is founded on the premise that a sustainable economic base can only be created in the inner city as it has been elsewhere, through private for-profit initiatives and investment based on economic self-interest and genuine competitive advantage instead of on artificial inducements, government mandates, or charity.

The Initiative's mission is to foster healthy economics in America's inner cities that create jobs and opportunity for local residents. To do so, the Initiative carries out research on inner-city economic opportunities and disseminates the findings to policy-makers in the public and private sectors as well as to the general public. The Initiative also provides critical assistance to inner-city businesses in a limited number of cities, demonstrating through first-hand experience that inner-city businesses can grow and generate jobs without government subsidies or mandates.

Headquartered in Boston, the Initiative has launched programs in Boston, Baltimore, and Oakland.

Making Comparative Advantage Work
for Economic Opportunity

by William Schweke

   Michael Porter's "The Competitive Advantage of the Inner City" is
one of the most important articles in the field of economic and community development authored in the last ten years. All development policy-
makers and professionals should look closely at the piece, reflect on its
message and decide how best to respond to its many recommendations.
The article provides a needed correction to the prevailing emphases in
the fields of economic and community development. It is animated by an
appropriate sense of urgency. It also begins at the right starting point: the
problem of jobs. Porter recognizes that the essential prerequisite for generating more and better employment opportunities is the creation of a
sustainable, export-oriented economic base. He asks some tough questions about the effectiveness of past approaches and offers a number of
appropriate criticisms of traditional approaches, such as the real estate
model, the location incentive model, the social conscience model, and
others. But it is not a complete and holistic framework for inner-city
development. Indeed, it insufficiently addresses the challenge of ensuring
that investments in economic clusters, business sectors, and anchors (for
instance, ports, downtowns, etc.) work for greater economic empowerment and opportunity.

About the Author:
   William Schweke is a program director at the Corporation for Enterprise Development and was president of Interchange, a firm specializing
in public policy exchange between the United States and Europe. He is a
specialist in development finance, plant closings, small and community
business, environmentally-compatible development, and local development planning. In the past, he has written reports on investing pension
funds in business development, operating small business initiatives, designing and running state-wide and local economic adjustment programs,
and launching urban low-income neighborhood development initiatives.
In his technical assistance work, he has advised a variety of state and
local governments, community-based organizations, foundations, trade
unions, chambers of commerce, private utilities, and governmental authorities in the U.S. and Great Britain. In the area of training, he has
developed courses on rural development, community economic develop-

ment, and local development planning. Mr. Schweke is currently writing two books, one on urban policy and another on positive business climate. (Corporation for Enterprise Development, 1829 E. Franklin Street, Suite 1200, Chapel Hill, NC 27514.)

Economic Development or Social Development? A Strategy for Rebuilding Inner Cities

by Arnold Graf

Recently there has been a growing chorus of voices focusing on various aspects of economic development as the primary means to revitalizing our inner cities. This essay, while recognizing the importance of inner-city capital formation, focuses on the importance of the social organization as the key to inner-city development. The essay examines the development of a new organization in Baltimore, Maryland, the Solidarity Sponsoring Committee, S.S.C.

About the Author:
Arnold Graf is on the national staff of the Industrial Areas Foundation (IAF). He has been with IAF since 1971. From 1971 through 1978 he organized for the IAF in Milwaukee, Wisconsin, and San Antonio, Texas. After teaching at the School of Social Work at San Jose College for two years, he returned to organizing with the Industrial Areas Foundation. Since 1980, Mr. Graf has built broad-based citizen organizations throughout the mid-Atlantic and southern regions of the United States. (Industrial Areas Foundation, 10117 Lakeside Court, Ellicott City, MD 21042.)

Mr. Porter's "Competitive Advantage" for Inner-City Revitalization: Exploitation or Empowerment?

by James H. Johnson, Jr., Walter C. Farrell, Jr., and Geraldine R. Henderson

Michael Porter has oversimplified the approach to successful economic development in the inner city. Following a discussion of ambiguities and questionable assumptions in his model, an alternative, business school initiated and managed strategy is presented, which seeks to: 1) build capacity for business development and job creation by providing aspiring and nascent inner-city entrepreneurs and community development practitioners with basic and advanced training in the nuts and bolts of sound business practices; 2) rebuild human capital through customized job training programs; and 3) reduce drug and crime problems through a new generation of social resource programs designed to mend the social fabric of the inner city.

About the Authors:

James H. Johnson, Jr., is the E. Maynard Adams Distinguished Professor of Business, Geography, and Sociology and the Director of the Urban Investment Strategies Center at the University of North Carolina at Chapel Hill. His research interests include the study of interregional black migration, interethnic minority conflict in advanced industrial societies, and urban poverty and social welfare policy in America. He has published more than 100 research articles and one research monograph, and has co-edited four theme issues of scholarly journals on these related topics. Prior to joining the UNC faculty, he was Professor of Geography and Director of the Center for the Study of Urban Poverty at UCLA. (The Frank Hawkins Kenan Institute of Private Enterprise, UNC Chapel Hill, Campus Box 3440, The Kenan Center, Chapel Hill, NC 27599–33440.)

Walter C. Farrell, Jr., is Professor of Educational Policy and Community Studies and a member of the graduate faculty in urban studies at the University of Wisconsin, Milwaukee, and a national research affiliate in the Urban Investment Strategies Center in The Frank Hawkins Kenan Institute of Private Enterprise at the University of North Carolina at Chapel Hill and in the Center for the Study of Urban Poverty at the University of California, Los Angeles. His research focuses on the race and class underpinnings of the urban underclass, urban education, public health, and urban social issues. Farrell has published more than 150 journal articles and scholarly essays on these and related topics. (Graduate Program in Urban Studies, University of Wisconsin-Milwaukee, Milwaukee, WI 53201.)

Geraldine R. Henderson is an assistant professor of marketing at the Fuqua School of Business at Duke University. She co-authored *The Economic Base of African-American Communities: A Study of Consumption Patterns*, which appeared in the National Urban League's *The State of Black America 1994*. Henderson also writes in the area of social networks and consumer brand associative networks. She has been an active member of both the National Society of Black Engineers (NSBE) and the

National Black MBA Association. (Fuqua School of Business, Duke University, Durham, NC 27708.)

A Dialogue on The Atlanta Project with Jane Smith, Executive Director

by Jane Smith

This essay is a dialogue between Jane Smith, Director of The Atlanta Project and Thomas D. Boston, co-editor of this special issue. During the course of the dialogue, Smith discusses the history, objectives and accomplishments of The Atlanta Project (TAP) and responds to specific questions asked by the editor. These include a discussion of the goal of TAP, its neighborhood cluster concept, its major accomplishments, and Smith's assessment of Porter's strategy. The Atlanta Project was founded by former President Jimmy Carter in 1991.

About the Author:
Jane Smith is a program director of The Atlanta Project (TAP), a program of The Carter Center in Atlanta, Georgia. In this capacity, she is responsible for the daily operations of TAP, which include supervising The Jimmy and Rosalynn Carter Collaboration Center, twenty neighborhood offices and over forty university and corporate partnerships. Dr. Smith earned her B.A. in sociology from Spelman College, her M.A. in sociology from Emory University and a D.Ed. in social policy analysis from Harvard University. She has served as Director of Development at The Martin Luther King, Jr., Center for Nonviolent Social Change, Inc., as a Senior Administrator at Spelman College and in the Atlanta and Detroit offices of INROADS, Inc. Currently, Dr. Smith is a member of the Atlanta Empowerment Zone Board. (The Atlanta Project, P.O. Box 5317, Atlanta, GA 30307.)

An Economic Strategy for America's Inner Cities:
Addressing the Controversy

by Michael E. Porter

Revitalizing America's inner cities requires a radically different approach. We must stop trying to cure the problems of these distressed urban areas by perpetually expanding social programs and hoping that economic activity will follow. An economic strategy is needed to build viable businesses that can provide sorely needed employment opportunities.

Economic development in inner cities will only come from enhancing the advantages of an inner-city location and building on the base of existing companies, while dealing frontally with the present disadvantages of the inner city as a business location (many self-inflicted by poor government policies). There is genuinely economic potential in inner cities that has been largely unrecognized and untapped.

The private sector must play a central role, as it has in successful economic development everywhere. The private sector is already investing in inner cities. By improving perceptions and addressing problems in the inner-city business environment, this trend can be accelerated.

Community-based organizations (CBOs) deserve much credit for helping to create the conditions under which the private sector would consider investing. Now, however, inner cities are ready to move to the next stage, which will require new CBO strategies. Rather than advising, financing, and owning inner-city companies, CBOs should facilitate private sector involvement, change attitudes, train residents and link them to jobs, and, where appropriate, develop sites.

There is a continued, vital role for government and for public resources in inner-city economic development, not a role focused on direct intervention and operating subsidies, but on creating a favorable environment for business (e.g., assembling and improving sites, training workers, upgrading infrastructure, streamlining regulation).

About the Author:

Michael E. Porter is the C. Roland Christensen Professor of Business Administration at the Harvard Business School and a leading authority on competitive strategy and international competitiveness. He received a B.S.E. with high honors in aerospace and mechanical engineering from Princeton University in 1969, where he was a member of Phi Beta Kappa and Tau Beta Pi. He also received an M.B.A. with high distinction in 1971 from the Harvard Business School, where he was a George F. Baker Scholar, and a Ph.D. in Business Economics from Harvard University in 1973.

Professor Porter is the author of 14 books and over 50 articles. His book, *Competitive Strategy: Techniques for Analyzing Industries and Competitors,* published in 1980, is widely recognized as the leading work in its field. In its 45th printing, it has been translated into fifteen languages. A companion book, *Competitive Advantage: Creating and Sustaining Superior Performance,* was published in 1985 and is in its 19th printing. His 1990 book, *The Competitive Advantage of Nations*, develops a theory of how nations and regions compete and their sources of economic prosperity. Professor Porter has also published books about the competitiveness of New Zealand, Canada, Sweden and Switzerland and has a book forthcoming on Japan. Professor Porter's *Capital Choices* (1992) and *Lifting All Boats* (1995) are studies of private capital investment in advanced economies. He has also written on the relationship between competitiveness and the environment. Professor Porter's most recent new research initiative is a study of economic development in America's inner cities, first published in the *Harvard Business Review* article "The Competitive Advantage of the Inner City."

Location Preferences of Successful African American-Owned Businesses in Atlanta

by Thomas D. Boston and Catherine L. Ross

This essay is motivated by Michael Porter's research on the "Competitive Advantage of the Inner City." The authors have assembled data on 722 of the most successful African American-owned businesses in the three county Atlanta MSA. Data includes information on the financial and employment characteristics of firms and the characteristics of their owners. This information is supplemented by a survey of 233 successful African American entrepreneurs. The objective is to determine where successful African American-owned businesses are located in Atlanta, the reasons behind their location decisions, and the employment and financial characteristics of businesses at specific locations. Zip codes within the three county Atlanta MSA are classified by median family income and racial characteristics. Businesses are mapped into these classifications. Contrary to the popular belief that successful African American-owned firms have abandoned black communities, the overwhelming majority in Atlanta are still located in predominantly black neighborhoods. In fact, the most successful businesses are established in some of the poorest neighborhoods, while one-fourth are located in neighborhoods where the median family income is $25,000 or less. On average, 21 percent of the employees in these businesses live in inner-city neighborhoods, and 77 percent of all employees are African Americans. Given the substantial employment capacity of these firms, along with their location preferences, the authors conclude that a key element of the strategy to revitalize inner cities must center on the promotion of African American-owned businesses.

About the Authors:

Thomas D. Boston is Professor of Economics in the School of Economics at The Georgia Institute of Technology in Atlanta, Georgia. He is the editor of *The Review of Black Political Economy,* editor of *A Different Vision: African American Economic Thought,* Vols. I & II (Routledge, 1996) and author of *Race, Class and Conservatism* (Unwin Hyman, 1988). (School of Economics, Ivan Allen College of Management, Georgia Institute of Technology, Atlanta, GA 30332.)

Catherine L. Ross is Professor of Planning at The Georgia Institute of Technology in Atlanta, Georgia. Professor Ross teaches urban policy and planning, transportation planning, environmental planning, and research methods. Ross has served in a number of administrative capacities and has also served as a senior policy analyst with the Transportation Research Board (TRB). Ross is currently on the Board of Directors of the Atlanta Economic Development Corporation (AEDC). (City Planning Program, College of Architecture, Georgia Institute of Technology, Atlanta, GA 30332.)

Part I:
Responses from the Academy

1

ECONOMIC DEVELOPMENT STRATEGIES FOR THE INNER CITY: THE NEED FOR GOVERNMENTAL INTERVENTION

Susan S. Fainstein and Mia Gray

For nearly fifty years scholars and policy-makers have lamented the plight of the inner city and proposed an ever changing set of policies aimed at reinvigorating it. These programs, commencing with the federal Housing and Urban Development Act of 1949, and culminating most recently in the establishment of empowerment zones, have contained one constant element—their basis in an unswerving faith that the private sector holds the key to urban revitalization. Thus, although the forms of governmental programs have changed and levels of subsidy have gyrated wildly, their purpose has always been the same—to renew the interest of private investors in places from which capital has fled. It is, therefore, nothing short of astonishing to hear from Michael Porter that "past efforts have been guided by a social model built around meeting the needs of individuals"[1] and that "government can assume a more effective role by supporting the private sector in new economic initiatives."[2]

To be sure, government has addressed the difficulties of impoverished individuals through various income maintenance and health-related programs. These have generally had the support of conservative economists, who have contended that any public intervention in the market creates distortions and undermines efficiency. But such benefit programs have not been justified as constituting a stimulus to economic growth; rather, they have been intended to supply a social safety net—now, of course, seriously jeopardized. In contrast, efforts aimed at replacing or enlarging the economic base of central cities have *not* provided direct assistance to low-income people. Rather they have consisted of a variety of direct and indirect subsidies aimed at attracting real-estate developers and other kinds of private firms into urban cores. These inducements have ranged from the provision of cleared land and supporting infrastructure to low-interest loans, tax subsidies and regulatory relief. The most frequent criticism of these programs has been that they benefited business rather than poor people.

Porter's argument starts with an incorrect premise—that the problem with inner-city revitalization programs lies in a failure to nurture the private sector. Some of his policy proposals also reflect myopia with regard to the history of past initiatives. Thus, he suggests, in the area of job training, that "the private sector must determine how and where resources should be allocated."[3] Perhaps Porter has forgotten that large-scale efforts at putting individuals to work under the Comprehensive Employment and Training Act (CETA) were quickly jettisoned in favor of Private Industry Councils (PICs), which carry out exactly this function, to no very great effect."[4] In another proposal he declares that

> [A] single government entity could be charged with assembling parcels of land and with subsidizing demolition, environmental cleanup, and other costs. The same entity could also streamline all aspects of building—including zoning, permitting, inspections, and other approvals.[5]

Professor Porter apparently does not remember the urban renewal authorities so roundly criticized by another Harvard Business School professor, Martin Anderson.[6] These authorities performed exactly these operations, often causing the displacement of low-income people, and subsequently finding that no private investor was interested in the land they had made available.

Since the days of urban renewal we have seen many programs designed to "leverage" private investment, as well as the development of public-private partnerships in which corporate officials and property developers play a dominant role.[7] These programs, however, have largely not targeted the worst-off areas of cities, because the business leaders involved see less potential profitability in peripheral locations than in city centers. Where major business investment has been attracted to very poor parts of the city, as in the case of Brooklyn's MetroTech, described by Porter, it has been at the cost of massive public subsidy.[8] It is largely wishful thinking to expect that businesses will discover the advantages of poor neighborhoods and will choose to locate within them without heavy governmental expenditure.[9] Such use of public funds, however, perpetually raises the question of the seemliness of assisting the already well-off with taxpayers' money.

ARE THERE GOOD STRATEGIES?

Although policy-makers have always held the view that they must entice private investors to the city, their conception of the appropriate role of government has changed. During the heyday of urban renewal, governmental authorities acted as master planners, decreeing what parts of the city should be transformed and specifying the character of the outcome. With the introduction of Community Development Block Grants (CDBGs) in 1974 and Urban Development Action Grants (UDAGs) in 1977, the governmental role shifted to soliciting private-sector interest first and then responding with grants, loans, tax relief, and infrastructure improvements. City officials became increasingly entrepreneurial in their activities; economic development corporations replaced the old urban renewal authorities; and deal-making rather than planning became the principal object of their exertions.[10]

Within this context, Professor Porter's advice starts to be helpful. The trouble with current attempts at inner-city economic revival is not in a failure to recognize the importance of "private, for-profit initiatives and investment based on economic self-interest and genuine competitive advantage."[11] Rather, it is in a frequent inability to understand wherein that genuine competitive advantage lies. Porter's more specific recommendations point in useful directions regarding fruitful revitalization strategies. Cities frequently succumb to slavish imitation of what worked elsewhere; thus, every metropolis now boasts a festive marketplace, a convention center, new sports facilities, subsidized office complexes, luxury hotels, and bio-tech centers. The predictable consequences are market saturation and disaster for those places that are unable to tap into a synergistic interaction between such projects and the existing assets of the locale.

Porter stresses the importance of strategic location, regional clusters, and human resources as assets possessed by inner-city areas in relation to export markets (i.e., for production of commodities to be sold outside the immediate area). Because inner cities remain dense places, even after decades of business and population outmigration, they can exploit agglomeration economies; because they possess a surplus of people eager to work, they can immediately fulfill the labor force needs of firms that have routine jobs to fill. There are a variety of often unglamorous, nonleading-edge, yet still viable industries that can profit from such niches. These include warehousing and distribution, recycling, automotive repair, and food processing. By creating the conditions for agglomeration of such industries, public investment can lower the costs of sanitation and security—the two greatest problems for inner-city operations. In order to do so, however, the level of governmental activity will usually have to be considerably higher than indicated by Professor Porter.

We turn now to the example of the Hunts Point Food Distribution Center in the South Bronx to indicate how government has stimulated economic growth and a substantial increase of employment in one of the most deprived sections of urban America. This largely unheralded development represents one of the great success stories in inner-city revitalization. The lesson of its story is that Porter does correctly identify the comparative advantage of an area like the South Bronx, but also that a much stronger governmental role than Porter prescribes underlies the creation of a new agglomeration.

HUNTS POINT MARKET

The Hunts Point Food Distribution Center, located in the heart of the South Bronx, is a prime example of a successful inner-city economic initiative based on sectoral clustering of small- and medium-sized firms.[12] Started in the 1960s, today the market is considered to be the largest food distribution center in the world, hosting more than 160 firms. In addition, auxiliary services such as packaging, trucking, and truck repair facilities crowd the area. Through the years, there has been surprisingly little decentralization of firms to the outlying suburban areas.

The New York City government was the main force in creating the Hunts Point Food Distribution Center, popularly referred to as the "Hunts Point Market." In the first half of the twentieth century, the city had a number of small, widely dispersed public food markets. In 1962 it acquired 329 acres of vacant marshland in the South Bronx from the local utilities company to develop a centralized site, into which it gathered most of the scattered markets. The immediate impetus was the displacement of markets in Manhattan by urban renewal activities rather than any particular intention of stimulating development in the Bronx. In providing spacious, modern facilities and shared support services, city officials felt that they could benefit both the general public health and the individual firms.

The city not only originated the plan and coordinated the move, but was, and remains, the property owner of the market complex. While remaining responsible for all infrastructure improvements, it leases the buildings and land to private companies, which operate, manage, and maintain the facilities. The cooperative management structure facilitates a unified approach toward the city and encourages the provision of services that help all the firms located in the complex.

The Hunts Point Market currently consists of two large cooperative markets (produce and meat) containing over 160 food companies and a number of larger, independent food-oriented concerns. The majority of these firms are in wholesaling, although some also manufacture food products. The complex, which occupies 329 acres, currently sells over $7 billion annually. It now handles over 75 percent of all fruits and vegetables and over 40 percent of all the meat and poultry that enter the metropolitan region (USDA, 1989).[13] Currently, the complex is operating at full capacity, and expansion plans are under consideration.

Although distribution to retailers is the major operation, wholesaling, institutional distribution (schools, prisons, hospitals), warehousing, food processing, and manufacturing all take place in the Hunts Points Market. The last few years have seen the growth of smaller specialty ethnic markets, such as the Caribbean Food Market. The multifunctional nature of its operations makes it a good location for smaller markets which benefit from preexisting infrastructure and trained labor.

Altogether, the firms in the Hunts Point Food Distribution Center employ over 11,000 people directly. If we include the entire complex around the market, local officials estimate 20,000 jobs are produced by the agglomeration of food firms and related services. A striking number of these employees live in the local community. Estimates from owners and market managers consistently cite roughly 20 percent of total employees as Hunts Point residents and 40 percent as Bronx residents. Many of the jobs are well paid, and a number of them are unionized; they range from inventory controllers, truck drivers, and warehouse people to sales and administrative staff.

The amount of employment generated within the local community is especially striking when compared to the relatively modest amount of money the city spent to create the market. Since its inception, New York City has spent roughly $117.6 million, in nonadjusted dollars, building and expanding the market facilities. Recently, the city committed another $35 million over the next five years to improving and updating the market's aging infrastructure. This equals a modest $13,900 per direct job created, including the current infrastructure commitment, and only $7,600 if the full 20,000 jobs in the food distribution agglomeration are included.

The Hunts Point neighborhood, where the market is located, would certainly qualify as an area of interest for Porter. The once vibrant working-class neighborhood experienced severe deindustrialization and white flight in the 1970s. The area's population hemorrhaged between 1970 and 1980. During this period, it lost 63 percent of its residents, declining from almost 94,000 to 34,000. As in many inner-city areas, poverty is overwhelming, and in 1992 over 57 percent of the population lived below the official poverty level, compared to 35 percent for the Bronx overall. Similarly, the unemployment rate is over 21 percent as compared to 13 percent in the Bronx as a whole; and 41 percent of the population is on public assistance. These factors result in a median annual income of only $10,165.[14]

At the same time, its location in the South Bronx has been extremely important to the success of the complex. In accordance with Porter's recommendations, the market has been able to take advantage of its central location within the region. The Food Distribution Center has its own rail links, excellent trucking access, and close port connections. Customers themselves have easy access and can reach the market from anywhere in the tri-state region.

Firms located in the Hunts Point Market also possess the advantages of agglomeration economies; indeed, they seem to benefit from each other's mere presence. By clustering together, smaller firms in the same industry realize economies of scale that are external to the firm but common to the entire cluster. When pressed to explain their continued presence in the market, owners explained the market's advantages. The main point that arose repeatedly was the usefulness of locating near competitors. As the owner of a meat-selling firm explained it, "If a product runs out...I run across the street to my competitor, buy what I need, and ship out a full order. They do the same to me." Many tenants mentioned that this arrangement not only helps keep customers satisfied, but also lowers costs, because each firm can keep a smaller inventory.

Agglomeration offers additional benefits. A common infrastructure, specialized business services, and a trained labor pool support all the firms in the complex. Trucking, truck service, and machinery repair firms crowd the streets around the market, resulting in quick response when equipment breaks down. Other benefits from clustering include the availability of joint training on computerized inventory control, offered by the co-op management, and a readily accessible, trained labor pool. Plus, the cooperative ownership of the produce and meat markets makes management very responsive to problems when they arise and fosters a spirit of common survival for the smaller firms. These factors tend to lower costs and raise quality for each firm. Porter points to this potential when he advocates that firms pursue integration with preexisting regional clusters.

As a whole, however, the benefits of the market go far beyond Porter's idea, because city sponsorship itself generated the agglomeration.

ECONOMIC DEVELOPMENT IN INNER CITIES

The spectacular success of the Hunts Point Market makes it important to reassess assumptions about economic development in the inner cities. First, wholesaling and distribution are often viewed as forming a decentralized industry, the location of which follows the population's distribution. Following this logic, the Hunts Point Market should have dispersed years ago to the suburban fringe of the metropolitan area. Instead, the market remains anchored and prosperous in its inner-city location. This is due to the continued importance of sectoral agglomeration, or clustering, for the food distribution industry. The advantages of such clustering outweigh the benefits gained from dispersion to lower cost locations. A parallel assumption is that the food distribution sector only serves a local market. However, the Hunts Point's success shows that food wholesaling can be an export sector that brings outside dollars into the city.

Second, some, like Porter, advocate a very small role for local government in economic development. The activist role played by New York City, in initiating the market complex and in continuing as an active partner in the South Bronx, is antithetical to Porter's model of success for the inner cities. Porter claims that local government's attempts at urban revitalization have failed because of its emphasis on social services rather than on economic imperative. He suggests that these attempts use up all the existing resources (entrepreneurship and capital), distort market mechanisms, and crowd out private sector efforts. Porter advocates an extremely limited role for government: assembling land parcels, subsidizing demolition, and reducing regulations. However, the success of the Hunts Point Market shows that an active local government can produce vibrant private sector economic growth.

If Hunts Point attracted even more governmental attention, it could do even better. The chief deficiency of the city's role has been its passivity with regard to fostering ancillary development around the market and its grudging commitment to further investment. Thus, it only agreed to the latest round of infrastructure improvements when aggressive relocation offers from neighboring New Jersey finally spurred it into action.

The city's economic development agency does provide considerable assistance to industrial and wholesaling facilities within the outer boroughs. Its highest-powered staff, however, concentrates on Manhattan;

the great bulk of its capital resources for economic development go to office and tourism complexes; and it does not deal with the problems that firms in the boroughs have with the endemic problems of inadequate parking, illegal dumping, and theft. For, even while one hand of city government is seeking to retain industry in New York, another is issuing summonses when infractions occur on properties located in industrial areas. And, understandably, the police pay more attention to crimes against persons than to those against property and are disproportionately deployed in residential and shopping areas.

Why have the economic development agencies of New York City and State given much higher priority to revitalizing downtown Manhattan and Times Square than to improving the industrial areas of the boroughs? In part, their predilections stem from a judgment that considers entertainment, tourism, business services, and finance to be the core industries of the city and the sectors in which it enjoys its greatest comparative advantage. But it is naive to think that the city's strategies are simply the result of objective policy analysis. Rather, they are responses to powerful constituencies. Real-estate developers, principals in bond houses, and hotel owners have the financial resources and access to governmental officials to insure that their interests receive substantial attention. The impoverished residents of Brooklyn and the South Bronx have far less influence.

Michael Porter criticizes community-based organizations for their ineffectiveness in fostering economic development. He assumes that these organizations have sprung up as a consequence of governmental initiatives. But, in fact, they are largely the result of governmental neglect. Once the federal Model Cities program ended and the War on Poverty ran down, public programs ceased to target low-income areas. Community groups formed local development corporations as vehicles for attracting capital into their areas when no other help was forthcoming. Once in existence, these organizations proved useful vehicles through which government could transfer what meager funds it was making available to poor neighborhoods. These then could be combined with funding from other sources, including philanthropies and national equity-providing organizations like the Local Initiatives Support Corporation (LISC). In the absence of either substantial private-sector interest or serious governmental attention, they will continue to be the principal mechanisms for fostering growth in the more deprived parts of the city. In most cases they will do so according to Porter's prescription, by aiding private firms. Although Porter is correct in arguing that the track record of community-based organizations is weak, they are becoming more experienced at what they do and are beginning to improve their performance.

Porter's suggestions for limiting and redefining government's role in local economic development resonate with readers of the *Harvard Business Review*. To the extent that they actually succeed in alerting business leaders to opportunities in poor areas, the hoopla that they have created can have a positive impact. But, if they prompt city governments to limit even further their willingness to invest in deprived parts of the city and to cease requiring that businesses receiving public benefits must make commitments to local residents in return, they will do more harm than good. The concept of simply turning land over to private investors harkens back to the urban renewal scenario of the 1950s and 1960s. During that period, cities gave carte blanche to the private sector to choose the type of activity it would carry out within the city. The result was the strengthening of the downtown core with no effect on urban poverty. Much the same outcome can be expected from Porter's recommendation of giving business a free hand. The very economic imperatives he stresses ensure that privately led economic development in inner cities, even when successful, rarely has much effect on overall urban poverty. Although Porter sees the private sector as the solution, its activities are not redistributive. At their best, when businesses enter the inner city, they can provide work for a portion of the population and can serve as an anchor for other firms. Too often, though, new economic ventures draw on skilled labor from outside the inner city, causing wages to leave the local area. Additionally, low wages paid for low-skilled jobs are insufficient to support most families. Only government intervention ensures that a minimum amount of redistribution accompanies economic growth.

In order to alleviate poverty, government's involvement in the inner cities must go beyond direct investment in economic development. While such efforts can help particular firms and sectors, many residents of the inner city will not benefit from increased economic activity without further help. To make a real difference in the dynamics of inner city economies and urban labor markets, the government must play a much larger role than that acknowledged by Porter. Governments need to ensure quality schools, daycare, and housing to enable the citizens of inner-city neighborhoods to truly benefit from increased private sector economic activity. Only with these structures in place will inner-city residents realize their true competitive advantage.

NOTES

1. Michael Porter, "The Competitive Advantage of the Inner City," *Harvard Business Review*, (May–June, 1995): 55.

2. Ibid,. p. 67.

3. Ibid., p. 66.

4. Like Model Cities, CETA is usually dismissed out of hand as a failure. No serious study, however, ever demonstrated it as such; it did provide direct employment to the otherwise unemployed, and the labor of CETA employees provided needed services in many localities.

5. Ibid., p. 68.

6. Martin, Anderson, *The Federal Bulldozer* (Cambridge, MA: MIT Press, 1964).

7. See Gregory Squires (ed.), *Unequal Partnerships* (New Brunswick, NJ: Rutgers University Press, 1989).

8. See Susan S. Fainstein, *The City Builders* (Cambridge, MA: Blackwell, 1994), chapter 7. As of mid-1992 New York city had spent $166 million in capital improvements in downtown Brooklyn, in support of the development of MetroTech and nearby Atlantic Terminal. It had also agreed to forego hundreds of millions of dollars in property taxes in future years in return for their developers' commitment to the area.

9. The exception is retailers and suppliers of entertainment, who, having saturated suburbia, are discovering that inner cities represent untapped markets that offer potentially very high rates of return.

10. See Peter K. Eisinger, *The Rise of the Entrepreneurial State* (Madison: University of Wisconsin Press, 1988); Fainstein, *The City Builders.*

11. Porter, p. 56.

12. Information on the Hunts Point Food Distribution Center is drawn from personal interviews with local officials, market managers, and tenants in 1994 and 1995 conducted by Mia Gray, and from three documents: City of New York, *Hunts Point Food Distribution Center Plan and Strategy for Expansion and Development* (New York: City of New York, Department of Ports and Trade, 1989); City of New York, *Hunts Point Peninsula: Planning Recommendations 1989* (New York: City of New York, Department of City Planning, 1989); and Hunts Point Local Development Corporation, *The Hunts Point Business Directory* (New York: Hunts Point Local Development Corporation, 1990).

13. US Department of Agriculture. *Wholesale Markets Development.* Washington DC: United States Department of Agriculture, 1989.

14. City of New York, *The City of New York Community District Profile: Bronx. Community District 2* (New York: City of New York 1993).

2

ENTREPRENEURSHIP AND THE ADVANTAGES OF THE INNER CITY: HOW TO AUGMENT THE PORTER THESIS

John Sibley Butler

Michael E. Porter has put the problem of "inner-city" economics on center stage in the public square. Although many researchers and practitioners have addressed this problem, there is nothing like an article in the *Harvard Business Review* by a top business scholar to get major players involved in the redevelopment of the "inner city."[1] The purpose of this essay is to think hard about the ideas of Michael E. Porter, with a major emphasis on whether or not they can make a contribution to solving problems of the "inner city." As we do this, we must understand that his ideas, in a modern way, have Booker T. Washington written all over them. After we give a consideration to Porter, we then move to a model that takes advantage of his work, but adds a strong consideration to the redevelopment of the entrepreneurial spirit among people who live in the inner city. As Porter's ideas now stand, they are predicated on the belief that American enterprise will come and reclaim the inner city so that jobs can be provided. While this is fine, people who live in the inner city actually developing enterprises, and networking with businesses throughout the world, must be a large part of the future of the inner city.

As we commence our effort, we must also explore how to reengineer the minds of intellectuals who analyze and write about the black experience. We must also look at the culture that represents black America in the public square.

INTRODUCTION

In "The Competitive Advantage of the Inner City," Michael Porter's major thesis is that most of the policies directed toward the inner city have failed because they have been guided by a social model that has taken as its main agenda relief programs such as income assistant, housing subsidies, and food stamps. In his own words, "We must stop trying to cure the problems of the inner city by perpetually increasing social investment and hoping for economic activity to follow."[2] Such a model, notes Porter, creates an entrepreneurial type who understands the importance of bringing social programs to communities for their own scale of economic stability.

Porter's major thesis, which is at the center of change, is driven by what he calls the competitive advantage of the inner city. The competitive model underscores the attractiveness of the inner city but also realizes disadvantages. The advantages included in the model are strategic location, local market demand, integration with regional clusters, and human resources.

Porter's major thesis, which stresses the importance of a business model for the "rebuilding" of the inner city, is excellent. It is difficult, if not impossible, to socially engineer economics. However, I think that people within the inner city will have to be major players as owners of enterprises for the cities to be totally rebuilt. Put another way, inner city residents themselves will have to replace the social welfare model, which is so much a part of the inner city, with the creation of entrepreneurial enterprises; they must become owners of major enterprises in inner cities. A jobs-only model will place residents in a situation where the jobs might once again leave their community. Also, jobs are usually associated with a degree of credentials. Entrepreneurship, on the other hand, levels the playing field by placing an emphasis on the entrepreneurial spirit. Thus Porter's discussion of the advantages of the inner city must be enhanced by stressing the point that residents should seek to own the invaluable land within the inner city. Then that land must blossom with business activity.

In order to understand the logic of my argument, we must explore historical as well as present models of urban living. We must also explore how paradigms influence research on black communities. Such an exploration will lead to a model that is wrapped around the importance of placing ownership of business enterprise, and entrepreneurship, at the center of communities.

BLACK ENTERPRISES: HISTORICAL CONSIDERATIONS

It is important to understand that what Michael Porter calls the social model, or the reliance on social programs to maintain communities, actually replaced a model that placed business at the center of communities. Research has shown that black Americans have one of the strongest histories of placing entrepreneurship and business ownership at the core of communities of any ethnic group in America.[3] Indeed, in a recent econometric test of this idea, Margaret Levenstein noted that "One of the most striking findings of [her] study is that in 1910 African-Americans were more likely than white Americans to be employers, and almost as likely as Whites to be self-employed."[4]

The fact that business enterprise once stood at the center of black communities is an historical fact that has been lost and neglected by scholars and commentators. At one time, the most important guiding research framework for the study of black communities was based on the success of business people and the development of self-help organizations. This research also gave a consideration to poverty, but the emphasis was on the importance of what was called racial "up-lift." The major works that were responsible for establishing this scholarship include W.E.B. Du Bois's *The Negro In Business (1898)* and *Economic Co-Operation Among Negroes (1907);* Henry M. Minton's "Early History of Negroes in Business in Philadelphia;" Abram L. Harris's *The Negro as Capitalist* (1936); Booker T. Washington's "Durham North Carolina: A City of Negro Enterprises;" and Monroe Works's annual studies published in *The Negro Year Book.*[5]

When the overall literature on black Americans is examined, it is clear that the emphasis on self-help and business activities switched to a framework that focused on failure. Instead of concentrating on strong black communities that kept enterprise at the center of life, or on how black Americas created institutions, educated children, and developed economic stability, the emphasis was on how blacks fail in America. For example, research on education prior to the mid-1960s placed an emphasis on how some black families, in the face of racial hostility, created business enterprises, and sacrificed by spending over 50 percent of their income on the education of children. This was the theme of Charles Johnson's 1938 study *The Negro College Graduate.*[6] At the present time it is almost impossible to find a study of black families, although there are thousands, who educate their children in the tradition of the findings of Charles Johnson. Instead, the emphasis is on how blacks cannot attend college in a racist society.

Related to this failure literature is how some commentators and "scholars" hold up the experiences of poor blacks to society as bait, but when the money comes for different well-meaning programs, economically secure blacks (because of the relationship between scholarships, test scores and family income) and their children benefit.

Failure frameworks, which are more concerned with the documentation of racism than with the creative energies of blacks, cannot deal with any kind of historical success within the black community. The research is usually associated with northern or western inner cities where the tradition of black institutional building (black colleges and universities, etc.) is very weak. The model is one that stresses the movement from the inner city to the suburbs, leaving blacks as victims of a changing economy. As blacks become economically secure, they leave this sea of nonopportunities and move to the suburbs.[7]

This model represents only one aspect of the black experience in America. The other model notes that historically, black long-term success has always stood on the shoulders of black entrepreneurs, community and family. This model is presented in more recent books, such as T.M. Alexander, Sr.'s *Beyond the Timberline*; Jonathan Greenberg's *Staking A Claim: Jake Simmons, Jr., and the Making of an African-American Oil Dynasty*; and John Sibley Butler's *Entrepreneurship and Self-help among Black Americans: A Reconsideration of Race and Economics*.[8]

All of these book, which are both popular and academic, bring out the fact that entrepreneurship was not only the anchor of black communities prior to the middle 1960s, but that it is also the source of the historic value that blacks place on education, a value that predates the Civil War. In a work by an historian entitled *Black Property Owners in the South,* Loren Schweninger was "surprised" to find that free black entrepreneurs placed a higher value on education than did whites. For example, he found that among 200 black families in one Louisiana parish, only 1 percent was illiterate. In the same parish, 20 to 25 percent of the white families were illiterate. Other works have shown that black business owners place a tremendous amount of emphasis on the education of children, a situation that is still true today.

It is important to reconstruct the history of black entrepreneurship and community building, and to replace the emphasis on failure, because placing business activity at the center of community is the only way to solve problems of the inner city. There are many traditions in the history of black America, and it is important to concentrate on the tradition that has had the most influence on educational and economic success.

For scholars and commentators who are in the public square pontificating on the black experience, this means that successful blacks, and their experience, will be just as importance as those who are defined as problematic. This also means that blacks who come from families that have been successful for generations must tell their stories; families that have produced three and four generations of college graduates and business people, must stand at the center of black America. Neglected books, such as Marian Wright Edelman's *The Measure of Our Success,* Dona L. Irvin's *The Unsung Heart of Black America,* T.M. Pryor's *Wealth Building: Lessons of Booker T. Washington for a New Black America,* George Fraser's *Success Runs in Our Race,* Robert L. Woodson's *On the Road to Economic Freedom,* Annalee Walker's *Reach Wisely: The Black Cultural Approach to Education,* T.M. Alexander's *Beyond the Timberline,* Dennis Paul Kimbro and Napoleon Hills's *Think and Grow Rich: A Black Choice,* Jonathan Greenberg's *Staking a Claim: Jake Simmons, Jr., and the Making of an Africa-American Oil Dynasty*, and Robert L. Wallace's *Black Wealth through Black Entrepreneurship*[9] must stand at center stage for the black community.

It is important to understand that studying failure produces nothing about living well in America. It is also true that failure studies have reached a point of saturation. As a result, for example, studies on poverty simply change the name of major concepts and produce the same result. Indeed, failure is so much a part of black literature and the popular press that television series such as the Cosby Show were criticized because they did not "represent" black America. To many blacks, however, the only thing wrong with the Cosby Show was that the family did not have a great country home, but rather lived in a glorified apartment house in the middle of a city. The most important thing for any policy is not to concentrate on failure, but rather to concentrate on degrees of success. Thus, the failure paradigm must be discarded and the success paradigm revitalized as the model for inner city black America.

We should also add that black successful entrepreneurship in America today can take place outside of the inner city. Thus, recent data from the Department of Commerce show that black-owned enterprises increased 46 percent, from 424,165 in 1987 to 620,912 in 1992. A great proportion of this increase is taking place outside of the inner city, an indication that there is not necessarily a relationship between business in the inner city and business growth in black America. Therefore inner-city entrepreneurship can be separate from the business activity of black entrepreneurs as a whole.

THE AUGMENTATION OF THE PORTER MODEL

Although Porter's ideas about the importance of creating a business model in the inner city are sound, we must add the importance of business ownership by people who live in the inner city; the strong historical culture of black entrepreneurship must anchor the effort to bring economic stability to the inner city. Indeed, every one of the advantages of the inner city discussed by Porter needs to be reengineered to the advantage of people who live there. When this is done, it can be seen that inner city-people, and people who choose to relocate there, can develop a very bright economic future. But, for this to happen, the education of inner city areas must also be reengineered.

It is very true that inner cities have an advantage of strategic locations. As noted by Porter, they are near transportation and communication centers and major business centers. The business leadership of black America, along with blacks in the inner city, could develop a strategy to buy all of this valuable land on which blacks live and do business. For example, the black community of Hunter's Point in the City of San Francisco overlooks the entire Bay area. This land, with an estimated value of over $3 billion, can be a bonanza for people who live there if it is developed. Land in Cleveland, Ohio; New York City, Washington, D.C., and Philadelphia stands in a similar light.

Ownership of property has to be the basis on which to rebuild the enterprises that could be the center of business activity for communities. Indeed, in cities where blacks own the land, such as Tulsa, Oklahoma; Jackson, Mississippi; Austin, Texas; Houston, Texas; and Atlanta, Georgia, redevelopment is much easier. For example, the Fifth Ward Redevelopment Corporation of Houston, Texas, has done wonders with land already owned by blacks. In addition to building over sixty new homes, they are redeveloping old ones and have a master plan for a commercial retail development. In Austin, Texas, the Praise Tabernacle Church is building a multimillion dollar complex that houses a private school, a recreation hall, and other amenities. This reconnects with a tradition that built historically black Huston Tillotson College, a private school that is the oldest institution of higher education in Austin, Texas. Tulsa, Oklahoma (Greenwood Section) rebuilt parts of its old black commercial community as an outdoor mall configuration that houses retail stores. On land where enterprises once stood, the black community developed a higher educational consortium, which is composed of The University of

Oklahoma, the traditional back college Langston University; and Oklahoma State. The key to all of this is that blacks own the land; land that was purchased and developed by their forefathers at the turn of the century is now paying great dividends. The only thing that had to be done was to teach the population to think as free people, as opposed to constantly creating masters.

Purchasing the land also means that blacks can sell to other immigrants who are newcomers to American cities, or can sell land as the city expands. For example, when blacks in Dallas created the outstanding community of Hamilton Park, they bought land and developed houses, enterprises, and community organizations. When the city of Dallas moved north, the residents of Hamilton Park were able to sell and make significant profits. One of the most sought after residential sections in Houston, Texas, is McGregor Park, an area near Texas Southern University that contains great mansions built by Jewish merchants in the 1920s. Black entrepreneurs purchased the homes and are now passing them down from generation to generation. Everything begins with ownership of the land, which creates a certain type of attitude toward economic success in communities.

It is true that black inner-city communities will vary according to land ownership. Thus, many black southern communities look like northern suburbs when compared to many inner-city communities of the north. This variation will determine the strategy for recreating the importance of ownership in communities throughout the country.

Porter also notes that there is great demand for goods by inner-city residents. Placing inner-city entrepreneurs at the center of community means that they would then strive to own the supermarkets, department stores, and other enterprises. Of course there is already an interesting ethnic literature that analyzes the structure of the black community and business enterprise. In Pyong Gap Min's book, *Ethnic Business Enterprise: Korean Small Business in Atlanta,* the author does an outstanding job of showing the importance of black areas in major cities for Koreans' business success.[10] In an interesting way, the immigrant ethnic entrepreneurs have already solved the problem of building community through inner-city entrepreneurship. This solution, which is also buried in black history, is based on the importance of business enterprise and stays away from those things that are social.

Perhaps the most important issue discussed by Porter is the need to increase the educational skills (both managerial and formal) of many inner-city residents. In order to do this, one must begin to reconstruct the educational system of the inner city. This can be done by concentrating on the development of excellent private schools to replace a public school system which, in many cases, has turned into a system of detention centers. It must be remembered that a great proportion of black education, especially in the South, has always been private. Most of the black colleges and universities are private. Catholic schools have always played a major role in the secondary education of blacks in all parts of the country.

As noted earlier, the development of business activity does not carry with it the same kinds of demands for educational credentials as do many other occupations. In many data sets, the relationship between business ownership and education is negative. Although this is true, traditional education of all people is very important.

In addition to traditional education, entrepreneurial education must be added to the curriculum. Professor James Todd of the San Franciso area has had tremendous success with an effort called "Step-To-College-Ascend." The program places entrepreneurship at the center of a traditional educational curriculum. In addition to having a high college matriculation rate, students learn to start and maintain enterprises. This could be the entire educational model for the country.

In 1947, Professor Joseph Pierce published a masterpiece entitled *Negro Business and Business Education.*[11] This book, because of its emphasis on business development in America, has been reprinted by Plenum Press. The work explores the relationship between community building and the development of business enterprise, and should be read by all interested in "rebuilding" the business spirit and know-how of inner-city America. In short, the reconstruction of education within the inner city must have a strong emphasis on business education and entrepreneurship.

Throughout America, there are communities that have been successful for years. It is important to place these communities on the marketing shelf as role models; it is also important to concentrate on successful individuals as role models. In a society that is becoming indifferent to old arguments about race and opportunity, it is important to rediscover the strong self-help tradition of black communities. Individuals who wish to concentrate on failure should have a voice in the public square, but we must understand that we cannot learn, as noted above, much from studying failure. The days are over when one can say that one is poor and black and someone will care. Even when this is said, certified new minority groups (sexual minorities, gender minorities, disability minorities) come to the table with arguments that are just as strong as those developed by racial groups, and in the long run seem to be more successful.

When enterprise is placed at the center of community, issues of capital formation, marketing, accounting and management information systems become the mechanisms by which an entire society is recreated.

Although many people have been concerned with rebuilding the inner city, Michael Porter should be congratulated for bringing the issue to the *Harvard Business Review* and placing the issue before the country. What is important is that inner-city residents themselves learn to understand the relationship between business activity and living well in America, a reality that is so much a part (and continues to be a part) of black America.

As this issue becomes more intensified in the public square, those who oppose the importance of placing enterprise at the center of community will become more vocal. For example, despite the fact that the country has spent billions of dollars on poverty programs, Bennet Harris (a visiting professor of political economy at Harvard's Kennedy School of Government) noted that he "feared that Porter's latest work will raise expectations about private-sector white knights that cannot possibly be fulfilled. In a time of growing cynicism and anger—especially among inner-city youth—the nation cannot risk still another round of bitter disappointment based on false advertising."[12]

Harrison's comments are typical of individuals who do not understand that blacks can be their own saviors in the business world. Also implicit in his comments is the idea that if the country tries to change, then inner-city blacks will have rising expectations about people coming to "save them." When this does not happen, then despair and disappointment will be produced. It is obvious that these things are already prevalent within inner cities. Thus, we must always be aware those individuals who are not willing to change.

Change was the theme of the recent Nissan-supported block of information on the importance of black entrepreneurship in America, and how black colleges and universities can help to rebuild communities. Tennessee State University in Nashville and Xavier University in New Orleans are among the historical black schools that are raising money for entrepreneurial programs—information that is designed to inform the student body of the importance of placing enterprise at the center of community. This, of course, is a return to the theme noted above that was outlined in

1947 by Joseph Pierce in his book *Negro Business and Business Education.* It is also the only theme that will bring economic life to one of the most depressed areas of the American Society.

Finally, the studies of Porter must be augmented by studies of entrepreneurship in the inner city—how to develop and maintain the importance of placing enterprise at the center of community.

NOTES

1. Michael E. Porter, "The Competitive Advantage of the Inner City," *Harvard Business Review* (May–June 1995).

2. Ibid., p. 57.

3. John Sibley Butler, *Entrepreneurship and Self-help among Black Americans: A Reconsideration of Race and Economics* (New York: State University of New York Press, 1991).

4. Margaret Levenstein, "African American Entrepreneurship: The View from the 1910 Census." Department of Economics, University of Michigan, Ann Arbor, Michigan, p. 2. Forthcoming in *Business and Economic History*, Vol. 24, no. 1, Fall 1995.

5. W.E.B. Du Bois, *The Negro in Business* (Atlanta: Atlanta University Press, 1898); *Economic Co-Operation Among Negroes* (Atlanta: Atlanta University Press, 1907); Henry M. Minton, "Early History of Negroes in Business in Philadelphia," Abram L. Harris, *The Negro as Capitalist* (1936); Booker T. Washington, "Durham North Carolina: A City of Negro Enterprises;" Monroe N. Work, *The Negro Yearbook* (Tuskegee Alabama: Tuskegee Institute, 1918).

6. Charles S. Johnson, *The Negro College Graduate* (Chapel Hill: The University of North Carolina Press, 1938).

7. For example, see William Julius Wilson, *The Declining Significance of Race* (Chicago: University of Chicago Press, 1988).

8. T.M. Alexander, Sr., *Beyond the Timberline* (Edgewood, MD: M.E. Duncan & Company, Inc., 1992); Jonathan Greenberg, *Staking a Claim: Jake Simmons, Jr., and the Making of an African-American Oil Dynasty* (New York: Atheneum, 1990); John Sibley Butler, *Entrepreneurship and Self-help among Black Americans: A Reconsideration of Race and Economics* (New York: State University of New York Press, 1991).

9. Marian Wright Edelman, *The Measure of Our Success: A Letter to My Children and Yours* (Boston: Beacon Press: 1992); Dona L. Irvin, *The Unsung Heart of Black America: A Middle-Class Church at Mid-century* (Columbia Missouri: University of Missouri Press, 1993); T.M. Pryor, *Wealth Building: Lessons of Booker T. Washington for a New Black America* (Edgewood, Maryland: Duncan & Duncan, 1995); George Fraser, *Success Runs in Our Race* (New York: George C. Fraser, 1994); Robert L. Woodson, *On the Road to Economic Freedom: An Agenda for Black Progress* (Washington, D.C.: Regnery Gateway, 1987); Annalee Walker, *Reach Wisely: The Black Cultural Approach to Education* (San Francisco: Aspire, 1993); T.M. Alexander, *Beyond the Timberline: The Trials and Triumphs of A Black Entrepreneur* (Edgewood, New Jersey: M.E. Duncan & Company, 1992); Dennis Paul Kimbro and Napoleon Hills, *Think and Grow Rich: A Black Choice* (New York: Fawcett Columbine, 1991); Jonathan Greenberg, *Staking a Claim: Jake Simmons, Jr., and the Making of an Africa-American Oil Dynasty* (New York: Atheneum,

1990); Robert L. Wallace, *Black Wealth through Black Entrepreneurship* (Edgewood, MD: Duncan & Duncan, Inc., 1993).

10. Pyong Gap Min, *Ethnic Business Enterprise: Korean Small Business in Atlanta* (New York: Center for Migration Studies, 1988): 117–123.

11. Joseph A. Pierce, *Negro Business and Business Education: Their Present and Prospective Development* (New York: Plenum Press, 1995).

12. "Why Business Alone Won't Fix the Cities," *Technology Review*, October, 1996, p. 71.

3

BUSINESS STRATEGY AND ACCESS TO CAPITAL IN INNER-CITY REVITALIZATION

Gary A. Dymski

INTRODUCTION

This essay discusses critically Michael Porter's proposals for inner-city economic revitalization—to make the inner city more open to market forces and more attractive to large firms, while eliminating economic-development subsidies. It is argued here that the inner city is already open to market forces, which have devastated its job and wealth structures. Further, large firms cannot be depended on to supply secure inner-city jobs. And it is not easy in practice to separate inefficient "social" programs from efficient "economic" programs for urban development, especially given the complex legacy of discrimination. Finally, even a hard-headed, market-oriented urban policy can only work in a more receptive political environment.

In sum, mechanisms of capital accumulation—including community-based institutions which Professor Porter finds to be inefficient—must be strengthened in the inner city. Among these mechanisms are institutions for channeling capital and credit to inner-city firms and individuals. This essay goes on to suggest some policy ideas for enhancing access to capital in the inner city, which Porter admits is in short supply. The same forces that have led nonfinancial firms to flee the inner city have been at work among financial firms; so financial market forces will only worsen the inner-city capital shortage if left alone. Accordingly, a number of methods for "greenlining"— the shifting of savings and credit into the inner city from outside it—are proposed, followed by an idea for recycling funds lent productively in the inner city.

THE HARVARD BUSINESS SCHOOL MEETS THE INNER CITY

According to Michael Porter, governmental programs for urban economic development—consisting primarily of subsidy and set-aside programs for inner-city and minority firms and organizations—have failed for three reasons: they have been fragmented; they have been aimed at individuals and firms, not just at impacted areas; and they have been formulated as both social *and* economic programs. These programs have nurtured small businesses and non-profit organizations, and have led many inner-city entrepreneurs to confuse achieving social goals with making profits. They have "treated the inner city as an island isolated from the surrounding economy and subject to its own unique laws of competition,"[1] isolating the inner city from the market forces remaking the "mainstream economy."[2]

However, pro-market public intervention based on hard-headed economics can stave off this bleak future. This intervention must begin with a realistic inner-city economic balance sheet. Porter identifies numerous inner-city disadvantages: costly and fragmented land; high building, operating, and security costs; antiquated infrastructures; weak workers' and managers' skills, and sometimes bad attitudes; and a shortage of capital. But, offsetting these liabilities are four competitive advantages: a sizable consumer market; location; proximity to industrial clusters; and underused human resources.

"Mainstream" firms have the know-how and capital to overcome these disadvantages and to exploit these advantages, either directly or through partnerships with inner-city firms. To spur their involvement, several changes in the landscape of urban economic development are needed. Government spending for economic development must be reshaped.[3] Programs that have targeted individuals and firms have sometimes worsened inner-city/suburban disparities; impacted areas should instead be targeted. Further, programs should not pursue joint social and economic goals, as in the case of subsidized housing construction; pursuing both goals does not spur market forces, it replaces them. In particular, government must cease using small firms and organizations to deliver capital and business services to the inner city; it must instead encourage "mainstream" firms to deliver these, in part through smart subsidies such as reduced capital gains taxes on equity investments in inner-city firms. Urban governments must reduce regulatory costs, bundle land into larger parcels, and rebuild infrastructures.

Further, Porter argues that community-based organizations and inner-city businesses must themselves recognize that their prosperity depends on the intervention of larger "mainstream" firms. They must seek out relationships and encourage "mainstream" firms to relocate in the inner city. Activist groups must use their organizing prowess to create business-ready sites.

Rosabeth Kanter, Porter's Harvard Business School colleague, has developed some complementary ideas.[4] Kanter argues that nation-states are becoming irrelevant; instead, regions and "citistates" must develop world-class levels of industrial knowledge, production capacity, or trading linkages. These are the three C's respectively—concepts, competence, and connections. Firms' survival, individuals' economic security, and region/citistate prosperity all depend on possessing one or more of these C's. Size alone does not guarantee success; indeed, small and flexible firms may be more competitively fit than large ones.

Kanter, like Porter, argues that small inner-city businesses and community development corporations are not viable because they are isolated from business clusters possessing one or more C's. Most minority-owned firms lack C's, and as such court extinction; and the absence of the three C's in inner cities is self-reinforcing.

In sum, Porter and Kanter argue that inner-city businesses can prosper primarily by servicing nearby business clusters and meeting inner-city market demand. Encouraging inner-city growth, Porter argues, does not require spending and the redistribution of wealth, but instead a (politically palatable) set of modest supply-side inducements to create wealth. It also requires local firms and organizations to be receptive to "mainstream" and even multinational firms.

ANOTHER VIEW OF INNER-CITY ISOLATION AND MARKET FORCES

At root, Porter provides an up-by-the-bootstraps exhortation to the racially oppressed that echoes Booker T. Washington's "five fingers and one hand" strategy and, indeed, Richard Nixon's "Black capitalism" program.[5] But, whereas Washington's and Nixon's programs suggested developing autonomous bases of black-owned capital, these authors call for developing dependent bases of inner-city capital linked to "mainstream" and multinational corporations.

At the level of individual cases, Porter has shown that his ideas have merit. The question is, will broad implementation of this prescription overcome inner-city economic stagnation? That is, does it offer a new U.S. urban policy? This section argues that it does not, for four reasons:

1. Social policies have not buffered the inner city from market forces.

The severity of inner-city stagnation reflects the unbridled operation of these forces.
2. Public policies enacted to achieve "economic" goals are not readily
distinguishable from those aimed at "social" goals, especially in
the case of antidiscrimination policies.
3. Ongoing reductions in government spending are undermining the
demand side of inner-city markets, undercutting any purely supply-side strategy.
4. Contemporary political rhetoric and the balance of U.S. political
forces may undermine Porter's inner-city strategy.

The "isolated" inner city and economic transformation. Porter asserts
that social spending has isolated minority businesses and the inner-city
economy from the competitive winds that have toughened the "mainstream" economy.[6] But this assertion is implausible. For one thing, it
vastly overestimates the scale of government spending on inner-city businesses. For another, two decades of private-sector deindustrialization have
exacted an especially terrible toll on the inner-city economy.[7] Industrial
job losses have been centered in the inner city; bank branches have
disproportionately closed there; and the governmental down-sizing and
benefits cuts of recent years has primarily affected (both sides of) inner-
city labor markets.

Both Porter and Kanter clearly appreciate the importance of path-
dependence in economic growth, which underlies their common advocacy of industrial clusters as growth nodes.[8] But it follows from the
inherently uneven character of economic growth that some areas' explosive growth (suburban growth areas) implies other areas' relative stagnation (inner cities).

In any case, it is unrealistic to think that new business connections
between inner-city firms and industrial clusters will reverse inner-city
decline. For one thing, contractual bridges now exist between the inner
city and the LA entertainment cluster, the New York financial cluster,
and so on. Thousands of janitorial, food-service, and other poorly-paid
service-sector jobs in these clusters are filled by residents of the inner
city, at wages that hardly leave them the option of entrepreneurship. For
another, industrial growth is increasingly multicentered; so the advantage
associated with proximity to any one industrial cluster is of decreasing
value.

The inner city is, then, hardly isolated from economic dynamics; its increasing deprivation relative to the "mainstream" economy is due precisely to these broader dynamics. Porter misses this point in arguing that the government should facilitate wealth *creation* in the inner city, rather than mandating wealth *redistribution*. Market forces themselves constantly create wealth in some places and destroy it in others. The differential trajectories of wages, real-estate prices, and equity values in different areas of any metropole all add up to market-driven wealth redistribution, with a vengeance. The entire economic process would grind to a halt if one allowed only wealth creation while barring wealth redistribution; so why should government alone play by this rule?

Discrimination and market processes. Contrary to Porter, there is no clear distinction between social and economic expenditures in urban policy. In principle, it may seem easy to distinguish, say, race-based lending aimed at reversing discrimination from market-based lending; and hence to follow Porter's advice and eliminate the former, which is economically inefficient. But this distinction is easily made only if discrimination consists entirely of acts by bigoted perpetrators, which are costly for perpetrators as well as for their victims.[9] An example is the case of white bankers rejecting loan applications by qualified black applicants; these bankers' bigotry decreases their profits. Efforts to pay reparations or to redress racial imbalances are unnecessary for discrimination of this sort, because nonbigots will eventually outcompete bigots in head-to-head competition.

But discrimination is not restricted to the acts of overt bigots; it may also consist of racially "neutral" acts that are economically "rational." For example, minorities who face unequal income-earning opportunities may be judged less creditworthy than whites, all else held equal. Similarly, minorities' disadvantage in obtaining home loans translates into fewer second mortgages financing higher education, and hence into unequal labor-market opportunity. And because of widespread residential segregation, these "rational" discriminatory processes reduce overall wealth levels—and hence entrepreneurial opportunities—in inner-city areas.

Again, market processes are anything but socially neutral. Discrimination based on bigotry and on "rational" calculation alike widens racial gaps in income and wealth. Overturning racial gaps requires policy interventions into market processes. Market processes inescapably have social effects, which only government can arbitrate.

Demand-supply feedback effects. Bennett Harrison has pointed out that government spending cannot be neatly divided into unproductive social spending and productive economic-development spending: much "unproductive" spending trains potential workers, provides day care for their children, and assures their health.[10] A further point should be made. Reduced government spending has another negative economic effect: it reduces buying power in inner-city consumer markets, thus reducing one of the sources of inner-city advantage identified by Porter.

Political realities and wealth-creation policies. Porter suggests dividing government economic-development spending into useful and extraneous, and then defending the former. Unfortunately, even if he were right about this division (see above), the political attack on government in 1996 makes no such fine distinctions. Racial and other divisions have fueled a political assault on those whose (assumed) profligacy and immorality can be blamed for decreasing wages and security in "mainstream" society.[11] There are many economically inefficient subsidies available outside the inner city; indeed, the really big subsidy money is to be had in suburban growth (notably via the mortgage deduction and FHA underwriting), not inner-city rescue. Lenders and developers hardly complain about distortions in suburban market forces; but then they are eager to compete in the greenfield markets these subsidies help to create.

And, even if business-friendly infrastructure spending could be substituted for social spending in U.S. inner cities, would the large, mobile corporations targeted by Porter and Kanter locate there? Kanter's description of regional success in South Carolina's Spartanburg area suggests otherwise. This region has prospered because local officials and business people have orchestrated effective vocational-training programs, educational reform, location incentives for overseas firms, and an integrated industrial clustering. Even so, Kanter admits that inner-city areas within this region have continued to deteriorate. Minorities have primarily taken low-wage jobs. German firms in the region have complained about the deterioration of downtown areas, but have expended no resources to make improvements there.[12]

Porter assumes mobile "mainstream" businesses will conform voluntarily with regulatory guidelines and incentives that tilt them to the inner city. He cites the CRA as an exemplar, since it guides financial firms into investments that are both socially and economically productive. But the CRA has been under sustained attack by the banking industry, and by many economists and legal scholars. Would other pro-inner-city regulations and subsidies be treated differently?

Another view. These second thoughts about the Porter/Kanter thesis lead to a different view of the role of government in inner-city reconstruction, of the need to nurture small inner-city firms and organizations, and of the relative importance of "mainstream" and inner-city firms.

The tendency of path-dependent market forces to redistribute wealth away from the inner city must be countered by strengthening mechanisms for inner-city wealth accumulation. This means making it easier both to preserve the value of existing wealth assets and to create new wealth. Preserving existing wealth means strengthening markets for housing exchange and financing, and making more flexible business financing in the inner city. Creating new wealth means new business incubators, technology and skill transfers, and venture capital.

Another conclusion of this analysis is that the in-migration of foreign firms and multinational corporations cannot be counted on to revive the inner city. Within the inner city, some neighborhoods with immigrants from Asia and elsewhere have, in some cases, enjoyed resurgent growth through two of Kanter's three C's—connections and competence. But the ability of Cuban or Chinese entrepreneurs to tap into global trading and manufacturing networks does not demonstrate that other minorities in the inner city can. Ethnic tension and bigotry appears to be quite robust in the face of inflows of people and capital from abroad into the U.S.; and historical patterns of locational and ethnic preference have been affirmed amidst these inflows.

For sustained prosperity, then, the inner-city economy needs its own autonomous or semi-autonomous clusters. This means an aggressive approach to antidiscrimination policy, which looks not just to punish economic bigotry but to redress racial inequalities. It also means reversing perverse path-dependent dynamics. This requires strategic coordination by a super-player able to discipline other players in the location game. Only government can play the super-player role; otherwise, no player has an incentive to buck established uneven-growth trends.

Finally, the problem of the political will to improve urban policies cannot be finessed. For one thing, cuts in social spending reduce the buying power on which, in part, inner-city renewal depends. For another, while the idea of a something-for-nothing inner-city policy is tempting, policies satisfying this criterion would be too tepid in practice to be effective. Any politician advocating meaningful policy shifts counter to established market interests and the politics of racial demonization must pay a political price, which a politically isolated inner city cannot cover.

FINANCIAL RESTRUCTURING AND ACCESS
TO CAPITAL IN THE INNER CITY

In essence, this critique argues, contrary to Porter and Kanter, that inner-city growth depends in part on autonomous inner-city development. Given their monumental disadvantage in wealth compared to their "mainstream" competitors, inner-city firms and organizations must obtain access to capital as a prerequisite to creating new inner-city growth clusters. Without slighting the importance of other aspects of generating growth clusters (such as job creation and skill enhancement), the remainder of this essay discusses access to capital in the inner city.

Interestingly, both Porter and Kanter agree that the unavailability of capital in the inner city is a barrier to economic renewal. These authors agree that small businesses (with one or more of the three C's) will play a role in the emerging global economy, and both agree as well that access to seed capital and to financing sources is crucial for such businesses. And while they argue that new sources of venture capital and financing are becoming available to smaller firms, they both admit that inner-city firms have limited access to these sources.

The U.S. banking system has traditionally provided the access to capital needed by smaller firms. To know what problems there are today in obtaining access to capital in the inner city, we must review the recent evolution of the U.S. urban banking system.[13]

Financial restructuring in the U.S. From World War II until the 1980s, the branch networks of U.S. commercial banks and thrifts served almost the entire urban population of households and firms. Small businesses obtained commercial and industrial loans, and households mortgage and consumer credit, from the same institutions at which they maintained checking and passbook savings accounts. Loan decisions were made locally by branch managers on the basis of personal information. This "New Deal" system functioned poorly in some minority neighborhoods, and was altogether absent in others; but for much of the inner city it constituted, in effect, an interlocking system of decentralized investment-savings mechanisms.

Since the 1970s, heightening competition from nonbank competitors and foreign entrants into U.S. banking markets has forced deregulation of the New Deal system. Banks and thrifts have faced the fiercest competition for the most profitable customers on both sides of their balance sheets. Wealthy depositors have been lost to equity-based and money-market mutual funds; blue chip firms now raise money directly from the money and bond markets, not just from bank loans.

Banks and thrifts failed in unprecedented numbers in the 1980s, in the wake of these changes. Those that now survive have adopted new competitive strategies. Among other strategic changes, banks have shed risk by making variable-rate loans and by bundling and selling fixed-rate loans. Indeed, banks and thrifts have moved from the traditional model of integrated financing into the era of "particle finance," wherein loans are made in many cases only if they can be sold off as securities. Further, banks have centralized loan decision making, which now often is based on standardized criteria evaluated by computer algorithms. In addition, banks and thrifts have eliminated cross-subsidies among their loan and deposit customers. The rates paid to wealthy depositors, and charged to blue-chip borrowers, once subsidized, respectively, lower-balance depositors and higher-risk borrowers; now each risk and cost class must bear its own weight. The upshot of loan centralization, customer loss, and the elimination of cross-subsidies is that many formerly profitable bank branches now generate losses. So bank branch networks have contracted rapidly in the past few years.

Banks and thrifts have effectively divided the New Deal customer bases into three segments. On the top are the super-included, the wealthy. These customers have access to personalized products delivered directly by brokers, account representatives, and advisors. In the middle are the process-included, the middle- and upper-income households. Their circumstances do not warrant personalized products or attention, but they are prime candidates for standardized transaction accounts and investment instruments. Banks and thrifts provide them with financial services as commodities, that is, impersonally and at low cost. Financial firms compete fiercely to provide for the transactions and investment needs of these two customers bases. At the bottom are the process-excluded, a group which includes not just the destitute, but also the working poor and the lower-middle class. Banks have made deposit accounts costly for low-balance customers, and the shift from "character" to balance-sheet criteria in loan decisions makes most of these customers uncreditworthy. So, whereas many of these households once had relationships with banks, an increasing number no longer do.[14] And as they have closed branches, banks and thrifts have largely withdrawn from the inner-city areas in which these households live.

Firms have also been profoundly affected by these changes in banking practices. "Mainstream" firms have available more lending and capitalization alternatives than ever before, at more competitive rates. By contrast, small firms have less access to capital in the new financial world: lenders will no longer make loans that are too small to be profitable, and their services can be obtained by inner-city firms only at higher out-of-pocket and/or shoe-leather costs.

The informal financial sector is growing to meet financial needs in the inner city. But, while check-cashing outlets and money orders provide (more costly) substitutes for banks' transaction services, the informal sector does not provide adequate credit and savings mechanisms. Pawnbrokers and "money stores" offer credit only on onerous terms, often to facilitate households' asset decumulation. Small firms cannot use even these options. Households without bank accounts have no secure means of conducting financial saving.

In sum, financial firms' strategic adjustments to changes in their own competitive terrain have been among the factors that have widened wealth and income differentials between the inner city and elsewhere; indeed, the differential availability of bank financing and venture capital is a principle mechanism of market-driven wealth redistribution. In effect, just as industrial expansion occurs in path-dependent clusters, so too does bank lending and expansion. It is no surprise that the areas of bank and industrial expansion and contraction neatly overlap. For this reason, Porter's idea for inner-city business incubation and expansion must be regarded with skepticism, for it requires that banks engage in against-the-herd behavior contrary to the growth patterns of nonfinancial firms. Financial structures, like nonfinancial clusters, will accentuate growth and worsen decay unless incentive structures are changed.

POLICIES TO FINANCE URBAN REGENERATION

We have argued that Porter portrays the possibilities for inner-city economic regeneration too optimistically because he overlooks some factors: market forces (deindustrialization and financial restructuring) have devastated the inner city and redistributed wealth elsewhere; "mainstream" and multinational firms have shown no great willingness to locate in the inner city; discrimination is not economically self-liquidating; inner-city labor supply and consumer demand are threatened by fiscal spending cuts; and the political terrain is hostile to pro-inner-city initiative. This section proposes some ideas for overcoming these further obstacles to realizing the competitive potential of the U.S. inner city. This section first takes up economic factors, especially financing mechanisms, and briefly discusses political factors.

Financial "push" mechanisms for inner-city wealth accumulation. It is useful to recall Kanter's skeptical view that the inner city is in decline because its residents and firms lack the three C's—world-class concepts, competence, and connections. If, as we have argued, "mainstream" and multinational corporations are unlikely to locate in the inner city, then mechanisms of inner-city wealth accumulation must create access to the three C's. Adequate financing can facilitate competence, and financial mechanisms can be a means of providing connections between the pools of savings and lending capacity outside the inner city, and the firms and individuals inside it. Connections in the form of more robust financing flows will require mechanisms *to push* financing into the inner city, and then mechanisms to *circulate and refresh* the financial flows thus engendered. Policies for "pushing" financing into the inner city include:

1. Preserve and strengthen the Community Reinvestment Act (CRA) of 1977.[15] Extend the CRA to all financial institutions, not just to banks and thrifts, and use simplified, results-oriented criteria for evaluation. Make bank CRA ratings public.
2. Establish a variety of loan funds for inner-city financing needs.
3. Reward financial institutions that contribute monies to inner-city loan funds or to community development banks, or financial institutions that make accumulation-oriented loans in specified low-income areas, with lower reserve requirements on a proportionate amount of their deposit holdings.
4. Require commercial banks and thrifts with over $50 billion in assets to offer and advertise special "Greenlining deposit accounts" wherein, for every dollar maintained by the depositor above some minimum amount (say, $500), the bank or thrift agrees to contribute a specified amount (say, 1 percent) into specified inner-city loan funds.
5. Establish investment pools that facilitate firm start-ups by entrepreneurs who live and work in specified low-income areas. These might include matching equity funds (wherein qualifying entrepreneurs receive an equity "bonus" for meeting specified performance goals) or equity-participation funds.
6. Create new mechanisms for community-based financial institutions of three kinds:
   a) microenterprise funds for the very poor—increase the number

of microenterprise funds, especially those that emulate the Grameen Bank strategy of targeting very low-income men and women. Make available to participants in such funds special assistance or grants covering day care, health benefits, and early childhood intervention;

b) community development corporations (CDCs)—expand the charters of CDCs to allow these firms more freedom to develop and invest in housing and businesses. Establish incentives for corporate capital and household infusions of equity to CDCs, on either a for-profit or not-for-profit basis. These incentives might include capital-gains or corporate-tax deductions up to some ceiling amount (following Porter's suggestion); and

c) community-based commercial banks and credit unions—create incentives for the founding or expansion of community-based, for-profit commercial banks and credit unions in communities underserved by the formal sector of financial intermediaries. Develop a criterion for a "financially underserved community," and encourage experimentation in institutional design. These incentives might include these institutions' equity participation in sponsored projects.

Diverse financial mechanisms are needed because of the diverse inner-city constituencies for such services. At one extreme are the small businesses and independent professionals who are cut off from networks of the sort Kanter and Porter discuss, and lack only access to capital to prosper. At the other extreme are adults with only sporadic contact with the formal labor force, who need a way "in" to become even proto-entrepreneurs. It is unlikely that these two constituencies, and those in between, can be serviced by the same financial-service providers.

All of the items in the above list suggest methods for accomplishing "greenlining"—attracting financing from "mainstream" communities to the inner city. Our analysis has highlighted the need for greenlining to compensate for unequal wealth. So does recent U.S. experience: even the most acclaimed U.S. community development bank, the South Shore Bank of Chicago, has relied on greenlined funds in its innovative lending practices. The erosion of inner-city branch networks makes greenlining essential. While public programs such as the Clinton administration's community-development banking initiative will provide some greenlining funds, the private sector is a much richer source. Incentives and subsidies like those proposed above can be used to bring monies into inner-city financing mechanisms. Even a government that has backed away from urban fiscal policy can provide incentives for taking risks in inner-city markets.

A financial "circulation" mechanism for inner-city wealth accumulation. Once "offshore" savings are extended to inner-city borrowers, they can be more efficiently used if the institutions holding them can recycle them—that is, can lend the same dollar more than once through a secondary-market exchange. Elsewhere, John Veitch and I have proposed a mechanism for circulating financing in the inner city, the Community Development Mortgage Association (Cindy Mae).[16] Cindy Mae would, if created, put in place a secondary-market mechanism like FNMA (Fannie Mae) for qualifying inner-city loans. Specifically, the government would buy up, bundle, and underwrite pools of qualifying inner-city loans from their originators; with appropriate guarantees in place, investors will purchase these pooled loans, and the proceeds they pay in will flow back to the institutions that originated the loans. To keep risk under control, the government would set prudential standards that lenders and borrowers alike would have to meet. Since many lenders will now originate only loans they can sell off, Cindy Mae should increase the number of inner-city lenders, as well as multiply the amount of inner-city credit.

Politics and inner-city renewal. We have argued above that reversing discrimination may require transfer payments to redress some racial gaps. This may be beyond the political pale. However, the various financing mechanisms suggested here, and entrepreneurship in the inner city more broadly, cannot succeed unless income flows and the supply of jobs in the inner city are increased. Further, spending for children, health care, and day care is crucial to prevent further social collapse in the inner city. Enhanced technical training and infrastructure improvements will similarly require a fiscal push, and micro-enterprise funds for the very poor necessarily run at a loss (even with zero default rates). This is to say, supply-side policy alone cannot renew the inner city; urban fiscal policy and/or redistribution must come back onto the political map.

Whether the suburban constituency will continue to take out its frustrations on an inner-city "other," and white workers will continue to vote with capital against minority workers, remains to be seen. A sufficiently deep recession could regenerate the political will to use stimulative demand-side policy, and to support social welfare and redistributive spending. But there is no guarantee that traditional Keynesian stimuli will put people back to work in the inner city.[17] Nor is there any guarantee that recession would not have the opposite political effect. The U.S. is, after all, two decades into a reaction to a brief period of liberal, pro-minority, pro-inner-city policy. In parallel events a century ago, white political reaction to Black Reconstruction in the South lasted over six decades. The racial and class divides now embodied in the split between the inner city and "mainstream" society are a hardy perennial in U.S. history.

NOTES

1. Michael E. Porter, "The Competitive Advantage of the Inner City," *Harvard Business Review* (May–June 1995): 54.

2. Both Porter and Kanter counterpose the euphemistic terms "inner city" and "mainstream" without defining them. The term "inner city" clearly refers to non-immigrant African Americans and Latinos located in lower-income urban areas; but the term "mainstream" is ambiguous. It could refer to "white" firms or areas, or to "large" firms regardless of their owners' color.

3. Porter makes it clear that he does *not* advocate cutting safety-net spending for individuals.

4. Kanter, Rosabeth, *World Class: Thriving Locally in the Global Economy* (New York: Simon and Schuster, 1995). Futurist John Naisbitt expresses ideas similar to those of Kanter in his *Global Paradox* (William Morrow and Company: New York, 1994).

5. Ironically, Nixon's program, framed as a conservative, market-oriented alternative to the more communitarian Community Action Programs of the 1960s, established some of the programs now attacked in Porter's analysis as oriented toward social and not market goals.

6. Kanter captures this idea in her phrase for those possessing none of her three C's—the *isolates*.

7. This is the central point of William Julius Wilson's *The Truly Disadvantaged* (Chicago: University of Chicago, 1987).

8. This point has been formally demonstrated by W. Brian Arthur, *Increasing Returns and Path Dependence in the Economy* (Ann Arbor: University of Michigan Press, 1994).

9. The legal and economic terrain of discrimination in credit markets was analyzed recently in this journal; see Gary Dymski, "The Theory of Credit-Market Discrimination and Redlining: An Exploration," *Review of Black Political Economy* (Winter 1995): 37–74. The discussion here is based on this analysis.

10. Bennett Harrison, "Why Business Alone Won't Fix the Cities," *Technology Review* (October 1995): 71.

11. Ronald Brownstein, "Voters in Growing Southern Suburbs May Determine GOP's '96 Nominee," *Los Angeles Times* (January 15, 1996): A5.

12. Kanter, *op cit.* Spartanburg's boom began with Roger Milliken's decision to relocate his family home and business from New York in 1954. A further cautionary tale is provided by South Central L.A.'s unsuccessful effort to woo a Mercedes-Benz factory in 1994, which lost out to a competing location in the South.

13. The impact of the continuing evolution of the U.S. banking system on urban development is analyzed in greater depth in Gary Dymski and John Veitch, "Financial Transformation and the Metropolis: Booms, Busts, and Banking in Los Ange-

les," *Environment and Planning A* (1996): 1233–1260.

14. John Caskey and Andrew Peterson, "Who Has a Bank Account and Who Doesn't: 1977 and 1989," *Eastern Economic Journal* 20(1) (1994): 61–74.

15. The Community Reinvestment Act of 1977 requires commercial banks and thrifts (savings and loan associations and mutual savings banks) to meet the credit needs of their entire market area, including low-income areas therein. The legislative intent and language is nonspecific; so regulators have interpreted compliance with the CRA as a procedural matter—filing the right forms in the right places. The Clinton administration has toughened CRA evaluations.

16. Gary Dymski and John Veitch, "Credit Flows to Cities," in *Reclaiming Prosperity: A Blueprint for Progressive Economic Reform*, edited by Jeff Faux and Todd Schafer (Armonk, NY: M.E. Sharpe, Inc., 1996): 227–235.

17. See Gary Dymski, "Economic Polarization and US Policy Activism," *International Review of Applied Economics* 10 (1) (1994): 65–84.

4

REBUILDING INNER CITIES: BASIC PRINCIPLES

June Manning Thomas

In 1994, Hartford, Connecticut, turned its public school system over to a private sector firm. Education Alternatives, Inc. promised to enhance student learning, improve test scores, introduce technological innovations, streamline school administration, and at the same time save the school district money. After one year, the Hartford Board of Education was so disappointed with the results that it wrested control of 26 of its 32 schools back from the private firm. Improving urban education, it seemed, was much harder, more complex, and more expensive than the company had imagined.[1]

This example is somewhat far afield from the *point* that Michael Porter is making in his 1995 *Harvard Business Review* article, "The Competitive Advantage of the Inner City." But it illustrates one of the dangers of the mindset that the private market, and by extension for-profit business, is the solution to all ills. While Porter is correct in asserting that unfairly negative attitudes toward the private sector are counterproductive, his claim that his pro-business approach to inner-city revitalization excels over all other options goes too far.

Here is what Porter does well: he offers critical insights into how central city economies work, particularly which firms survive within distressed areas of inner cities. Simply by documenting business survival in these environments, he has provided a valuable service. Because of his research, those who work to encourage economic development in areas that the private market has abandoned can benefit from a much stronger set of directives than existed before. Indeed, if Porter is correct, local governments need to overhaul their business attraction operations, which have relied too heavily on expensive government incentives, and to apply his suggestions. These are in fact not far astray from procedures that some local governments are already using, but Porter brings greater focus to the factors underlying successful business development.

His comments also assist the private and non-profit sectors, helping businesses, or those who would interact with the world of business, make intelligent choices about how to survive and thrive in distressed central cities. It is easy to envision a new generation of business plans and ventures founded upon the information he provides. This can improve the economic and social status of distressed neighborhoods, beset as they are by lack of viable employment opportunities. The strength of Porter's suggestions is their strong empirical connection to the natural workings of business, allowing public and private sector organizations to avoid trudging uphill, working against the laws of (economic) gravity.

Here is what Porter's work does *not* tell us: we have no evidence, yet, that this particular approach triumphs over other strategies for revitalizing distressed areas. Porter eagerly leaps from the firm grounding of his excellent research in the motivations of businesses into the uncertain stratosphere of urban revitalization. His claim that his economic model offers "a new and comprehensive approach to reviving our nation's distressed urban communities" is apparently based on hope and little else. Where is the evidence that this approach is the best framework for urban revitalization, the most suitable pivot upon which development strategies should center?

Before accepting such a claim, we need experiential testing of Porter's precepts in the urban context. That is, someone needs to try his "economic model" prescriptions and carefully document their results compared to other *urban revitalization* (as opposed to simply business development) strategies.

In the meantime, what do we know about revitalization? A first step might be to consider what urban revitalization is. Then it will be important to outline a few key principles that should guide our assessment of proposed urban revitalization strategies. These principles are not in disharmony with Porter's ideas, but offer some dimensions that need further emphasis.

URBAN REVITALIZATION

No generally agreed-upon definition exists for urban revitalization. But at its broadest level, urban revitalization surely means the bringing back of life, or "vitality," into areas of the city or metropolis that have lost such life. For inner-city areas that have lost people and commerce, we might see, instead, a healthier mix of people, commerce, industry, and viable community life.

We have gotten into trouble in the past by defining urban revitalization too narrowly. Targeting central business district revival, the focus for many decades, left residential neighborhoods open to neglect and decline. Turning to neighborhoods only as sites to be cleared and reconstructed for middle- and upper-class owners and renters—or, in earlier years, for overcrowded and segregated public housing residents—caused massive political conflict and social turmoil. Chasing smokestack industries, or sports stadiums, or casinos, yielded limited gains. Expecting distressed area businesses to bring life back to dead areas could also prove to be too optimistic.

We must instead come back to a vision of a revitalized urban area. This basic step of visioning—required, by the way, of all communities that applied for U.S. empowerment zone/enterprise community designation—yields an image that is really quite complex. That image certainly includes businesses and opportunities for adults to work. But it also includes good housing, adequate community services and facilities, and viable transportation. It includes schools that adequately prepare youngsters for meaningful and purposeful lives. It includes safe streets, where women and children need not fear to walk.

The issue is larger than economic and physical rejuvenation. Etzioni argues that we must promote the "spirit of community," aiming for strong families, positive "core" social values taught in schools, and citizen involvement in the life of the community.[2] An excellent example of such sentiments is the spirit that moved African American men to converge in Washington, D.C., for a Million Man March, to reinforce male commitment to family and community. Who can deny that their changed thinking, translated into action, could have major effects on the well-being of distressed urban communities?

Another way of saying this, according to a recent statement by the Bahá'í International Community, is that concepts of development must allow people to become better human beings as well as answer their physical wants, because a "materialistic conception of life" may not be "capable of meeting humanity's needs."[3] It is blind pursuit of materialism, for example, that has fueled the inner-city drug culture, since inner-city youths who crave expensive things know that legal job opportunities could never match the princely sums available from drug sales. So this concept of urban revitalization is no simplistic matter, but rather one that gets at the heart of what it means to create a good community, a good city, a good society. We must consider what might be some basic principles governing such revitalization. Following are a few ideas.

Use Holistic Strategies

Perhaps one of the most important concepts is to use multifaceted efforts. While it is no longer possible to claim the ability to undertake "comprehensive" strategies, as urban planners promoted in the past, a systems view of the world suggests that various facets of urban distress are interconnected, and that those connections must be recognized, acknowledged, and addressed.

In the 1950s and 1960s (and beyond), some physical development strategies for central cities led to disastrous consequences for the social fabric of low-income city residents. In the 1960s the nation turned to the "social needs" model that Porter disparages, aiming to bring inner-city residents into the process of urban improvement. Also generated were strategies associated with sectors such as housing (subsidized construction, rental, or purchase programs), or economic and business development (notably minority business development and business attraction efforts).

Perhaps these strategies are not equally effective, and perhaps it is impossible to coordinate their execution perfectly. It may also be that, if we could choose only one candidate among them, economic development would prevail, since its absence affects so many other components of urban systems. Economic restructuring has had a pernicious effect upon the social, economic, and physical well-being of inner-city neighborhoods.[4]

Yet practical evidence and common sense indicate that urban distress problems are interrelated, as must be their solutions. We cannot yet trust one-dimensional efforts. What would happen, for example, if a distressed area received new businesses, but had no effective strategy to combat urban crime? Or if the educational system's ineffectiveness prevented inner-city youngsters from gaining access to new inner-city jobs?

The 1960s program Model Cities, an unfairly maligned innovation, attempted to combine social, economic, and physical solutions for inner-city revitalization.[5] The newest federal urban program, Clinton's as yet untested Empowerment Zones and Enterprise Communities, reflects the counsel of numerous urban scholars and practitioners in its encouragement of holistic approaches to urban reform in target cities.[6]

The engine of these programs may be economic development, but critical to their shape, direction, and velocity are such efforts as community policing, family support programs, housing and neighborhood development, improved elementary education, and job training.

Those in faith-based development would add that urban rejuvenation must involve the whole human being, implying a spiritual dimension as well. This is one reason that, within many inner-city black communities, faith-based community development is a rising star.[7]

Involve Residential and Institutional Partners

A second basic principle: involve local residents and institutions in solving the problems their communities face. A recent report by the Committee for Economic Development (C.E.D.), an independent research and policy organization, explains this principle in "Rebuilding Inner-City Communities: A New Approach to the Nation's Urban Crisis." C.E.D. calls such involvement the key principle for revitalizing urban areas.[8] A decided turn-around has occurred in several deteriorated inner-city areas around the country. An important characteristic of many of these successes is that they involved "community building." Resident partnership in problem-solving is one important facet of community building; another is involvement of local institutions.

Porter notes that retail businesses that come to know their customers' tastes, and that hire local residents as employees, can build very successful ventures and loyal clientele within inner cities. This is true because such practices recognize the importance of partnership with local residents. He also correctly points out that community-based organizations can assist greatly in the process of economic development, by changing community and resident attitudes, creating work-readiness and job-referral systems, and serving as a catalyst for commercial and industrial development.

But the significance of resident involvement is even more important than these examples would suggest. Porter presents them as activities that can support business development. An alternative way of thinking about this inverts the relationship: business development can support community development. An even better conceptual framework, perhaps, is of a partnership. It is true that communities benefit from business development, and that they cannot expect businesses to be more concerned about local needs than about making a profit. But businesses lose by interacting with local inner-city residents merely as passive customers or employees. Firms may find it to their benefit to participate with local residents in problem-solving efforts involving training and unemployment, youth development, public safety, or community services.

The Committee for Economic Development (CED) also points out the importance of community-based institutions. These include not only community development corporations, referred to in Porter's article, but also public schools, religious communities, hospitals, universities, and financial institutions. Community-based institutions must be involved because of their longevity. Unlike most businesses, which could move or shut down because of whim or markets, many such institutions have sunk considerable long-term investment into inner-city areas. It would be foolish *not* to involve institutions with long-term standing in the area, and with access to resources that could assist with the myriad facets of urban revitalization. The challenge is to coordinate and focus activities so that they add up to significant results.

Improve Social Justice

A final key principle is perhaps the most controversial for business advocates. It is controversial because, as Porter notes, in its name society may place inappropriate demands upon businesses that are simply trying to do what they do best, or may develop government programs that appear to fail. But social justice *is* an important principle to consider concerning urban revitalization strategies.[9] When urbanist Kevin Lynch laid out the principles for designing good cities in his last published book, he called justice a "meta-criterion," one that underlay all other components of good cities.[10] For what good is it to "revitalize" cities if all the benefits accrue to the prosperous?

As noted in the Bahá'í International statement cited above, development must avoid sacrificing the well-being of the general citizenry "to the advantages…available to privileged minorities."[11] It is a matter of justice for a city's low-income and distressed area residents to expect their concerns and needs to merit full consideration in the dialogue of urban revitalization. Or, as promoted by urban planner Norman Krumholz, a major purpose of redevelopment must be to open choices to those who have few.[12]

This does not mean that each and every redevelopment initiative must be judged only by its distributional effects—as Porter notes, in many cases this is neither possible nor sensible—but that, on balance, a city's redevelopment agenda must take into account the goal of equity.

One way to insure this is to honor the first and second principles listed above. If we combine strategies in several different areas, we have a better chance of tackling the issue of social justice. If we make urban problem-solving *participatory*, involving residents who live in distressed areas, we can be sure that issues of social justice will not fade away unnoticed.

Another way to promote social justice is to think carefully about the equity possibilities of any particular strategy, and to build program components that take advantage of those possibilities. "Linkage" programs are not the only possible equity response to business development. For example, since we now have better ideas about what kinds of businesses succeed and fail in distressed inner cities, it might be possible to revisit the possibilities of opening ancillary opportunities for minority business owners, or to consider the implications for microenterprise. Another strategy would be to strengthen school partnerships with local firms in order to bring young people into the world of commerce and shape their education in ways that are useful. Perhaps this would be a stepping stone to something like the German model, which provides internships for high schoolers that usher them directly from school to the world of work, giving meaning and purpose to their high school diplomas.

CONCLUSION

In summary, Porter's concepts offer a welcome framework for improving the business vitality of inner-city areas. He does this by highlighting the natural advantages such areas enjoy, and by offering empirically based advice about which firms could do well in areas others have given up for lost. Undoubtedly his concepts will have a major impact upon how we think about, and carry out, economic development in central cities.

What Porter does not yet give us is a well-tested "new" model of urban revitalization. In fact, what we know about revitalization suggests that it must be holistic, expanding beyond economic issues; that it must be participatory, involving local residents as well as local institutions in the business of urban rejuvenation; and that issues of social justice remain important. Porter's concepts could provide an extremely important component of a well-rounded effort. But the three principles we have described suggest the need for supplementing business development initiatives with more holistic, more participatory, and more consciously equitable strategies for urban revitalization.

NOTES

1. Elizabeth Gleick, "Privatized Lives," *Time*, November 13, 1995, p. 88.

2. Amitai Etzioni, *The Spirit of Community: The Reinvention of American Society* (New York: Simon and Schuster, Touchstone Books, 1994).

3. Bahá'í International Community, "The Prosperity of Humankind" (Haifa, Israel: Bahá'í International Community, Office of Public Information, c. 1995), p. 2.

4. William Julius Wilson, *The Truly Disadvantaged: The Inner City, The Underclass, and Public Policy* (Chicago: The University of Chicago Press, 1987).

5. For alternative perspective on Model Cities see Robert Woods, "Model Cities: What Went Wrong—The Program or its Critics?" in *Neighbourhood Policy and Programmes: Past and Present*, ed. by Naomi Carmon (New York: St. Martin's Press, 1990), pp. 61–73; Rufus P. Browning, Dale Rogers Marshall, and David H. Tabb, *Protest is Not Enough: The Struggle of Blacks and Hispanics for Equality in Urbana Politics* (Berkeley: University of California Press, 1984); and June Thomas, "Model Cities Revisited: Race and Empowerment," chapter in a book edited by June Thomas and Marsha Ritzdorf, *Urban Planning and the African American Community in the Shadows* (Thousand Oaks: Sage Publications, 1996).

6. June Thomas, "Applying for Empowerment Zone Designation: A Tale of Woe and Triumph," *Economic Development Quarterly* 9 (August 1995): 212–224.

7. June Thomas and Reynard Blake, Jr., "Faith-Based Community Development and African-American Neighborhoods," *Revitalizing Urban Neighborhoods*, edited by Dennis Keating, Norman Krumholz, and Phil Starr (Lawrence: University Press of Kansas, forthcoming 1996).

8. Research and Policy Committee, Committee for Economic Development, "Rebuilding Inner-City Communities: A New Approach to the Nation's Urban Crisis" (New York: Committee for Economic Development, 1995).

9. For an excellent definition of "social justice," see Robert Mier and Howard M. McGary, Jr., "Social Justice and Public Policy," in Robert Mier, *Social Justice and Local Development Policy* (Newbury Park, Calif: Sage Publications, 1993), pp. 20–31.

10. Kevin Lynch, *Good City Form* (Cambridge: M.I.T. Press, 1984), pp. 118, 225–35. Lynch's book focuses on city design, but his comments on justice are very instructive. For a more focused discussion of the relationship of social justice and economic development policy, see Mier, *Social Justice*, op. cit.

11. Bahá'í International Community, "The Prosperity," p. 6.

12. Norman Krumholz and John Forrester, *Making Equity Planning Work: Leadership in the Public Sector* (Philadelphia: Temple University Press, 1990).

5

DÉJÀ-VU ALL OVER AGAIN: PORTER'S MODEL OF INNER-CITY REDEVELOPMENT

David S. Sawicki and Mitch Moody

Dr. Michael Porter has advanced a model for the redevelopment of the inner city that relies heavily on private sector and natural market forces, diminishing the role of government in social programs. Since Porter's assertions are apparently being taken seriously by some American civic and business leaders who may make substantial investments of time and other resources into some manifestations of his theory, we think it important to provide coherent criticism of its failings. Upon close examination, little he recommends is new or stands the scrutiny of thirty or more years of research and practice in inner-city economic redevelopment. Here, we first place Porter's ideas in historical context, then discuss six major assertions from his writings. In our opinion, Porter contributes to another misformulation of the problem of revitalizing ghetto economies, and therefore provides a sure loser of a solution. His theory, should the corporate world accept it and give it a real test, is tailor-made for another lesson, true or not, on how the ghetto cannot be redeveloped.

INTRODUCTION

We would like to begin this essay by paying Dr. Porter the usual compliment: "Michael Porter has made an important contribution to the research and practice of inner-city economic development." Though many have found new merit in Porter's proposals, we cannot. What the policy debate does not need is yet another model for urban redevelopment that raises unrealistic expectations about what can be accomplished and which directs potentially productive players (young, black, business school graduates) into private sector-initiated activities without real roots in the inner city. The idea that minority alumni of business schools might come to the aid of minority businesses is solid and reasonably timed, given the growing cadre of maturing professionals. Those business persons should be prepared, however, with the knowledge garnered in over thirty years of research and practice in urban redevelopment—an experience Porter substantially ignores. His resurrection of a large number of well-worn ideas about inner-city redevelopment, some of them previously discredited, invites our critical review.

Our self-imposed agenda is to inform readers about the issues Porter raises. In doing so, we are aware of Robert S. Browne's observation in "The Origin, Birth, and Adolescence of *The Review of Black Political Economy* and the Black Economic Research Center":

> An examination of the contents of the RBPE over its twenty-three year lifetime reveals that a subtle shift has taken place in both the focus and tone of the articles. In the early issues, macro-perspective articles looking at the black community as a whole . . . predominated. . . . But as time passes, the preponderance of the articles shifts toward more narrowly focused topics; the articles become less discursive and more scholarly. . . . Largely disappeared are the wide-ranging, somewhat ideological, somewhat polemical prescriptions for restructuring the black community and its relationship to white America.[1]

Porter chooses to admonish investors to locate black businesses in the inner city as a way to create jobs for poor black people (we presume). His choice of strategies is curious, though. Our contribution begins with a brief review of Porter's strategy, placing it in the larger historic context of economic development theory and practice. Following that review, we discuss six core assertions he presents and assess their contribution to the existing knowledge base of community and economic development.[2]

THE CONTINUING VITALITY OF THE PEOPLE-VERSUS-PLACE DEBATE

There is a long-standing debate, "place prosperity versus people prosperity," in both research and economic development practice about the strategies of targeting places (usually inner cities) or targeting people with the goal of improving the fortunes of the poor, especially minorities.[3] Apparent failures, especially in the place-targeting approach both in the United States and overseas, have led the Clinton administration to develop a mixed approach, which Ladd calls a "place-based people strategy."[4] As background for his proposals, Porter implicitly chooses a place-based minority business strategy. Because it is essential to understand the people-vs.-place debate before analyzing any redevelopment model, we will give it a brief review.

A pure people-based economic development strategy would attempt to help people or households wherever they were located. State and federal programs that provide education or social services for the poor are examples of aid for persons no matter what their location. This people-based strategy has led to both a dispersal tactic and a mobility tactic. Downs[5] is the best-known advocate for the dispersal of the ghetto, and the integration of residential areas. Programs that discourage housing segregation and provide vouchers to low-income renters, rather than public housing located in the central city, work toward that end. Hughes is the principal advocate for integration of suburban work places, suggesting strategies that encourage the mobility of central-city workers.[6] Job-listing and information programs as well as subsidized commuting programs from center city to suburb are examples of his proposals. There are at least three strong reasons for preferring people-based strategies. There is a large literature, begun by Kain in the 1960s that discusses these three things: "(1) residential segregation affects the geographical distribution of black employment; (2) residential segregation increases black unemployment; and (3) the negative effect of housing segregation on black employment is magnified by the decentralization of jobs."[7] It is the latter point that has been well documented by many, but especially well by Ihlandfelts[8] and Kasarda,[9] that has tilted preferences recently towards people versus place-based strategies. Jobs, especially entry-level jobs, have decentralized to outlying suburban areas. This fact, coupled with the relative immobility (e.g., lack of automobiles, inadequate public transportation, relatively high reservation wages, and impossibly long commutes) of the minority poor have created serious employment problems, especially for young inner-city black males. However, physical isolation from appropriate jobs has greater impacts than simply higher commuting costs; it also means isolation from social and job networks and peer groups that sustain employability. These changes in the nature of work in America and its microlocation within metropolitan areas has brought new life to person-based strategies that encourage mobility to suburban residences and workplaces.

In our own work, so far concentrated in Atlanta, we found that despite the incredible growth of the metropolitan economy, arguably the first or second best in the nation in the 1980s, a large proportion of central-city blacks remained either unemployed or not in the labor force at all. The prime explanation found was that large numbers of inmigrants to Atlanta, mostly whites, were getting the entry-level jobs. Young and relatively uneducated blacks, both in-migrants and natives, suffer much higher rates of disconnection from the labor force than similarly aged and trained white in-migrants. In addition, in-migrants located disproportionately closer to the new entry-level jobs in the north central suburbs.[10]

A pure place-based strategy makes investments in a physical place at a particular location. Interestingly, the approach need not involve a needy population. There are many reasons these strategies are preferred in practice.[11] By far the most important reason is that places are represented by elected officials, and elected officials do not want their places to deteriorate. Short terms of office make it essential to achieve tangible results that voters can see with their eyes; thus physical projects are preferred. In addition, place-based strategies keep blacks contained in the center city. This result is favored by many black elected officials who do not wish to see their power base eroded, and by some whites who do not want to integrate the suburbs. However, the result is often that those in the city who own the land and capital, not poor (renting) residents, are the beneficiaries. Probably the most disturbing aspect of the acceptance of place-based strategies is the *de-facto* acquiescence to racial segregation.

The enterprise zone approach, as it was conceived and implemented in England, provides a good example of how place-based policies can fail to benefit poor residents.[12] First, there are questions about whether the incentives actually are successful in attracting jobs to poor areas. Second, there is substantial evidence that when there are net new jobs to the enterprise area, they are simply jobs being transferred from other poor areas. And finally, the jobs that do get created do not usually go to poor residents of the zone. Some research cites "skills-mismatch" as the reason, but Kasinitz and Rosenberg provided a convincing case in Red Hook in Brooklyn that physical proximity to jobs was unimportant compared with social and ethnic networks.[13] Just as the English program focused on blighted nonresidential areas with declining industrial and warehousing facilities, the American version focused on failing downtowns in large central cities. Wolman, Ford, and Hill have shown that, with few exceptions, cities that had successfully revitalized their downtown areas did no better than those that did not in terms of benefiting their residents with better economic circumstances.[14] The key, again, is confusing the benefiting of places with the benefiting of people. Presuming that changed tax policies and regulatory relief or incentives like land write-downs could bring new economic activity and employment, the question of which individuals get those jobs remains. Programs that have specified that jobs must go to local residents have proved either unsuccessful or unattractive to businesses.

Given the failings of both pure strategies, the Clinton administration has chosen to implement a place-based people strategy. Within a number of zones in cities (roughly 50,000 population) and a few rural areas in the country, federal and state governments will relax regulations, reduce taxes, and provide job training money in an effort to entice businesses to locate in the zones and employ local residents. Simultaneously, the legislation provides a block grant that can be used for social services for needy residents in the zone.

What is curious about Porter's work is that he never provides a rationale for why he adopts a place-based business strategy. He eschews the pure people-based strategy, recommending that governments direct their energies to helping central-city businesses rather than to providing aid for human services in central cities. However, presuming his ultimate goal is to attack the problems of persistent poverty in minority communities, and his approach is to attack poverty by improving business practice, Porter could have elected either of two possible methods: a place-based business strategy, or a people-based business strategy. The latter, of course, would involve strategizing about how to provide innovative help to minority businesses.

There are many strong arguments that could be made against a place-based business strategy, especially if the places are America's large central cities, beyond the fact that incentives geared to moving businesses there have largely failed. We will illustrate with the work of three researchers. The most compelling condemnation of the approach is provided by research published in this journal by Timothy Bates.[15] Analyzing a sample of records from the Characteristics of Business Owners survey compiled by the U.S. Bureau of the Census in 1987, Bates concludes the following: "Most of the nonminority-owned small businesses operating in large urban areas do not employ minorities. Even among the businesses physically located within minority communities, the majority of the workers in the nonminority small firms are white. Black-owned businesses, in contrast, rely largely on minority workers even when their firms are located outside of minority neighborhoods." In Atlanta, Boston[16] found that the most successful minority businesses are located in suburban areas. Finally, using a dataset of firm records, White, Binkley, and Osterman[17] showed that during the expansionary period of 1983 to 1987 net gains in employment in the city of Milwaukee came almost entirely from firm expansions. The authors differentiated types of suburbs, and showed that, in the outer suburbs, employment growth came mostly from expansions, but also from migrating businesses and new startups. Migration was not an important factor in any area, however. Should the Milwaukee experience be a model, it is clear that trying to recruit new firms to the central city is definitely an activity akin to swimming against the tide. The strategy of helping to grow minority businesses in the inner city seems to place an additional (geographic) burden on a task that doesn't need more challenges.

A people-based business strategy would seem to make more sense given our reading of both research and practice. Such a strategy would encourage successful businesses to offer aid to needful minority businesses wherever they were located, inner city or in exurbia. If we believe Bates's argument, such businesses would hire minorities at a much greater rate than would nonminority firms. Suburban black businesses would provide the mechanisms for opening up the suburbs for black suburban workers to live in the suburbs;[18] urban black businesses could employ many stuck in the central city because of housing discrimination.

This people-based strategy helps to partially solve the problems of spatial mismatch, job discrimination, and housing discrimination, described in great detail by researchers over the last thirty years. Viewed generationally, with more blacks living in the suburbs with children attending suburban schools, the historic problem with skills mismatch might be reduced as well. Why Porter chose to constrain his strategy of aiding minority businesses with the requirement of locating them in central cities is difficult to understand.

PORTER'S CENTRAL ASSERTIONS ABOUT INNER-CITY DEVELOPMENT

Several threads of thinking permeate most of Porter's writings: 1) economic initiatives should be preferred over social initiatives; 2) market forces should replace government subsidies; 3) non-profits should not specialize in business development; 4) export-based development is superior to local-serving economic development; 5) the inner city has four areas of competitive advantage; and 6) agglomeration economies and clusters can spawn more development. Each of these assertions by Porter has important implications for inner-city development. The validity of these claims should be central to critical acceptance of his ideas. The following discussion places several of Porter's assertions in proper historical context and addresses the merits of his proposals. Where appropriate, the people-vs.-place dichotomy will provide an informative conceptual framework for understanding the placement of Porter's prescriptions on the policy spectrum.

Economic Initiatives Should Be Preferred Over Social Initiatives

In Porter's opinion, none of the economic development strategies for the inner cities have worked, and thus should be replaced by programs that deal directly with the economics of the ghetto. True, the creation of a sustainable economic base in inner cities still eludes policy-makers. But what Porter fails to acknowledge is that past efforts, numerous as they have been, were never designed or funded to fully resurrect the inner-city economy.[19]

Two aspects of past policies have been particularly detrimental to inner-city residents. First, public sector social and employment programs were never intended to supply jobs in the quantities demanded by the ghetto unemployed (i.e., unemployed, underemployed, and not-in-the-labor-force but desiring work), so we should not be surprised that ghetto economies have continued to languish. Over 21,000 black males (not counting the underemployed) in such circumstances were reported in Atlanta's inner city in 1990.[20] Second, for several decades, social programs directed at the poor have been remarkably successful at maintaining, without prolonged insurrection, a substantially jobless population at a minimum short-term financial cost to society. Each of these critical points will be discussed in turn.

First, Porter criticizes current social policy, which operates under "the implicit assumption that if social needs are met, then economic revitalization will follow." This criticism ignores the circumstances under which current programs have evolved; in truth, few policy-makers have labored under that assumption. More realistically, social spending has served to ameliorate some of the damage caused by the failure of free-market economic development of the inner city and, most importantly, the disappearance of living-wage jobs for the unskilled in these areas.

As the problem is defined, so goes the design of the solutions. If the problem becomes defined as "too-generous social programs eroding the will of ghetto residents to work," then "tough-love" solutions that severely restrict benefits to the poor may be the appropriate policy. If, however, the problem is that the private and public sectors are unwilling or politically incapable of generating living-wage jobs for lower-skilled people, then tough-love, austerity economics and "information society" jobs are final insults to the economically disenfranchised.

For thirty years after World War II, the federal government, at least in rhetoric, supported the goal of full employment. The appointment of Paul Volcker by President Jimmy Carter in the late 1970s to head the Federal Reserve signaled abandonment of a national goal of full employment.[21] About the same time, the Full Employment and Balanced Growth Act, also known as the Humphrey-Hawkins Act, was signed into law, making the government the "employer of last resort." The Act had little impact, however, because an enforceable job guarantee had been eliminated in the version finally enacted. The federal government, under substantial private sector and conservative influence, was unable to pass effective labor legislation guaranteeing decent jobs, in the private or public sector, for those willing to work. This failure is indicative of a true struggle for economic fairness, one that blacks and other unskilled persons have been steadily losing for fifty years.

The failure of blacks, and the poor generally, to secure guarantees of employment meant that social programs would be required to do what had been ruled out-of-bounds for national employment policy—provide at least a minimal level of living for the persistently unemployed. Social programs should not be blamed for the failure of national leadership, both private and public, to provide economic futures to inner-city residents. Notably, current conservative "solutions" for the jobless poor still do not include job guarantees even while the social safety net is dismantled.

Second, given the lack of national resolve regarding employment policy, the problem after the ambitious Great Society programs of the Johnson administration was to find a least-cost solution for the "problem of the ghetto." The least expensive solution, which denied all public and private sector responsibility for the joblessness of the urban poor, was simply to discontinue public assistance. Considered a politically risky strategy at the time because of the possibility of renewed urban riots, this solution was not implemented, waiting for a more propitious time to introduce such a radical approach (1994 and the 104th Congress). The next least costly solution, and the one adopted as *de facto* national policy for twenty-five years now, was to contain inner-city residents in poor-quality housing in segregated areas, providing little real hope of joining the economic mainstream. Considering the relatively modest magnitude of funds directly expended on the poor, it can be argued that thirty years of relative domestic tranquillity have been purchased at a reasonable cost, at least to the taxpayers. Most public funds expended on the poor have been for health and housing programs that have widely benefited many groups, including the medical, insurance and construction industries. Direct trickledown to the poor has been much too little to permit their rebuilding of the ghetto economy.

Porter's indictment that government-backed social programs have failed ignores the history of how present policies evolved. He claims that economic programs should now prevail where the social programs of the 1960s and 1970s have fallen short. But the need for social programs in the ghetto arose from the failure of the private sector to provide new economic opportunities to unskilled and blue-collar inner-city residents more than twenty years ago when manufacturing employment began to decline rapidly. Private sector failure, infrequently discussed today, is even more likely now, given the well-documented diminishing number of jobs that demand lower-skilled workers. Unfortunately, as we will show, Porter's ideas are neither so innovative nor so powerful that private sector success at revitalizing inner-city economies can reasonably be expected in the near future.

Market Forces Should Replace Government Subsidies

Michael Porter states that the only way to promote a sustainable economic base is through for-profit initiatives based on economic self-interest and true competitive advantages, not through artificial inducements, charity, or government mandates. In fact, we are in basic agreement on this point, but for two reasons Porter does not mention. First, place-based incentive programs have not proven to be very effective in the inner city. With many levels of government offering incentives, the only strategies that make sense are those that try to organize those governments to eliminate incentives (a nonstarter in game theory terms), or to match incentives when they prove to be important to private sector location decisions. Second, as discussed previously, the beneficiaries of incentive programs are seldom the poor and unskilled, but rather the owners of land and capital in the designated areas and activities.

Porter's role for the public sector follows conventional business ideology. To quote again from Porter, "Governments should cut across geographical and political boundaries to assemble land to turn back to the private sector," "strident environmentalism will make the problem worse by further scaring away business investment," and "community input is important in development, but it should take place on the overall plan for an area rather than an individual project." However, if the ghetto is really a good deal, then why has investment-hungry capital not found a way to make a profit? Appeals for environmental regulatory relief is an old locational incentive that has worked often to the detriment of poor people. And stifling public discussions of community development plans could be read as an attempt to defer sincere and relevant popular input on important issues, not a democratic, much less empowering, act.[22] The skepticism of ghetto residents that Porter decries is not without some foundation.

Dr. Porter's strategy for solving the problem of access to capital for firms in the ghetto is simple, if inconsistent with the free-market approach he seems to prefer rhetorically. The ideal role for government in solving the decades-old problem of lack of ghetto capital, as Porter sees it, is for government to "address the high transactions cost of making the relatively small loans . . . through . . . incentives. To provide incentives, a bank closing a qualifying minority or inner city-based business loan might receive a transaction fee to offset the cost of working with inner city entrepreneurs. . . . An additional fee might be earned if the loan were performing 18 months later." At odds with his professed business program, Porter does not lose a step as he prescribes a form of corporate welfare to take the place of the human welfare programs. Porter seems content to maintain some traditional forms of public sector involvement in inner-city development—and substantial public incentives to private firms is one of the oldest and still-popular forms of public-private cooperation—if they benefit influential business constituencies.

Non-profits Should Not Specialize in Business Development

On this topic, we will defer to our fellow writers, who represent community-based organizations (CBOs), and keep our observations to a minimum. Porter saves some of his harshest criticism for the community development banks and some community development corporations, citing their lack of expertise and resources to become major business lenders. Porter states that "a better approach would be to create the conditions for private, mainstream financial institutions to be profitable in minority and inner-city business lending." Certainly, attracting financial institutions back to the inner city is a desirable goal but not one that will be achieved in the short term. In the meantime, what institutions are available to make up for the failure of financial markets to serve the ghetto businesses that are there? CBOs have simply filled the vacuum created by the lack of private lending institutions.

Though community-based organizations have a spotty record with inner-city lending, it must be remembered that economic survival in the ghetto environment is difficult for all concerned. As Bates has noted, minority enterprise assistance programs are largely failures. Lending to blacks is typically in small, marginal, low-profit businesses, many retail, with a relatively high propensity to fail. Private lending institutions, fearful of high default rates, rationally hesitate to make funds available.[23] Most CBOs probably do reasonably well, considering the hostile circumstances in which they operate.

Export-based Development Is Superior to Local-serving Economic Development

Porter believes that inner-city businesses should be capable of competing on regional, national and international scales. Inner-city businesses must go beyond local markets and begin to export to the outside world (i.e., outside the ghetto, the city, the region, and the country). This thinking is consistent with his popular book, *The Competitive Advantage of Nations*,[24] and traditional export-based growth economics, which emphasize the importance of recirculating within an area dollars derived from the external economy to achieve a multiplier effect that raises the incomes of area residents.

Not a new idea, over twenty years ago Bennett Harrison surveyed the state of ghetto economic development and found that most groups actively engaged in community economic planning were already "consciously seeking 'export linkages' and externally located assets to complement their internal activities." He also mentioned the "possibilities for 'exporting' goods and services to nearby institutional customers . . . "[25] Harrison and Porter are not alone in observing the desirability of export ties for the ghetto economy; many others have explored, and exploited, the obvious advantages.[26]

It is significant that Porter's theorizing in *The Competitive Advantage of Nations* addresses only the industrialized countries of Europe, North

America, and East Asia; virtually no mention is made of the lesser-developed countries of Africa and much of Asia and their general failure to integrate with the world economy. As Harrison and others have noted, it is the economies of the Third World that are most analogous to the inner city, but about them Porter has little to say. Like the populations of lesser-developed countries, most ghetto residents have too few skills to market to the national and world economies. It is not clear why Porter expects that lessons from the international economy can be successfully applied to the inner city given the core-periphery relationships that have evolved between the industrialized and the majority of lesser-developed countries. Export-based economic development will not work for inner-city residents unless their skills and labor are embodied in the products exported. If skills are few, then benefits to the people of the ghetto from exports will be minimal unless the political process intervenes. This is as true in New York as in New Delhi.

Finally, Porter criticizes the development strategy counterposed to export-directed import substitution (IS). First, he is incorrect when he suggests the total failure of IS as an economic development strategy. Import substitution is usually viewed as a temporary expedient to jump-start an economy that has less than a critical threshold of internal industry to stimulate its own economic growth. Successful and unsuccessful examples abound. Successes include Brazil and the post-World War II Los Angeles area. Most IS failures, India for example, are due to a tendency to keep such programs in place after the initial stimulation to growth has occurred. The problem is not so much the concept of IS but how it is implemented.

Many economists and planners are not as predisposed as is Porter to reject IS as an inner-city development strategy, at least as part of a more comprehensive solution. Persky et al., for example, used regional economic models to estimate the effects of IS on a group of forty selected firms in Chicago.[27] Their results were positive, indicating both the feasibility and utility of selected IS intervention strategies for the economic development of the ghetto. As they note, "Ideally, a program of IS mobilizes local resources in a fashion that greatly enhances their productivity." Porter admits his export-oriented program does not guarantee jobs for ghetto residents; perhaps import substitution has more promise for bringing those human resources into the economic mainstream.

The Inner City Has Four Areas of Competitive Advantage

Porter has identified four areas of potential competitive advantage for the inner city:

Strategic location. Porter's theory on the competitive advantage of the inner city reflects the thinking of many practitioners in the field of economic development, which sees locational (space and time) factors as the most important, and amenable to control, of all the factors related to economic development. Inner cities are located near major business, transportation and communications nodes and would be ideally situated if such effects were economically important. But increased geographic mobility and improved communications and distributions systems have lessened the advantage of central locations over the suburbs and exurbs, where most economic activity now occurs. The importance of locational centrality has waned for almost all economic activities. What is left—governments, medical institutions, and educational facilities—are constrained either politically or by enormous investments in buildings and land.

Local market demand conditions. Opportunities exist to serve the inner-city markets but what special, new competitive advantage results? Porter is least impressive when he goes on at great length about the "special" market of the inner city with its consumer preferences for beauty care products and certain food products. There are elements of truth here. Ethnic marketing is an accepted business practice, but this is really nothing new in economic development theory or practice.

Integration with regional clusters. By definition, clustered firms should exhibit a complex pattern of complementary and competitive behaviors. How these linkages are discerned and formulated into a detailed implementation plan that specifies linkages to new firms, Porter leaves substantially unaddressed. These details are the nuts-and-bolts of a credible plan to make clustering work in any environment, especially the inner city. Even in *The Competitive Advantage of Nations*, Porter's methodology relies primarily on the *ad hoc* adjustment of location quotients based on international trade patterns. Porter's few examples of inner-city export clusters in Boston and Los Angeles, mostly food distribution, laundry and toy importing, do not clearly suggest a specific methodology of identifying clusters. Access to which clusters by which inner city firms is an important question that must be answered clearly and accurately if Porter's ideas are to be implemented.

Human resources. The inner-city labor force has almost no real competitive advantages in a globalized economy. The black middle-class continues to abandon the inner city as a place of residence (and commerce). Porter rejects exploiting unskilled labor—the only real, short-term product of the ghetto—because of its wide availability in the global market. However, not all unskilled labor is replaceable in global markets; much unskilled labor, such as personal and home repair services, can only be delivered locally. Maximizing these types of locally delivered unskilled jobs is not mentioned in Porter's scheme, in part because it would not be consistent with his preference for export over income substitution and other internal development strategies. Instead, he implies that poor inner-city residents should find jobs in the new information and other industries identified as part of export-based clusters.

Porter correctly warns against a rising tide theory, avoiding pinning inner-city revitalization hopes on general improvements in the regional economy. Full regional employment should create strong forces to employ unskilled inner-city residents. But first, as Porter notes, "there would still be a large surplus of better qualified unemployed or underemployed people that would need to be absorbed before the benefits to inner-city residents would be realized. If the demand for labor rose enough to approach local supply, migration and immigration of unskilled labor into the region would limit the benefits for inner-city residents." Porter's speculation about the deleterious effects of unskilled in-migration as a factor that effectively denies the unemployed jobs has been demonstrated for the Atlanta region, as noted previously.[29] But what are the objectives of inner-city revitalization if employment of current residents is not the central focus? Inner-city industry employing suburbanites or new migrants to the metropolitan region benefits most inner-city residents very little. And without work for its residents, the physical, social, and economic conditions of the inner city will not be renewed.

Agglomeration Economies and Clusters Can Spawn More Development

At the center of Porter's prescription for economic development of the inner city is the idea of industrial clusters. For the past decade, there has been a great revival of interest among academics and a few policy-makers in industrial districts and clusters. This has been fueled by the rapid growth and competitive success of clusters in parts of the Third Italy, Germany, the U.S., and Japan.[30] Earlier, Harrison described certain "operational solutions which had been in use by development planners for years," which use the "'industrial complex' or 'cluster'. . . ."[31] The intent is to exploit the positive externalities, consumption interdependencies and economies of scale, to link together different firms; a cluster of competitive and complementary industries becomes more than the sum of its parts. A potentially powerful idea for inner-city economic development, economies of agglomeration have yet to be purposely exploited in a systematic and widespread way by economic developers. The major obstacle to use are methodological complexities that make difficult the specification of concrete prescriptive measures.

Doeringer and Terkla address the controversy regarding the implementation of clustering in particular settings.[32] The difficulty of translating clustering concepts into economic development practice is evidenced by the *ad hoc* techniques commonly used to identify specific clusters. Doeringer and Terkla describe the official Massachusetts state growth policy, which specifies desirable clusters as those that "compete nationally and internationally and have the size, sophistication, productivity, and national and international positions to drive economic upgrading." Functional, quantifiable criteria defining clusters and linkages were not in evidence. Likewise, in an appendix of *The Competitive Advantage of Nations*, entitled "Methodology for Preparing the Cluster Charts," Porter is similarly vague; a "revealed competitive advantage" was evident if an industry ranked above average in terms of national output. Further adjustments were made, including the *ad hoc* addition of "industries where there was a clear indication of substantial competitive strength."[33] Other adjustments, not detailed here, seem plausible but arbitrary. These procedures are not an adequate basis for practical economic development planning in the inner city or elsewhere and, because of the human judgment involved, currently remains more of an art than a science with an explicit theoretical basis.

Finally, Porter does not confront the issues of scale and distance. At the metropolitan regional scale, can a cluster be formed in an area of one hundred square miles? Five hundred square miles? How close must clustering activities be; how much accessibility to each other do they need? And do these ideas carry over to the inner city and its neighborhoods in, say, five square miles?

DISCUSSION AND CONCLUSIONS

While it is easy to agree with many of Porter's criticisms of past economic development efforts in the inner city, his new "model of competitive advantage of the inner city" is based on familiar ideas of private sector leadership in the inner city that have had great political currency, especially during the 1980s and early 1990s. Whatever the ills of the inner city now, widely perceived as growing alarmingly worse, the present environment has been most recently and directly shaped by conservative shifts in government policies during the 1980s, which emphasized the preeminence of the private sector as the controlling influence over the economy.

For example, President Reagan's Job Training Partnership Act (JTPA) program, which ceremoniously displaced the liberal Comprehensive Employment Training Act (CETA) program in 1982, mandated high levels of industry participation in both curricula development and administration. Often criticized as merely performing a prescreening service for participating firms, the JTPA is now widely acknowledged as ineffective by conservatives and liberals alike. A frequent criticism of the JTPA is the fact that training is for low-paid, entry-level positions, most often with no job ladder for advancement.[34] Clearly, private industry involvement is no panacea for the problems of the inner-city economy, at least when it comes to job training.

Porter's calls for more private sector initiatives, and fewer by the public sector, seem incongruous with the failure of this and other conservative policies. Porter offers a limited amount of anecdotal evidence of successful inner-city firms, but, beyond blaming government, fails to explain why these have not been more widely replicated. The absence of more reports of the successful application of competitive advantage at the city-region level simply reflects the underlying fact that the revitalization of the inner city defies simplistic solutions. Porter has greatly underestimated the obstacles to revitalizing inner-city economies, and has ignored the people in the place. Less than revolutionary, his proposals essentially readvance probusiness ideology of less government, leaving basic economic patterns in the ghetto unchanged.

Porter's fundamental practical recommendations amount to little more than general statements: identifying location-sensitive industries with potential for growth; promoting ethnic marketing to capture inner-city consumers; supplying more dynamic areas of the regional economy from the inner city and stimulating and supporting more entrepreneurship in the inner city. Rather than a concise theory of competitive advantage, Porter's exhaustive tabulations of national data and industry descriptions in *The Competitive Advantage of Nations* touch on almost every aspect of international and national competitiveness and, precisely because of their generality, do not seem to provide much practical illumination, especially at the scale of the inner-city neighborhood.

Porter has repackaged his remedies for the decline of the United States in the international trade arena, and now speculates that the same answers will prevail in America's inner cities. It is not at all obvious that techniques that work in one situation will work in another, thoroughly dissimilar, situation. Unfortunately, little confirmative evidence of Porter's theories is available in the literature. In one study by the New Hampshire Industry Group, Kaufman et al. found that suppliers in New Hampshire's leading industries pursued differentiation strategies that minimized competitive rivalry within the state, a result at variance with Porter's ideas. The study also recommended that state government in New Hampshire should take a strong leadership role in restructuring the state's post-Cold War economy.[35] New Hampshire is probably not the only geographic area where Porter's theory would be problematic in practice. While Kaufman found that Porter's ideas were useful in framing the problem, the fact that "the (Porter's) model itself cannot provide answers" makes it of dubious value to economic development planners and practitioners. In fact, in a literal sense, it is impossible even to prove that Porter's ideas about international trade advantage are true; they just seem plausible in light of the many observed changes in international industrial organization. Finally, the application of these ideas on trade advantage between industrialized countries to the inner city (leaving out the regional and other intermediate levels of analysis) is a distant reach offered without any real theoretical basis.

In "The Competitive Advantage of the Inner City," Porter tells his audience, presumably influential business and civic leaders, what they wanted and expected to hear: the private sector should be assisted by the public sector, and otherwise government should not interfere with private sector initiatives and control. This is a message we have been hearing for almost two decades from conservatives and free market advocates. There really is nothing here in the way of a radical reformulation of the problem of economic development of the inner city. What Porter brings to the table is credibility within the business community, though not much with those specializing in economic development research or practice.

For whatever reason, Porter has chosen a place-based business strategy that focuses on the place and its problems rather than on the people who remain there. In our opinion, all the evidence suggests that his energies and formidable ability to marshal business persons would be better directed at black-owned businesses, wherever they located. Coupled with governmental programs that prevented racial discrimination in housing, banking, and hiring, some progress might be made in providing jobs for the less-skilled, including blacks stuck in the inner city. However, the country needs a more radical look at the changing nature of work, private- and public-sector hiring policies, and an attitude that should hold our society to blame for creating too few jobs, rather than blaming those that lose in the competition for those jobs. In our opinion, Porter contributes to another misformulation of the problem, and therefore a sure loser of a solution. His theory, should the corporate world buy into it and give it a real test, is tailor-made for another lesson, true or not, on how the ghetto cannot be redeveloped.

NOTES

1. R. Browne, "The Origin, Birth, and Adolescence of the *Review of Black Political Economy* and the Black Economic Research Center," *The Review of Black Political Economy* (Winter 1993): 22.

2. See Dr. Porter's writings on inner-city redevelopment, M. Porter, "The Competitive Advantage of the Inner City," *The Harvard Business Review* (May-June 1995); M. Porter, *The Competitive Advantage of the Inner City* (Boston: Harvard Business School, November 1, 1994); and M. Porter, *The Competitive Advantage of the Inner City* (Boston: Harvard Business School, June 22, 1994).

3. See, for example, R. Bolton, "'Place Prosperity vs. People Prosperity' Revisited: An Old Issue with a New Angle." *Urban Studies* 29(2), (1992): 185–203; M. Edel "'People versus Place' in Urban Impact Analysis," in *The Urban Impacts of Federal Policies,* edited by N. Glickman (Baltimore: Johns Hopkins University Press, 1980), pp. 175–191; L. Snow, "Economic Development Breaks the Mold: Community-Building, Place-Targeting, and Empowerment Zones," *Economic Development Quarterly* 9(2), (1995): 185–198; M. Whitman, "Place Prosperity and People Prosperity: The Delineation of Optimum Policy Areas," in *Spatial, Regional, and Population Economics: Essays in Honor of Edgar M. Hoover* (1972), edited by M. Perlman, C. Leven and B. Chinitz (New York: Gordon and Breach 1972), pp. 359–393; L. Winnick, "Place Prosperity and People Prosperity: Welfare Considerations in the Geographic Distribution of Economic Activity," in *Essays in Urban Land Economics in Honor of the Sixty-fifth Birthday of Leo Grebler,* edited by the Real Estate Research Program, University of California at Los Angeles (Los Angeles: Real Estate Research Program, University of California at Los Angeles 1966), pp. 273–283.

4. H. Ladd, "Spatially Targeted Economic Development Strategies: Do They Work?" *Cityscape* 1(1), (August 1994): 193-218.

5. The clearest rationale for the "dispersal strategy" is provided in Anthony Downs, "Alternative Futures for the American Ghetto," *Daedalus* (Fall 1968): 1331–1379. In *New Visions for Metropolitan America* (Washington: The Brookings Institution, 1994), Anthony Downs details six basic policy strategies directed at inner cities: present-policies, adjustment, area development, personal or human capital, household mobility, and worker mobility.

6. See, for example, M. Hughes, "Fighting Poverty in Cities: Transportation Pro-

grams as Bridges to Opportunity," (Washington, D.C.: National League of Cities, 1989).

7. See J. Kain, "The Spatial Mismatch Hypothesis: Three Decades Later," *Housing Policy Debate* 4(3), (1992): 371–460.

8. Kain, at a recent conference, commended Ihlanfeldt's understanding of Kain's three hypotheses (quoted from Ihlanfeldt in *Cityscape* 1[1] "The Spatial Mismatch Between Jobs and Residential Locations Within Urban Areas" [August 1994] above), the difficulty of obtaining appropriate data to test those hypotheses, and Ihlanfeldt's proper interpretation of the results. He was especially generous in his praise for Ihlanfeldt's "Housing Segregation and the Wages and Commutes of Urban Blacks: The Case of Atlanta Fast-Food Restaurant Workers" (Atlanta, Georgia: Policy Research Center, 1992).

9. Kasarda showed that the movement of jobs from central city to suburb was not the same for all occupations. Especially important was the disproportionate movement of entry-level jobs to the suburbs, and vice versa the movement of high-level jobs in telecommunications and information processing to the central city. Kasarda has many articles. See, for example, John D. Kasarda, "Entry-Level Jobs, Mobility, and Urban Minority Employment," *Urban Affairs Quarterly* 19, (1983): 2140; and "Urban Industrial Transition and the Underclass," *Annals* (1989), *AAPSS*, 501:26–47.

10. D. Sawicki and M. Moody, "The Effects of Intermetropolitan Migration on Labor Force Participation in Poor Communities," forthcoming in *Economic Development Quarterly*.

11. The most comprehensive analysis of these reasons is provided in Matthew Edel, "'People versus Place' in Urban Impact Analysis," in *The Urban Impacts of Federal Policies*, edited by N. Glickman (Baltimore: Johns Hopkins University Press, 1980), pp. 175–191.

12. B. Rubin and C. Richards, "A Transatlantic Comparison of Enterprise Zone Impacts: The British and American Experience," *Economic Development Quarterly* 6(4), (November 1992).

13. P. Kasinitz and J. Rosenberg, "Why Enterprise Zones Will Not Work," *City Journal* (Autumn 1993): 63–49.

14. H. Wolman, C. Ford III, and E. Hill, "Evaluating the Success of Urban Success Stories," *Urban Studies,* 31(6), (1994): 835–850.

15. T. Bates, "Utilization of Minority Employees in Small Business: A Comparison of Nonminority and Black-Owned Urban Enterprises," *The Review of Black Political Economy* (Summer 1994): 113–121.

16. T. Boston, *Strict Scrutiny: The Conservative Challenge to Minority Set-asides* (London: Routledge, forthcoming).

17. S. White, L. Binkley, and J. Osterman, "The Sources of Suburban Employment Growth," *Journal of the American Planning Association* 59(2), (1993): 193–204.

18. Mark Alan Hughes provides a clear argument that separates moving out of the ghetto and into the suburbs as an end versus moving as a means. He then recommends integrating the workplace first, suggesting residential integration could then follow. These ideas are contained in "Moving Up and Moving Out Confusing Ends and Means About Ghetto Dispersal," *Urban Studies* 24, (1987): 503–517.

19. N. Lemann, "Rebuilding the Ghetto Doesn't Work," *The New York Times Magazine, (*January 9, 1994): 26–58.

20. D. Sawicki and M. Moody, "The Effects of Inter Metropolitan Migration."

21. M. Weir, *Politics and Jobs: The Boundaries of Employment Policy in the United States* (Princeton: Princeton University Press, 1993).

22. W. Rosenbaum, "The Politics of Public Participation in Hazardous Waste Management," from *The Politics of Hazardous Waste Management*, edited by J. Lester and A. Bowman (Durham: Duke Press, 1983).

23. T. Bates, "Why Do Minority Business Development Programs Generate So Little Development?" *Economic Development Quarterly* 9(1), (February 1995).

24. M. Porter, *The Competitive Advantage of Nations* (New York: Free Press, 1990).

25. B. Harrison, "Ghetto Economic Development: A Survey," *Journal of Economic Literature* 3(2), (1975): 6, 19.

26. M. Streit, "Spatial Associations and Economic Linkages between Industries," *Journal of Regional Science* 9(2), (1969).

27. J. Persky, D. Ranny, and W. Wiewel, "Import Substitution and Local Economic Development," *Economic Development Quarterly* 7(1), (February 1993).

28. Ibid., p. 21.

29. D. Sawicki and M. Moody, "The Effects of Inter Metropolitan Migration."

30. F. Pyke and W. Sengenberger, *Industrial Districts and Local Economic Regeneration* (Oxford: International Labor Organization, 1992); and Michael Storper and Richard Walker, *The Capitalist Imperative: Territory, Technology, and Industrial Growth* (Oxford: Blackwell Publishers, 1989).

31. B. Harrison, p. 21.

32. P. Doeringer and D. Terkla, "Business Strategy and Cross-Industry Clusters," *Economic Development Quarterly* 9(3), (August 1995).

33. M. Porter, *The Competitive Advantage of Nations,* pp. 739–744.

34. G. Orfield and C. Ashkinaze, *The Closing Door: Conservative Policy and Black Opportunity* (Chicago: The University of Chicago Press, 1991).

35. A. Kaufman, R. Gittell, M. Merenda, W. Naumes, and C. Wood, "Porter's Model for Geographic Competitive Advantage: The Case of New Hampshire," *Economic Development Quarterly* 8(1), (February 1994).

6

TAKING BACK THE INNER CITY: A REVIEW OF RECENT PROPOSALS

William W. Goldsmith

INTRODUCTION

While it would appear that only a minority of white public figures today pay attention to urban issues, recently several prominent groups have come forward to recommend public policies and ways of understanding urban problems—problems of areas variously called the inner city, the central city, poor black neighborhoods, or the ghetto. Such prestigious and influential groups as the Committee for Economic Development, the Twentieth Century Fund, the *Harvard Business Review,* and the Woodrow Wilson Center have issued reports and proposals calling for a fresh look at inner cities.

Some of those who explain the causes of inner-city problems or who propose policies to resolve them observe correctly the importance of larger social orders. They acknowledge that politics and economics beyond the inner city, beyond the metropolis and nation, in the global economy, are replete with defects that create nearly impossible conditions for poor people, especially when they suffer enforced isolation in large central neighborhoods. Unfortunately, a majority among those who dominate the crafting of public policy seem not to pay attention or are ignorant of the relevant social influences. They ignore layers of causation, such as joblessness resulting from lack of opportunity; they lay blame on those pushed to the bottom of a biased social structure rather than on those who design or dominate that structure; they attack those who struggle to survive decently but cannot; and they focus hostile attention on the small minority who adopt anti-social strategies for survival.

In what follows I identify and discuss five sets of ideas—positions on public policy, really—about central-city poverty and underdevelopment. Taken as admonitions, the first insists on the importance of community institutions, the second on meeting the requirements of private investment, and the third on reducing suburb-city inequities. The fourth argument turns our attention to the powerful harm caused by residential segregation. The fifth contends, more broadly, that the central city is filled with people who suffer from the country's great inequalities of income and wealth. Taken together these five arguments—on institutions, investment, suburban disparities, racial discrimination, and inequality—encompass the peculiar dilemma of the American inner city. They leave little doubt that our society needs profound change. Can they be woven into a politics that will produce that change?

TAKE LOCAL INITIATIVES TO BUILD COMMUNITY

In a 1995 proposal for urban policy entitled *Rebuilding Inner-City Communities,* the Committee for Economic Development recommends mildly progressive changes—no radically conservative suggestions to appeal to the far-right Congress, but nothing either that threatens main prerogatives of corporate America.[1] This well-written, brief, and well-informed document has numerous strengths, and, as I will argue near the end of this essay, one debilitating weakness.

Perhaps the report's greatest strengths are its descriptions.[2] First, it lays out clearly and in very few pages the multiple miseries that confront people living in the poorest of America's neighborhoods—poor schools, high crime, high unemployment, and physical blight. Second, the study lists some basic and proximate causes for these miseries—employment discrimination; residential segregation; redline and greenline exclusion by realtors, banks officers, and insurance agents; bad public housing; poor social services; the placement of undesirable NIMBY[3] facilities; and ineffective policing, specifically, the absence of the beat cop. Nearly six million people live in badly distressed neighborhoods in the 100 largest cities in the country.[4] Many millions more live nearby in conditions nearly as bad.

The CED report focuses on the need for *social capital,* "the attitudinal, behavioral, and communal glue that holds society together through relationships among individuals, families, and organizations."[5] Social capital is defined by three processes or qualities: information sharing, trust engendered through generalized reciprocity, and norms and values that maintain social order. These important community qualities are in short supply in the poorest of city neighborhoods. When a neighborhood is missing social capital, its social order collapses. This is the case when residents cannot share information (e.g., to find jobs), trust one another (to watch neighborhood streets so that each other's kids behave and come to no harm), or get positive reinforcement from peers (to work hard to succeed in high school).

In response to this view of the world, the report urges public authorities and private businesses to support community development corporations, arguing that CDCs can expand their problem-solving skills from housing to other areas, including "employment, education, health, youth development, [and] public safety." The report notes the need for enhanced "leadership, managerial, and organizational capacity of community-based organizations," for enhanced coordination, and for the redirection of "public and philanthropic funds," as well as creative mobilization of "market forces and incentives," to expand good but limited programs to meet a much larger need. In this context, the report acknowledges that even in the area of housing, while CDCs produced nearly 23,000 units in 1990, the need is an order of magnitude larger, in the millions.

CREATE CONDITIONS TO ATTRACT BUSINESS INVESTMENT

Also in 1995, the *Harvard Business Review* published an article by Michael Porter on attracting private investment, seeking conditions that will make the inner city a competitive business location.[6] Porter warns against piecemeal approaches and calls for an overall strategy; he opposes subsidies and preference programs; and he believes that "social programs"—for housing, real estate, and neighborhood development, or charity or government mandates—"undermine the creation of economically viable companies." Instead, he says:

> We should be asking how inner-city businesses and nearby employment operations for inner-city residents can proliferate and grow. A sustainable economic base can be created . . . but only . . . through private . . . investment based on economic self-interest and genuine competitive advantage. . . . [I]nner-city businesses should be profitable and positioned to compete on a regional, national, and even international scale.

Porter believes businesses should find it attractive to locate in the inner city, where they can secure strategic location, fill local market demand, integrate with regional clusters, and utilize human resources, but only with guaranteed physical security. Inner-city neighborhoods have the advantage of easy access to downtown, but they must overcome superior suburban access to highways and airports. There is room for "market penetration," especially to meet "cultural and ethnic needs of inner city customers" and to "export" products like Latino and African American foods. Porter favors specialized "major business employing the latest in technology, marketing, and management techniques," and he urges "[i]ntegration with regional clusters," e.g., in health care, as "potentially the inner city's most powerful and sustainable competitive advantage over the long term." The hard-working, loyal, honest and entrepreneurial labor force should redirect their energy away from "social services" and toward business.

Porter argues that business firms should tailor products to the market, hire locally, use local suppliers, redirect philanthropy from social services to business-to-business efforts, improve training, assist management, and invest in "such mundane but potentially profitable projects as supermarkets and laundries." Government should direct resources to the areas of greatest economic need, improve transportation, simplify and reduce regulations, offer tax exemptions, and deliver services through private institutions. Community-based organizations should stay out of business, teach the workforce and community to respect business, create work-readiness and job-referral systems, and facilitate commercial site improvement and development.

REORGANIZE THE METROPOLIS

American cities suffer a huge deficit to the suburbs. The city limits constitute a political artifact inappropriate to dense metropolitan patterns of interdependence, an arrangement guaranteed to produce city misery. David Rusk argues this with considerable force in his little book *Cities without Suburbs*.[7] Rusk, mayor of Albuquerque before conducting this study of the country's 100 largest metropolises, finds roughly half of them working reasonably well, with central-cities capable of solving their problems. He uses the term "elasticity" for the capacity of the city to expand its limits or to densify. A city that literally stretches its limits or adds density internally "captures" its suburban growth, whereas cities that keep stale boundaries and do not densify "contribute" to suburban growth but themselves decline. "Inelastic" cities are hobbled by bad state laws, they are trapped by their surrounding neighbors, and they are more highly segregated by race and income.

Rusk's argument is deceptively simple: without the artificial wall that separates suburb from city, their mutual dependence can be mutually productive, their costs of service and development fairly shared, and the benefits more widespread. European cities serve as examples, with authorities likely to stretch municipal boundaries so as to incorporate outskirts, and with national agencies likely to increase allocations so as to accommodate expanding urban population. Indeed, in the United States elastic cities not only deconcentrate their poverty and diminish their racial segregation, but their inclusiveness seems to affect the economy, causing entire metropolitan areas to grow more successfully. Perhaps the most notable case of elastic city growth is New York State's creation of New York City in 1898, merging five mostly empty boroughs and abolishing all other municipalities, including Brooklyn, then one of the largest cities in the country. Many decades of successful growth followed for the entire metropolis, mostly inside city limits, a growth so powerful it absorbed the energy of countless immigrants. New York's severe problems began to mount only later, when its physical, fiscal and political growth were choked off by the suburbs.

Fifty-five years later, in 1953, Ontario created Metro Toronto, an authority that dominates its five constituent parts, including the City of Toronto.[8] Metro Toronto sought the advantages of growth, of rationalized services, and of fair distribution of burdens and benefits. Observers judge the experience to have been extremely successful, but by the 1990s the population had spilled far beyond the fixed metropolitan boundaries, leaving only half of four million inhabitants still in Metro Toronto, half now in separate suburban jurisdictions. Recent economic downturns and quests for efficiency and fairness have yielded new efforts to expand Metro boundaries and have engendered resistance by suburbanites, conscious of their hidden subsidies. The strains between "inner" city and suburbs are pronounced. Advocates of Metro Toronto fear that unless boundaries are expanded, ethnic and social contrasts between the multiracial city and its overwhelmingly white suburbs will lead to a circular decay: neglect of central neighborhoods, social harm to their residents, and economic harm to the area as a whole. There is speculation that this might lead to deplored U.S.-like urban conditions.

DISMANTLE APARTHEID

The problem is not so simple as city-suburb boundaries. These boundaries stand for deeper conflicts. As Rusk writes, "racial and economic segregation is the heart of America's 'urban problem.'" Until we confront "deep-rooted fears about race and social class" we will not be able to reshape urban America.

> Segregating poor urban Blacks and Hispanics has spawned physically decaying, revenue-strapped, poverty-impacted, crime-ridden "inner cities." These inner cities are isolated from their "outer cities"— wealthier, growing, largely White suburbs.[9]

In his dissent from the Supreme Court's 1974 decision in *Milliken v. Bradley,* Justice Thurgood Marshall agreed with lower court arguments that Detroit's suburbs should share responsibility with the city for its needy school children. Marshall warned that:

> In the short run, it may seem to be the easier course to allow our great metropolitan areas to be divided up each into two cities—one white, the other black—but it is a course, I predict, our people will ultimately regret.

Twenty years after Justice Marshall's dissent, the problem remains unresolved.[10] The City of Detroit has one-million residents, 76 percent of whom are black. In the surrounding suburbs there are 3.3 million people, more than 90 percent white. City and suburb are like a black neck choked by a white collar. The city is poor, conditions near hopeless for its majority, the schools terrible.

Although rarely demarcated so starkly by city boundaries, segregation by race is the rule everywhere in the United States, including *inside* the separate municipal jurisdictions that make up the metropolis.[11] In twelve of Cleveland's suburbs the black population constitutes more than 2 percent. The eleven of those twelve suburbs that are adjacent to Cleveland's black neighborhoods, on the city's east side, house 96 percent of the suburban black population. In each of them the black proportion of the population increased between 1980 and 1990,[12] threatening to segregate fully all but a very few stable integrated areas.

Throughout the United States, in fact, black Americans live in the *ghetto,* a "set of neighborhoods that are exclusively inhabited by members of one group, within which virtually all members of that group live. By this definition, *no ethnic or racial group in the history of the United States, except one, has ever experienced ghettoization, even briefly.* For urban blacks, the ghetto has been the paradigmatic residential configuration for at least 80 years."[13]

In *American Apartheid,* a thoroughly documented and forcefully argued 1993 monograph published by Harvard University Press, Douglas Massey and Nancy Denton show why nearly all black Americans find their residential options tightly restricted: discriminatory laws and social practices reinforce one another in housing, schools, labor markets, and commerce in a destructive circle of mutual causation. They write: "[A]t critical points between the end of the Civil War in 1865 and the passage of the Fair Housing Act in 1968, white America chose to strengthen the walls of the ghetto." And, later, "[T]he black ghetto was constructed through a series of well-defined institutional practices, private behaviors, and public policies by which whites sought to contain growing urban black populations." Aside from small numbers of black families that have moved to suburbs, there has been no improvement in the last thirty years, and race continues to overpower social class as the main determinant of residential immobility.[14]

REDISTRIBUTE INCOME, TAX WEALTH

Although mainstream commentators challenged Bennett Harrison and Barry Bluestone when they first asserted that the wages of American workers had fallen since the 1970s, that dismal finding is now virtually undisputed: the inability of many hardworking couples to support a family has become a staple of the media.[15] The gap between rich and poor has grown fantastically, the historical comparison reversed, so we might *today* contrast a "Jeffersonian" Europe with an "aristocratic" America. While social democracy has protected Europeans from the worst ravages of the global market, in the United States bad social and economic policy has generated new classes of very rich and very poor. The maldistribution of income is so extreme that William McDonough, the president of the Federal Reserve Bank of New York, inclined by occupation toward conservative statements, allowed these remarks to become public:[16]

It is deeply troubling that during the nineteen-eighties the real wages of low-skilled workers in the United States have fallen sharply, both in absolute terms and relative to the wages of highly skilled workers. . . . We are forced to face the question of whether we will be able to go forward together as a unified society with a confident outlook or as a society of diverse economic groups suspicious of both the future and each other.

Wealth is maldistributed even more badly than income. Edward Wolff's 72-page report for the Twentieth Century Fund, *Top Heavy*,[17] provides astonishing summary statistics on worsening disparities in wealth. Between 1983 and 1989 *all* of the increase in financial wealth and 99 percent of the increase in marketable wealth accrued to the top one-fifth of the population. The bottom *four-fifths* gained nothing! Of the *total* wealth (including homes, automobiles, and other such property, as well as finance), the top one-fifth own 86 percent (data for 1989); they own 94 percent of financial wealth (the top *one* percent of the population own nearly half); all of these figures have increased since 1983. This represents the top-side of American economic change in the last two decades.

With only 15 percent of total wealth and 6 percent of financial wealth held by 80 percent of the population, the real bottom-side, that is, the lowest one out of five persons of the population, simply disappears from view—the underclass becomes practically invisible, except when some of its members become disruptive for the majority.

African Americans and dark-skinned Latinos, and, among them, women with children, are pushed to the very bottom of the distributions of income, wealth, and financial power. In 1988, when the median white married couple owned more than $62,000 in household wealth (home, auto, appliances, clothing, savings, etc.), the median African American and Hispanic woman with children owned practically nothing—less than $750![18]

HOW TO DEVELOP THE INNER CITY

As I asserted in the introduction, these are sensible admonitions— to develop competent institutions, attract investment and new jobs, reduce city-suburb disparities, fight racial discrimination, and reduce income inequality. Those who make the proposals present ample evidence, which leaves little doubt that our society needs profound change. But each on its own, the proposals seem either terribly partial or hopelessly utopian. I am thus moved to ask again, can these ideas be woven into a politics that will produce change?

The picture is not promising. Isolated into segregated neighborhoods, without adequate income or wealth, unable to share the growth of the

suburbs, shunned by investors, and with few robust institutions, is it any
wonder that "inner-city" people are in trouble, or that they have difficulty
finding political allies? Can the separate suggestions for improved policy
be combined? Is there a way to define objectives and work for political
actions that citizens might take to move the country in the right directions? In what follows I suggest several strategies for focusing attention
and perhaps building the political coalitions that will be required, if all of
these problems are to be tackled in a way that each reform reinforces
some others. Without the hope for such progressive ratcheting, the solution appears distant, indeed. My first suggestion is that those concerned
mainly with inner-city actions, with local decisions and local politics,
spend more time and give more credence to extra-city forces, to external
elements.[19]

Look Upstream

Answering those who asked him to help Cleveland's poor in the first
decade of the twentieth century, the mayor, Tom Johnson, said that while
it was a noble thing to help drowning people out of the river, it might be
more useful "go up the stream . . . to see who is pushing the people in."[20]

In today's terms, such a shift of focus can highlight the need for efforts
to improve the distribution of income, by assuring full employment at
decent pay. An upstream focus would lead to demands for the correction
of tax and revenue biases against central cities and their school districts.
Such a focus would identify the need to overcome residential segregation, by fighting against continuing discrimination in housing markets. In
the absence of success in these and parallel endeavors, people working to
build institutions and to attract investment will find their efforts come to
naught. To be successful, advocates of inner-city development must identify, point out, and then resist *external and imposed* pressures that maintain poverty, that reduce municipal revenues and increase costs, and that
restrict residential options for people of color.

The CED report, *Rebuilding Inner-City Communities,* as it acknowledges real difficulties in the inner city, admits of external causes, and,
perhaps most important, insists that federal, state, and local governments
should take action—to control guns, shift drug programs from incarcera-
tion to prevention and rehabilitation, fight racial discrimination, coordinate neighborhood services, and support research and the monitoring of
neighborhood conditions. Furthermore, the report points out that inner-

city problems are *national* economic and ethical problems, quoting HUD
Secretary Henry Cisneros's observation that the country and the cities
have "interwoven destinies."

But in spite of these accurate and useful observations and its strikingly
positive and generally progressive recommendations about repairing communities, *Rebuilding* displays a debilitating and conservative weakness—
it ignores the main forces that produce poor neighborhoods to begin with.
The report does note that "[s]ocial capital, in and of itself, is not sufficient to reverse urban decay," and that no effort will succeed "if poor and
disadvantaged Americans live in isolation from the larger national community."[21] But even in this context, in the same paragraph, the report
turns the issue inward, suggesting if not quite saying that the problem is
with the people in the neighborhoods, who "must be brought back into
the social and economic mainstream," must not be so isolated "from each
other, and from shared national values, purpose, and hope." Statements
like this can be interpreted to perpetuate the myth that the problems are
rooted in the communities themselves, that is, in the nature of their
people, and that these residents hold bad values, exhibit lack of purpose,
and are debilitated by absence of hope. So, my second suggestion:

Do Not Lend Support to Those Who
Would Blame Victims

There is a similar dilemma in the *Competitive Advantage* propositions
by Porter, in spite of superficial disagreements with *Rebuilding* about
community organizations. In a sense, he's right: if inner-city poor people,
with their need for "social programs," would either improve attitudes or
step aside, then "development" energy could create attractive conditions,
locational advantages could be seized, and business would invest.

Unfortunately, it is precisely the poverty of the people, and their
crowded isolation, that generates community organizations needing to do
remedial work to deal with "social" problems.[22] Certainly, the impoverishment of inner-city communities is related to poor investment climate
just as it is to lack of social capital, but what neither Porter nor the CED
report admits is the extent to which ghetto impoverishment, which wipes
out social capital and ruins the investment climate, is not caused by
weakness on the inside so much as by damage from the outside. Advocates of inner-city development must demonstrate in their proposals and
actions a conviction that strong majorities of inner-city residents hold
mainstream, correct values and behave with as much dignity and com-

mon sense as do better-off residents in other parts of the metropolis.[23]

One unavoidable example here is street crime. Porter observes that security problems discourage businesses from investing in inner-city neighborhoods, or cause them to fail. But fixing the problem of street crime is not, in the first instance, a matter of improving the social attitudes of neighborhood residents. Nor is street crime a problem noticed by potential investors, but not by residents. Indeed, a recent poll found that 80 percent of the nation's secondary school students would join "programs that could help reduce or prevent crime."[24] Street crime is a plague to residents, and it will be reduced by improving police procedures, dealing sensibly with the drug problem (prevention and rehabilitation, as the CED urges, rather than prison terms), improving schools and youth programs, and creating jobs, reducing poverty, and defeating discrimination.

Eliminate Unfair Subsidies to Suburbs

Three of the most damaging outside forces that benefit suburbs and harm cities are public subsidies, residential exclusion, and maldistribution of income. Advocates of inner-city development must apply persistent political, legal, and economic pressure to correct for biased and unfair subsidies that support segregated, well-off suburbs. This means undertaking a broad and sustained political attack on cherished privileges—a difficult task, especially when these advantages are perceived as birthrights and as natural ways of ordering social life, especially when the conventional wisdom suggests that the subsidies are available to all.

There are enormous subsidies provided in the United States for housing and transportation. The annual federal subsidy to homeowners through the income-tax deduction for payments of interest on mortgages and property taxes is mammoth. This subsidy transfers between $50 and $80 billion each year.[25] These funds are available only to those who own their homes (two homes qualify, and the second can be a yacht, as long as it is large enough to afford sleeping accommodations), hold mortgages, and earn enough to be able to make use of detailed tax reports (the IRS "long form"). The subsidy therefore goes disproportionately to well-off suburban residents. Adding it up, over the last decade, the federal government has transferred more than a half-trillion dollars to middle-class and wealthy citizens, but not to poor (and minority) residents of inner cities.

Subsidies are also granted for transportation, more generously for suburbanites than city residents, for the well-off rather than the poor, and for whites rather than minorities. Problems of the inner city are increased when it is hard to get to work by public transit: systems are expensive, inconvenient, and, if the rider must go to work from the city to the suburbs, nearly impossible to use. The standard judgment by the public, reinforced by orthodox, marginalist analysis from the social sciences, is that mass transportation, whether by train or bus, is too costly to the public purse, requiring unjustifiably large subsidies, and that expenditures for public transit should be cut. As it turns out, the massive subsidies are for *private* transportation—the automobile. How much? Estimates put the figure in the tens of billions of dollars per year, very likely larger than the housing mortgage subsidy.[26] Even ignoring indirect costs, such as damages to the environment, destruction of communities, or defense appropriations to protect petroleum companies,

> roadways and private car use have been massively subsidized . . . at every government level. Private car users pay an artificially low price that reflects virtually none of the private car's enormous social and environmental costs . . . [T]axes . . . cover only 60% of the direct economic costs. . . . The overwhelming government support for private car use . . . has placed all forms of public transport at an unfair competitive disadvantage.[27]

Just as in the case for housing, the subsidy bias in urban transportation is overwhelmingly in favor of the suburbs and against the cities.

Fight Against Residential Segregation

Not only have government and business failed to establish effective remedial actions to provide people of color with the residential choices available to all other Americans, but there is scant public recognition even that coerced segregation lies at the core of the U.S. inner-city problem. As Dennis Keating concludes, "a variety of race-conscious housing policies aimed at racial and economic integration in the suburbs is required if residential segregation is to be reduced significantly."[28]

> [I]t is critical that affirmative housing policies be initiated and implemented at the metropolitan level . . . [with] the possibility of forcing or persuading all suburbs . . . to eliminate barriers to a more open housing market and society. . . . through either mandates or incentives that emanate from the federal and state governments. This

means that there must be a much stronger political constituency for affirmative policies aimed at greater racial diversity.

Establish Better Wage, Income, Tax
and Transfer Policies

Pro-rich and anti-poor tax and wage policies of the federal government influence the maldistribution of income and wealth, and the results show: ratios of high to low incomes are extreme. Average incomes of the top 10 percent of Americans are six times as high as those of the poorest 10 percent, a much broader gap than in Western Europe: France, Australia, and Norway are about 4-to-1; West Germany, Britain, Austria, Finland and Italy are roughly 3.5-to-1; and Sweden and the Netherlands are less than 3-to-1.[29] The ratios of *top* U.S. incomes to normal earners are outrageously large, worse than feudal:

> In 1688, England's 300 temporal lords averaged 300 times their countrymen's median income.
> Three hundred years later, in 1988, American junk bond kingpin Michael Milken made $500 million. In the same year, America's Teacher of the Year earned $36,000, fourteen thousand times less than Milken.[30]

Such huge and barely taxed differences define the conditions of poverty in America. Among the major industrial nations, the United States is the only one without a national health plan—one result is that poor people are made significantly poorer. U.S. laws provide minimum wages that are inexcusably low, even lower in value than decades ago, and unemployment protections are minimal. Without intervention, or worse with the onslaught of regressive changes under consideration by the Congress, bad policies will continue to create a large mass of poor people.

CONCLUDING REMARKS

Without new policies to narrow these wage and salary ratios or to provide massively generous income transfers, without a shift of subsidies away from current, well-off recipients toward those in deepest need, without convincing suburbs they must pay their due to cities, and without an end to our separate societies created by poverty and racism—America will not solve the " inner-city problem."

The ten bills proposed by the Republican party in its "Contract with America" run in precisely the wrong direction. In the summary version issued by the party, not one of the items even mentions problems of cities, much less inner cities, racial minorities, or the poor.[31] The problems, the people, are invisible except as euphemistically worded targets for invective. Instead of focusing on serious urban problems, the Contract bills would cut social spending for such things as summer jobs and would shift the money to prison construction and law enforcement (#2); they would cut welfare payments to young mothers and "additional" children and terminate welfare after two years to "promote individual responsibility" (#3); they would further subsidize the well off with personal tax and capital gains exemptions (#5 & #8); and they would shift a daunting financial burden to ordinary citizens should they challenge corporate irresponsibility (#9). On top of these direct attacks, the bills mount two more general attacks: they would cut nearly all social programs through a particular version of budget balancing (#1) and would *increase* military spending (#6).

Anyone genuinely interested in inner cities and the fate of their residents must work to defeat such proposals. What coalitions will arise, what possibilities there are for attracting suburban allies for the solution of city problems, which whites will ally for the solution of problems suffered by people of color, and whether such coalitions will form before further destruction of people and their urban habitat—only time will tell. But there can be little doubt that all progressive citizens should work in these directions.

NOTES

1. *Rebuilding Inner-City Communities: A New Approach to the Nation's Urban Crisis* (New York: A Statement of the Research and Policy Committee of the Committee for Economic Development, 1995), 70 pp., funded by the Ford Foundation and 16 other foundations and corporations. The CED is a nonprofit, nonpartisan, and "nonpolitical" organization of some 250 blue-ribbon corporate leaders and educators that researches and proposes policies to support, among other things, economic growth, high employment, reasonably stable prices, and "greater and more equal opportunity for every citizen." In its own words, "CED believes that by enabling business leaders to demonstrate constructively their concern for the general welfare, it is helping business to earn and maintain the national and community respect essential to the successful functioning of the free enterprise capitalist system."
2. *Rebuilding,* ch. 2.
3. NIMBY = Not In My Backyard!
4. The list is from John Kasarda, "Inner City Concentrated Poverty and Neighborhood Distress: 1970–1990," *Housing Policy Debate* 3 (1993), 253–302, who

designates a Census tract distressed when it is considerably, i.e., one standard deviation above, the national average on four indicators—the proportion of poor households, single women with children, welfare cases, and unemployed men.

5. *Rebuilding*, p. 3.

6. Michael E. Porter, "The Competitive Advantage of the Inner City," *Harvard Business Review* (May-June, 1995): 55–71.

7. David Rusk, *Cities without Suburbs* (Baltimore: Johns Hopkins, for the Woodrow Wilson Center, 1993), 146 pp.

8. Ian J. Bromley et al., "Agenda Seven: An Urban Centered Economic Strategy for Greater Toronto," mimeo, November 1994, 11 pp.

9. Rusk, *Cities*, pp. xiii–xiv, and p. 1.

10. In March 1992, the Supreme Court *(Freeman v. Pitts)* again overruled an appeals court to void an order to bridge municipal lines in order to overcome racial segregation, this time in the Atlanta metropolis. See W. Dennis Keating, *The Suburban Racial Dilemma: Housing and Neighborhoods* (Philadelphia: Temple University Press, 1994).

11. Douglas S. Massey and Nancy A. Denton, *American Apartheid: Segregation and the Making of an Underclass* (Cambridge: Harvard University Press, 1993), p. 10 and chaps. 3–4.

12. *The Suburban Racial Dilemma*, table 3, p. 63. Eunice S. Grier and George Grier surveyed the 37 metropolitan areas with more than one million population, finding "most of the black suburban growth . . . merely an extension of previous segregated patterns," *Minorities in Suburbia: A Mid-1980s Update* (a report to the Urban Institute, 1988), p. iii.

13. *American Apartheid,* pp. 18–19, emphasis added.

14. *American Apartheid,* Chaps. 4 and 6.

15. Bennett Harrison and Barry Bluestone, *The Great U-Turn: Corporate Restructuring and the Polarizing of America* (New York: Basic Books, 1988).

16. Quoted in John Cassidy, "Who Killed the Middle Class?" *The New Yorker*, (October 16, 1995):113. Oddly, in an otherwise excellent summary of the worsening of the distribution of income, Cassidy *never* mentions race.

17. Edward N. Wolff, *Top Heavy: A Study of the Increasing Inequality of Wealth in America* (New York: A Report from the Twentieth Century Fund, 1995), 93 pp. The Twentieth Century Fund, a nonprofit and nonpartisan group, "sponsors and supervises timely analyses of economic policy, foreign affairs, and domestic political issues."

18. William W. Goldsmith and Edward J. Blakely, *Separate Societies: Poverty and Inequality in U.S. Cities* (Philadelphia: Temple University Press, 1992), figure 2.7, p. 29.

19. In the terms of many social scientists, this is a plea for considering both agency and structure.

20. Johnson's words appear in the *Cleveland Policy Planning Report, vol. 1,* (1975) p. 1, quoted in Robert Mier, *Exclusion and Inadequacy Indexes: Labor Market Indicators for Social Planning* (Ithaca: Cornell Dissertations in Planning, 1975), pp. 1–2.

21. *Rebuilding*, p. 9

22. For a review of the way "complexity" theorists view the pernicious dynamics of information flow in large and crowded cities, see Edward L. Glaeser, "Cities, Information, and Economic Growth," *Cityscape: A Journal of Policy Development and Research* 1(1), (August, 1994).

23. There is a long-standing and highly detailed anthropological literature sup-

porting these views. See *Separate Societies*, chap. 1.

24. Louis Harris, October–November 1995, conducted for Teens, Crime and the Community of Washington, D.C. These results are in spite of the murder rate doubling among 14–17-year-olds over the decade. *Ithaca Journal*, (January 11, 1996).

25. The spread comes about from price inflation, different methods of evaluating tax incidence, and different estimates of how the housing market would adjust were the tax expenditure to be eliminated. One recent comparison puts the entire HUD budget at $26 billion, compared to $54 billion of IRS deductions for mortgage interest and property taxes. Nearly two-fifths of this tax expenditure goes to the 5 percent of taxpayers with incomes over $100,000, while half the homeowners in the country claim no deductions—and tenants don't qualify. See Peter Dreier and John Atlas, "Reforming the Mansion Subsidy," *The Nation* (May 2, 1994): 592–95.

26. See estimates in John Pucher, "Urban passenger transport in the United States and Europe: A comparative analysis of public policies," parts 1 and 2, *Transport Reviews* 15(2/3), (1995).

27. Ibid., part 2.

28. This sentence and the following quote from *The Suburban Racial Dilemma*, p. 5.

29. From the newsletter *Too Much* 1(3) (fall 1995).

30. Henry Phelps Brown, *Egalitarianism and the Generation of Inequality* (Oxford: Clarendon Press, 1988), p. 139; and Molly Ivins, "Deep Voodoo," *Mother Jones*, January/February 1991, p. 10; both cited in Sam Pizzigati, *The Maximum Wage: A Common-Sense Prescription for Revitalizing America—by Taxing the Very Rich* (New York: Apex Press, 1992), p. 79.

31. The Contract's second bill, the "Taking Back our Streets Act," does mention neighborhoods and schools, but only to propose that summer social spending be cut and shifted to prison construction and law enforcement.

7

POLITICAL ECONOMY OF URBAN POVERTY IN THE 21st CENTURY: HOW PROGRESS AND PUBLIC POLICY GENERATE RISING POVERTY

Timothy Bates

Increasing the incidence of poverty is rarely the primary purpose of public policy decisions, but it is often a byproduct. When HUD Secretary Henry Cisneros calls upon local governments to improve their business climates by "lowering operating costs, reducing unreasonable regulatory burdens . . . ", his objective is job creation generally, but achievement of that objective may entail increasing the ranks of the urban poor (Cisneros, 1995, p.5). Rising poverty in urban America is increasingly rooted in the fact that officially sanctioned economic development policies are working. Understanding why this is true is a precondition for formulating pragmatic political-economic strategies for attacking the causes of this tragic situation.

POVERTY IN VIBRANT CENTRAL CITIES

The nature of expanding poverty is most apparent in central cities that have experienced substantial central business district growth in the past thirty years. Problem cities, such as Detroit, Michigan; Newark, New Jersey; and Gary, Indiana, have undergone severe declines in their traditional economic base, industrial production, but their status as sick cities today reflects their limited success in building a new economic base. Despite the real problems of population and job loss typifying these declining cities, this study focuses upon cities that *have* coped with manufacturing decline by generating rapid central business district (CBD) growth.

In the CBD of Chicago, Atlanta, Boston, New York and others, an economic base of white collar employment has taken hold because of the proximity to complementary businesses and amenities, appropriate infrastructure, and favorable labor market conditions for managerial and professional employees. CBD-based corporate headquarters, in particular, have thrived in the midst of dense networks of business service providers, such as commercial and investment banks, advertising agencies, corporate law firms, and CPA firms. These skill-intensive service industries have often proliferated in the CBDs of "global" cities, including Miami, Los Angeles, and New York. Whereas poverty in Gary is heavily rooted in the decline of area steel mills, the poverty of blighted inner-city areas of Los Angeles and Atlanta more often reflects the fact of employment at very low wages. Working poverty, more than joblessness, is the growing malaise in America's urban centers of high wage white-collar employment.

Analyses of low-wage employment growth in cities like New York and Los Angeles often confuse the symptoms of working poverty with its causes. For example, the informal economy is portrayed as a sweatshop revival phenomenon: destitute people work in off-the-books enterprises concentrated in immigrant population centers. A common sense definition of the informal economy is a set of small-scale business activities conducted in a manner that evades government regulation and taxation. The rise of the informal economy is not principally associated with the illegal employment of poor immigrants. Opportunities for generating income in evasion of prevailing government rules and regulations are widely available throughout society. A true understanding of why such evasion has been expanding in recent decades sheds light on the causes of the indecently low wages, declining benefits, and loss of job security that typify a rising share of American's employment opportunities.

THE NEED FOR RISING POVERTY IN URBAN AMERICA

America's metropolitan areas benefit from the presence of a large labor force employed at low wages. Metropolitan area industries can be sorted into three broad groups. First, the export industries provide the raison d'être for the regional economy. They are oriented to national and international markets—autos in Detroit, financial services in New York, motion pictures in Los Angeles. The second major industry group complements the export industries by selling them the inputs used to produce the exported products. Both of these groups tend to be dominated by large firms utilizing high technology production processes. A third group of industries supplies the local economy with food, shelter, clothing, recreation, education, and the like. Many are low-wage industries dominated by small businesses, and this is the sector most likely to employ central city minority residents.

An inherently exploitive relationship is established (Fusfeld and Bates, 1984). Living costs in the metropolitan area are held down by the presence of low-wage service industries. Costs of production in the export industries and their supplier firms are limited because the services they buy are provided, in part, by low-wage workers. The low wages paid to ghetto residents are embedded in the prices of products and services that the entire community relies upon. If one large city (or state) were to undertake a serious effort to eliminate ghettos and the poverty found there, base costs of the area's export industries and their complements would increase. Higher government expenses, rising distribution costs, and more expensive services would increase the cost of living for those employed in the export and complementary industries. Higher living costs would necessitate higher wages in order to attract appropriately skilled managers and professionals to the region.

Higher costs could reduce the region's comparative advantage (relative to other metropolitan areas), thereby slowing local economic growth. Maintaining the poverty inherent in low-wage industries is an important component of regional viability, and this is particularly true in America's emerging global cities. If worker incomes increase in the low-wage industries, then the cost of living will rise for affluent, white-collar workers, and their standard of living will fall. The observation that "someone has to clean the floors" reflects the widespread realization of the need for a ghettoized, impoverished subsector within a healthy urban economy.

Preferences of highly educated women to pursue managerial and professional careers interact with the high cost of living in corporate-headquarters cities, such as New York and Los Angeles, producing a rise of affluent two-earner households that voraciously consume an array of services. Often lacking sufficient time to cook their own meals, clean and press their clothes, raise their children, clean their houses, and so forth, these affluent households rely heavily upon the services forthcoming from the low-wage sector. The result is a vast infrastructure of restaurants, gourmet food stores, domestic services, messenger services, laundries, dog walkers, child-care centers, and the like. The resultant low-wage jobs in the labor-intensive service industries are critically important to maintaining the quality of life for the urban elite working in the managerial and professional jobs that are proliferating in the expanding CBDs.

The new urban labor aristocracy requires the presence of a vast low-wage labor force because they purchase more and more of the consumer services that, in earlier generations, would have been produced within the household, often by housewives. Work that was previously internal to the household—raising children, cooking meals—is increasingly done by low-wage workers in the major corporate-headquarters cities of America. In this context, "immigrants represent a desirable labor supply because they are relatively cheap, reliable, willing to work on odd shifts, and safe," (Sassen-Koob, 1981, pp. 28–29). Providing the "large cohort of restaurant workers, laundry workers, dog walkers, residential construction workers, and the like," immigration helps to lower the cost of maintaining the elite lifestyle of the new urban labor aristocracy (Feagin and Smith, 1988, p. 15).

THE INFORMAL ECONOMY: APPARITION TODAY, MAINSTREAM TOMORROW

Kasarda's observation that "virtually all of New York's employment expansion was concentrated in white-collar service industries," (1985, p. 65) is based upon standard statistical series reported by federal government agencies. His skills-mismatch hypothesis—that central city net job growth was found solely in occupations that demanded college credentials, while minority job seekers disproportionately were high school dropouts—seemed out of synch with trends in global cities. If job opportunities for the unskilled really were shrinking rapidly, as the official statistics suggested, why were immigrants continuing to pour into New York City from places like the Dominican Republic and China? Why were sweatshop manufacturing industries growing rapidly (Waldinger, 1986)? Departure of working class whites from the central city was creating some opportunities for immigrants and indigenous minorities to enter New York City's workforce, but rapid growth of the informal economy was widely seen as creating jobs for unskilled workers. These jobs are often invisible to agencies that compile employment statistics (Waldinger and Lapp, 1993).

This view of the informal economy tends to focus attention on the misfeasance of the immigrant-entrepreneur sweatshop owners and the tax-evading dog walkers among the urban poor. Viewing the informal economy thus serves to divert interest and attention from the broader role being played by wealthier and more powerful groups that are promoting "legal employment at indecently low wages and in abhorrent conditions" (Waldinger and Lapp, 1993). What is that role?

There is a disenfranchisement underway, of the institutionalized power captured by labor over the past century in the U.S.: the rise of the informal economy is a *symptom* of the decline of labor, not a cause. The informal economy is a specific form of relations of production embedded in a specific historic context: the context is an attenuating system of institutionalized regulation. This system includes a set of laws and rules enforced by active intervention of government into the private employment realm. It encompasses established relations between employers and employees nationwide embedded in union contracts, normal employment practices of nonunion employers, custom, and workplace tradition. It is the social contract.

The social contract is being substantially rewritten. The rise of the informal economy is a reflection of fundamentally changing political-economic processes at the core of society. Immigrant entrepreneurs may benefit from such changes, but do not cause them. Although informal activities may be periodically harassed by the state, the "informal sector as a whole tends to develop under the auspices of government tolerance" (Castells and Portes, 1989, p. 27). Decline in enforcement and subsequent rise in minimum wage law violations, for example, was a serious problem by the early 1970s (Levitan and Belous, 1979), well before the growth of the informal economy was observed. Immigrant entrepreneurs were quick to realize that declining government enforcement of an array of worker health, safety, wage, and similar regulations provided them with a foot in the door, a comparative cost advantage in certain small business sectors (Bonacich and Light, 1988). Reaping cost savings from "lax enforcement of wage and sanitary provisions of the labor code" (Light and Rosenstein, 1995, p. 77), Korean-owned small businesses became dominant in small-scale retailing in Los Angeles county in the 1970s and 1980s, a development that went far beyond mere creation of off-the-books firms. Having a desperate, often destitute immigrant labor pool to draw upon (partially due to government tolerance of illegal immigrant workers), of course, facilitated exploiting the advantage conveyed by the de facto demise of enforcing laws protecting workers in Los Angeles. As the personnel director of an Asian-owned fast-food chain described the Los Angeles labor market, "The Latinos in our locations, most are recent arrivals. Most are tenuously here and here on fragile documents. I see them as very subservient." Blacks, by contrast, were "far more aware of the regulatory system and far more aware of remedies if they've been wronged" (Waldinger, 1996, forthcoming). This firm employed a workforce made up largely of immigrant Latinos.

UNDERMINING ORGANIZED LABOR

Proliferation of maquiladoras along the Mexican border reflects the same political-economic dynamics that produce a growing informal sector in Manhattan. Both patterns of business growth reduce the costs of labor substantially. Informalization in the labor market tends to reduce wages, but the greatest savings occur from nonpayment of fringe benefits and employee-related payments to government. The power of labor is falling in all spheres: bargaining with employers, social organization, and political clout. "Undeclared, unprotected labor, small units of production, networks rather than socialized labor processes, homework rather than factories, unstable relations of production, multiple intermediaries between workers and capital, segmentation of labor along age, gender, and ethnic lines, dependence of the job on the absence of legal control"—all of these factors are contributing to the de-collectivization of the labor process, the decline of the labor movement as an organized force (Castells and Portes, 1989, p. 31).

Declining ability to compete in the labor market is commonly blamed upon the deficiencies of individuals: they need to acquire more education and skill so that they will be more productive workers. Although the link between high worker productivity and high earnings has prevailed throughout most of the twentieth century, it is increasingly being severed. In the U.S. durable goods manufacturing sector, for example, average output per worker rose 37.2 percent over the 1982–1991 period, but this greater productivity coexisted with declining real hourly compensation for manufacturing workers nationwide (U.S. Bureau of Labor Statistics, 1992). The automotive assembly and auto parts industries in the U.S. cut their ranks of low-skilled workers dramatically over the 1975–1990 period while, simultaneously, *low-wage* employment grew substantially (Howell, 1994).

Twenty years ago, bureaucratic trade unions represented most of the nation's manufacturing production workers. In the durable goods manufacturing areas, particularly where large corporations were most dominant, labor and corporate America coexisted in relative harmony. The crux of the social contract in manufacturing was that unions:

1) permitted management to have complete control over production;
2) accepted increased worker productivity as a key goal; and
3) kept workers on the job.

In return, the large manufacturers provided high and gradually increasing wages for their workers (O'Conner, 1973). When productivity gains occurred, they were not ordinarily passed on to the customers in the form of lower prices; instead, they were retained to support higher wages and profits. This social contract between labor and capital had evolved in the post-World War II period. The deal began to unravel in the 1970s.

Increased international competition is often blamed for undermining corporate America's social contract with its workforce. Key unionized sectors, such as autos and steel, lost market share to foreign rivals in the 1970s, and the profits of the impacted companies often suffered. Intentional competition, however, was only part of a more fundamental phenomenon that was remaking corporate America. In a world of rapid technological advancement, some entrenched firms adapt and prosper, while others lag behind and experience rising costs and, or falling market share (hence, falling profits). Sometimes an entire industry lags, as did steel. New, more innovative competitors—foreign and domestic—move in to replace the industry laggards: thus, newcomer Nucor Steel is a giant today, while industry giants of the 1970s, like Republic Steel, have been cut back and merged out of existence.

Rapid technological change has helped to spur growing competition—both domestic and international—and many of corporate America's giants have had to cut costs and innovate to remain competitive. Innovation has often meant less reliance upon unionized blue collar workers. The previous era of corporate giants sharing monopolistic profits with unionized workers has been replaced by a modern era in which the high wage costs of unionized labor have become a prime target for corporate cost cutters.

Former Secretary of Labor Ray Marshall captured the spirit of corporate America's new attitude towards blue collar labor when he noted that "Since the early 1970s, U.S. companies have been competing mainly through reducing domestic wages and by shifting productive facilities to low wage countries" (Marshall, 1992).

Fraying of the social contract between corporate America and its workforce has produced dramatic uncouplings of historic relationships between worker productivity and compensation. A $15 per hour unionized job with General Motors is a prime candidate to become a $6 an hour nonunionized job with a small manufacturing firm: the same worker may be working at the same machine in the same building; the wage reduction reflects the altered labor relations of the 1990s. Worker productivity changes did not produce the $9 per hour wage cut. Rather, the $15 per hour wage was rooted in the social relations of production of a bygone era; the $6 wage reflects the emerging reality of blue collar manufacturing work in the 1990s.

Strategies for converting high-wage jobs into low-wage jobs include:

1. downsizing the corporate labor force and contracting out to low-wage suppliers work that was previously done in-house;
2. relying more heavily upon part-time and temporary workers, while not providing traditional fringe benefit coverage to these employees (Appelbaum, 1992);
3. playing hardball with the existing work force, reducing their wages and fringe benefit compensation; and
4. shifting operations to low-cost sites, both within the United States as well as globally (Howell, 1995).

This transformation in the relations of production has been greatly facilitated by government's pro-market ideological climate. The Reagan revolution and ensuing events at all levels of government have produced an array of government policies favoring corporate America's push for revamped employment and employee compensation practices. America's institutional arrangements for protecting workers—labor unions, labor laws, minimum wage levels—have eroded severely, freeing corporate employers to rewrite their social contract with labor (Goldfield, 1987; Appelbaum and Batt, 1993). What began most commonly as a corporate attempt to reduce their reliance on high-cost, unionized blue collar employees has become, in the 1990s, an all-encompassing revision of the relations between labor and capital in U.S. society.

RISING URBAN EMPLOYMENT INCREASINGLY COEXISTS WITH RISING POVERTY

The dominant political-economic conventional wisdom today suggests that the U.S. must increase its ability to compete globally. This entails decreasing government regulation of business, government sanctioning of corporations shifting productive facilities to low-wage areas such as Mexico, declining influence of labor unions, and a host of related polices. The common denominator is that these policies serve to reduce the costs of labor substantially. Not all workers are equally impacted.

Earlier in this essay urban industries were divided into three groups—export firms, suppliers to the export firms, and firms serving the local economy. Downsizing, contracting out, and the like are strategies whereby the export firms cut their reliance on expensive white-collar employees and unionized blue-collar workers. Many of these jobs continue to exist, but they are now found in group two, the complementary firms that serve the export industries. The net effect of the job shift has been to cut costs for the export firms. The displaced workers are often re-employed at lower wages, sharply reduced fringe benefits, and lessened job security. Intense pressure imposed by the export industries upon supplier firms to cut costs forces them to squeeze their employees: wage cutting, relying increasingly upon part-time and temporary workers, and slashing fringe benefits are common responses. The complementary supplier firms, in particular, are moving away from institutionalized employment practices emulating large corporations, and towards laissez-faire employment practices. Laissez-faire practices have always been the norm in the informal economy. Among the group-three firms—those serving the local economy—small businesses are widespread, unions are weak, and protection of workers depends heavily upon government enforcement of legally-mandated employment safety standards. It is in this sector that the lines between the informal economy and above-ground economy are blurring. The movement to lessen government regulation of business has its greatest impact on workers employed in the small retail and service businesses that serve the local economy.

How can inner-city ghetto areas attract employers and strengthen their economic base in the prevailing political-economic milieu? The consensus seems to be shifting towards acceptance of the Reagan administration's initial conception of enterprise zones. The crux was that a reduction of government presence within the inner-city zones would create fertile grounds for indigenous entrepreneurial activity. This reduced public presence would be achieved by largely eliminating government regulation within the zone, in conjunction with tax relief. As James Johnson notes, the federal government under Reagan made substantial progress towards this laissez-faire ideal when it "aggressively relaxed environmental regulations and reduced the budgets and slashed the staffs of governmental agencies that were charged with enforcing laws governing workplace health, safety, and compensation, as well as hiring, retention, and promotion practices" (p. 152, 1995).

Adopting the laissez-faire practices of the informal economy, narrowing the gap between the off-the-books sweatshops and the inner city, above ground small business sector may increase employment in poor urban areas, but poverty will not decline. Growing informalization and sustained high levels of job creation typified Los Angeles County during the 1970s and 1980s, with the incidence of working poverty growing substantially. Between 1969 and 1987, the proportion of male, year-round, full-time (YRFT) workers in L.A. County earning less than $10,000 annually (in 1986 dollars) doubled, rising from 7 percent to 14 percent of YRFT workers. Whereas only six percent of L.A. manufacturing jobs were low-wage (defined in conjunction with the poverty level) in 1969, over 20 percent were low-wage in 1987 (Schimek, 1989). Low-wage workers "increased in total numbers from 114,000 in 1969 to 467,000 in 1987, a rate of growth 16 times that of the total population of Los Angeles County" (Soja, 1991, p. 364). The illegal immigrants working in the informal economy that did not respond to applicable government population surveys are not counted in these figures, but their presence increased poverty levels well beyond official estimates. According to those official estimates, Los Angeles County, while experiencing sub-stantial economic growth in the 1969–1987 period, went from a situation of below-average poverty (1969) to above-average poverty (1987) rela-tive to the country as a whole.

The informalization of a growing share of America's small business (and big business), is the expression of new forms of social control being imposed on America's workers, often with the acquiescence of the state. A political consensus in Washington calls for increasing global competi-tiveness of America's businesses and reduced regulatory burdens. In prac-tice, these goals often manifest themselves as declining job security, falling wages, plummeting fringe benefits, poor working conditions, and failure to enforce worker employment, health, and safety regulations; in the inner-city context, this increasingly causes working poverty. There is nothing on this list of consequences that is upsetting to the large corpora-tions that make up the export base of America's large cities. The broad-based lowering of labor costs coexists with an expanded supply of low-wage service workers to clean houses, cook meals, raise children, and walk the dogs of the managerial and professional elites that run these large corporations. Challenges to this emerging status quo, if they are forthcoming, will arise when younger generations of workers put forth a class-based agenda to reverse the decline of the institutionalized power of labor. Observing government's activist and reformist response to labor radicalism in the 1930s, a famous economist observed that "instead of a revolution, we had a budget deficit." Our presidential contenders tell us that the budget deficit will disappear in seven years. Will revolution once again be on the agenda?

REFERENCES

Appelbaum, Eileen, "Structural Change and the Growth of Part-Time and Temporary Employment," Virginia duRivage, ed., *New Policies for the Part-Time and Contingent Workforce*. Armonk, N.Y.: M.E. Sharpe, 1992.

————, and Rosemary Batt, *The New American Workplace*. Ithaca, ILR Press, 1993.

Bonacich, Edna, and Ivan Light, *Immigrant Entrepreneurs: Koreans in Los Angeles*. Berkeley, University of California Press, 1988.

Castells, Manuel, and Alejandro Portes, "World Underneath: Origins, Dynamics, and Effects of the Informal Economy," *The Informal Economy*, A. Portes, M. Castells, and L. Benton, eds. Baltimore: Johns Hopkins University Press, 1989.

Cisneros, Henry, "Urban Entrepreneurialism and National Economic Growth" U.S. Department of Housing and Urban Development essay (September 1995).

Feagin, J. and M. Smith, *The Capitalist City*. New York: Blackwell, 1988.

Fusfeld, Daniel, and Timothy Bates, *Political Economy of the Urban Ghetto*. Carbondale: Southern Illinois University Press, 1984.

Goldfield, Michael, *The Decline of Organized Labor in the United States*. Chicago: University of Chicago Press, 1987.

Howell, David, "The Collapse of Low-Skill Male Earnings in the 1980s: Skill Mismatch or Shifting Wage Norms?" (unpublished manuscript, 1994).

————, "Collapsing Wages and Rising Inequality," *Challenge* (January/February 1995).

Johnson, James, "The Competitive Advantage of the Inner City: Comment," *Harvard Business Review* 73 (July–August 1995).

Kasarda, John, "Urban Change and Minority Opportunities," *The New Urban Reality*, Paul Peterson, ed. Washington, D.C.: Brookings Institution, 1985.

Levitan, Sar, and R. Belous, *More than Subsistence: Minimum Wages for the Working Poor*. Baltimore: Johns Hopkins University Press, 1979.

Light, Ivan, and Carolyn Rosenstein, *Race, Ethnicity, and Entrepreneurship in Urban America*. New York: Aldine De Gruyter, 1995.

Marshall, Ray, "The Future Role of Government in Industrial Relations," *Industrial Relations* (Winter 1992).

O'Conner, James, *The Fiscal Crisis of the State*. New York: St. Martins, 1973.

Sassen-Koob, S. "Exporting Capital and Importing Labor: The Role of Caribbean Migration in New York City," Center for Latin American and Caribbean Studies Occasional Paper, New York University, 1981.

Schimek, Paul, "Earnings Polarization and the Proliferation of Low-Wage Work," Graduate School of Architecture and Urban Planning, UCLA, 1989.

Soja, Edward, "Poles Apart: Urban Restructuring in New York and Los Angeles," *Dual City: Restructuring New York*, J. Mollenkopf and M. Castells, eds. New York: Russell Sage Foundation, 1991.

U.S. Bureau of Labor Statistics, *Productivity and Costs*. Washington, D.C.: U.S. Department of Labor, 1992.

Waldinger, Roger, *Through the Eye of the Needle: Immigrants and Enterprise in New York's Garment Trades*. New York: New York University Press, 1986.

————, "Who Makes the Beds? Who Washes the Dishes? Black/Immigrant Competition Reassessed," *Immigrants and Immigration Policy*, Harriet Duleep and Phanindra Wunnava, eds. Greenwich: JAI Press, 1996.

————, and Michael Lapp, "Back to the Sweatshop or Ahead to the Informal Sector," *International Journal of Urban and Regional Research* 17 (1993).

8

PROMOTING ECONOMIC DEVELOPMENT IN THE INNER CITY: THE IMPORTANCE OF HUMAN RESOURCES

Carla J. Robinson-Barnes

In his essay entitled "The Competitive Advantage of the Inner City," Michael Porter proposes a model for the revitalization of inner cities. The proposed model relies on business development as a strategy to promote revitalization and assigns a leadership role to the private sector. This essay critiques the Porter model and suggests some additional factors that will need to be addressed by a model attempting to promote the comprehensive revitalization of inner-city communities. Such a model will need to acknowledge that the issues confronting these communities are not only economic in nature. Moreover, efforts to address the economic issues must not be limited to Porter's business development strategy. These efforts must be capable of responding to a range of other important economic issues, most notably human resource development.

THE PORTER MODEL

Porter views "a coherent economic strategy" as being central to efforts to revitalize the inner city.[1] In his opinion, past revitalization efforts have, for the most part, failed largely because they "have been guided by a social model built around meeting the needs of individuals."[2] He claims that efforts emphasizing economic development have failed as well, partly because they were not effectively integrated into a coherent strategy and partly because they assumed that basic principles of business and competition do not apply within inner-city economies. According to Porter, neither the emphasis on individuals nor the belief that "unique laws of competition" are at work in inner-city economies is likely to take us very far in our efforts to revitalize inner cities.[3] As he sees it, the real issue at hand is "how inner-city-based businesses and nearby employment opportunities for inner-city residents can proliferate and grow."[4]

Porter believes that this issue can be effectively addressed by a revitalization model that emphasizes the development of viable businesses. In order to be viable, the businesses must be able to compete within the general economy (and not only within the inner-city economy), and they must be profitable. He states:

> These businesses should be capable not only of serving the local community but also of exporting goods and services to the surrounding economy. The cornerstone of such a model is to identify and exploit the competitive advantages of inner cities that will translate into truly profitable businesses.[5]

He posits that his model, by creating profitable businesses, will result in a situation in which wealth is created within (and not simply redistributed to) the inner city. He describes this model as "a new and comprehensive approach to reviving our nation's distressed urban communities."[6]

ECONOMIC DEVELOPMENT VERSUS BUSINESS DEVELOPMENT

Porter's model offers numerous insightful and instructive principles for the design of business development programs in inner-city areas. The emphases on the competitive advantage of inner-city locations and on the importance of "clusters of companies" in spurring local economic development are particularly helpful. By focusing attention on the economic (and not just geographic) environment in which businesses function, the model provides an important and practical perspective that can improve the effectiveness of business development programs.

Like the models Porter criticizes and attempts to improve upon, however, his model still only takes us part of the way (albeit down a somewhat better paved road) in our efforts to revitalize inner-city areas. Part of the model's inability to take us farther results from its almost exclusive focus on economic issues. The issues present in inner-city communities are complex, resulting from and involving a historically rooted combination of economic, political, and social forces. Although Porter's model will likely be effective in addressing some of these issues, its failure to recognize the complexity of the array of issues present in inner-city communities limits the extent to which it can function as a "comprehensive approach" to inner-city revitalization.[7]

The model's inability to take us farther also results from its conceptualization of the economic issues in inner cities solely in terms of business development. While business development issues are a very important subset of the economic issues facing inner-city communities, they are not the only type of economic issues facing them. Consequently, a model built on efforts to foster the broader economic development of these communities is needed. Economic development strategies typically involve efforts to restructure, sustain, or expand local economic activity and resources. Although business development is the central element of many economic development strategies, by itself it has little potential to tackle the full range of economic issues confronting many communities, especially inner cities. A crucial issue, and one that is not adequately addressed by the Porter model, is human resource development. Porter recognizes that employers offering "moderate-wage jobs" can "find hardworking, dedicated employees in the inner city"; that some inner-city residents have entrepreneurial talents; and that attractive business opportunities in the inner cities can lure well-trained African-American and Latino managers.[8] He also outlines roles the private sector and community-based organizations can play in training workers and in creating work-readiness and job-referral systems. However, this perspective views human resources primarily as an input for the business development strategy rather than as an important economic resource with the potential to contribute to the economic development of these areas in ways other than the business development strategy.

THE ROLE OF HUMAN RESOURCE DEVELOPMENT

Human resource development is an often overlooked aspect of economic development. Frequently, human resource issues are regarded as being more closely related to social development than they are to economic development. This perspective notwithstanding, the ability of the residents of a community to cultivate skills that enable them to be productive and to secure incomes that allow them to support themselves and their families is fundamentally an economic development issue. In this context, inner-city communities must be viewed as more than potential locations for businesses able to exploit competitive advantages in ways that allow larger markets to be served profitably. Inner-city communities must also be viewed as areas containing various resources (including human resources) that can potentially contribute to the further development of the communities.

An inner-city economic development strategy that recognized the importance of human resource development would address a number of issues that affect the productivity of area residents. Efforts to reduce the high dropout rates common in many inner-city high schools would be made not merely as gestures to assist "at-risk" youth, but also as measures to ensure that the area's valuable stock of productive human resources will be developed to its full potential. Steps to forge genuine partnerships between businesses and schools would be taken not simply to provide businesses with "community service" photo opportunities, but rather to ensure that students will have access to state-of-the-art equipment and will have early exposure to practical applications of their knowledge in the world of work. Programs to train workers would focus not only on very basic skills, such as job readiness and job retention, but would also emphasize retraining and skill upgrading in areas in which participants are likely to find stable employment opportunities. Each of these initiatives could conceivably be undertaken in conjunction with business development strategies designed in accordance with the principles proposed by Porter. However, each could also be undertaken as part of a strategy emphasizing the fullest possible development of the community's human resources in an effort to provide residents with access to meaningful employment options, whether in the inner city or elsewhere.

The broadly defined approach to economic development requires the perceived boundary separating social issues and economic issues to be removed so the full set of economic issues facing the inner city can be recognized and addressed. Education, training, and other activities that can develop human resources are frequently regarded as social programs. This perspective limits the ability of these activities to make significant contributions to economic development. Because this perspective is so ingrained, it is not likely to be easily changed. Many city officials and economic development practitioners do not see the relationships between their efforts to promote growth and the economic circumstances of the residents of their communities, particularly the poor. The notion that economic development could be related to an issue like poverty alleviation escapes many city officials, to whom "the latter seems like just another social objective that obstructs entrepreneurial deal making and business attraction."[9] This situation is reinforced by the structural separation of public agencies handling economic development issues and those handling human resource issues.[10] Barriers between training agencies, educational institutions, and employers further exacerbate the situation.[11]

Despite the perceptual and structural obstacles to the linkage of economic development and human resource development, progress is being made in some places. In Baltimore in the late 1980s, for example, a coalition of African-American churches and labor groups called Baltimoreans United in Leadership Development (BUILD) was successful in placing human resource issues on the city's policy agenda.[12] Prompted by concern that the city's economic renaissance of the 1970s and early 1980s had not significantly improved the economic circumstances of many poor and African-American residents, BUILD set out to improve the city's school system, which had a 50 percent dropout rate. In partnership with the local business community and the mayor, BUILD developed programs to help high school students prepare for college and to help high school graduates find jobs with local companies. What makes this example significant is BUILD's ability to place these issues on the local policy agenda. During the 1970s and early 1980s, downtown revitalization and the development of the Inner Harbor and Harborplace dominated the city's policy agenda. That BUILD was able to forge a coalition around human resource issues in this context and begin to highlight relationships between economic development and human resource development suggests that a broader perspective for addressing inner-city economic development is possible.

"Targeted economic development" provides another recent example of an approach that signals hope for the emergence of a broader perspective toward inner city economic development. This approach "refers to the combining of employment training, human services, and enterprise development to enhance access to and creation of jobs, careers, and self sufficiency for the disadvantaged."[13] It is targeted in that it emphasizes not only the development of specific geographic locations, but also the creation of "decent jobs and incomes for the disadvantaged as short-term outcomes."[14] One of the important characteristics of this approach is that it is market-oriented, meaning that "job access and creation efforts recognize the economic dynamics affecting jobs and occupations—paying attention, in particular, to what businesses want in job skills and work preparation."[15] Types of initiatives undertaken within this approach include the creation of employment opportunities in specific economic sectors through business development and targeted training and the provision of assistance to businesses likely to employ economically disadvantaged residents.

The broader approach to the economic development of the inner city will also require the policy framework typically used to foster urban economic development to be expanded in ways that permit inner-city economies to be understood in the context of their surrounding metropolitan economies. Porter contributes to this effort by pointing to the importance of such economic factors as industry clusters, the comparative advantage of inner-city locations, and the size of inner-city markets. In doing so he draws attention to potential development opportunities in the inner city. These opportunities are frequently overlooked by city officials, who have a tendency to concentrate their development efforts in central business districts, and by business people, who tend to assume that inner-city locations cannot be profitable.[16] An expanded policy framework for urban economic development would recognize that issues concerning inner-city development are central to, and not separate and apart from, issues concerning the development of metropolitan economies. Within such a framework, the comparative advantage of various types of locations (including inner-city locations) could be recognized, and appropriate strategies could be designed to capitalize on those advantages.

The administration of Mayor Harold Washington of Chicago provides one of the best examples of an expanded policy framework for urban economic development. The administration's development plan for the city emphasized the creation of benefits for residents and locations that had historically been left behind or adversely affected by development.[17] Among the plan's goals were the promotion of balanced growth, the creation of job opportunities for residents, and broad public participation in the development process. The administration relied on strategies aimed at specific economic sectors and at specific geographic areas in its efforts to ensure that disadvantaged residents and areas would receive benefits.[18] In relying on both types of strategies the administration acknowledged that, often, sectoral strategies do not benefit some geographic areas and that some areas may require focused attention. Both strategies were central to the administration's policy approach.

CONCLUSION

Economic revitalization strategies for the inner city must be based on sound economic principles. Porter makes an important contribution in this regard by identifying basic economic principles upon which a business development strategy for the inner city can be built. However, to be effective, economic revitalization strategies must address the range of economic issues present in the inner city. Porter's model addresses the issue of wealth generation within inner city communities. Another important issue involves the ability of inner-city residents to contribute to the wealth-generation process. Strategies based on a broad economic development perspective that recognizes the importance of human resource development are needed in order to address this issue.

NOTES

1. Michael E. Porter, "The Competitive Advantage of the Inner City," *Harvard Business Review* (May–June 1995), p. 55.

2. Ibid.

3. Ibid.

4. Ibid.

5. Ibid., p. 56.

6. Ibid., p. 71.

7. A more thorough presentation of this point may be found in June Manning Thomas, "Rebuilding Inner Cities: Basic Principles," in this special edition of *The Review of Black Political Economy.*

8. Porter, pp. 61–62.

9. Robert Giloth, "Social Investment in Jobs: Foundation Perspectives on Targeted Economic Development during the 1990s," *Economic Development Quarterly* 9 (August 1995), p. 281.

10. Roger Friedland, Frances Fox Piven, and Robert Alford, "Political Conflict, Urban Structure, and the Fiscal Crisis." In *Comparing Public Policies: New Concepts and Methods,* Sage Yearbooks in Politics and Public Policy, Vol. 4, edited by Douglas E. Ashford (Beverly Hills, CA: Sage Publications, 1978).

11. Giloth, p.281.

12. Marion Orr, "Urban Regimes and Human Capital Policies: A Study of Baltimore," *Journal of Urban Affairs* 14 (1992), pp. 173–187.

13. Giloth, p. 280

14. Ibid., p. 279.

15. Ibid., p. 282.

16. Carla Jean Robinson, "Municipal Approaches to Economic Development: Growth and Distribution Policy," *Journal of the American Planning Association* 55 (Summer 1989), pp. 283–295.

17. City of Chicago, Department of Economic Development, *Chicago Works Together: 1984 Development Plan* (City of Chicago, 1984).

18. Robert Mier, Kari J. Moe, and Irene Sherr, "Strategic Planning and the Pursuit of Reform, Economic Development, and Equity," *Journal of the American Planning Association* 52 (Summer 1986), pp. 299–309.

9

THE PORTER MODEL OF COMPETITIVE ADVANTAGE FOR INNER-CITY DEVELOPMENT: AN APPRAISAL

C. Michael Henry

Harvard's Michael Porter has joined the growing number of academics in search of a model that will solve the problems of material deprivation and degradation of racial minorities in the inner cities. We should add, however, that this search is not merely for a model, but for a model that is "politically" acceptable to the majority. This condition of political acceptability is not unique to the inner city. Recently, we read that Presidential candidate, Senator Bob Dole, importuned Jack Kemp, chairman of a Committee on Tax Reform, to keep the Committee's report free of incendiary specifics, presumably to prevent loss of support among voters—the devil remains in the details. But a politically acceptable model does not necessarily solve the problem. Indeed, it may impair the efficacy of the model and exacerbate the problem. Hence, perhaps, the enduring nature of inner-city poverty. This is, therefore, an important problem in political economy. To be sure, political economists do not necessarily provide the "solution key" to this problem. But, we are informed, neither do sociologists or historians, both of whom tend to be pessimists because, unlike economists, "they take their bearings from past failure." Economists, on the other hand, cannot be characterized as a dismal lot; actually, they are optimists, "because they suffer from almost total historical amnesia."[1] The British political scientist, Kenneth Minogue, mused that economists (the problem solvers) consider themselves equipped with a portable science, and he therefore pointedly raised the following question: "Does the world consist merely of societies navigating their way through history in terms not of religion or morality or philosophy but of whatever model currently happens to impress economists and politicians?" Alas, for the most part, response to this query may very well be in the affirmative. In this essay, we appraise the applicability of the Porter model to the inner city by addressing the following: Can the model be deemed politically acceptable, and if so, what are its implications for inner-city development? Can Porter be considered merely a champagne socialist, in the sense of a patrician who assumes that he knows what is best for the inner-city residentiary better than the residents themselves know? And, if emulating material success is the basic drive of the inner-city populace, will the Porter model effect or subvert achievement of this objective?

According to Porter, "economic distress of America's inner cities" is due to "lack of businesses and jobs," which effects "not only a crushing cycle of poverty but also crippling social problems such as drug abuse and crime."[2] Porter's solution lies in "creation of a sustainable economic base in inner cities" through mobilization of the private sector in an economic environment made conducive to viability of enterprise by government policy. This joint effort of the private and public sectors will lead to economic betterment of the inner-city residentiary and will at once make the inner city an "integral part of the regional and national economy. . . . "[3] Now, what is the socioeconomic reality that would give rise to this diagnosis cum solution to the problem of inner-city poverty? To begin with, we provide a brief depiction of the forces of inner-city impoverishment as reflected in the model. Second, we present a brief rendition of the model. And, in the light of *the* reality of the inner city, we will appraise the process of inner-city development rendered in the model. Finally, we suggest an alternative model and assess its likely efficacy relative to the Porter model.

THE PORTER MODEL

The model is based on an inner-city reality viewed almost exclusively through the prism of the majority experience. This reality may be characterized as follows: With respect to the inner-city community as a whole, the lack of businesses is due to a lack of debt and equity capital—and hence, a low level of investment. Further, the lack of businesses gives rise to a lack of jobs as well as to a paucity of skills, which give rise to low productivity which, in turn, gives rise to low real income and hence to widespread impoverishment and, concomitantly, to a large number of recipients of welfare and other forms of public assistance. Furthermore, the low productivity and attendant high costs give rise to low investment which, in turn, gives rise to a lack of businesses, and the cycle is complete. Crime and drug abuse may be treated at the individual level. Over time, these straitened circumstances may adversely affect the individual's

health (say, depression, etc.) and induce use of illegal drugs for ameliora-
tion—and owing to a low real income or unemployment, this usage may
lead to drug abuse which, in turn, may lead to crime to support the
addiction. In Porter's world, there are no significant racial barriers to
socioeconomic progress. Hence, if the composition of the inner-city populace were changed from a "predominantly minority community" to a
"predominantly majority community," the model would be equally appli-
cable.

Circular relations may also be observed on both the demand and supply sides of debt and equity capital in the inner city. On the supply side,
the low level of real income results in a low level of savings on the part
of inner-city residents and hence, if not an absence, at most, a modicum
of equity capital. But the low level of real income is due to low productivity which, in turn, is due to the lack of debt and equity capital. And the
lack of capital, especially equity capital, is due to the small capacity to
save. This completes the circle on the supply side. On the demand side,
the lack of investment is due to small consumer demand, which is due to
low real income which, in turn, is due to low productivity. And the low
productivity is due to lack of debt and equity capital, which effects the
lack of investment. This completes our cycle on the demand side. Thus,
the low level of inner-city real income that reflects a low level of productivity is common to both demand for, and supply of, debt and equity
capital. On the supply side it ill-affects the supply of debt and equity
capital, and on the demand side it ill-affects the inducement to invest.
Hence, the solution key to inner-city development is enhancement of the
level of inner-city income. How is this objective achieved in the Porter
model?

Before focusing on this aspect of the model, it would perhaps be
instructive to summarize Porter's appraisal of past efforts in this regard.
In his view, past efforts at inner-city development failed because they
were *misguided* "by a social model" in which aid was provided in "the
form of relief programs such as income assistance, housing subsidies,
and food stamps." These programs "treated the inner city as an island
isolated from the surrounding economy and subject to its own unique
laws of competition," which "encouraged and supported small, subscale
businesses designed to serve the local community but ill-equipped to
attract the community's own spending power." Accordingly, the social
model "undermined the creation of economically viable companies."[4]
And, given the community's prickly insistence on continuation of programs that provide a safety net for its residentiary, it follows that the

community is, in large measure, responsible for its impoverishment, which is banished in the model by proliferation and growth of businesses in the inner city and nearby employment for its residents.

To increase inner-city real income, the model brakes the cycle of poverty by exploiting spacial attributes unique to the inner city to establish a sustainable economic base. Hence, given its proximity to "downtown business districts, logistical infrastructure, entertainment or tourists centers, and concentrations of companies,"[5] location-sensitive enterprises with potential for growth and expansion will be "persuaded" to establish branches in these areas where they provide jobs to inner-city residents. Given this creation of jobs, local market demand grows in significance and becomes the second major advantage that makes for viability of inner-city enterprises. This subset of enterprises will be established to satisfy the needs of inner-city consumers. This holds in regard to activities in retail trade, and financial as well as personal services. Porter cites a number of enterprises that have succeeded in this regard. These include Goldblatt Brothers (Chicago), CareFlorida (Miami), Universal Casket (Detroit), Americas' Food Basket (Boston), and a number of others, all of which have served the inner-city market admirably in areas such as food products, beauty care, and media. Additionally, inner-city serving enterprises have the potential to provide services to consumers beyond the inner-city. This is facilitated by establishing links between inner-city enterprises and similar enterprises that form part of a regional cluster and are competitive nationally and globally. This "integration of enterprise" makes it possible for inner-city enterprises to compete in the future in downstream products and services.

The fourth advantage exploited in the model is the human resource endowment of the inner city. The very large and capable inner-city labor force is tapped for production of goods and services. In addition to this relatively deep well of labor, Porter points out that the inner city is a rich source of local entrepreneurs which, when coupled with the growing number of black and Hispanic MBA graduates, will grow considerably greater in the future as these graduates take opportunities to serve inner-city needs. It is this confluence of forces in the model that underpins inner-city development. Well, you may ask, why have enterprises failed, so far, to seize these opportunities? The answer, we are informed, lies in the real inner-city disadvantages.

REAL DISADVANTAGES AND MEASURES
TO OVERCOME THEM

The forces of competitive advantage have failed to induce inner-city development owing to a number of real disadvantages created, in part, by government regulations. These disadvantages relate to lack of land development, exorbitant building costs as well as other high factor costs, lack of security, poor infrastructure, a paucity of both managerial and labor skills, lack of debt and equity capital, and an antibusiness attitude on the part of the community. In the model, disadvantages are addressed directly, and not indirectly, through "subsidies and mandates."

Lack of access to land for businesses, as well as poor land development, militates against business development, in part, because they ill-affect building costs that are considerable in the inner city relative to the suburbs. These costs arise from "delays associated with logistics, negotiations with community groups and strict urban regulations," including "restrictive zoning, architectural codes, permits, inspections, and government-required union contracts and minority setasides."[6] Furthermore, regulatory costs create uncertainty for entrepreneurs owing to the length of time endured waiting for approval, permits, and so on. Other costs (e.g., costs of water, health care, real estate and other taxes, workers compensation, etc.) of doing business in the inner city are also high relative to the suburbs, especially the cost of property insurance. The model incorporates measures taken by government to remove regulatory barriers, as has been successfully undertaken recently by the Indianapolis Regulatory Study Commission (in Indiana). In this regard, a government department is used "to provide building-ready sites at market prices . . . assembling parcels of land and subsidizing demolition, environmental clean up, and other costs."[7]

Another significant disadvantage lies in lack of security, which ill-affects costs of doing business. More specifically, these costs are ill-affected by crimes against property, employees and customers. To be sure, "crime ranks among the most important reasons why companies opening new facilities failed to consider inner city locations and why companies already located in the inner city left."[8] In the model, problems of security are dealt with by having concentrations of enterprises spread the costs of security. In other instances, firms have formed organizations to increase the effectiveness of security and to spread security costs while others, such as Americas Food Basket (Boston), have reduced security costs by employing residents of the community and by having strong relations with the community.

The transportation infrastructure in the inner city is seriously wanting in adequacy. In the model, this infrastructure is essential to: a) linkage of the inner city to the downtown business centers; b) linkage of the inner-city enterprises to regional clusters; and c) development of export oriented enterprises that "require the presence of strong logistical links between inner-city business sites and the surrounding economy."[9] This infrastructural inadequacy impedes the mobility of workers, shoppers, and goods and services. In the model, the unit of government responsible for land development is also deployed for development of adequate transportation infrastructure.

Lack of a skilled inner-city labor force as well as management skills is also a significant disadvantage to business development. This deficiency is addressed by the private sector. In the model, private sector programs for the inner city are not driven by preference programs and charity as they have been in the past. On the contrary, corporations undertake job training and management assistance as part of their endeavor to create and support "economically viable businesses built on true competitive advantage." Examples are cited in inner-city Boston, where job training has been done by corporations around industry clusters (e.g., restaurants, food service, and food processing) and the regional economy (e.g., financial services and health care). Additionally, professional associations and business schools could develop advisory programs for inner-city managers.

Another formidable disadvantage is created by lack of access to debt and equity capital. This impedes development of entrepreneurship in the inner cities. Lack of access to debt capital by inner-city businesses is due, in Porter's world, to "limited attention that mainstream banks paid them historically." In order to overcome bias in lending in the money and capital markets, government is enlisted to create an economic environment whereby private mainstream financial institutions can lend and invest profitably to inner-city enterprises. This holds especially with respect to reduction of the high transaction costs of inner-city loans. Recent legislation, like the Community Reinvestment Act, has led to greater attention being given by banks to inner-city areas. So far, however, direct lending by government has been ineffective. In order to increase equity capital, the model employs the government "to eliminate the tax on capital gains and dividends from long term investments in inner city enterprises that employ some acceptable number of inner city residents."[10]

Similar to the private sector, in this model, government preference programs are not utilized because they "in effect guarantee enterprises a market." In this model, such programs do not make for growth and efficiency of enterprise.

Anti-business suffuses the attitude of workers, community-based organizations (CBOs), community leaders, and social activists in the inner city, and this constitutes a significant barrier to development of inner-city enterprises. "Some workers perceive businesses as exploitative, a view that guarantees poor relations between labor and management."[11] This attitude, according to Porter, has dissuaded some businesses from locating in the inner city. For example, Porter notes that some enterprises refused to locate in inner-city Boston "because of demands to build playgrounds, fund scholarships, and cede control of hiring and training to community based organizations."[12] The model does, however, include a role for CBOs, but this role excludes ownership and management of businesses since, in Porter's view, their record in this regard is abysmal. CBOs are assigned to change workforce and community attitudes and to "act as a liaison between the community and enterprises to promote business development." In addition, CBOs participate in preparing, screening, and referring employees to local businesses, and in work-readiness training. This training includes training in communication skills, self development, and workplace practices. Furthermore, CBOs may facilitate commercial site improvement and development. This holds in regard to facilitating "environmental cleanup and development of commercial and industrial property."

At this point, we may conclude that in Porter's world the intense poverty and immiserization of minorities in inner cites is effected, in large measure, by antibusiness attitudes of minority residents that subvert business development in the community; outdated government regulations that create barriers to inner-city development; a dearth of managerial skills and skilled labor in the community; a lack of debt and equity capital; crime and an attendant lack of security; inadequate transportation infrastructure; undeveloped land; and relatively high factor (including building costs) and nonfactor costs of doing business. These constitute the real disadvantages to inner-city development. If this formidable array of barriers to realization of competitive advantage were supplanted by a set of government policy measures to mobilize the private sector and to foster establishment, growth and proliferation of enterprises in the inner city, then poverty and its debilitating concomitants in the inner city will be significantly alleviated.

APPRAISAL OF THE MODEL

In our appraisal of the model, we address the following questions: Is the model politically acceptable? Does it dictate to the inner-city populace what is best for their development? And, will this model transform the inner city for the economic betterment of its residentiary?

With respect to political acceptability, we focus on the role of government, the private sector and inner-city residents. The model deemphasizes government; government serves mainly to ensure that the inner city is made conducive to profitability of enterprise. In the past, government "assumed primary responsibility for bringing about the economic revitalization of the inner city,"[13] but these efforts have come to nought. Indeed, according to Porter, government has been and is part of the problem of inner-city poverty. Its "priorities run counter to business needs." The traditional private sector is now assigned the leading role. Subsidies and mandates are now eliminated and replaced by "market place realities." To be sure, if these subsidies were continued, "the inner city will continue to drain our rapidly shrinking public coffers." This, however, is a view of the inner city from a rather distorted prism. Only a negligible portion of government subsidies accrue to the inner-city populace. The major portion of expenditure and tax subsidies goes to the private sector. Indeed, if calls for tax and expenditure reform for reduction of subsidies were heeded, over time, reduction of these subsidies to the private sector would exceed $200 billion. Tables 1 and 2 portray a five-year savings (billions of dollars) in subsidies to industry from spending and tax reforms, respectively, computed by Robert Shapiro.[14] These savings are disaggregated by industry and given in Appendices (A) and (B).

Except, perhaps, in the cases of public housing in the miscellaneous category of industry, and mass-transit in the transportation industry, none of these spending subsidies directly affects the well-being of inner-city residents. And, with respect to tax subsidies, the only industries to which these subsidies may bear some relevance to inner-city residents is the construction industry. In this industry, some inner-city residents may receive direct tax subsidies in mortgage interest deduction and deductibility of interest paid on consumer loans secured by home equity. But, given the relatively small portion of inner-city residents who are home owners, to all intents and purposes, this population may be considered relatively unaffected by this subsidy. In Tables 1 and 2, we observe substantial tax and expenditure subsidies accruing to private sector enterprises. Yet Porter claims that the inner city must develop in the same

TABLE 1
Five-Year Savings from Reform of Spending Subsidies to Industries

Industry	Five-Year Savings in Subsidies
Energy	16.1
Other Natural-Resource Industry	1.4
Agribusiness	18.3
Transportation	31.1
Aerospace & High-Tech	12.9
Miscellaneous	31.2
Total Savings from Spending Reforms	**$114.2 (billions)**

TABLE 2
Five-Year Savings from Reform of Tax Subsidies to Industries

Industry	Five-Year Tax Subsidies
Natural-Resource	17.1
Construction	41.4
Agribusiness	2.4
Financial-Industrial	3.3
Miscellaneous	46.9
Total Savings from Spending Reforms	**$111.1 (billions)**

Source: Based on Shapiro, "Cut-and-Invest to Compete and Win," pp. 13–19.

manner that other segments of society have developed, by "market place realities," and not by way of subsidies because "subsidies to business don't work." Total savings in subsidies from expenditure and tax reform are approximately $225.3 billion. Clearly, emphasizing a pivotal role for the private sector and declaiming subsidies to inner-city residents enhance the political acceptability.

Another important factor that enhances acceptability of the model is its denouncement of so-called anti-business attitudes of CBOs and community leaders, and enlistment of their efforts to make the community less guarded in relations to the private sector. In short, like the government, participation of CBOs and community leadership is to make the inner city conducive to profitable business activity. The profit motive is of overriding importance in this model of inner-city development.

It is eminently clear that emphasis on reduction of subsidies to the inner city, elimination of antibusiness attitudes of the inner-city commu-

nity and the pivotal role of private sector activity that satisfies the profit
motive makes the model highly acceptable and will engage substantial
interest and support (financial and otherwise).

Will implementation of this model foster economic betterment of
inner-city residents? In this case, we focus on Porter's real disadvantages
and how they prevent realization of competitive advantage in the inner
city. To begin with, the community is characterized as having an antibusiness attitude, which constitutes a real disadvantage. Is this a legitimate characterization? Historically, practices of private sector enterprises
have actually militated against minority development and, by extension,
inner-city development. In this sector, wage discrimination on the basis
of race is as common as it is significant.[15] Minority workers are under-
paid relative to their white counterparts regardless of skill or experience.
For example, on the average, black college graduates are paid less than a
white high school graduate, and white college graduates are paid more
than blacks with graduate degrees, once again, regardless of skill and
experience.[16] Second, this sector practices discrimination on the basis of
race in the product market. A recent Harvard study reports that white
automobile dealers charge blacks premium prices for new automobiles
and accessories relative to prices paid by white males for automobiles of
the same make, year, and so on.[17] Hence, the real costs of cars to blacks
are considerably higher regardless of location (in or outside the inner
city) of the dealership. Third, a homeowner's equity (the appraised value
of a home less liens) is a significant part of one's wealth. Families use
this equity to finance the college education of their children, to establish
a business enterprise or a relatively riskless investment portfolio (say,
mutual funds and the like). Yet, the appraised value (determined by
appraisers in the private sector) of homes owned by blacks is considerably lower than white-owned homes of identical size, in the same neighborhood, on the same block and on the same street. Fourth, traditional
private sector enterprises established in the inner city, on the average,
charge prices for goods and services to inner-city consumers that are
considerably higher than prices paid by non-inner-city consumers for the
same goods and services in other areas. This price differential cannot be
due to differences in factor costs (enumerated by Porter) between the two
locations unless the supply elasticity of these goods and services is infi-
nite. In general, price is not cost determined. Fifth, this sector indulges in
the pernicious practice of discriminating between job applicants based on
race. In this case, the level or quality of education, etc., is irrelevant.
Moreover, a recent ABC television program (prime time) showed two

Ivy League graduates, one black and the other white, accorded quite different treatment, in the rental office, when applying to rent an identical apartment. The black graduate, whose application was considered first, was told that there were no vacancies, and if I recall correctly, he was quoted a higher rental price, whereas his white counterpart was told that the apartment was available at a rental price lower than that quoted to the black applicant. This treatment by landlords is meted out to blacks regardless of education, income, job security, and so on. Indeed, the overriding determinant in this and the foregoing cases is pigmentation of skin.

Given the foregoing practices by private sector enterprises to black citizens, why must community-based organizations, community leaders, and inner-city labor expose themselves to this outrageous fortune and further degradation? This seemingly antibusiness attitude is simply a wary response of the community to traditional enterprises entering the community to provide "services" to residents. In the late 1960s, Senator Goldwater was dubbed an extremist and rejected by "Republican moderates" for his statements, "extremism in defense of liberty is no vice" and "moderation in pursuit of justice is no virtue." On subsequent reconsideration, however, Goldwater thought that he would have been more acceptable to voters if he had said, "wholehearted devotion to liberty is unassailable and halfhearted devotion to justice is indefensible." In this regard, CBOs and community leaders are merely showing wholehearted devotion to both liberty and economic justice.

Thus, to suggest that blacks must change their attitude to permit competitive advantage to prevail, while private sector enterprises continue their traditional practices as if they were atavistically programmed to treat blacks with disdain assures the failure of Porter's endeavor. To await modification of this healthy response by blacks to a pernicious practice which will remain unchanged, is equivalent to waiting to hear the sound of one hand clapping.

To what extent do government regulations that create barriers to achievement of competitive advantage, pertain to the whole city as opposed to the inner city *per se*. If they pertain to the whole city, then why do they not create the same formidable barriers to growth and proliferation of enterprise in the center of the city? If these regulations pertain only to the inner city, then it seems that they pertain only to the areas peopled by impoverished blacks and Hispanics. Or, perhaps by some obscure element of chance, the impoverished have moved to areas where these regulations apply. I, therefore, find it somewhat difficult to grasp the relationship between this subset of urban space and the government regulations. Moreover, if the inner-city residentiary relocated to other areas in which these disadvantages to achievement of competitive advantage are absent, would they enjoy the same measure of economic prosperity to which their white counterparts have grown accustomed? Or, if this residentiary relocated to other areas (outside the inner city), would these regulations still remain a significant barrier to establishment of enterprises here, or would they be dismantled with great facility for economic progress? It is most unusual for a government to have enduring regulations that strangle development of enterprise in a capitalist economic environment and at once give rise to a growing group of impoverished citizens who are either unemployed or underemployed. This would be an enormous waste of human resources. Such waste "is a terrible thing to mind."

The paucity of managerial and labor skills is neither a real disadvantage to achievement of competitive advantage nor a cause of inner-city poverty and degradation. Actually, it is a result of poverty. There is no demand for these skills, hence, the inconsiderable number of skilled workers. Indeed, if a large proportion of the inner-city labor force were to acquire skills, there is no certainty that a significant portion of this skilled labor would acquire gainful employment beyond the boundaries of the inner city. The record of the absorption rate of black workers by the private sector does provide grounds for optimism. The banality of discrimination in employment discourages some blacks from acquiring high-powered skills because the rate of return does not justify acquisition of the skill. A structure must therefore be put in place whereby the absorption rate of skilled black personnel is determined by their qualifications and years of experience and not on criteria irrelevant to this consideration. Given the history of discrimination in employment, however, it may not be fair to blacks if experience loomed large as a factor in their consideration for employment and promotion over the next three decades, everything else congenial.

In the Porter world, lack of debt capital to inner-city entrepreneurs is euphemistically described as due to "limited attention that mainstream banks paid them historically." Shortage of debt capital is dealt with by government policy that facilitates lending to inner-city entrepreneurs by reducing transaction costs of inner-city loans. This measure may augment the supply of debt capital over the short run but not over the long run because the supply of debt capital is governed by a significant number of factors and, therefore, is a considerably more complex relationship than that presented. This is not simply a matter of overcoming "bias" by banks. Over the years this so-called bias or "limited attention" did not simply shift the supply curve of debt capital. This deliberate creation of a void of capital also created a void in entrepreneurial skills and experience and, by extension, the skills and experience of that cadre of workers who would have been employed in these activities. Hence, the flow of debt capital must be related to enhancement of general entrepreneurial skills and knowledge specific to the activity in which the entrepreneur will be engaged, along with the general and specific skills required of the employees. This ensures that funds borrowed by inner-city entrepreneurs are utilized most efficiently by the enterprise and that the community, as a whole, gets the maximum possible benefits from the investment.

Over the short run, crime and lack of security may be dealt with effectively in ways suggested in the Porter model. But clearly, this addresses crime with respect to the cost of doing business; it does not address the problem of crime *per se*. Over the long run, however, crime has to be dealt with by generating significant gainful employment (for inner-city labor) with opportunities for advancement, while at the same time making the inner city a more inviting, congenial and healthy environment for its residents. A good portion of the crime is due to lack of employment opportunities, but as we pointed out above, the record of the private sector is not particularly good with regard to absorption of black labor in gainful employment with opportunities for advancement. Some crimes are part of the pernicious effects of racial discrimination and its attendant degradation. These effects include depression and other forms of mental and emotional maladies. Perhaps a most significant effect of degradation is anger which is quite evident nowadays among some of the black youth. This anger is sometimes evinced in rebellious forms of behavior, for example, in dress codes, playing music fortissimo in the streets, lack of interest in academic pursuits, and so on. Treatment of this anger by psychotherapy involves a rather grim irony in the sense that the patient is taught to deal with his anger by using it creatively for the benefit of society. The "regenerated" individual is then reimmersed in society to function wholesomely, but this approach is seriously deficient because it leaves untouched and uncured that subset of society that is the fundamental cause of these problems—anger and all that. Laterally, we have been informed that society has grown more tolerant of violent crime, but this is somewhat doubtful. Prior to the end of World War II, lynching and other forms of inhuman behavior to blacks were quite common, yet the banality of this evil never caused any uprising on the part of the populace for good to prevail, or perhaps the pusillanimity of those who knew better prevented them from speaking up. Indeed, during this period, as with that sizable quotient of the German populace, this brutality was quietly accepted. Thus, the society has always glorified existential extremity. D.H. Lawrence once mused that "the essential American soul is hard, isolate, stoic and a killer."

In summary, the model fails to account for the widespread discrimination that has historically ill-affected blacks in the labor market, in employment and opportunities for advancement on the job. Hence, there is no reason to expect that a significant number of skilled and unskilled inner-city labor will secure gainful employment after the proliferation and growth of enterprise. Some augmentation of employment will be effected, but not at a level that absorbs a significant portion of the inner-city labor force and, given wage discrimination, on the average, levels of remuneration will fall significantly short of those of their white counterparts. Moreover, according to an example given by Porter, inner-city labor may earn only $7 to $8 per hour (plus contributions to pensions and health insurance), which is a relatively low-wage rate. But, he states, "the fact is that they are jobs; and the inner city and its residents need more of them . . . ," even though these jobs provide "limited opportunities for advancement."[18] Porter therefore fails to distinguish between creating jobs and creating jobs with incomes that permit the poor to work their way out of poverty. Second, the model fails to come to terms with the underlying nature of what it designates an antibusiness attitude of CBOs and community leaders. This so-called attitude is part of the response to degradation. But the model suggests elimination of this attitude without dealing with the inimical forces that gave rise to it. The two must be addressed concurrently. Third, the model suggests shifting the supply curve of debt capital to inner city entrepreneurs by a government policy that reduces the transactions cost of lending to these entrepreneurs. But there are many significant factors other than high transactions costs that ill-affect the availability of debt capital to the inner city. Finally, the principal focus of the model is satisfying the profit motive of private sector enterprises. The role of government policy, CBOs and community leaders is to make the inner city conducive to viability of these enterprises. Development of the inner-city populace is secondary. The crisis in the inner city, however, requires a comprehensive model of inner-city development that addresses a wide range of issues affecting development of the inner city *in toto*. In the light of these and other failings of the Porter model, we suggest an alternative model, to which we now give focus.[19]

AN ALTERNATIVE MODEL OF INNER-CITY DEVELOPMENT

To put an end to widespread immiserization in inner cities, we suggest an alternative model that will generate a significant and stable circular flow of income in the community. This model is designed for a community in which a significant portion of its residents is impoverished and subject to a color bar. The first step in economic transformation of the community is creation of productive activities in the community that effect direct inflows of resources, which will induce expenditure and establishment of additional viable productive activities (within the community). In this model, activities that spawn resource inflows are fundamental to the transformation process since they give rise to earnings that induce strong local consumer demand as well as establishment of enterprises to satisfy this demand. In this respect, two significant barriers must be considered: a) racial barriers (color bar); and b) skill barriers. These barriers may be causally linked in the sense that the former affects the latter. However, the latter may be overcome by endowing inner-city labor and entrepreneurs with skills specific to activities undertaken. But racial barriers are enduring and problematic. Thus, in this model, the resource inflow is effected by awarding procurement contracts (from government) to qualified inner-city entrepreneurs. (The procedure for qualification of entrepreneurs is given later in this essay.) In short, given the significance of resource inflows, in order to avoid this barrier— encountered regularly in the private sector by racial minorities—long-term contracts between qualified inner city entrepreneurs and the government are deemed necessary to generate significant and stable inflows. Such contracts are fundamental to diffusion of labor market opportunities to inner cities to foster socioeconomic development.

In this conceptual scheme, the inner-city economy is bifurcated into a *basic* and a *nonbasic sector*. These sectors are portrayed in Figure 1, where the basic sector includes procurement industries and provision of medical services. The latter is included in this sector because it gives rise to a significant inflow of resources to the inner city. The nonbasic sector satisfies inner-city (internal) demand. In the basic sector, entrepreneurs earn a return from provision of contractual services to public institutions—federal, state and local government. The nonbasic sector is adaptive. Initially, it arises primarily to satisfy household demand induced by income earned in the basic sector; but subsequently, it satisfies demand induced by earnings from basic as well as nonbasic activities. To be viable, the latter activity must supply qualitatively adequate goods and services, at competitive prices, to inner-city households.

FIGURE 1
Schematic Depiction of the Alternative Model

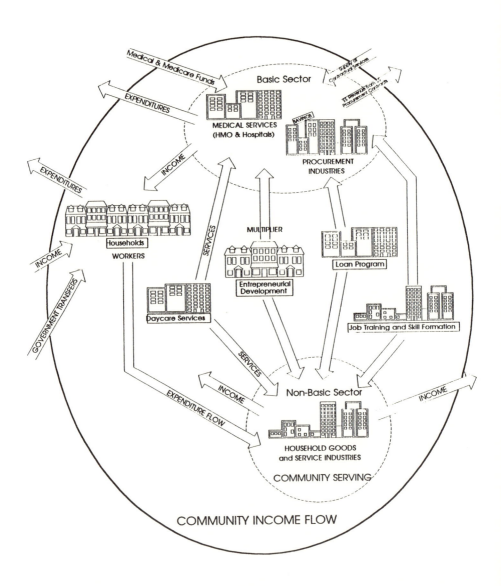

Note: diagram showing the circular path of income flow through the community.

Necessary conditions for efficient supply of goods to households and services to institutions are: qualified inner-city entrepreneurs, skilled inner-city labor and availability of adequate debt capital to entrepreneurs. Skill endowment of labor comprises: a) general training for job readiness, which involves development of behavioral traits (discipline, punctuality, etc.) appropriate to gainful employment; and b) acquisition of skills specific to sectoral activities. In Figure 1, job training and skill formation serves both sectors, hence the direction of the arrows. Entrepreneurial development encompasses endowment of general skills as well as organizational, managerial and technical skills specific to activities satisfying institutional and household demand. This development of entrepreneurs requires provision of managerial, organizational and technical courses to the entrepreneurs. The content of courses is determined by the specific activities in which entrepreneurs will be involved and by a survey of the entrepreneurs. Data from the survey will be analyzed to uncover entrepreneurial and other requisite skills in which they are deficient. The loan program (see figure 1) provides debt capital to entrepreneurs. This program is quite nontraditional in approach. For example, harsh financial experiences suffered in the past by entrepreneurs, such as bankruptcies, etc., will not be considered in the same manner as is done traditionally by banks in determination of eligibility of entrepreneurs for loans. Subsequent to course completion, a five-year entrepreneurial extension service will be established to give counsel and guidance to entrepreneurs engaged in sectoral activities. Entrepreneurial development as shown by arrows in the diagram serve the basic as well as the nonbasic sector. In this model, successful course completion and participation in the extension program are prerequisites to ownership of a sponsored enterprise (an enterprise formally included in the basic or nonbasic sector) and eligibility to participate in the debt capital program.[20] Gainful employment of labor by entrepreneurs to supply goods and services will establish a circular flow of income and will enhance the standard of living of the community.

An approach to development of minority entrepreneurship, similar to that suggested in this model, has been successfully undertaken by an alliance of public agencies, including the Port Authority of NY and NJ, and by private firms—The Regional Alliance for Small Contractors. This Alliance was established in response to formidable barriers to participation in construction (in the NY–NJ subregion) by enterprises owned by minorities and women. The Alliance offers technical assistance, loan programs and information on business opportunities to enhance performance of these contractors in the construction industry. Technical assistance encompasses practical classroom instruction to enable contractors to compete successfully for larger contracts from the Port Authority. Course instruction is given at the basic, intermediate and advanced levels in courses such as bidding strategies, contract law, contract administration, construction management, financial management, and so on. Courses are taught by executives of member-firms of the Alliance as well as by procurement officers of public agencies.

The Alliance has resulted in a significant increase in the dollar volume of contracts awarded to minority proprietors who successfully completed courses relative to a control group of minority contractors. For example, in 1991, a sample of 27 participating minority contractors were awarded $1.48 million in prime contracts and $1.64 million in subcontracts (as Port Authority contractors), whereas the control group (30 contractors) won no prime contracts and received $.82 million in subcontracts. Furthermore, in 1992, a sample of 27 participating minority contractors won $5.20 million in contracts, of which $1.56 million were prime contracts and $3.64 million subcontracts, while the control group won only $.41 million, of which $75,000 were prime contracts and $335,000 were subcontracts.

In the model, the vector of viable nonbasic activities (inner-city serving) is obtained from an inner-city household expenditure survey, for analysis of household expenditure patterns, to determine commodities and commodity groups that may be profitably supplied, over time, at competitive prices, to households with different characteristics (age composition, education of head of household, etc.) and income levels.

Implicit in the basic-nonbasic sectoral division of the inner-city economy is a causal link. The basic sector is considered the prime mover of the economy; indeed, it determines the economic health of the community. Hence, it is important that the government play a role in creation of this sector and of programs for provision of debt capital to entrepreneurs to undertake these activities. Two points should be noted in regard to basic activities. First, the basic sector primarily supplies services for which demand is cyclically stable and for which production is relatively labor intensive as well as skill intensive. Cyclical stability implies that inner-city basic income and employment are not subject to extreme swings. In short, the policy objective is a mix of basic activities that are not highly sensitive to cyclical fluctuations. That is, a significant part of the mix of procurement contracts must be made up of contracts for which the dollar volume is not cyclically sensitive. This provides ballast to the inflow of resources and thus gives a stable multiplier over time. Increasing the employment of minorities has implications for countercyclical policy, macro and monetary, particularly with respect to downward adjustment of the unemployment target (back to an aggregate unemployment rate of 5 percent or less) of policy makers. Second, basic activities serve a market whose level, to inner-city entrepreneurs, is set by political decisions. Given the assumption that policy-makers are favorably disposed to inner-city development and to long-term contractual arrangements between government (or quasi public agencies) and inner-city entrepreneurs, the dollar volume of basic activities is determined by the effective skill capacity of entrepreneurs and labor, and the availability of debt capital. The larger is the dollar volume of basic activities; the greater is inducement to establish nonbasic activities. And, the larger are: a) the proportion of basic sector labor income spent on goods and services, and b) the proportion of the wage bill in total costs of nonbasic activities; the larger is the nonbasic sector.

In Figure 1, day-care services are actually part of nonbasic activities, but given their significance to households in which both spouses are employed, they assume considerable importance. Management and staff in this activity are trained in a manner similar to that for other activities.

By way of example, assume inner-city entrepreneurs secure annual procurement contracts of $20,000,000, of which 60 percent pays wages and salaries (net of taxes) to inner-city labor. This $12,000,000 represents annual household income (from the basic sector). In addition, assume households spend 50 cents of every dollar of income (propensity to consume) on goods and services supplied by the nonbasic sector. That is, households spend $6,000,000 of income *locally* on goods and services generating internal (inner-city) sales revenue of $6,000,000. Furthermore, assume every dollar of sales revenue creates 70 cents of income (local income created per dollar of sales) in the nonbasic sector. That is, $4,200,000 of sales revenue pays wages and salaries to inner-city labor (employed in the nonbasic sector) and, given the propensity to consume, households spend $2,100,000 of this income on goods and services (supplied internally), of which 70 percent or $1,470,000, pays wages and salaries to inner-city labor.

This process of *internal income generation* will continue until annual inner-city income increases by approximately $18,461,538 as a result of external injection of $12,000,000 of basic sector income. It is important to note, however, that this income will be created, *if and only if*, inner-city entrepreneurs are developed and are provided with adequate financial capital, inner-city labor are skilled for gainful employment by entrepreneurs, and profitable household (inner-city) markets are identified.

Internally generated income may be increased by raising the dollar volume of basic activities, everything else constant. Endogenous increases in income may also arise by increase in local income created per dollar of sales, or by increase in the propensity to consume goods supplied locally, or by both. From the above example, if the propensity to consume were to increase from .5 to .65, and local income created per dollar of sales increased from .7 to .8, then the multiplier for exogenous increase in basic income increases from 1.54 to 2.1. That is, income increases by $2 for a dollar increase in exogenous expenditure as a result of increase in these parameters. Moreover, a larger increase per dollar change in exogenous expenditure may obtain if, in addition to the propensity to consume, the model were expanded to include propensities to invest in local business, human capital, local housing, and so on. The income stream swells as more dollars change hands locally. Prior to establishment of viable nonbasic activities, the dollars flow to enterprises outside the community. Thus, a policy that induces greater consumption of goods supplied locally will augment income created per dollar of sales and make for a more self-sufficient (with respect to government transfers) inner-city community.

In this model, the basic sector is of overarching importance. In its absence the community will remain mired in poverty. Thus, current efforts to establish retail shopping centers and like enterprises in inner cities cannot be an effective means for the poor to earn their way out of poverty. Inner-city residents cannot prosper by taking in each other's washing; i.e., there must be a net inflow of funds to stimulate and support secondary activities. Clearly, retail shopping centers and similar enterprises are secondary activities that do not spawn viable markets in the absence of basic activities. In the long run, nonbasic enterprises per se do not have the capacity to supply qualitatively adequate, and price competitive, goods and services unless they are provided large government subventions. But, alas, such subventions to the inner city are considered politically unacceptable, "a drain on the public purse." Moreover, over time they will not spawn opportunities that effect economic self-sufficiency of the community.

As noted in the foregoing, basic sector activities effect net inflows of resources. If a large proportion of labor in the inner city were gainfully employed beyond its boundary and annual earnings provided significant net inflows, an effect would be engendered equivalent to that of basic sector activity. But presently, such equivalence does not obtain owing to barriers previously noted. Figure 1 shows inflows of resources in the form of transfer payments and income, but presently flows from government largess are relatively weak, and thus, do not give rise to nonbasic activities of significance. Thus, inner-city serving activities are, in the main, nonviable and therefore fail. This nonviability is due, in part, to anemic market demand and lack of business know-how coupled with inadequacy of debt capital. According to recent findings,[21] black-owned enterprises enjoying some degree of success serve markets (outside the inner city) made up of white and nonwhite clientele (but disproportionately white). For example, mean sales ($52,308) of black enterprises with predominantly minority clientele are approximately 51 percent less than mean sales ($102,207) of black enterprises with mixed clientele. But the number of the latter enterprises is statistically insignificant.

Efficacy of the Model

Implementation of this model is eminently worthwhile. It has several advantages, and its costs are not exorbitant; in fact, the cost of not undertaking it can be very high. In addition to economic transformation of the community, it effectively reduces the gap in wealth between blacks and whites through development of black entrepreneurship and provision of employment opportunities to inner-city labor. Entrepreneurial development will reduce differences in inherited wealth between blacks and whites, for example, differences in *inter vivos* transfers for defrayment of costs of college education, downpayment on a house or a share in the family business. Indeed, intergeneration transfer of household wealth can only be made if there is wealth in the family to transfer, hence the relatively large wealth-gap observed between blacks and whites. Second, black enterprises employ primarily black labor. Recent evidence shows that 74 percent of black businesses employ a work force comprised of at least 75 percent blacks.[22] Thus, entrepreneurial development in the inner city will augment employment of black labor, enhancing their prospects for long-term employment and provide blacks with opportunities for advancement. Third, the model addresses elements of both demand and supply. The demand side relates to decomposition of demand for goods and services supplied by inner-city entrepreneurs. The supply side deals with the nature of the inner-city economic environment. This, for example, has to do with availability of adequate finance for entrepreneurs and development of inner-city entrepreneurship, as well as a skilled labor force. Fourth, the analysis of the model may be cast in terms of income, employment or sales. Albeit, sales are problematic since, in effect, they double count. That is, the volume of recorded sales is lower if producers sell directly to retailers than if they sell to wholesalers who, in turn, sell to retailers. This shortcoming may be avoided if value-added (roughly, sales less cost of materials purchased from other enterprises) were used. Nonetheless, consider a sales tax. Given its rate and coverage, the revenue depends on local sales. Hence, use of sales as a unit of measurement provides a basis for forecasting sales volume, and in turn, tax revenues. And if income is the unit of measurement, this makes possible a forecast of the yield (local) of an income tax. Such forecasts would be a boon to city (as well as state and federal) planners in regard to public expenditures in the urban community.

In addition, implementation of this model serves to remedy labor market and related problems peculiar to minorities. The effectiveness of the two large-scale job placement and training programs, the Job Training Partnership Act (1982) and its predecessor, the Comprehensive Employment and Training Act (1973), designed to remedy labor market problems of minorities has, so far, been limited in terms of significant impact on labor market participation or earnings levels of minorities. This is due, in part, to discrimination in the hiring practices by white employers. In short, the capacity of the private sector to absorb minorities, whether skilled or unskilled, on an equal footing (earnings, etc.) with whites remains limited. This absorptive capacity is enhanced, in part, through development of black entrepreneurship. Indeed, implementation of this model changes the composition of the inner-city labor force in terms of skilled relative to unskilled labor as well as the occupational structure of the labor force in terms of entrepreneurs relative to labor.

In the initial stage, procurement contracts (in the basic sector) between government and qualified inner-city entrepreneurs may be considered *setasides*, but as these entrepreneurs gain experience, after a quinquennium or so, they will be able to compete for contracts in the "open market," albeit with a level playing field. This approach has been successfully undertaken by the Port Authority of NY and NJ, and minority contractors have competed with signal success. These entrepreneurs will always succeed in winning contracts on merit when the ugly head of racism is not raised to deny them opportunities to compete. We may infer from Appendix A that federal procurement contracts constitute an enormous sum. If a portion of this sum were allocated for provision of services to the government by qualified inner-city entrepreneurs, this would bode well for development of the inner city and its residentiary.

Finally, this model allows for integration of inner-city enterprises with "regional clusters of enterprises" without leaving the community totally dependent on the traditional private sector with which its relations historically have been, at best, poor. It is therefore important that the basic activities be, in the main, between the community and the government, the role of which is, in part, to protect the well-being of the citizenry. This model does not rule out inclusion of the traditional private sector. To be sure, inclusion of the traditional private sector is very important. But, assuming that the historical behavior towards blacks has been transformed, the model merely provides protection to this subset of the citizenry in the event of a reversion to inimical practices towards them.

In summary, therefore, we may conclude that the Porter model of competitive advantage is an ill-conceived attempt at inner-city development. Indeed, it will not effect development. The model fails to reflect a firm grasp of the character of the inner cities and the characters who reside in them. Inner-city development involves considerably more than provision of a hospitable environment for private profit-seeking enterprises. This approach *per se* will simply add to the sum of human misery already in the inner city. Inner-city development requires a broad, innovative and refreshing approach in which the socioeconomic well-being of the residentiary is paramount. Porter, on the contrary, provides a rather banal treatment of a very important subject.

APPENDIX A
Spending Subsidies

Energy-Industry Subsidies	5-Year Savings
• *Rural Electrification Administration (REA):* Created to electrify rural America, today it subsidizes private utilities in selected areas with low-cost loans. Reduce the subsidy by charging near-market rates on loans.	$0.7 b.
• *Tennessee Valley Authority (TVA):* Much like the REA, TVA subsidizes electricity consumption and certain recreational activities in the Tennessee Valley. Reduce these subsidies.	$0.6 b.
• *Clean Coal Technology Program:* End this program, which subsidizes practical research for one segment of the coal industry, which could finance it on its own.	$0.3 b.
• *Energy Supply, Research and Development grants:* Cut funding of these grants, which since the late-1970s have subsidized research with little industry participation and often little commercial value.	$6.9 b.
• *Fusion research grants:* Reduce these grants and require more private-industry support for research projects.	$1.0 b.
• *Uranium enrichment services:* Recover the government's cost of enriching uranium for nuclear power firms.	$1.6 b.
• *Strategic Petroleum Reserve:* Suspend new purchases.	$1.1 b.
• *Naval Petroleum and Oil Shale Reserve.* Suspend new purchases.	$1.3 b.
• *Advanced light-water reactor:* End federal subsidy for utilities' reactor design costs and regulatory aid.	$0.3 b.
• *Sales of federal hydroelectric power to private utilities in certain regions:* Raise rates to cover the government's cost of providing the power.	$2.0 b.
• *Nuclear waste disposal fees:* Index for inflation government fees to dispose of utilities' nuclear wastes.	$0.3 b.

Other Natural-Resource Industry Subsidies

• *1872 Mining Act subsidies:* Set a 12.5% royalty to mine on public lands and extend hardrock mining holding fees.	$1.2 b.
• *Timber sales from national forests:* Raise price of timber from public lands to cover costs to prepare the timber.	$0.2 b.

Agribusiness Subsidies

- *Agricultural target price programs:* Lower price-subsidy supports for basic commodities by 3% a year. $11.2 b.
- *Agricultural subsidies to wealthy farmers:* Eliminate subsidy payments for individuals with taxable incomes of more than $120,000 and firms with incomes of more than $5 million. $1.0 b.
- *Export-enhancement agricultural subsidies:* End U.S. taxpayer subsidies for food purchased by foreign consumers. $3.2 b.
- *Grazing fees:* Raise fees for grazing on public lands so time commercial users pay market-based rates. $0.2 b.
- *Dairy-support program's milk marketing orders:* End government-set minimum pricing for fluid milk, which raises consumer prices and increases costs of price support program for milk products. $1.1 b.
- *Irrigation programs:* Water subsidies created for family farms now subsidize many suburbs and agribusinesses. Impose a surcharge on water sales from Bureau of Reclamation projects and charge market rates for water used to irrigate surplus crops. $1. 1 b.
- *Meat and poultry inspection fees:* Require slaughterhouses and processing plants to pay for government inspections. $0.5 b.

Transportation-Industry Subsidies

- *Airport grants-in-aid:* End direct taxpayer subsidies for projects to upgrade or expand airline terminals, which in a deregulated environment should be privately financed. $6.7 b.
- *Federal Aviation Administration:* Charge airlines and private plane owners user fees to cover the marginal cost of FAA air-traffic control services on their behalf. $6.8 b.
- *Highway demonstration projects:* Rescind funding for projects not eligible under state transportation plans or highway grant programs. $7.9 b.
- *Inland-waterway programs:* Charge firms using inland waterways user fees to cover federal costs to maintain, operate and upgrade these routes. $2.2 b.
- *Harbor maintenance programs:* Strictly enforce current fee collection for harbor maintenance charges. $0.2 b.
- *Mass-transit operating subsidies:* Mass-transit construction is public investment, but operating subsidies are not and should be phased out. $4.0 b.
- *Maritime Administration operation subsidies:* Phase out subsidies that protect U.S. shippers from competition. $1.3 b.

- *Amtrak operating subsidies:* Reduce current subsidies by 50% so the system becomes more self-supporting.
- *Essential Air Service program:* Reduce subsidy to airlines to serve 125 small cities.

$1.3 b.

$0.7 b.

Aerospace and High-Tech Industry Subsidies

- *National aerospace plane:* End this program, which is not supported by the Pentagon as a defense project.
- *Sematech:* Phase-out research funding for consortium of semiconductor firms after 1997, as urged by the Defense Advanced Research Projects Agency.
- *NASA advanced solid rocket motor:* End this program, which has virtually no support in scientific community.
- *NASA space station:* Cancel the program, which has dubious prospects.

$0.7 b.

$0.1 b.

$1.7 b.

$10.4 b.

Miscellaneous Industry Subsidies

- *Federal procurement:* Allow federal agencies to buy goods and services directly from private firms at market prices, as urged by the National Performance Review.
- *Overhead payments for federally-supported university research:* Cap payment rate for overhead costs at 50%.
- *Davis-Bacon Act:* This 1931 law requires all federal construction projects pay union wages, raising the cost of federal contracts by 30 percent. Limits this subsidy to projects of $100,000 or more.
- *Market-promotion program:* End this program, which subsidizes foreign advertising costs of U.S. businesses.
- *Superfund:* Require polluting firms pay more of the cost of cleaning-up their toxic wastes.
- *Grants for constructing wastewater-treatment plants:* Phase-out grants in favor of a revolving fund.
- *FDIC examinations of state-chartered banks:* Charge for this service.
- *Public housing:* End operating subsidies for vacant public housing and substitute vouchers for new construction.
- *Commodities Futures Trading Commission:* Impose a fee on futures exchange transactions to cover costs of overseeing the exchanges.
- *Federal Communications Commission:* Raise fees for private media using FCC services to cover costs.

$16.8 b.

$1.0 b.

$0.2 b.

$0.9 b.

$1.1 b.

$6.3 b.

$1.4 b.

$0.9 b.

$0.3 b.

$0.4 b.

- *Securities and Exchange Commission:* Raise current charges
  to cover SECs costs of registering and monitoring securities
  transactions. $0.2 b.
- *Travel and Tourism Administration* and *International Trade
  Administration:* Charge firms for using tourism export promotion services. $0.8 b.
- *Export-Import Bank programs:* Reduce loan subsidies to foreign purchasers of U.S. products by one-third, increase fees
  based on credit-risk, and direct loans to credit-worthy firms in
  growing countries. $0.9 b.

Total savings from spending reforms: **$114.2 b**

APPENDIX B
Tax Subsidies

Natural-Resource Industry Tax Subsidies	5-Year Savings
• *Special tax credit for producers of fuel from non-conventional sources:* Phase-out taxpayer subsidy for one particular source of energy.	
	$5.7 b.
• *Expensing of oil, gas, and mineral firms' intangible drilling, exploration and development costs:* Phase-out extractive industry's special right to fully deduct certain capital costs instead of depreciating them.	
	$5.9 b.
• *Percentage depletion cost-recovery for oil, gas and non-fuel mineral firms:* Repeal the extractive industry's special right to deduct a percentage of their gross income.	
	$4.1 b.
• *Special tax credit for timber companies' reforestation costs:* Phase-out subsidy for timber industry expenditures to prepare sites, seeds and seedlings, labor and tools, and depreciation.	
	$0.2 b.
• *Timber-industry exception from uniform capitalization rules:* Reduce by half benefits from timber firms' special right to expense all indirect costs of production.	
	$1 .2 b.

Construction-Industry Tax Subsidies	
• *Private-purpose revenue bonds:* End ability of state and local governments to raise funds loaned to private developers by issuing bonds exempt from federal tax.	
	$5.3 b.
• *Mortgage-interest deduction:* Lower ceiling from $1 million to $300,000, to end the taxpayer subsidy of very high-priced housing for the top 4 percent of homeowners.	
	$12.5 b.
• *Exclusion of capital gains on home sales:* Cap this exclusion at $125,000.	
	$2.3 b.
• *Deductibility of interest paid on consumer loans secured by home equity:* Phase out this special provision.	
	$12.8 b.
• *Tax credit for rehabilitating older buildings:* Reduce credit for historic structures to 15% and repeal the special tax benefit for older, non-historic structures.	
	$0.4 b.
• *Tax depreciation on rental housing:* Treat depreciation of rental housing on same basis as other structures.	
	$8.1 b.

Agribusiness Tax Subsidies

- *Exclusion of cost-sharing payments:* Phase-out farms' ability to exclude state or federal support payments from income if they are used for conservation. $0.1 b.
- *Exclusion of "cancellation of indebtedness" income:* Reduce ability of farm firms to exclude income from debt repayments. $0.5 b.
- *Cash accounting:* Phase-out farm firms' special right to defer tax on income from crops to be delivered the following year. $1.2 b.
- *Dairy and breeding cattle exclusion:* End special tax exclusion for costs of raising dairy and breeding cattle. $0.6 b.

Financial-Industrial Tax Subsidies

- *Exemption of credit union income:* Tax credit unions' income on same basis as mutual savings banks and thrifts. $1.7 b.
- *Exemption of certain income for small property and casualty insurance companies: Ta*x all property and casualty insurers on the same basis. $0.2 b.
- *Taxable income adjustment for small life insurance firms:* End ability of small life insurers to be taxed on investment income rather than adjusted gross income. $0.6 b.
- *Special deduction for certain health insurers:* End special deduction of one-fourth of annual claims and expenses for health insurers who accept all applicants, when health care reforms universalize this requirement. $0.8 b.

Miscellaneous Industry Tax Subsidies

- *U.S. territorial possessions tax credit:* Repeal tax credit exempting from tax any income earned by U.S. firms on operations in Puerto Rico and other U.S . possessions. $21.5 b.
- *Expensing of advertising costs:* End firms' right to fully deduct advertising costs by amortizing 20% as a capital cost to build brand recognition. $17.5 b.
- *Foreign sales corporations:* End ability of firms to exclude 15% of income on exports sold through special foreign subsidiaries set up as paper corporations. $7.9 b.

Total savings from tax reforms: **$111.1 b.**

Source: Robert J. Shapiro, "Cut-and-Invest to Compete and Win: A Budget Strategy for American Growth," Policy Report 18, Progressive Policy Institute, Washington, D.C., January, 1994.

NOTES

1. See Robert Skidelsky, *The Road From Serfdom: The Economic and Political Consequences of the End of Communism* (New York: Viking Press, 1996).

2. Michael E. Porter, "The Competitive Advantage of the Inner City," *Harvard Business Review,* May–June, 1995, p. 55.

3. Ibid., p. 56.

4. Ibid., p. 55.

5. Ibid., p. 57.

6. Ibid., p. 63.

7. Ibid., p. 68.

8. Ibid., pp. 63–64.

9. Ibid., p. 64.

10. Ibid., p. 69.

11. Ibid., p. 65.

12. Ibid., p. 65.

13. Ibid., p. 67.

14. Robert J. Shapiro, "Cut-and-Invest to Compete and Win: A Budget Strategy for American Growth," Policy Report 18, Progressive Policy Institute, Washington, D.C., January, 1994.

15. Alan S. Blinder, "Wage Discrimination: Reduced Form and Structural Estimates," *Journal of Human Resources,* VII (1993). William A. Darity, Jr. and Samuel L. Myers "Racial Earnings Inequality and Family Structure," paper presented at the Western Economics Association Meetings, Lake Tahoe, Nevada, June 12–24, 1933.

16. Andrew Hacker, *Two Nations: Black and White, Separate, Hostile, Unequal* (New York: Macmillan Press, 1992); and William A. Darity, Jr. and Samuel Myers, "The Problem of Racial Inequality," paper presented at the American Economic Association Meetings, Boston, 1993.

17. See Ian Ayres, "Fair Driving: Gender and Race Discrimination in Retail Car Negotiation," *Harvard Law Review* 104(4), (1991): 817–72.

18. Porter, op cit., p. 61.

19. For a detailed treatment of this model, see C. Michael Henry, "A Framework for Alleviation of Inner City Poverty," in Thomas D. Boston, (ed.), *A Different Vision: African American Economic Thought* (London: Routledge Publishers, 1996).

20. These include sponsored enterprises, i.e., those owned by entrepreneurs who are participating in the program as well as nonparticipating entrepreneurs.

21. See Timothy Bates, "An Analysis of Korean-Owned Small Business Start-ups with Comparisons to African American and Nonminority-owned Firms," unpublished paper, 1992.

22. Ibid.

10

MICHAEL PORTER: NEW GILDER OF GHETTOS

Edward J. Blakely and Leslie Small

Michael Porter is in the vanguard of a new ghetto economics. It is interesting that Porter, one of the nation's leading economists, developed his intrigue with the ghetto after the most recent urban violence in Los Angeles in 1992, just as the earlier interest in the ghetto was galvanized by the Watts riots in 1965.

The nation was shocked and confused by the Watts outbreak but considered it an isolated incident until similar and even more frightening eruptions occurred across the nation like a wild fire in the summer of 1967. These conflagrations of ghettos in Detroit, Newark, Cincinnati, Sacramento, Chicago, Atlanta, and Tampa were not mere uprisings but had the makings of revolution.

Why these riots in Los Angeles and in many other cities, just when middle class Negroes[1] were moving into civil service positions and moving out of the historic ghettos and some few into surrounding suburbs of major metropolitan areas? Why were these insurrections occurring, as economic conditions for some, if not all, were improving? In part, the differential movement of some Negroes only made the larger and visibly trapped group feel more neglected, more frustrated, and more angry at a system that the Kerner Commission depicted as one in which "segregation and poverty have created in the racial ghetto a destructive environment totally unknown to most White Americans. . . .White institutions created it, White institutions maintain it, and White society condones it."[2] It is still here. No matter how much the ghetto is romanticized or depicted as a new economic engine for its occupants, the underlying pathology remains the same. In some respects, the latest twist on ghetto gilding by Porter and others takes a direction dismissed by the Kerner Commission. The Commission rejected the notion of ghetto as platform for economic revitalization three decades ago because of the "disability of race."[3]

Race as place, in the form of black community, no matter how organized or presented is a restrictive attribute in this nation. Thus, the defects of urban places associated with African Americans as the base are debilitating for the people of these zones. This pattern is clear in Porter's own description of the advantageous economic and geographic attributes of American ghettos. Many ghetto areas are, as Porter aptly notes, on the edge of major transportation corridors with superior access to sea and airports. Until recently, major sports franchises, museums and other cultural facilities were located within easy walking distance of the center of the city and near low-income inner-city communities. This is no longer true. Strategic relocation choices based on race are being made every day. Seaports, like Los Angeles, are investing billions of dollars to transport goods through the ghetto for reassembly and shipment to other destinations, when some suggest there is ample space in nearby minority communities like Compton. The Chicago Bears, Houston Oilers, and other sports franchises are moving away from inner-city areas for more suburban locations, for so-called security and access reasons. Even in Los Angeles, where the City and County spent nearly $200 million to rehabilitate the historic Los Angeles Coliseum, in the heart of the second largest media market in the United States, no NFL team will play there because of its geographic undesirability (code for ghetto location). The new Getty museum perched high above Los Angeles will be both a new visual icon and a blow to the heart of the city. In essence, race and space remain deeply intertwined in American political economy. Mr. Porter is not alone in suggesting that racism is not the only factor holding back the ghetto. Let's turn to some of the other more recent arguments that are shaping this debate. We will bring Porter's and other restoration concepts into a clearer historic tradition of ghetto economic scholarship and the contemporary failures of various schemes to rekindle these communities. Finally we will offer our own principles upon which economic revitalization of the inner city should be based.

RACE AS SPACE

Race is an increasingly volatile topic in the nation. One reason for this is the reemergence of literature based on the issue of race, character, intelligence and morality. Booker T. Washington and W.E.B. DuBois at the end of the last century set off an historic divide regarding economic and social independence of black Americans that is still the core of the debate over black progress. These two thinkers differed on the means, but both assumed that the collective improvement of blacks was the only vehicle for their economic survival in the United States. They were forceful spokesmen for black capacity building and later economic integration in various forms. This led them to place much of the burden of self-development on the Negro community. Booker T. Washington believed that self-help and self-respect formed the core of any Negro economic development. "If," as he said, "Negroes believed in themselves, stood together, and supported each other, they would be able to shape their own destinies."[4] He held that blacks could accommodate and be accommodated by the white community. W.E.B. DuBois, formed the Niagara Movement to oppose Washington's concept. Instead he proposed the notion of political separate power to promote " . . . the abolition of all caste distinctions based simply in race and color."[5] His view was that blacks had to form their own economy and separate politics from whites to command white attention but maintain a separate resource base. Martin Luther King and Malcolm X took up these same themes nearly fifty years later because the causes of ghetto pathology remained and the cures both via education and politics had few tangible results in what was then called the ghetto and today relabeled the inner city.

WHITE-NOMICS VS. BLACK-NOMICS

Washington and W.E.B. DuBois started an economic discussion of a black economy or black-nomics that has been joined by a more secular and neo-social Darwinistic white-nomics.[6] Percy Steele, Tom Sowell (both at the Hoover Institute at Stanford University), and Charles Murray (Heritage Foundation) form the base of this new white-nomic. Steele traces the current black malaise to a lack of social fiber among blacks that limits their desire to achieve within the societal construct. Tom Sowell, like Porter, views social welfare as the culprit in limiting the economic and social aspirations of blacks and creating a more damning culture of socioeconomic turpitude. These prominent black intellectuals have become idols of the most conservative forces sweeping the nation.

Sowell has been particularly outspoken on such issues as affirmative action and set-asides for minorities, arguing that these programs merely deepen the divisions between black and white economies, creating a "reservation" mentality for the recipients of such aid and casting doubts on the real attributes of those who achieve on their own. The notion of ghetto as social and intellectual reservation captures many of the contemporary thinkers on the problems of the inner city. Charles Murray goes even farther in his assessment of the debilitating aspects of the ghetto, labeling the residents as intellectually inferior in his *Bell Curve*.[7] His analysis, supported by an array of statistics, shows that black inherent sociobiological problems lead to underachievement in a technocratic world. As Murray describes it, "low intelligence (among blacks) means a comparatively high risk of poverty."[8] The problems of inner cities, in the opinion of Murray and his co-author, can only grow worse, trapping millions in the poverty and perversity of the inner city unless drastic measures are taken to break up the ghetto and reeducate its inhabitants.

The inner city is not merely a problem for its residents; it is increasingly a drag on the nation's economy. Anthony Downs, among others, has demonstrated that the inner city's ills are the problems of the entire metropolitan region.[9] If the inner city decays, it has dramatic implications for its region. There is no better and more visible example of this than Los Angeles where the decay of the core has reached well into the suburbs and beyond. Many of the nation's regions can now be categorized in international competitive terms by the health and economic vitality of their inner core.

As we enter a new century, we will also enter an era of internationalization that will surely test the notion of the nation-state economy, let alone that of a neighborhood or inner city or even a city economy. The real issue is: What is the role of small, economically detached and socially distant disadvantaged communities in this brave new economic world? Focusing on the ghetto alone or its occupants provides no economic theory for understanding the dynamics or the potential for redevelopment of these communities. Porter's lack of a theory grounded in the realities of the ghetto is the basis of the shortcomings in his and similar approaches to solving the problems of the inner city.

GHETTO GILDING THEORY

There are three macroeconomic theories competing for our attention in inner-city neighborhood or ghetto transformation. One theory holds that the ghetto is a pool of labor with current problems related to the position of that labor in the labor market. According to this theory, if human capital is improved and worker mobility enhanced, the ghettos will be changed by the residents' rising incomes. Another thesis is that the causal factor in ghetto residents' low performance is the social distance of inner-city residents from the nation's values and economic structure. This view is best articulated by William Julius Wilson's work on the truly disadvantaged underclass. Finally, the structural view advanced by Bennett Harrison, William Goldsmith, and Edward Blakely, sees the economic organization of the nation as having systematically frozen out blacks from participation in the growing portions of the economy. This argument suggests that the latest wave of globalization has had an even more devastating impact on ghetto residents because their manual and low-skilled labor is pitted against low-wage, low-skill labor pools worldwide. Let's examine these concepts through the Porter lens.

Labor/Human Capital

As Michael Porter points out, there is a readily available workforce in inner cities with more skills than most employers acknowledge. Nonetheless, the ghetto remains a high unemployment and underemployment zone. Address discrimination plays a very large role in who gets jobs. A ghetto street address is an almost certain disqualification for most employers. Inner-city youth with similar skills to those of their suburban peers, as Quigley has shown, have very different job outcomes.[10] Suburban minority youth do slightly better in the labor market than their inner-city counterparts with similar skill levels. This is, of course, related to job knowledge and networks, but it is also due to employer perceptions of certain areas producing "bad labor." It is interesting to note that the unemployment rate in the ghetto in 1967 was 26.5 percent, about the same as it is today (1996), even before so-called global economic restructuring.[11] Nationwide, unemployment for African Americans in 1994 was three times that of whites' 4.5 percent. In hardcore ghetto areas depicted in Table 1, the rate of unemployment reaches more than 50 percent for adult males without a high school education. This is the labor pool that Porter suggests can and will be absorbed by increasing inner-city job options. We think, to the contrary, this is the very labor pool that only large employers, like the government, with significant training and long-term capacity, can absorb.

Unemployment is ascribed to a skills and information mismatch in the ghetto. Kasarda has provided clear documentation for the disequilibrium for both skills and job location.[12] Neither of these issues is new. Unemployment is very much related to the personal skills developed by association with people within the labor force. The lack of employment opportunity and the visible access to it were prime causes of the riots in the '60s. Even in the late 1960s the movement of firms out of the city was already well underway. As a result, the spatial mismatch had already begun. It is interesting to note how the spatial mismatch lines up with the skills mismatch. In essence, the de-industrialization is directly related to the skills mismatch.

According to Porter, "a pressing need among inner city residents is work readiness, training which includes communications, self development and workplace practices."[13] Government and nonprofit programs have been providing precisely this form of training for more than three decades with only marginal impacts. The real reason for the continuing distance from the labor market among a large segment of the ghetto population is that there is little connection between work and better outcomes for ghetto dwellers or for their communities. The signals are very clear. To move up economically requires moving out. As a result, the link between job and social betterment is lost collectively as achievers move out of the ghetto rather than pass on social and networks skills to the community or act as the magnets for community human resource recovery. Porter does not suggest ways to capture this social capital in the community as it is developed. Surely, decades of racial oppression have taught the rising middle class minorities that the route to acceptance is to leave the ghetto and not to contribute to its gilding.

Socio-spatial Distancing

Porter scarcely acknowledges the social pathologies that undermine the most noble efforts for economic reform. The ghetto, as William Julius Wilson points out, is an economic and social community with its own guiding or misguiding philosophy. To treat the ghetto as a value-free zone is a serious error in comprehending the limitations of adapting any economic model to it. "Living in the ghetto means being more socially isolated."[14] This is collective isolation; isolation from the value structures of the dominant society. Social and economic marginalization is an attribute of the ghetto that forms the backdrop for a culture that is violent, with dysfunctional families with few ties to the world of work, or the aspirations of the middle class. As Wilson puts it, "[the]inner city in recent years has created a fictitious normative divide between urban Blacks . . . which . . . cannot but pale when compared to the objective structural cleavage that separates ghetto residents from the larger society . . . "[15] These conditions are scarcely changed by the introduction of work opportunities within this environment. Wilson goes on to say,

> It is the cumulative structural entrapment and forcible socioeconomic marginalization resulting from historically evolving interplay

TABLE 1
Hardcore Black Unemployment
Unemployment–Black Adult Males with less than 12 Years' Schooling
Inner-City Suburb 1969–1992

Regions	1969	1977	1982	1987	1992
All Regions					
Inner-city	18.8	38.3	49.5	49.5	44.8
Suburb	18.3	31.4	31.4	33.4	34.6
North west					
Inner-city	21.1	42.8	44.8	44.0	45.1
Suburb	15.1	27.0	34.4	30.8	31.2
Midwest					
Inner-city	19.5	42.6	54.3	55.3	53.3
Suburb	8.0	44.3	43.6	41.3	42.7
South					
Inner-city	15.4	32.0	47.3	45.8	46.9
Suburb	15.9	24.9	37.9	32.1	33.8
West					
Inner-city	27.4	42.3	60.4	60.8	55.5
Suburb	38.9	44.2	37.7	43.2	43.6

Source: Bureau of the Census, Current Population Survey, Annual Demographic File
1969; 1977; 1982; 1987; 1992.

of class, racial, and gender domination, together with the sea changes in the organization of American capitalism and failure of social policies, not a "welfare ethos," that explains the plight of today's ghetto Black.[16]

If there is to be any plausible alternative to the ghetto pathology it must attack and break the cycle of poverty and underclass values that permeate it. Porter assumes that some indigenous miracle among American business will form new competitive clusters of firms in an uncompetitive environment with technologically inferior infrastructure that can transcend this morass. These new clusters will presumably arise to take advantage of both the locational assets of market access or proximity; or,

possibly existing ghetto entrepreneurs will use this labor pool and overcome the cultural vicissitudes of the labor force to propel their firms into
the regional and international economy. While Porter can cite instances
of food outlets expanding within the ethnic marketplace, he has few
illustrations of other goods or service firms making such a transition. The
cost, emotionally, of operating in the ghetto is very high even for minority entrepreneurs.

Structured out of the Economy

A growing number of policy scientists are coming to the conclusion
that the ghetto and its residents have been structured out of the international economy. Blacks who came from the South were valuable adjuncts
as laborers, maids and even assembly line workers for an expanding
industrial economy. The movement of blacks from the South to the North
took place only after European immigration stopped providing the requisite labor pool for industrial expansion. This movement of blacks was
expedited by the Second World War. Black labor was needed and blacks
were valuable for direct or indirect employment necessary to the expansion of manufacturing. As the economy has transformed to a more infor-
mation-dependent service base, the need for black labor has diminished.
International pools of low-skilled labor now compete successfully for
manufacturing and even service employment. Not only are computer and
electronic components made overseas, credit card bills are processed in
the Caribbean and Asia. Black labor was never really accepted in white
America, so as the need for it declined, there were no attempts to repair
this economic damage. The riots of 1967 were the first sign of this
problem. Even the Kerner Report acknowledged, as early as 1968, the
destruction of black jobs due to new manufacturing technologies. The
corrosive nature of this transitional economy has been especially destructive to the ghetto. The nation lost almost eight million jobs to lower wage
and more competitive foreign nations between 1980–1990. These losses
had both their trickle down and trickle out effects. By trickle out, we
refer to the spatial impact of the job losses on certain communities within
the city or metropolitan region. For example, Los Angeles in the 1970s
and 1980s was a net job producer for most inhabitants, but the geography
of employment changed location from East and Southeast Los Angeles
manufacturing belts to the financial and entertainment nodes of Downtown, Westwood, and Century City. Entire communities, Goldsmith and
Blakely assert, have been structured out of the economy.[17] These com-

munities are effectively redlined from the American dream. Goldsmith and Blakely opine,

> Observers of the American scene know, however, it is not just wealth, income, and social mobility, but race and ethnicity, too, that are essential forces in the physics of neighborhood change . . . Occupational status is a key explanatory variable. City neighborhoods become differentiated even along occupational lines.[18]

Business locating within prescribed urban redevelopment boundaries may receive various forms of government assistance but these inducements scarcely offset the social and economic cost of doing business in a ghetto environment. As Goldsmith and Blakely go on to say,

> . . . changes in the composition and organization of the national economy have led to further separation in the economic, social, racial and political patterns in metropolitan areas. Rapidly growing industries and firms are most often located at the urban fringe, while traditional city employers . . . such as textiles and apparel, prefer the city, where they can take advantage of larger concentrations of immigrants as low-wage employees . . . These are not the general trend, and they also eventually reinforce stagnation.[19]

Nowhere is the pattern of fringe expansion more clear than in the Chicago metropolitan area where the region, as depicted in Figure 1, has more than doubled in size, while the population has grown less than 3 percent.

The situation in Chicago is both dramatic and sad. The famous Sears Tower is no longer occupied by that corporate giant. "Sears," says Christopher Leinberger, "is moving its merchandising division to Hoffman Estates, which is unreachable by public transit—twelve miles beyond Schaumberg and thirty miles from the Sears Tower . . . the primary reason for the move is that the company wants to rid itself of the predominantly Black workforce downtown."[20]

These structural divisions are now deeply entrenched. They are impervious to any form of incentives such as enterprise zones and similar blandishments. Ghetto locations are simply not desirable space for most enterprises irrespective of the economic fillips government offers.

Porter rightfully cites the failure of government incentives aimed at revitalizing the ghetto as wrong headed. He suggests pretty much what

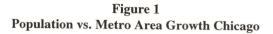

Figure 1
Population vs. Metro Area Growth Chicago

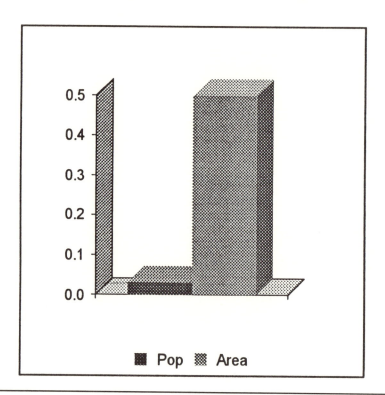

Source: Christopher Leinberger, 1994.

local governments have long ago figured out; that is, make it easier to do business in these locales. Nonetheless, there is no rush for new or existing firms to minority communities anywhere. The simple fact is that low-income communities are at a structural disadvantage in the restructuring competition with low-wage suburban and exurban areas. There is a perceived danger for workers of doing business in inner cities; moreover advanced technology allows the use of more reliable labor pools to perform the same tasks anywhere in the world.

Being Critical or Being Correct

We have been critical of the concepts that underpin Michael Porter's dicta. It is, admittedly, far easier to be critical than correct. We acknowledge his work has restimulated thinking about the ghetto. His personality and his prestige are important resources for refocusing a serious reexamination of the ghetto and its role in the nation's political economy. However, we must build any new programs and policies by repositioning the inner city on a more solid and long lasting prescription than Porter's model.

Many of the most critical condemnations of government efforts are aimed at the earlier antipoverty and Great Society projects. These programs and their surviving counterparts are panned by Porter and others as failures. We do not hold that view. It is true that the ten or more billion dollars spent on ghetto revitalization in the Johnson-Nixon era did not provide very many visible physical or social reforms. Black inner-city poverty rates are back to where they were pre-War on Poverty. Inner-city areas are even more violent and physically deteriorated than they were in the 1960s. But let us not be too quick to label these programs overwhelming failures. They did some good. Minority politics has changed because of them. Black political figures from Marion Barry to Jesse Jackson and Andrew Young ascended to political prominence in large measure because of the political and social education of these programs. The number of black elected officials who attained their skills in the antipoverty movement is legion. Moreover, these programs catapulted many black social workers, educators, and other professionals into new roles and responsibilities in government and the private sector. Unfortunately, the programs that liberated people from the ghetto seem to have been far less beneficial to those left behind. The expectations of these early efforts are best described by Robert Moriarty:

> The representatives of the poor have had to dash many false hopes in what the anti-poverty program would mean and do. A Fishtown representative said that when the program was announced, many had visions of increased relief grants. In South Philadelphia's Ramcat district, a woman representative said some of her poor assumed they would have jobs and new homes within weeks.[21]

The poor were not the only ones with such lofty expectations. The national anticipations were exaggerated as well. As a result, the programs have fallen into disfavor and contemporary advocates for them are looked upon with increasing suspicion. Nicholas Lemann has completed the most scathing and penetrating analysis of those efforts. Lemann's critique in the *New York Times* of government efforts since Johnson to cure problems of the ghetto promised too many big things and did not do well on delivering the little things in the ghetto that make a real difference in these communities "like improving schools, housing, and police protection."[22] Instead the programs placed their emphasis on economic development, and as Lemann points out, "What is gained in the short run by making a promise that sounds appealing—economic development—is far outweighed by what is lost in the long run when the idea doesn't come true."[23]

The essential flaw in these and similar revitalization programs lies in the assumptions about the problems and the range of solutions. Similarly, Porter's diagnosis adopts the place hypothesis from among the two competing assumptions regarding ghetto malaise. On one side there are those who believe it is a *people* problem. In this camp, we find the welfare reformers like Lawrence Mead who believes forcing work on aid-dependent ghetto residents will generate sufficient voluntary momentum for welfare recipients to individually and collectively leave the ghetto or reshape it. Among the most promising programs in this regard is the Chicago Gautreaux experiment in which ghetto housing authority residents are placed in suburban neighborhoods with some transitional assistance. Like new immigrants to a new country, these pioneers in the suburbs have done surprisingly well even as minorities in a white sea. This is not to say that there are no problems, but the strong and mobile black ghetto dweller breaking out of the inner city may be one possible solution. However, there are two problems with this approach. First, racism limits the suburban neighborhood choices for ghetto escapees in many parts of the nation. Second, the numbers will not work. There are simply too many potential candidates for this program. Third, not all blacks want to live in a largely white environment. Finally, the cost of relocation is too high.

"Cold Turkey" welfare reform is the most recent answer to changing the culture of poverty. Conservatives and liberals alike, including President Clinton, are embracing some form of time limited terminal welfare for women and their dependent children. While there are variations in this approach, the main thrust of it is to move people off welfare with cash grants, some limited multiyear benefits, job training and some form of universal health care. The assumption is that the welfare recipient will find work if there are few other options. It is meant to be coercive.

"Workfare" is often associated with the above approach. Under the Workfare approach, all able-bodied men and women would be forced to work or attend training programs to receive any welfare benefits. The goal of this effort is not to necessarily place every welfare recipient in a self-sufficient job but, as Lawrence Mead, the architect of this concept says, "to increase work effort, to raise the share of employable recipients who are doing something to help themselves, whether or not they leave welfare, whether it be training, looking for work, or actually working."[24] This logic is very compelling for many policy makers, both liberal and conservative. It is not opposed by all welfare rights groups. However, the basic thesis has several shortcomings. First, most welfare recipients already go to work after a very short term on welfare. Second, the residual group of persons on welfare has multiple social and physical disabilities that will keep them out of the workforce under almost any regime. Third, this program is aimed at men. Men do not usually receive welfare. While some men prey on women who do receive welfare, the programs do not touch men. If the idea is to get more men to work, then the number of women on welfare could be reduced by increasing male work options. We have already shown that the number of young uneducated black men out of work varied little by urban or suburban locations. Finally, there simply are not enough jobs to go around. If all the able-bodied black men and women in the nation were actually seeking work, the unemployment rate would exceed 20 percent. Katherine Abrahams, who analyzed U.S. Department of Labor data, provides careful and conservative research on the relationship between unemployment and jobs. She says,

> If it could be assumed that the vacancy rate/unemployment rate relationship observed . . . mirrored the vacancy rate/unemployment rate in the United States over the same time period . . . the number of unemployed persons in all sectors of our economy (would balance) . . . most likely (in fact) the unemployed actually exceeds the number of vacant jobs by a factor of 10 or more.[25]

Thus, the fact is that black males and females who do not seek work may be a drag on the economy, but they also create less competition for available work and reduce social tensions.

The second competing hypothesis for dealing with inner-city issues is to move away from people and race-based affirmative action, welfare, and employment programs to place-based programs. Place programs put the emphasis on changing the economic and social structure in areas of the city or region. Under such regimes, special incentives such as place-oriented affirmative action would provide blighted areas with business incentives. Or, residents of these areas can be given special assistance in the form of specialized training. Employers in the same zones might receive very substantial tax breaks for employing local labor and for locating in the affected zone. The new federal empowerment and enterprise zones are the first steps in this direction. The results of the enterprise zones have been very disappointing, from all available evidence. While firms do move into such zones, they are only local relocations that scarcely affect new employment or build new jobs. Most of these firms do not hire any more local individuals than do other firms in the same areas.[26]

Critics of the place approach say that it penalizes upward mobility. They also suggest that these programs promote certain types of easy fraud, such as the use of ghetto addresses to receive vouchers or employment subsidies. Moreover, setting the boundaries of low income areas entitled to relief would be an intensely political process. On the other hand, proponents note that the current schemes, including welfare, are subject to massive abuse and plenty of politics.

These two concepts are not mutually exclusive. It is possible to merge the people and places concepts into operational programs. That is, the notion of work for welfare could be merged with a strong subsidy in a targeted zone for hiring former welfare recipients and the like. We think people- and place-based concepts can be molded into a single paradigm with fewer defects than either.

A NEW PARADIGM—MAKING BETTER PLACES WITH BETTER PEOPLE

Porter, as nearly all prescribers of ghetto revitalization, in our view, proposes solutions that are either place- or people-oriented. It is unclear why so few analysts mix place and people prescriptions but this is precisely what is required. As we have described above, the ghetto has a complex mix of both people with social pathologies in defective places associated with dying industries and deteriorating infrastructure combined with severe environmental problems. Integration or separation theories proposed by various pundits have these similar defects. They assume an economy that no longer exists. The ghetto is simply not an economic unit by itself. We live in an economically and politically interdependent world. Any attempts to separate a neighborhood economy from the regional or world economy are fruitless. Connecting the economy with people and opportunity to create wealth and net new jobs must be the goal of any form of ghetto economic development.

Our paradigm recognizes Porter's economic interconnectivity but moves beyond it to reposition the ghetto as a sustaining economic competitor with the regional, national, and global economy. We assert that there are five interrelated domains that must be addressed—employment development; locational infrastructure formation; social capital building; a new set of developmental institutions; and reductions of dependency. All of these must be attacked simultaneously, not just one or two. Uneven starts and stops for the people and place improvements in the ghetto will collapse into an economic and human wasteland.

Employment Development

The old focus of more firms, more jobs is repeated in the Porter treatise. It is true that more firms may produce jobs. But even Porter knows that job shedding, not job creation, is the dominant movement for internationally competitive firms. Moreover, we are entering a period of "jobless" economic expansion. For the most part the jobs that are promoted and promised for low-income communities are those that are projected for either technological or international competitive downsizing or de-skilling. Most of the jobs slated for inner-city areas are those described by Porter—food processors and food retailers, and local community services. None of these are good jobs, and there is little competition from other communities for them. Ghetto economic isolationists may see this as local income capture, but a realist must view this as an expensive trade-off for new enterprises with good wages that locate elsewhere.

Our paradigm promotes the establishment of new employers in ghetto communities, employers with new technologies and new job opportunities in the fast-rising sectors of the economy. As Table 2 shows, the rising sectors of the economy are information-based. These sectors will provide the best long-term jobs. It is silly to suggest that any job, as Mead proposes, is a good start. Obviously, work ethics need improvement, but they improve faster if the prospective employee can envision an economically viable future.

New jobs can best be created in the ghetto by the use of regulatory changes that make it easier and profitable for new technology firms to locate in inner-city communities. An example is allowing some ghetto communities to be designated "telecommunication and media free zones" aimed at permitting new telecommunication firms to operate in such areas outside the regulatory authority of local public utilities commissions for new product development. Such zones have a real international competitive advantage and thus stimulate the formation of new firms and reuse existing ghetto real estate. Similarly, we suggest engaging the intellectual resources of urban universities with grants to establish "software, media, telecommunications, bio-health" or other incubators in low-income communities. Bringing universities into these communities can add human capital infrastructure and regional networks for neglected communities. In fact, many of these areas already have major teaching hospitals but no assembled land for the location of experimental ventures. In these zones certain longterm tax advantages would flow to firms spinning out of the incubators into nearby space. Similarly, new sectors like media and environmental industries could be provided with special permits for local development and exemptions from a plethora of local rules and regulations and taxes that stymie their development. In essence, we are promoting the stimulation of new jobs in the ghetto and not merely the leftover jobs in a transformed economy.

Locational Assets

While it is true that many ghetto communities occupy traditionally significant real estate, the deterioration continues. The reasons for this are related to the continued reduction in importance of proximity factors. Computers and telecommunications have diminished the asset value of location. As work can be accomplished off-site, ghetto space cannot overcome the other disadvantages of crime, crumbling streets and old technologically inadequate buildings. These are real structural disadvantages. The only way this can be overcome is for ghetto communities to gain strategic advantages.

We propose a New Community Development program for inner cities. This program would focus on the building of new technology infrastructure such as optic cable, telecommunications, and transportation improvements for both mass and goods transportation. Such improvements would be funded through capital infrastructure banks (underwritten by both government and interstate banks) that would issue community revitalization bonds designated for physical upgrading so that those communities can become internationally competitive. These bonds could support land assembly as well as redevelopment of sewers, electric power undergrounding, building upgrades for new truck docking, and computer technology improvements. In essence, making ghetto communities "smart communities" with smart buildings would be the goal of this effort. Building

TABLE 2
Employment Growth by Macro-Sector 1976–1990 (000's)

Sector	1976	1981	1985	1990	net % change
Old Line Industry	18,548	20,306	19,274	18,345	-6.1
High Tech	3,074	4,075	4,280	5,354	+5.0
Energy	758	1,085	987	762	-9.0
Services	26,354	33,288	37,961	42,584	+18.0
Govt.	15,322	16,408	16,468	16,321	+.01
Trade and Distribution	13,675	15,655	17,075	18,472	+9.1

Source: Author compilation of data from Bureau of Labor Statistics.

owners could receive substantial tax relief and guaranteed loans to upgrade their buildings.

Quality infrastructure is the stimulus for business location and formation. It is our assessment that, "concentrating on building the (physical infrastructure) . . . creates the inducing *environment* for firms to develop or locate in a community"[27] (italics in text). Quality, technologically efficient infrastructure will compete for new firm and new job formation. This will be good for the economy as a whole as well as for the ghetto communities where it occurs.

Skills and Human Capital Development to Social Capital Formation

Government and foundations are placing more resources in human capital formation. Skills declines are associated with community deterioration. There is no doubt about this. What is unclear is the remedy. Billions are being spent on school reform. There is increasing talk about "school to work" transitions and better remedial job training. Unfortunately, most of these efforts are unlikely to succeed because of the contradictory results of skills improvement on community enhancement. Educational and job improvements lead out of the ghetto, thus constantly denuding the community of these resources. The Urban Institute concludes that, during the 1980s alone, black population suburbanized 38 percent in the nation's largest metropolitan areas.[28] Big cities like Miami, Cleveland and Detroit lost half or more of their black middle class from city centers to the suburbs. Keeping human capital, as opposed to forming human capital, is the problem for most ghettos. Minorities who enter the labor force do go up the economic ladder at a rapid pace. Recent data are based on cohort income movements of new migrants and native-born minorities over a decade. Native-born individuals residing in Southern California, who were twenty-four years of age in 1990, experienced tremendous job and income growth, while the older cohort reaching sixty-five had a lower but still generally improved status up to age fifty-five. While the data are for Southern California, we are confident that similar patterns hold true for most regions outside the deep south for blacks.

As age and skill formation increase, so does income for most groups. While many of these individuals start out in the ghetto, they certainly do not remain there. In essence, the real loss in the ghetto is social wealth, not human capital alone. We need strategies to capture human social capital in the ghetto without trapping people in it. Poor communities remain poor markets because of the loss of social capital. As Avis Vidal puts it,

> Social isolation increases with the degree of neighborhood poverty. (There are) . . . higher rates of employment among innercity survey respondents who have friends and family members who are employed.[29]

Incentives for human capital wealth formation are required to overcome the problems of the lack of social capital in distressed communities. William Julius Wilson, Goldsmith and Blakely, among others, point to the social capital drain as a fundamental impediment in community network formation. It is human networks that provide access to work and alter aspiration levels, not rhetoric or educational programs. Our proposals in this area are modest. First, we suggest the expansion of the new programs of Fannie Mae and Freddie Mac to increase home ownership in distressed communities. These programs would be coupled with other schemes, such as the increased use of sweat equity. Second, a set of new savings instruments should be devised for residents of these communities that allow the pretax accumulation of capital in local savings institutions by local residents up to $9,000 per year. These funds could be used without paying any tax on them for home purchase or business starts within the same zone or for higher education of residents and similar purposes. Moreover, local governments might forgive property tax increases for up to five years for residents who change homes within the same zone. Residents of these zones who fall below metropolitan poverty levels might be provided school vouchers for education at any accredited school within the zone and discounted vouchers for use in schools out-

FIGURE 2
A New Paradigm for Inner City/Ghetto Development

Component	Porter Concept	New Paradigm
Employment	more firms = more jobs	Firms with quality jobs that fit the population
Locational assets	Comparative advantage of physical assets	Competitive advantage based on quality infrastructure
Human capital building	Improved schooling and training programs	Social capital formation
Development base	Sectoral clusters	Creating local economic institutions
Dependency reduction	Reduce or remove welfare	Establish incentives for independence

side the zone. A myriad of other proposals might be advanced with similar aims of stabilizing minority communities as incomes rise. Critics will suggest that these incentives are chaining people to undesirable circumstances. Our retort is, why is it better to give business incentives over individual incentives? Or, why is it all right to subsidize suburban homeowners with a variety of indirect subsidies and not use similar subsidies for inner-city residents? Finally, can and will this lead to more rapid gentrification of the ghetto, displacing the poor? This is unlikely since the subsidies would be tied to existing residents and not aimed at new residents.

Development Base

Porter is not alone in suggesting the development of firm clusters for low-income communities. In some respects, this is not new. Local governments have chased "smoke stack" industries and more recently "retail box" industries for many years. None of these have had any real or beneficial employment or wealth-building impacts. As the incentives disappear or the markets change, these firms evaporate.

There is nothing wrong with the cluster concept if the firms locating in the ghetto use local infrastructure such as optic cable, seaports or local universities as competitive advantage factors. Such clusters need to be cultivated within the community. In almost no instances, as Porter suggests, are there institutions designed to bring together community interests and business interests to promote mutual economic advantage in the inner city. Equity capital is the most important vehicle for facilitating such goal-sharing. Historically, African Americans have been denied real ownership. Therefore, this proposal would provide this kind of opportunity and perhaps compensate African Americans for the "forty acres and a mule" that was promised but never given to freed slaves over one hundred years ago. In other words, community ownership can promote far more communal and long lasting exchanges. Money talks, and ownership commands respect.

We propose the use of foundation and some limited government funding via industrial development bonds to promote community development corporation equity investments for the purpose of creating new local industries. Community development corporations have little experience in industrial or commercial development. The new Community Development Banks could become appropriate vehicles for community development corporations to gain the necessary expertise to form partnerships with new industries that increase regional and international competitiveness.

No new money need be allocated for this purpose. There is sufficient money available in existing small business and other resources for such programs. One approach to this concept is to expand the employee ownership tax devices to community ownership programs.

Dependency Reduction

There is now welfare reform. The question is whether it will create or destroy incentives. Lifting the underclass out of poverty by welfare reduction seems very unlikely to us.

We propose augmenting the current reforms with existing resources of the welfare system. Rather than reduce welfare, we need to give men incentives to form or live in families. Basically, the more incentives we can provide men to relate to their pseudo families, be they fathers, brothers, cousins or uncles, the better for all. This involvement has the best chances of breaking the cycle of intergenerational poverty. Rather than end welfare, we propose using welfare funds as family-forming resources.

Our suggestion is to use the existing welfare grant structure to promote work effort by men who stay in or enter poverty families. The grant would include health care assistance with an HMO or equivalent, modest family assistance and tax relief similar to the existing Earned Income Tax Credit (EITC) program that provides quarterly payments to families below the poverty line who earn some portion of their income. This incentive would continue for a low-income family as work efforts increased. A number of formulas and sliding scales might be devised to promote independence and limit assistance by family size. There could be a five-year limit for any family, including all adult members of the family, for such assistance. Some details would have to be worked out, but the notion would be to provide a floor for father/male-based families to work into self-sufficiency. The program would allow savings from earnings and other inducements to lead the family into housing ownership, better education and self-improvement.

Many will question, why reward men with low skills and low attachments to work? The obvious answer is that inducing men to work is better and cheaper than paying for prisons, out-of-wedlock births and other social maladies. The link between male-based households and family stability is very clear. Another alternative might be for such benefits to be accorded any combination of adults within a family setting, whether male or female. We reserve judgment on this approach but note the male-based household relationship is well established.

CONCLUSIONS

Michael Porter has opened an old argument. He has proposed a mixture of old and new cures for the continuing problems of inner-city America. Porter is right when he asserts that these areas offer exceptional infrastructure, human resources, and new market opportunities. However, his analysis and prescriptions are incomplete. The ghetto is a far more complicated place than Porter depicts. We suggest a more comprehensive approach to deal with the debilities of the market structure, the community pathology and the economic development potentials of these communities in an era of international competitiveness. All Americans are victims of the current ghetto economy. We are appalled by the violence, crime, and signs of physical and social deterioration. We will all continue to pay a high price for this deterioration.

We applaud Michael Porter for his courage in bringing this issue to the forefront because he has recognized the need to be part of the solution rather than being victimized by the problem of ghetto America.

NOTES

1. Negro was the official term used at that time.

2. *Report of the National Commission on Civil Disorders*, Governor Otto Kerner, Chairman (New York: Bantam Books Publishers, 1968), p. 2.

3. Ibid., p. 278.

4. Booker T. Washington, in *Report of the National Commission on Civil Disorders*, op. cit., p. 216.

5. W.E.B. DuBois, in *Report of the National Commission on Civil Disorders*, op. cit., p. 217.

6. We add *nomics* as in economics to provide a literary bridge to the concepts espoused by the authors based in various political economic notions stemming from either an African-American black-nomics, or white free market white-nomics perspective.

7. Richard Herrnstein and Charles Murray, *The Bell Curve: Intelligence and Class Structure in American Life* (New York: Free Press, 1994).

8. Ibid.

9. Anthony Downs, *Metropolitan Visions* (Washington, D.C.: Brookings Institution, 1994).

10. Katherine O'Regan and John Quigley, "Labor Market Access and the Labor Market Outcomes of Youth," *Regional Science and Urban Economics* 21 (1991): 277–293.

11. *Report of the National Commission on Civil Disorders*, p. 114.

12. John D. Kasarda, "Urban Industrial Transition and the Underclass," *Annals of the American Academy of Political and Social Science* 501 (January 1989).

13. Porter, p. 70.

14. Loic Wacquant and William Julius Wilson, "The Cost of Racial and Class Exclusion in the Inner City," *Annals of the American Academy of Political and Social Science* 501 (January 1989), p. 23.

15. Ibid., p. 25.

16. Ibid., p. 25.

17. William Goldsmith and Edward J. Blakely, *Separate Societies: Poverty and Inequality in U.S. Cities* (Philadelphia: Temple University Press, 1992).

18. Ibid., p. 116.

19. Ibid.

20. Christopher Leinberger, "Business Fleeing to the Urban Fringe," *The Nation* (July 1992).

21. Robert Moriarty, *New York Herald Tribune*, cited in *New York Metropolitan Council Report: A Relevant War Against Poverty*, 1968, p. 118.

22. Nicholas Lemann, "The Myth of Community Development," *New York Times*, January 9, 1994, p. 50.

23. Ibid., p. 54.

24. Lawrence Mead, "The Logic of Workfare," *Annals of the American Academy of Political and Social Sciences* 501 (January 1989), p. 47.

25. Katherine Abrahams, "Too Few Jobs," *Washington Post*, May 25, 1982, p. A-17.

26. Rodney Erickson and Susan W. Friedman, "Comparative Dimensions of State

Enterprise Zone Policies," in *Enterprise Zones: New Directions in Economic Development*, ed. Roy E. Breen (Newbury Park: Sage Publications, 1991), pp. 155–176.

27. Edward J. Blakely, *Planning Local Economic Development* (Newbury Park: Sage Publications, 1994), p. 62.

28. Avis Vidal "Reintegrating Disadvantaged Communities into the Fabric of Urban Life." *Housing Policy Debate* 6 (1) 1995, p. 178.

11

REVITALIZING THE INNER CITY:
A HOLISTIC APPROACH

Usha Nair Reichert*

The economic and social distress of America's inner cities is one of the most challenging problems of our times. There are many diverse and often conflicting views on how to break the debilitating cycle of economic poverty, psychological despair, and violence that has crippled and blighted these communities. Despite investment of considerable resources and skills, extensive government programs for inner-city revitalization, such as Urban Renewal, Model Cities Community Block Development Grants, CETA, Small Business Administration (SBA) and Enterprise Zones, efforts by social nonprofit groups and other private initiatives have met with limited success. Few would deny that there is a critical need to reexamine these efforts, analyze the reasons for their successes and failures, and develop a new thinking on solutions to the inner-city problems. The inner city with its history, culture and enormous human resources is an integral and vital part of our country. Its continued deterioration places the economic, political and social fabric of our nation at great risk. For this reason, Michael Porter's "Competitive Advantage of the Inner City" is a welcome initiative.

Let us first examine the significant contributions of Porter's model to the debate on inner-city revitalization. His article has helped refocus attention on the pressing problems of the inner city and highlights factors necessary for successful revitalization efforts. This is especially important in light of the current debates on welfare, health reform, and affirmative action programs, all of which may have major implications for inner-city communities. His research helps to highlight profitable private business opportunities available in the inner city at a time when private business initiatives in the inner city are somewhat scarce. It also provides a well-documented survival guide to succeeding in the inner-city business

* I would like to thank John Pomery, Don Reichert, Tom Reichert and Jon Willner for some interesting discussions.

environment. He identifies the kinds of businesses that are more likely to succeed in the inner city. His research shows how market-based policies can be used to revitalize and reclaim the competitiveness of inner-city America by providing appropriate incentives. It focuses on overcoming the disadvantages of the inner city, as well as on the strengths of the inner city, and attempts to leverage these strengths into vehicles for economic development.

The change in focus also places the inner city in a more positive role as compared to many existing models. Instead of being passive recipients of welfare and other forms of aid, and being unemployed and perceived as unemployable, this model calls for a new approach towards inner-city communities and their latent strengths in the process of rebuilding. New attitudes would in time help to end the economic and social isolation of the inner city, build bridges across community boundaries, and attract resources and skills into the community. Porter also argues that the negative attitudes of government and social agencies are often impediments to attracting business ventures into the inner city. This indicates a need for continued dialogue between the government and private businesses to restructure inner-city business development programs.

So, what are the missing pieces to this picture of inner-city revitalization fueled by private business initiatives? It is a rather significant leap of faith to assume that private businesses will vigorously pursue opportunities available in the inner city, if they are not obstructed by government and community organizations. There is also no concrete evidence as yet that Porter's approach is distinctly superior to other programs for inner-city revitalization. Before dismantling or restructuring other developmental programs in the inner city, it is necessary to conduct pilot studies of Porter's model in selected inner-city communities, to ascertain its applicability, strengths, weaknesses, and sustainability as compared to other models. Porter's model sharply distinguishes between economic and social policies and argues that the role of government and community agencies should be to support private business initiatives. He also argues against race-based minority support programs. But his model does not propose any alternate methods to promote social justice or ensure that minorities are afforded a reasonable opportunity to participate in the new business prosperity.

Although Porter's research offers valuable directions and resources for inner-city revitalization, it does not fully address the inner city's complex and wide ranging problems that are deep rooted in its unique social and economic dynamics. For example, his plan for inner-city revitalization focuses on business development and consequent job creation as the engine of inner-city revitalization. He argues that "Over time successful job creation will trigger a self reinforcing process that raises skill and wage levels."[1] It is very difficult to imagine that workers earning $6–$10 per hour at low-skill jobs will be able to enhance their job skills, raise stable families, become upwardly mobile, and break the crippling cycle of poverty. The ultimate objective of any inner-city development program should be sustained revitalization of *all* positive aspects of the inner-city community, as opposed to anticipating that the effects of business development will over time permeate the inner-city community. What is really needed is a critical mass of diversified and sustained economic activity that will jump-start the inner-city economy. Let us outline a few key aspects of a more holistic approach to inner-city revitalization: an approach based on the competitive advantages of the inner city, as discussed by Porter, but also incorporating within its framework the unique social dynamics of the inner city and the need to promote social justice.

INNER-CITY REVITALIZATION: THE KEY FEATURES

What is our vision of sustained revitalization of all positive aspects of the inner-city community? It involves redefining inner-city revitalization in a holistic manner by focusing on the economic, social and psychological needs of the inner-city communities, coordinating developmental efforts, and efficiently allocating available resources so as to allow for sustained growth. The problems involved in coordinating a game plan that addresses several complex needs are undeniable; yet previous experience has shown that piecemeal efforts offer only temporary solutions and do not eliminate the cause of the problems. We need to rebuild the social and economic fabric of inner-city communities so that inner cities are vital, dynamic, self-sustaining engines of growth. Part of our holistic vision implies that we need to define a set of long-term goals and plans and dovetail our efforts to be consistent with these goals, instead of focusing on potentially short-term, piecemeal remedial measures.

The growth of businesses as envisaged by Porter is certainly a vital part of this vision; but it is not the whole vision. The inner city needs to be transformed into safe neighborhoods where families can live in peace and harmony without fear of crime. We need to empower inner-city communities to value their gifts and abilities, to develop a strong sense of self-worth, and to create a core set of positive social values that encourage good citizenship. The inner-city youth need positive role models—adults who care and are willing to reach out and touch the lives of young people who may otherwise slip through the cracks. A holistic vision of inner-city development is a complex one. What are some additional measures that will enable us to develop a more complete picture of a revitalized inner-city community, on a stable path to sustained growth?

INTEGRATING SOCIAL JUSTICE INTO THE FRAMEWORK OF INNER-CITY REVITALIZATION

The first step towards a holistic vision may be the need to integrate social justice into the framework of inner-city revitalization. This implies that inner-city residents are empowered to participate fully and enjoy the benefits of the development process. How does Porter's model address this issue? It highlights opportunities for businesses in the inner city, but forces of competition do not necessarily lead to economic, social and distributive justice. His model does not ensure that inner-city residents have a reasonable chance to participate in new opportunities as entrepreneurs and owners, rather than merely as workers. It does not address the specifics of how the wealth generated by exploiting the competitive advantages of the inner city can be used to largely benefit inner-city communities, instead of being enjoyed only by wealthy entrepreneurs.

Porter also argues that the antibusiness attitudes held by workers, community leaders and social activists are debilitating. He critiques community leaders as "mistakenly viewing businesses as means of directly meeting social needs; as a result they have unrealistic expectations for corporate involvement in the community."[2] It may be advantageous to businesses to accept social responsibility along with the rest of the community, so long as it is in a way that does not threaten their economic viability. It is neither prudent nor feasible to judge each and every new business plan solely on the basis of its redistributional effects. However, it is important to remember that equity issues may be an integral part of any sustained developmental effort. Let us examine how empowering the local communities, restructuring affirmative action programs and targeting vulnerable groups such as teenagers and women can create a more holistic framework for inner-city revitalization.

EMPOWERING LOCAL COMMUNITIES

Local residents and communities should be an integral part of the ongoing effort at community building. The 1992 OECD Conference on the Economic, Social and Environmental Problems of Cities has observed that "Community spirit, civic pride, and the opportunity to influence decision making are key elements in creating the sustained momentum required to improve our cities."[3] Thus, it is argued that individuals and communities should have a voice in the process of change that affects their lives. As the Committee for Economic Development argues "failure to enlist local institutions and citizens as partners in problem solving leaves essential resources untapped, ignores local priorities, and misses opportunities to strengthen communities' own problem-solving capabilities."[4]

Porter notes that the inner-city entrepreneurs with their specialized knowledge of the local community have the unique ability to understand and address the needs of the inner-city markets, create employment opportunities and build a loyal customer base. He acknowledges that social service providers, social, fraternal, and religious organizations represent a vast pool of entrepreneurial talent and energy. They also have well-established, long-lasting roots in the community. Porter envisages that community development organizations can use their intimate knowledge of and influence within inner-cities communities to promote business development. They potentially can help to change community and workforce attitudes, create workreadiness and job-referral systems and facilitate establishment of businesses within the community.

While this idea has considerable merit, a partnership between CBOs, businesses, local communities and the government that uses all available resources in an efficient and coordinated manner, may be more sustainable and productive in the long run. In addition to expecting support from CBOs and government agencies, private businesses may also have a responsibility to be good citizens of their local communities.

RESTRUCTURING AFFIRMATIVE ACTION PROGRAMS

Porter's arguments on the role of affirmative action programs assume a special significance in view of the debate on policies based on location and economic criteria versus those based on race. While Porter acknowledges the importance of the role of minority businesses, he argues that government programs that support businesses on the basis of race, ethnicity or gender rather than economic need are inherently inefficient and can direct resources away from the inner city. They also "reinforce inappropriate stereotypes and attitudes, breed resentment and increase the risk that these programs will be manipulated to serve unintended populations." Government assistance should be based on location in the inner city and employment of a significant percentage of its residents.[5]

As we argue about the merits of affirmative action programs, we need to ask ourselves some key questions. Do minority entrepreneurs face severe and unique hardships based on their minority status, over and above those who are financially disadvantaged? Is it fair to say that after about thirty years of affirmative action, we have created a more equitable business and social environment, where minorities no longer face significant discrimination? Or can we say that even though the playing field is far from level, these programs are so inefficient and costly that it makes economic sense to permit the marketplace to function independently, in anticipation that the benefits of wealth creation will eventually reach the disadvantaged sections of society? The answer largely depends on how we define our goals for inner-city revitalization.

If the ultimate objective of inner-city development is sustained revitalization of all positive aspects of the inner-city community, then there may be a legitimate role for affirmative action programs. In their absence, minorities may have access to only a disproportionately small fraction of new growth opportunities. This might lead to a widening disparity between the economic and social conditions of the minority and the nonminority communities. We may not want to abandon the goals of affirmative action completely; rather, it may be appropriate to find a more efficient and socially acceptable way to achieve these goals and create a level playing field for all members of our society. Special efforts may be made to help vulnerable groups in the inner city, such as teenagers and single mothers, to avoid high-risk behavior.

CONCLUDING REMARKS

Porter's work provides a welcome opportunity to rethink the issue of inner-city revitalization. His extensive research offers insights on the scale and scope of potential private business initiatives in revitalizing the inner city. His views on the role of affirmative action programs and the benefits of private business initiatives are valuable contributions to the current debates on these issues.

If the ultimate objective of inner-city development is sustained revitalization of *all* positive aspects of the inner-city community, then we need to add a few other dimensions to Porter's model. A more holistic approach should not only create opportunities, but also raise the expectations of the people, forge bonds of community and trust, improve social justice and equity, and establish a sense of accountability and ownership within the community. Our vision includes justice, both social and economic, education and training, special programs for vulnerable children in schools and colleges, job creation, rebuilding infrastructure, and providing a safety net for the disadvantaged during the transition period. The complex and wide-ranging problems faced by the inner city are deeply rooted in its unique social and economic dynamics. We may need to develop a critical mass of integrated policies that lead to sustainable, long term solutions. This can perhaps be best achieved by a broad-based community building effort, which involves pooling of resources and commitment by government and community-based organizations, local residents, and private businesses.

NOTES

1. M. Porter, "The Competitive Advantage of the Inner City," *Harvard Business Review*, May-June 1995, p. 62.
2. Ibid., p. 65.
3. OECD (1994), "Cities for the 20th Century," OECD, Paris.
4. Research and Policy Committee of the Committee for Economic Development (1995), "Rebuilding Inner-City Communities: A New Approach to the Nation's Urban Crisis," CED, New York.
5. Porter, op. cit., pp. 67–68.

REFERENCES

Bates, T. (1994). "Utilization of Minority Employees in Small Businesses: A Comparison of Non-Minority and Black-Owned Urban Enterprises." *Review of Black Political Economy* (Summer): 113–121.

——— (1989). "The Changing Nature of Minority Businesses: A Comparative Analysis of Asian, Non-Minority, and Black-Owned Businesses," *Review of Black Political Economy* (Fall): 25–41.

Katz, M. (1995). "Improving Poor People: The Welfare State, the 'Underclass,' and Urban Schools as History." Princeton, N.J.: Princeton University Press.

OECD (1994). "Cities for the 20th Century," Paris: OECD.

Porter, M. (1995). "The Competitive Advantage of the Inner City." *Harvard Business Review* (May–June): 67–68.

Research and Policy Committee of the Committee for Economic Development (1995).

Rebuilding Inner-City Communities: A New Approach to the Nation's Urban Crisis. New York: Committee for Economic Development.

Vidal A.C. (1995). "Reintegrating Disadvantaged Communities into the Fabric of Urban Life: The Role of Community Development," *Housing Policy Debate* 6(1): 169–230.

12

REPARATIONS AND THE COMPETITIVE ADVANTAGE OF INNER CITIES

Richard F. America

SUMMARY

Michael Porter adds weight to disparate attempts to stimulate and accelerate investment, business development, and job creation in chronically distressed urban areas. But his discussion of the problems and his proposed alternative policy have two important defects. First, the paper fails to appreciate the powerful role of nationalism in promoting economic development as a collective enterprise with overarching goals. Second, it fails to acknowledge the full thrust of economic history in white-black relations. Hence, it misunderstands the fundamental problem that gives rise to the economic stagnation described. That means the paper avoids the issue of reparations. And it shows no grasp of the restitution principle. Without that, public policy on race-related distributive justice issues will continue to stumble.

DISCUSSION

Michael Porter has struck a nerve by carefully reviewing the strategies that have been tried to stimulate inner-city development. He has produced a constructive model that he calls the economic model. It is not novel. Most of the model has been proposed,[1] debated, and tried before. And much is actually being applied in many places.

But Porter has articulated this model and presented it in a way that has attracted wide attention. And his timing has been good—we need more heavyweight attention to the chronic problems of distress.

So, Porter reaches largely correct conclusions, but surprisingly, often for the wrong reasons and by the wrong route. But, all in all, he has reinforced a set of arguments that have needed extra force. His stature will help bring private and public resources to these programs.

But, this article concentrates not on the areas of agreement, which are many, but on the areas of disagreement, which are few, but profoundly significant.

Porter says:

- Location in economically distressed areas, and employment of a significant percentage of their residents, not race, should be the qualification for government assistance and preference programs.
- Preference programs too often are designed to support business development based on the race, ethnicity and gender of their owners rather than on economic need.
- The policies reinforce inappropriate stereotypes and attitudes.
- They breed resentment.
- They are designed in ways that increase the risk that such programs will be manipulated to serve "unintended" populations.
- Inner cities continue to " . . . drain public coffers."
- Redistributing wealth from haves to have nots, from whites to blacks, "is a trap."

All these beliefs, findings, and assertions are either false or reflect a weak grasp of the real problems.

The article also shows no understanding of the role of nationalism in development. And it seems to imply that Western advanced development was based on pure market processes alone—although there is a passing acknowledgment of past injustices—rather than heavily on public sector-supported private exploitation of other peoples' land, labor, and capital.

The key missing ingredient is the concept of reparations. The Restitution Principle is fundamental to understanding social policy. Without this understanding it is not possible to properly appreciate, and analyze the problems of race and the inner city. To understand poverty we must understand income and wealth creation. Present income and wealth distributions are invariably based, in part, on past systemic class injustices. Only by viewing these problems through the restitution lens can we derive the comprehensive policies needed to accelerate development.

The fundamental problem that blocks inner-city development, and "minority" business progress, is a history of wrongful exclusion and discrimination. This produces current unjust enrichments to a large class of people who live outside the inner city. And it results in a moral obligation to make restitution.

We need to first get this basic principle right. Then we can employ

Porter's analysis and model to modify the programs administratively, and correct the practical weaknesses he highlights.

Inner-city, and minority business programs, federal, state, county, and local—especially those that require contract set-asides or set lending targets—do exhibit the kinds of defects he describes. Political opponents are attacking all affirmative action programs. And they want to end contract set-asides both because of these real problems and for ideological reasons.

Some governors have moved to end all small business racial "preferences" by executive order. Some legislators have offered proposals to do the same. And the courts are taking a harder look, and narrowing the application of preferential programs.[2]

Furthermore, many corporate managers are ambivalent about the policies and the programs. Even many supporters seem uncomfortable, unable to articulate a clear rationale, and unsure how to respond to opponents.

Guidance from courts and legislatures is confusing and contradictory, and public attitudes are divided, murky, and uncertain.

Programs built over thirty years are attacked by opponents emboldened by Supreme Court rulings and the 1994 mid-term congressional elections. And many corporate executives, who want to help in some way, are unclear about the benefits to themselves or to inner cities from the approaches they have been using.

THE LACK OF A FIRM ENOUGH POLICY BASIS

Public and corporate policies since 1965 have been based on widely shared assumptions. Porter shows that many premises were weak. But in addition to being unworkable or subject to sabotage by ideological opponents, they also avoided the basic moral issue.

Porter's economic model makes sense, using market principles and rational self-interest to create local investments based on perceived real competitive advantage rather than on artificial inducements, subsidies, and mandates. But public redistributive subsidies are also part of the answer. The trouble is, they haven't been argued for properly. They should be defended on the grounds that the public funds involved, directly or indirectly, are really payments on a long-standing social debt, and are a way to make restitution; and that long resident, indigenous and "quasi-indigenous" minorities—Native, African, Hispanic, and Asian—of three or more generations, ought to be the target groups.

REDEFINING THE PROBLEM

The way society in general has looked at the inner-city problem fundamentally misses the point and avoids the real issue.

We should ask this question—Why are we involved in this activity in the first place? And with whom should we be trying to work? But the way the policy debate frames the problem is this—"Minorities have been kept from participating fully in business. And now we need to help them overcome their lack of entrepreneurial background and lack of access to markets, financing and consulting assistance, and give them a hand in setting up so they can grow, compete and create some jobs, but in ways that don't displace existing businesses or create unfair reverse discrimination."

But that's not the problem. The problem, instead, is this. There are several indigenous and quasi-indigenous groups, including all Native Americans, most African Americans, many Mexican Americans, and some Chinese Americans, whose ancestors have lived in the United States for generations. They have, for long periods, been actively prevented by the majority of European background from creating and accumulating financial and human capital, and from developing competitive businesses. The interests of the European majority group, relative to minorities' interests, have been served by limiting participation and competition by race.

This historical exclusion, over at least three centuries, therefore, systematically benefited "majority" businesses. And the process produced income and wealth, market share, and a kind of overwhelming ethnic monopoly position. It was characterized by extremely high barriers to entry. These wrongfully produced benefits were then bequeathed, i.e., transferred intergenerationally, and the situation continues today.

That is, past discrimination, exclusion and exploitation, in labor and capital markets, and in education and training—human capital development—produces a large, measurable,[3] aggregate benefit—ill-gotten gains—currently, to investors, managers, professionals and some high-skilled workers, as a class.[4] It is wrongful, and it's an *unjust enrichment*.

If we believe that the practices are wrong, then ethically it is not acceptable to receive and retain benefits that flow from them. Those benefits should be returned. That is the Restitution Principle.

The remedy is through redistributive justice, including affirmative action and set-asides. These programs should consciously and explicitly use the tax and budget process to change the relative racial distributions of income and wealth and business ownership and participation. It would amount to reparations.[5]

So, the first reason for stimulating inner-city development is that it will be good for the overall economic development of the country as well as the regions and communities targeted.

But, the second reason for minority business and inner-city assistance, is similar to the reasons for affirmative action in education, housing and employment. It is that these are avenues for making restitution, for paying the social debt. There is an increasing body of analytical work that points in this direction, and that will be useful in sorting out policy options.[6]

We want a healthy competitive economy in inner cities. But the racial monopoly in business has produced some of the same harmful consequences as monopoly in the usual sense. It has distorted prices, restricted output and limited innovation. So, inner-city and minority business policy is, or should be, interested in helping to remedy that general economic defect. The policy should be consciously concerned with helping remedy these monopoly tendencies.

HOW POLICIES HAVE BEEN JUSTIFIED

For thirty years, government at all levels, and major companies have taken sometimes extraordinary steps to help inner-city and small businesses owned by managers and investors who are African-, Mexican-, and Native American. These are commonly called "minority" or "disadvantaged" businesses. The policies and programs have also often included women-owned businesses. This article focuses on racial minorities, because they are the real target of the attack.

They've been helped for reasons well known or at least given frequent high-level lip service. Briefly, the reasons are that such programs would:

- generate jobs in distressed communities;
- supply visible institutional anchors in otherwise unstable social environments;
- serve local retail and service requirements;
- provide role models in capitalism to young people who might otherwise be tempted to embrace radical political alternatives, crime, or the underground economy; and
- create steady and reliable vendors and suppliers to large busi-

nesses, providing goods and services based on normal competitive price and quality, thereby diversifying the supplier base.

These are also largely Porter's objectives, and they are widely shared, as far as they go. Corporate interests, broadly defined, were to be served in all these ways. And public policy rested on these bases. But corporate and public policy also has been based, in part, on a general but uneasy sense that society has some obligation, based on historic patterns of systematic injustice—slavery and discrimination—to help groups who have been displaced, exploited, excluded, and prevented from participating in regular business and community development on account of racial prejudice. The trouble is that this is the real basis for a redistributive policy like affirmative action set-asides, and most mandates, but it has not been the main articulated argument in favor because supporters have not been sure themselves about how they feel about the full implications of that approach.

Despite this cloudy policy background, corporate and public programs have expanded steadily. Assistance takes the form of purchasing, financing, and technical assistance. The programs, as Porter notes, though flawed, have endured and have had some positive results.

But there's evidence that commitment is weaker below the corporate CEO level, that is, at management levels where day-to-day decisions are made. It is also weaker at management and implementation levels in the public sector. There, commitment is shaky, shallow, and often quietly opposed, characterized by half-hearted performance, footdragging and sabotage.

A STRONGER PREMISE

There has to be a better fundamental reason than any of those pragmatic ones cited. Otherwise, inner-city and minority business policy will always struggle to find any kind of broad public, executive, legislative, and judicial support. There has to be a principled rationale for such policies, because they are widely perceived as racially redistributive in a zero sum fashion.

Unless the basic rationale is principled, these policies will continue to be diluted and distorted, subject to avoidance, corruption, and continuing controversy, resentment, bad faith dealing, and suboptimum performance, or defeated and outlawed altogether.

Minority business set-asides, and other forms of affirmative action in contracting and lending, should be based on policies that recognize that:

- there is a kind of quantifiable social debt,
- something we can think of as restitution is owed based on 375 years of history, and
- set-asides and minority business programs, including some of the kind that Porter specifies as counterproductive, are ways to help pay that debt.

This formulation offers several benefits. It will permit increased resource commitment, sharper focus on just who the intended beneficiaries are, and a time limit, a sunset, that will be beneficial for all concerned.

THE STATE OF THE ART—A FEW ILLUSTRATIVE EXAMPLES

The practical objective is to accelerate the development of reliable suppliers, and of competitive, growing, job generating firms in all industrial sectors, at significant scale, that help stabilize communities. Effective public policies and programs at all levels have the goal of creating solid competitive businesses, at every scale, in inner cities. The policies, when they are effective, as Porter rightly observes, are not social welfare. And corporate assistance to inner cities and to minority businesses has been significant and increasing through prime and subcontracting, direct and indirect financing, debt and equity, and through consulting and technical assistance. But despite this record, many of those who support the policies remain dissatisfied that they have not accomplished more. Those who want to end public set-aside requirements, also want to end private ones as well, if they can, because they believe that these, too, are unfair to white competitors. Policy-makers, public and private, are caught in the middle.

THE HISTORY OF BLACK BUSINESS

It is healthy to pause here to clarify a frequently confused point. African Americans have known entrepreneurial success historically. There have been at least two major periods in which businesses developed, flourished, and competed for market share in the mainstream economy.

From about 1820 to 1860, there were African Americans in numerous ventures that did well, such as caterers, builders, and furniture and leather goods makers. Later, from 1890 to about 1930, again black businesses succeeded in areas such as banking, insurance, publishing, and other fields.

In each case a powerful combination of adverse public reaction, coupled with macro phenomena, including panics, depressions and wars, and new immigrant waves, shut down the budding success, and eliminated the beachhead that had been achieved. But in each case, too, public policy was consciously used to prevent the emergence of permanent, strong, competitive black firms, and to turn back this competition.

So it is ahistorical to suggest that African Americans lack a history of entrepreneurial interest or lack native talent. The fact is that the white majority systematically prevented African American participation *in order to enjoy unjust and wrongful benefits*. The motive was essentially to maintain a social monopoly.

BASIC MISUNDERSTANDINGS AND PROGRAM WEAKNESSES

Our confusion about inner-city development is based on the way basic assumptions have gone unquestioned. The assumptions derived in part from the legislated and regulated atmosphere in which programs evolved. The key premises were that:

- programs should help the economically disadvantaged, meaning marginal, inexperienced, undercapitalized entrepreneurs;
- they should be given continuing management consulting and technical assistance; and
- resources and opportunities should be allocated largely first-come, first-served, rather than targeted by industrial sector, the characteristics of the entrepreneurs, or by an overall development strategy. Government should not "pick and choose," in other words.

Porter finds those premises to be weak and part of the problem. And he is right, as far as he goes. But we have learned from the more successful corporate, and federal, state and local government programs that targeting is appropriate and effective, and that programs should seek and work with the stronger potential participants, who can use this assistance efficiently to grow and create jobs.

Too many corporate and public policies have common weaknesses.

They operate on the wrong scale, wasting resources on very long-shot businesses, and on would-be entrepreneurs rather than on well-qualified investor/managers in manufacturing, construction and sophisticated services. Their time horizons are not well thought out, but appear to be hazy and laissez faire rather than based on growth rate and market share targets set in careful plans. Moreover, the fundamental problem in the inner city and in society generally, that they presumably have been trying to help solve, has been poorly defined. That problem, correctly defined, is that past racial injustices create a current social debt. It should be paid by making restitution, in part through capital transfers and subsidies. But the issue is typically framed, instead, in terms of charitable, compassionate assistance, or, as Porter does, in terms of hard-headed business self-interest, rather than of moral obligation. Both rationales apply.

Most critics, unlike Porter, are actually opponents masquerading as objective analysts. They dwell on several perceived defects in the operations of corporate and public programs. Their common criticisms can be summarized in this way:

- Benefits too often go to people who aren't personally "economically disadvantaged," and they are thereby unfairly made "rich."
- Benefits tend to be geographically skewed and concentrated rather than more evenly distributed nationally, statewide or citywide.
- Beneficiaries are allowed to participate in programs for too long. They should be forced to "graduate" so there can be "turnover" and others have a better chance to participate.
- Unqualified minority firms are allowed to receive large contracts or subcontracts for which other small businesses should have as much right to compete.
- Minority firms and individuals, that are no more than "fronts", are permitted to receive contracts, most of which are, in turn, passed on to larger "nonminority" firms, or more experienced individuals.
- Corporations pay an unwarranted premium in doing business with many minority vendors and suppliers. This distortion costs shareholders. And it's unfair to losing bidders, and often results in poor quality work.
- There is a significant quality gap, in any event, and most minority firms that do get contracts, financing or technical assistance, are not able to supply competitive quality goods and services, and are thus wasting resources and shortchanging customers.

Those frequent complaints are based, to some extent, on accurate assessments. Porter, correctly, makes several. But to some extent, they are also flawed, because they proceed from flawed assumptions about the underlying basic problem. Those who complain assume that somehow, inexperienced, relatively untrained people can be assisted to create strong competitive firms, and that this can be done with meager resources. Porter shows that this is untenable. Related to this is the assumption that middle- or upper-middle-income individuals should be ineligible because they have overcome whatever personal disadvantages they may have started out with in life. Furthermore, there is an assumption that contracts, financing and other corporate or public assistance should be more or less evenly distributed over the nation, state, county or city. In fact, there is no reason to insist on such geographic dispersal of program benefits, or to expect federal resources to be so distributed since there are clusters of population and of business opportunities, and of fertile business conditions in which minority firms will have maximum prospects for success. Others argue that businesses should be forced to "graduate." The rationale given for this assumption is that it allows others the opportunity to participate. But this is disingenuous because the critics who express this view often disapprove of the basic notion of minority assistance. So their motivation really seems to be to try, by rear-guard action, to make sure no firms receive program benefits long enough to become truly competitive and strong.

Obviously, there have been abuses. Firms have become content to get corporate or public sector contracts, and have not bothered to develop competitive marketing capability, or to diversify products or services. But there's reason to believe the real motive of those who push for stringent graduation requirements is to prevent the use of corporate or public resources to build real competitors who might win market share. That's an understandable motive. But it ought to be defended explicitly rather than pursued covertly.

Critics point to favoritism, political and personal cronyism, and the like, for wrongfully influencing contract and financing awards. They argue that this must be monitored, prevented and violators punished. Where inside decision makers have participated in schemes to benefit friends, political supporters or relatives, the injustice should be dealt with. They also point to the presence of fronts. There is no excuse for fronts. This practice is cynical and corrupt. But often the accusation of fronts becomes a convenient scapegoat and tool for managers who fundamentally disagree with the key objectives of the basic corporate public policy in the first place. They seem to take a perverse interest in subverting the intent of the policy by turning a blind eye to front applicants and front operations, and allowing them to enter the programs. The way to make sure there are no fronts is not through monitoring and investigations, the usual bureaucratic response to problems. Instead, the most useful method is to do away with the notion that personal economic "disadvantage" is a requirement for participation.

If minority investors and managers who are personally strong and experienced are allowed to participate, in order to build strong competitive businesses, and generate jobs and income, then opportunities for fronts will dry up. Fronts occur when the truly talented are excluded from the programs in the mistaken belief that they have personally done well and need or deserve no further assistance.

Those who complain cite cases and evaluative studies suggesting that, in too many instances, affirmative action procurements or "set-aside" contracts go to minority firms that are not the lowest bidders. The argument is that this is plainly harmful to the general public interest. The counter-argument, however, is that awards are not always made to the lowest bidder. Contracts are often based on considerations of quality, convenience to the purchaser or other factors thought to be important corporate or public objectives. Minority businesses need a foot in the door from which they have been wrongfully excluded historically. There is sufficient justification for the additional cost, as long as it is within reasonable bounds, and as long as this practice has a sunset provision.

That is, we would not expect to continue to make contract decisions this way beyond, say, a generation or two, forty years. By then, it is hoped, enough firms will have become established and competitive, on normal terms, so that these kinds of allowances will not have to be continued.

This concept of sunsetting has too often been missing from the operation of these programs. It should be decided and announced that such programs are not indefinite but are designed to accomplish set goals. Afterwards, they will be terminated.

Reformers generally fall into two camps. The first camp includes most corporations, trade associations, politicians, bureaucrats and journalists. They believe reform should be in the direction of:

- fewer set-asides and strict justification, as suggested by the Supreme Court in the case of *City of Richmond v. J.H. Croson Co.*;
- accelerated graduation criteria;

- greater inclusiveness (meaning more emphasis should be placed on making eligible categories of demographic groups defined as "disadvantaged"; and
- tighter restrictions on the personal net worth and income of program participants (limiting inclusion generally to less well off minority investors and managers).

The second camp includes most minorities and their advocates. They generally propose,

- expanding the scope of set-asides,
- a narrower definition of eligible "minorities," and
- greater allowance for individuals with higher net worth, and management experience, i.e., a higher threshold of personal economic disadvantage.

Solutions to the perceived problems have tended to quiet Camp One and mollify Camp Two, by perpetuating programs that seem to help primarily small, marginal businesses. But these programs do not address the historic problem of monopolistic exclusion from full participation in major sectors.

The problem we face in finding a better way to support minority and inner-city business development is not unusual. We often have to reconcile conflicting values and conflicting rights.

In this case, Camp One essentially wants to be able to pursue a solution through unfettered traditional free enterprise. Camp Two, while also sharing basic beliefs in free enterprise, wants to see social justice done through payment of restitution, though few would yet explicitly put it that way.

The idea is not to force a zero sum solution through the courts or legislatures. But instead, the idea is to research, debate and find a basis for consensus that balances the objectives of Camp One with those of Camp Two.

THE RESTITUTION PRINCIPLE

Until now there has been sustained corporate involvement and public policy support. But there is much room for improvement, and this is where Porter adds tremendous value.

Porter, correctly, attacks the tendency to see these kinds of "disadvantaged" and inner-city business programs as matters of social compassion, altruism, and charity. But, unlike Porter, we believe such programs should be based on the restitution principle, as well as on basic economic development objectives with long-term implications for the country's general well-being.

Only with such a basic rationale will we be able to strengthen this business sector so it can develop and compete fully and fairly. We do not need to merely continue to tinker and adjust the programs incrementally.

If we accept most or all of the logic in the restitution principle, and the problem redefinition that flows from it, we will understand that current unjust enrichments enjoyed by those at the top of the wealth and income distribution are based on past injustices, exclusionary discrimination, exploitation and favoritism and thereby create an obligation to repay. With this in mind, we will be able to develop a program that could, over a reasonable time, say, forty years, produce lasting benefits, and that could then be terminated.

The restitution principle eliminates the false and diversionary controversy over the need to produce specific evidence or proof of past discrimination. This requirement is used to prevent remedies to individuals where there has obviously been a clear broad pattern of exclusion. The restitution principle can also help remove the hairsplitting semantics over who is "economically disadvantaged."

CONCLUSION

Tinkering has been useful over the years at achieving incremental improvements. But inner-city and minority development financing and set-aside programs and policies remain basically unsatisfactory. If we take this opportunity, during a broad national debate, to step back and ask basic, difficult, and, perhaps, touchy questions, we'll invite short-term controversy, but likely long-term clarity and strategic success. The review must rest on a clear, tough-minded and principled problem definition.

NOTES

1. See Richard F. America, *Developing the Afro American Economy* (Lexington Books, 1977).
2. Paul M. Barrett and G. Pascal Zachary, "Budding Backlash? Race, Sex Prefer-

ences Could Become Target in Voter Shift to Right." *Wall Street Journal*, January 1, 1995, p. 1.

3. Lester Thurow, *Poverty and Discrimination* (Washington, D.C.: Brookings, 1969).

4. Richard F. America, editor, *The Wealth of Races: The Present Value of Benefits from Past Injustices* (New York: Greenwood, 1990).

5. Boris Bittker, *The Case for Black Reparations* (New York: Random House, 1972).

6. Richard F. America, *Paying the Social Debt: What White America Owes Black America* (New York: Praeger, 1993).

13

POTENTIAL WELFARE GAINS FROM IMPROVING ECONOMIC CONDITIONS IN THE INNER CITY

James Peoples

I. INTRODUCTION

A large source of potential employees, customers and employers reside in the inner city. However, conditions such as high unemployment, low per capita income, and low educational attainment indicate the difficulty of making this potential a reality. These conditions are especially problematic for blacks since they comprise a disproportionate share of the inner-city population. While improving these conditions in the inner city would clearly benefit its residents and also strengthen the city's overall economy, current policies apparently have not generated appreciable welfare gains.[1]

Porter (1995) suggests a greater role for the private sector and a new focus for government as a more effective approach to improving the economic development of inner cities. He reaches this view by examining the advantages and disadvantages inherent to the inner city. Such an analysis allows him to indicate how the private sector could do a better job than the government at unlocking the potential gains to be realized from improving the economy of the inner city.

This article reexamines the competitive advantages and disadvantages of the inner city with the objective of uncovering the potential welfare gains that can be realized from encouraging greater participation by the private sector. Initially, we categorize the competitive advantages inherent to the inner city as factor input and product market outcomes. Such an approach can help identify the differing mechanism by which business use of these advantages can improve the local economy. Furthermore, this distinction reveals how the enhancement of these positive inner-city characteristics can benefit its residents. The disadvantages are then classified as labor and nonlabor production costs and as externalities that flow from these costs. The rationale for making these distinctions is based on the assumption that correcting these problems should attract business, but it will do so in different ways and may therefore vary in its influence on the welfare of individuals living in the inner city. Lastly, concluding remarks are made on the possible effectiveness of Porter s approach to improving the economic condition of the inner city.

II. INNER-CITY ATTRIBUTES AND POSSIBLE BENEFITS TO RESIDENTS

Porter lists abundant availability of human resources, strategic location, integration with regional clusters, and local market demand as major advantages to locating businesses in the inner city. These attributes are classified in Table 1 as factor input markets and product market outcomes.

In Table 1 the large supply of potential workers in the inner city is classified as a favorable labor market condition. The availability of workers from these localities, as reflected by high inner-city unemployment rates, should lead to more competitive labor markets. It follows then that businesses would benefit from lower unit production costs that are typically associated with more competitive labor markets because they could hire at lower wages. The extent of wage reduction, though, is partly dependent on the labor demand elasticity.

Residents would directly benefit from wage payments associated with enhanced employment opportunities if they received enough to compensate for the loss of any government transfer payments. Despite these benefits a possible drawback from businesses taking advantage of the large supply of potential workers is the opportunity for employee exploitation in the form of below-market wages. Such employer behavior occurs if there are few local employers because the absence of competing firms limits the employment opportunities for workers. In keeping with Porter's free market approach, sustaining a business friendly environment that encourages a significant influx of companies can help mitigate this behavior by reducing employers' monopoly control over the labor supply.[2]

Table 1 lists strategic location and ease of integration with regional clusters as production cost advantages because they lower transportation costs and create a work environment that allows for a greater likelihood of cost saving synergy effects. Increased business formation derived from firms taking advantage of these opportunities improves the economic

TABLE 1
Classification of Inner-City Advantages

A. *Advantages Derived from Factor Input Market Conditions*
1. Labor market conditions center on the large supply of potential employees (Human Resources)
2. Production techniques center on:
   a. Strategic location
   b. Ease of integration with regional clusters

B. *Advantage Derived from Product Market Conditions* center on the large pool of potential customers

---

well-being of inner-city residents if entering employers are committed to hiring workers residing in these localities. In addition, the extent of employment gains by residents is dependent on the preparedness of the workers. Hence, while it is possible for businesses to benefit from these cost-saving strategies, this behavior may do very little to improve the welfare of inner-city residents without policies that create added incentive for new businesses to employ these workers.

The inner cities' large pool of potential customers is the attribute that has a much different welfare effect on residents. As reported in Table 1, this advantage is considered a condition of the product market. Depending upon the product, locating business operations near concentrated populations may increase product demand by improving shopping convenience of inner-city residents. Prices may even decline if enough retailers enter this market. As Porter contends, even though per capita income is low in this locality, businesses still benefit from taking advantage of this opportunity because the nontrivial number of potential customers is enough to generate profits. Thus, in contrast to the other inner-city advantages, the large pool of potential customers does not directly improve residents' welfare through wage gains and increased employment. Instead, welfare gains are by-products of increased retail business activity.

Taking advantage of the opportunity to hire from the large pool of inner-city workers has the potential to generate the greatest welfare gains for residents. But it is also necessary to provide businesses with incentives for employing inner-city residents or to develop programs that enhance the competitiveness of these workers.

III. BARRIERS TO BUSINESS FORMATION

Despite the competitive advantages of the inner city, few companies have established business there. This apparent aversion is due in part to substantial barriers to business formation. Porter lists the high cost of land, construction, product distribution, stringent environmental standards, lack of skilled workers, security risk and high barriers to equity capital as major competitive disadvantages of the inner city. These problems are classified in Table 2 as sources of high production cost, and as externalities that residents and businesses face.

Purchasing land, constructing buildings, distributing products and meeting environmental standards are considered as nonlabor inputs in Table 2. Under these circumstances, the high production cost experienced by businesses operating in the inner city is partly influenced by government regulation. While these policies are intended to protect workers and the environment, the additional cost to business can be prohibitive. Indeed, Porter contends that companies considering new operations in the inner city face unreasonably high costs due in part to regulation. Regulatory reform that removes these barriers to business formation, then, could improve the economic conditions of the inner city by increasing the demand for workers from these localities.

Even if regulatory reform leads to increased business formation in the inner city, residents still may not experience meaningful employment gains. The ability of inner-city businesses to employ local workers is severely limited if residents have not acquired the skills needed to successfully compete in the labor market. As Porter contends, the employee and management skills of inner-city residents pose major competitive disadvantages. Indeed, information from the Current Population Survey reveals that by 1991 black residents of the inner city acquired on average 10.92 years of schooling compared to 12.02 for other SMSA residents. The difference in years of schooling is also prevalent for black inner-city residents employed as managers; on average they acquired 10.82 years of schooling compared to 13.86 for other SMSA residents. Increasing the level of educational attainment in the inner city benefits employers by lowering unit production costs, since more years of schooling is typically associated with more productive workers. By enhancing their qualifications residents acquiring more years of schooling are more likely to find alternative employment, even if companies do not locate operations in the inner city. Evidence reveals the benefits from schooling. Blacks receive significantly higher earnings for additional years of schooling, and

TABLE 2
Classification of Inner-City Disadvantages

A. *Disadvantages Originating from the Production Process*
   1. Nonlabor factor input costs
     a. Cost of land acquisitions
     b. Construction costs
     c. Poor infrastructure
     d. Cost of meeting environmental standards
   2. Labor Costs
     a. Employee skills
     b. Managerial experience

B. *Negative Externalities Associated with Poor Economic Conditions*
   1. High security risks
   2. Difficulty acquiring equity capital

the return on this investment does not differ appreciably from that of their white counterparts.[3] Hence programs such as Head Start that increase the likelihood of higher educational attainment are essential for improving the economic well-being of individuals residing in the inner city.

Reducing high production costs in the inner city has the added benefit of reducing security risks and lowering barriers to acquiring equity capital, externalities that arise partly from poor economic conditions. For instance, high poverty rates and chronic unemployment are usually associated with high crime rates. Thus, any improvement of employment opportunities and earnings derived from lowering production costs should reduce security risk in the inner city. Additionally, increasing the earnings potential of inner-city residents lowers barriers to acquiring capital.

In sum, correcting production inefficiencies caused by regulations and enhancing the skills of inner-city residents provide welfare gains by attracting more business to distressed areas.

IV. CONCLUDING REMARKS

There is little argument on the need to improve economic conditions in the inner city. Debate arises, however, over the approach towards enhancing the welfare of inner-city residents. Porter provides compelling reasons for encouraging greater involvement of the private sector, while reducing that of the government. This article addresses Porter's list of competitive advantages and disadvantages with the objective of examining the potential gains to be realized from stepped-up business formation in the inner city. While creating an environment that is more conducive to business growth would surely improve economic conditions, this article suggests that these benefits are heavily dependent on residents acquiring the schooling and training required to succeed in a more competitive labor market.

NOTES

The author thanks John Heywood, Richard Perlman and Harold Rose for valuable comments.

1. Welfare gain for inner-city residents is defined as their improved standard of living.

2. Larger numbers of competing employers also reduce the probability of collusive behavior.

3. Baldwin and Johnson (1996) find that each additional year of schooling is associated with a $0.485 and $0.553 hourly increase in wages for black and white men, respectively. Anderson and Shapiro (1996) find that each additional year of schooling is associated with a 5.6 and 5.8 percent increase in hourly wages for black and white women, respectively. It should be noted that these studies also find evidence of racial wage differentials, especially for men.

REFERENCES

Anderson, Deborah and Shapiro, David. "Racial Differences in Access to High-Paying Jobs and the Wage Gap Between Black and White Women," *Industrial and Labor Relations Review* (January 1996), pp. 273–286.

Baldwin, Majorie and Johnson, William. "The Employment Effects of Wage Discrimination Against Black Men," *Industrial and Labor Relations Reviews* (January 1996), pp. 302–316.

Bates, Timothy. "Analysis of Survival Rates among Franchise and Independent Small Business Startups." *Journal of Small Business Management* (April 1995), pp. 26–36.

Porter, Michael. "The Competitive Advantage of the Inner City," *Harvard Business Review* (May–June 1995), pp. 55–71.

14

IS THE INNER CITY COMPETITIVE?

Margaret C. Simms and Winston J. Allen[1]

Michael Porter's article in the *Harvard Business Review* (May–June 1995) on "The Competitive Advantage of the Inner City" in many ways is a valuable contribution to our thinking about economic redevelopment in metropolitan areas. Its appearance in a mainstream journal read by corporate and public policy leaders puts the discussion of one of our major economic policy challenges back on the table. However, the main issue is: Does it make a positive contribution in terms of designing a "coherent economic strategy," which he says is so sorely needed at this point in time (p. 55). Unfortunately, it does not.

From a series of anecdotes or case studies (each one different), Porter weaves a rationale for inner-city competitiveness that is internally inconsistent and perhaps unduly confining as a development strategy. For example, he asserts that businesses can be successful catering to the inner-city market because the relatively low income of residents is offset by high density. Yet this is likely to be in conflict with other guidance that he offers, such as the establishment of businesses that export goods to other markets. Porter also suggests that the ideal company is one that "is not small and high-cost but a professionally managed major business employing the latest in technology, marketing and management techniques." By the end of the article, a reader could conclude that virtually any business can be successful in the inner city. While that may be true, this information does not help a policymaker or lender develop a focused economic development strategy.

Part of the problem with the Porter analysis is that it does not distinguish clearly the different ways in which success can be measured. A strategy that is effective in reaching one goal may not move us very far along in terms of achieving another objective. Sorting out and analyzing each objective separately has taken on greater importance as federal policymakers have begun to consider "place-based" not "race-based" business development strategies. A public policymaker might have at least four objectives in mind when considering economic development strategies. They could include:

1. Job creation or job upgrading for inner-city residents;
2. Increasing tax revenues received by the central city through increased property values and/or increased business taxes;
3. More goods and services for inner-city residents;
4. Creation or expansion of the entrepreneurial class among minority groups.

While it may be possible for some firms to meet most or all of these objectives simultaneously, it is more likely that some types of firms will be relatively successful in some areas and not so successful in achieving other goals. In addition, the overarching question is the long-term viability of the firms; can they be profitable in the inner city? The answer in most cases is: it depends.

IS THE INNER CITY COMPETITIVE?: FINDINGS FROM A NEW STUDY

In late 1993, the Joint Center for Political and Economic Studies began a study of the employment potential within minority-owned businesses. One of the primary objectives was to expand our knowledge of the hiring patterns within such firms. From pioneering studies by Timothy Bates,[2] we know that minority firms are more likely to employ minority workers than are nonminority firms, but little is known about the characteristics of those workers and which types of firms are more likely to employ workers from low-income communities. The Joint Center study was designed to provide answers to those questions by surveying a sample of medium-sized and large minority firms and comparing them with similar firms owned by whites. While the focus was on characteristics of the workers, information on firm location allows us to match up firms and their employment patterns with the characteristics of the neighborhoods in which they are located.[3] We used some of the data from that study to determine whether a narrowly targeted place-based strategy leads to job creation for inner-city residents.

The Joint Center's sample of minority-owned firms consisted of a total of 3,060 firms, nearly 600 black-owned businesses surveyed annually by *Black Enterprise* magazine when it constructs its BE 100 industrial/service firms and just over 2500 minority-owned firms that are affiliated with regional councils of the National Minority Supplier Development Council in four states—California, Florida, Illinois, and Texas.[4] Surveys were also sent to 2,000 nonminority firms that were similar in sales volume and industry distribution.[5]

The responses to the survey confirmed Bates's findings; minority firms are more likely to employ minority workers. Moreover, they are more likely to recruit in low-income neighborhoods. Nearly one-quarter of minority respondents said that they always recruited in these neighborhoods, while only 10 percent of the nonminority firms said that was the case. Another 37 percent of the minority firms said they sometimes recruited there, in contrast to only 24 percent of nonminority firms that did so. Substantial proportions of the employees in minority firms had a high school education or less, indicating that these businesses are providing jobs to people with education levels comparable to those of many inner-city residents.

It is clear then that a strategy that focuses on minority firms can make a positive contribution to job creation for individuals who live in low-income neighborhoods. The next question is: Are these firms actually located in those neighborhoods? Indeed, are they located in the central city at all? Our findings in this regard are mixed. A substantial proportion of minority-owned businesses are located in minority neighborhoods. For example, 41 percent of black-owned businesses responding to our survey are located in zip codes where the proportion of blacks in the population is higher than blacks' representation in the U.S. population. However, very few of these firms are located in high poverty areas. Therefore, requiring firms to be located in high poverty areas may be unduly restrictive if the major objective is to provide employment for residents of those areas.

Our findings with regard to central city location are not as easy to interpret. Overall, over one-half of all minority respondents were located in the central city. An examination of black-owned firms by themselves shows a similar distribution. While firms located in the central city tended to have been in that location longer than those in the suburbs, location did not appear to affect sales volume significantly one way or the other. When the firms are disaggregated by industry, it turns out that a majority of firms in the emerging industries (as the nontraditional industries are known) are in the central city, including 65 percent of construction firms and 72 percent of business services firms. So central city firms can be as viable as those in the suburbs and central city location is not necessarily disadvantageous for minority entrepreneurs entering new industries.

TABLE 1
Percent of Firms that Always or Sometimes Recruit in Low-Income Neighborhoods by Location and Industry

	Central City	Suburbs	All Firms
All Minority Firms*	66.2**	52.6	60.2
Manufacturing	67.3	58.2	62.8
Construction	72.1	79.2	74.6
Business Services	71.9	53.9	66.7
Professional Services	62.0**	30.3	47.6

** Statistically significant central city-suburban difference at the 99% confidence level.

The central city firms were more likely to derive more than 50 percent of their sales from state and local government, but few firms overall cater exclusively to government. Only about 7 percent of firms received more than 50 percent of their revenue from either federal or state and local governments. So one can hardly conclude that minority firms are being sustained by noncompetitive government contracts. Suburban firms were more likely to be heavily focused on national markets than were their central city counterparts. Therefore, suburban firms could be said to be somewhat more "export" oriented. It would appear then that when proximity to local consumers or businesses is not an issue, firms tend to locate where intercity transportation and land use costs are lower. In other words, they make profit-maximizing decisions that are similar to those of nonminority firms.

Our data indicate that central city firms are significantly different from their suburban counterparts in ways which suggest that a strategy promoting central city (over suburban) location can be more effective than a general minority business strategy—if the objective is to increase employment of residents of low-income communities. Minority firms located in the central city were significantly more likely to target low-income neighborhoods when they recruited and have a significantly larger proportion of black employees. There are no significant differences for any other minority group in terms of employment. The difference for recruitment in low-income areas was particularly noticeable in professional services firms, one of the emerging industries for minority entrepreneurs. However, among all minority firms, even 50 percent of those in the suburbs indicated that they always or sometimes recruited in low income neighborhoods.

What is not clear is whether the employment pattern is the result of

TABLE 2
Percent of Firms in which More than 50% of
Employees are Black by Location and Industry

	Central City	Suburbs	All Firms
All Minority Firms	50.9**	37.2	45.6
Manufacturing	40.0	24.1	34.2
Construction	44.2	23.1	38.3
Business Services	33.3	55.5	39.4
Professional Services	46.5	37.2	42.5

** Statistically significant central city-suburban difference at the 99% confidence level.

differential recruiting patterns or differences in access to transportation since minority firms that are located in the central city were more likely to be on or near a public transportation route than were their suburban counterparts.[6] If it turns out that recruiting patterns are affected by business location then making assistance location-specific may be critical to achieving the employment objective. However, if the problem is merely one of transportation, then lowering that barrier may be sufficient.

A policymaker may be more interested in the total number of jobs created than in the racial or neighborhood characteristics of those employed. In other words, if the total numbers are high, more people from all groups may have a better chance of being employed. Although that does not necessarily follow, the number of jobs created is an issue of concern. If we use Porter's criterion of fifteen or more employees as a measure of a firm that has crossed the threshold between "mom and pop" and "big" business, then nearly 40 percent of the minority respondents to our survey were in that category.[7]

Among firms in the emerging industries, manufacturing companies were more likely to have large workforces: over 50 percent of firms in both the central city and the suburbs had at least sixteen employees.[8] (Just over 30 percent had fifty or more.) Minority firms in the manufacturing industry were also more likely to have increased their workforces recently, with a large proportion of the increase among blue collar positions.

While service industries also showed large increases in employment, their expansion was more heavily concentrated in white collar jobs. Within the service industry, business services ranked second (behind manufacturing) in terms of high employment and for these companies there was a significant difference between city and suburb. Firms located in the city

Table 3
Percent of Firms with 15 or More Employees by Location and Industry

	Central City	Suburbs	All Firms
All Minority Firms	39.7	39.6	39.6
Manufacturing	52.3	59.6	55.8
Construction	36.4	31.8	34.8
Business Services	47.1*	23.1	40.5
Professional Services	39.5	33.2	36.8

* Statistically significant central city-suburban difference at the 95% confidence level.

were much more likely to have large workforces. This may be related to the high proportion of these firms that are janitorial services firms, although this cannot be confirmed by our data.

POLICY IMPLICATIONS

Our data does indicate that location patterns for minority-owned businesses differ by industry, market orientation, and employment. Porter's location-based strategy is an imperfect but not totally incorrect way of looking at economic development issues. Our study confirms the fact that race is important; minority firms are more likely to employ individuals from populations with high unemployment rates. If the major objective is one of creating jobs for inner-city residents (as opposed to generating tax revenue or providing services to residents) then a general locational strategy can have a positive impact on employment. Firms in the central city are more likely to recruit in low-income neighborhoods and employ black workers. However, firms do not have to be in high-poverty neighborhoods in order to generate these employment gains.

The fact that suburban firms are less likely to employ black workers and have higher proportions of their employees living in the suburbs suggests that black workers may be disadvantaged by limited housing choices or higher transportation barriers. An alternative policy might focus on building low-moderate income housing near suburban plants or reducing transportation costs. However, the former strategy does not help the central city policymaker achieve the objective of improving the economic conditions of central city residents if it results in employed residents relocating in the suburbs.

For local policymakers, incentives that increase minority business formation in central cities may be successful in creating jobs. Our study would suggest that, even though the U.S. manufacturing sector provides fewer jobs overall, minority firms have identified profitable niches within the industry and are among those minority entrepreneurs providing the largest number of jobs. Identifying the types of incentives that may be more important to these firms could be a particularly fruitful exercise, at least for some cities. Land assembly might be a necessary incentive. However, given the new technology used in many manufacturing plants, another incentive could very well be higher expenditures on "social" services, such as education and training, which Porter feels have received a disproportionate share of government resources.

NOTES

1. The authors are Director of Research Programs and Research Associate, respectively, at the Joint Center for Political and Economic Studies. The findings reported here are based on research supported by the Ford Foundation, grant #930-0798. The views expressed here are those of the authors and not necessarily those of the Ford Foundation, the Joint Center's Board of Governors or any of its sponsors.

2. Timothy Bates, "Do Black-Owned Businesses Employ Minority Workers? New Evidence," *Review of Black Political Economy* 16 (Spring 1988).

3. Two variables allow us to determine neighborhood characteristics: responses to a survey question about location—"central city," "suburban," etc., and a Joint Center-created file that matches zip code to selected neighborhood characteristics taken from the Census of Population and Housing; 1990 (Summary Tape file 3 on CD-ROM).

4. In 1987, over 50 percent of all minority-owned firms included in the Census Bureau *Survey of Minority-Owned Businesses* were in these four states. In 1992, the same four states included 30 percent of all black-owned businesses. (At the time this article was written, the Census Bureau had not released data for other minority-owned businesses.)

5. The overall response rate for the minority firms, which are the focus of this discussion, was 21.9 percent, for a total of 669 minority respondents.

6. A recent study by the Joint Center indicates that non-Hispanic blacks are over four times as likely as whites to depend on public transportation for the worktrip. Hispanics were somewhat less dependent, being slightly less than three times as likely as whites to use public transit to get to their jobs. Joint Center for Political and Economic Studies, *The Trip to Work: A Demographic Profile of Public Transit Users*, A Report to the Federal Transit Administration under Cooperative Agreement No. DC-26-6020, May 1995.

7. Porter's other measure is one million dollars or more in sales. In our sample the two measures were highly correlated.

8. This size difference was statistically significant at the 99 percent confidence level.

Part II:
Responses from
Community Service Providers

15

OVERVIEW OF THE INITIATIVE FOR A COMPETITIVE INNER CITY

Initiative for a Competitive Inner City

The mission of the Initiative for a Competitive Inner City is to foster healthy economies in America's inner cities that create jobs and economic opportunity for local residents.

BACKGROUND

The Initiative for a Competitive Inner City is a national, nonprofit corporation founded in June 1994, after several years of research on the economic distress of America's inner cities. Harvard Business School Professor Michael E. Porter became convinced that the current approaches were not working, and that a fresh look at inner-city economic development using some of his ideas on strategy and competitiveness might prove fruitful. Utilizing the forces of the marketplace and the resources of the private sector, he believed there had to be a way to restore the economic health of our inner cities and create jobs and economic opportunity for residents. Just as important was the need to develop the perception of America's inner cities as places of economic opportunity and vitality. The negative perception today divides us as a nation, impedes the growth of inner-city communities, and severely limits the opportunities for the most disadvantaged among us to become self-sufficient. The inner city has been overlooked as a place with genuine economic opportunities.

Extensive research has been conducted on this issue, examining the economies of nine inner cities, including Atlanta, Baltimore, Boston, Chicago, Los Angeles, New York City, Newark, Oakland, and Washington, D.C. This research led to a new model for thinking about inner-city economic development, summarized in the *Harvard Business Review* article "The Competitive Advantages of the Inner City." The vast majority of past and current efforts to revitalize inner cities take a social perspective, focused on areas such as housing, health care, crime and education. However, an economic strategy is *also* a necessity if jobs accessible to inner-city residents are to be created that will allow the social investments to pay off. The desire to reform welfare only raises the sense of urgency.

A sustainable economic model for inner cities must be based on genuine profit, not artificial subsidies and mandates. It must focus on the position of the inner-city economy in the regional economy rather than treat inner cities as separate. Instead of starting with the premise that inner cities are devoid of business and cannot compete, the new model starts with the premise that inner cities must compete. Otherwise, economic activity there will not be sustainable. The research suggests that inner cities *can* compete, drawing on potential competitive advantages of inner cities such as a prime location for logistically sensitive businesses and the presence of large, unmet local demand. Economic development efforts should build on these advantages, and concentrate on improving the inner city as a place to do business. There are numerous government and business policy implications that flow from this overall framework.

The research suggests, however, that simply changing government policy will not be sufficient. Professor Porter came to believe that it would also be necessary to *engage the private sector* in new approaches to addressing the inner city. The notion that government and non-profits can, or should, drive economic development in inner cities is, in our view, open to serious question. Sustained economic development in our country has always come from the private sector driven by the pursuit of profit. There is no evidence that this should be different for America's inner cities.

The ICIC model represents a significant new approach to inner-city business development. The ICIC model has generated significant response from both the private and public sectors and is rapidly being disseminated throughout the country. This way of framing the problem seems to have hit a responsive chord, and there is increasing evidence that it can reshape the national debate and help transform the approach in dealing with the distressed areas of this country. We believe that this model, which is driven by the forces of the private marketplace, can be applied in all of America's inner cities.

THE INITIATIVE FOR A COMPETITIVE INNER CITY

The Initiative was founded, first, to continue the research and communication process on inner-city business development. Its focus on inner-city economies and inner-city businesses remains, and there is much more to be learned about inner-city businesses, and much knowledge and best practices to be disseminated. For example, the Initiative has developed a methodology for studying a city, understanding its economic potential, and developing action recommendations. This methodology is being continually enhanced and disseminated.

More importantly, however, we believed that the formation of an organization with strong credentials in the business community was needed to develop and participate in the implementation of a series of private-sector initiatives focused on inner cities around the country. A central concept of the Initiative is to connect the inner-city economy with the surrounding economy in order to upgrade the quality and capability of inner-city based companies. This occurs through the creation and strengthening of business-to-business relationships within the inner city, involving not only companies but leading business schools, professional service firms, and financial service providers.

Through our research, we have discovered that there are hundreds and even thousands of existing companies of some scale in inner cities ($1 million or more in annual revenues and fifteen or more employees, the majority of whom must be inner-city residents). Many of these companies have significant growth potential. There are also many other potential *new* businesses of scale, in areas such as retailing and rapid-response service delivery, that could benefit from an inner-city location.

The Initiative's initial goal is to mobilize the private sector in business-to-business efforts to enhance the growth of the existing companies; these existing companies are the Initiative's core clients, because they offer the greatest potential for near-term job creation. Over time, we also hope to stimulate new business formation through partnerships with franchisers and other means. Other programs with similar aims, such as they exist, focus primarily on microenterprises and small neighborhood retailers.

The Initiative addresses the economic distress of America's inner cities with a two-pronged strategy: 1) research and communication to extend our ideas and recommendations on inner-city business development and disseminate them widely to the important constituencies; and 2) programs that put ICIC's ideas into practice via the private sector.

RESEARCH AND COMMUNICATION

Providing information and inspiration to others is perhaps the Initiative's most leveraged activity. Lasting change will happen only as new ways of thinking are adopted by many individuals and organizations from every relevant sector on a national basis. Research and communication will continue as one of the Initiative's most important functions in order to reshape the debate about inner-city economic development, transform the approach that cities are taking to address their distressed communities, and change behavior in the private sector.

The Initiative's research has led to wide-ranging recommendations about business practice as well as inner-city economic development efforts. We are developing a standard template of how to study the economy of an inner city and develop action recommendations. This template will be made available to cities across the country. ICIC is unique in its research focus on inner-city development; we know of no other organization devoting primary attention to this critical issue.

The Initiative's research will be shared with businesses, policymakers, scholars and leaders of programs and institutions affecting inner-city economic development across the country. The Initiative's learning will be shared through articles, editorials, speeches, seminars and events.

Finally, the Initiative plans to establish a training and educational component, offering courses in inner-city economic development. These training programs would be made available to inner-city entrepreneurs, businesses interested in doing business there, community organizers, public officials, academics, foundations and community leaders. Training and education can potentially provide a source of ongoing fee income to the Initiative.

PROGRAMS: PUTTING THE NEW MODEL INTO PRACTICE

To achieve its mission, the Initiative has developed four programs: *Inner City Advisors,* the *National Business School Network,* the *Corporate Partners Network* and the *Equity Capital Network.* Each program can stand alone, but the four programs are mutually reinforcing.

Each of these programs is aimed at bringing the resources together with entrepreneurs in inner cities for the purpose of business expansion. Each of the programs involves a set of unique relationships which have never been made available to America's inner cities. We believe that bringing new resources to inner-city businesses, and bringing new businesses to inner cities, can transform the economics there as well as change attitudes about the inner city as a viable place to live, work and do business. This potential to change perceptions is among the most powerful benefits of the Initiative.

Inner City Advisors

Inner City Advisors is a small management advisory organization established in each participating city, staffed with a few highly sophisticated, experienced managers called managing directors. The strategy of the program is to bring private sector resources to inner-city businesses.

The managing directors provide some management assistance directly, but their principal role is to act as a market maker. Inner City Advisors coordinate access to the Initiative's other programs including the *National Business School Network,* the *Corporate Partners Network* and (eventually) the *Equity Capital Network.* Managing directors are responsible for identifying, qualifying and prioritizing inner city-based companies with the greatest promise, and building relationships with them. They then connect inner-city entrepreneurs with field study teams from local business schools *(Business School Network)*, access assistance and resources from regional companies *(Corporate Partners Network)* and assist in approaching capital providers *(The Equity Capital Network).*

Requests from cities to bring the Advisors model to their communities far exceeded our ability to respond. To date we have established pilot *Inner City Advisors* programs in Boston, Oakland and Baltimore. Our initial part-time efforts in Boston, with about fifteen clients, have yielded heartening results. We have recently hired full-time managing directors in each of these three cities and have begun developmental and research efforts in Atlanta and Kansas City that will likely lead to the establishment of a formal program within the year. Interest has also been expressed from such cities as Newark, New York, Chicago, Philadelphia, Pittsburgh and Dallas, just to name a few. A strategy for expansion to these cities, including the raising of the resources required, is under development.

National Business School Network

The *National Business School Network* aims to motivate and assist graduate business schools around the country to develop field-based courses to work with inner-city companies. Such courses provide analytical resources to companies and help draw them into corporate networks, while dramatically changing the perceptions of the inner city among faculty and students who will be tomorrow's corporate leaders.

There were almost no such efforts three years ago, but today there are established or emerging programs at such schools as Harvard, Babson,

MIT, Yale, Columbia, Vanderbilt, and numerous others. The Initiative champions such programs and provides assistance in designing and launching them. We hope that with greater resources the Initiative can also operate an ongoing network among the schools which would involve, among other things, an annual conference, assistance with fundraising, computer-based information sharing, and other services. As with *Inner City Advisors,* the demand for our services far exceeds our ability to deliver. A recent grant from Bankers Trust will enable us to expand this program.

Corporate Partners Network

The private sector can provide crucial resources to inner-city economies, while the inner city represents a major unmet business opportunity for the private sector. The *Corporate Partners Network* establishes a framework for business-to-business partnerships between regional corporations and inner-city businesses. Corporate Partners come from regional companies, financial institutions, and accounting, consulting and law firms. *Inner City Advisor* managing directors identify the needs of inner-city clients and match them with Partners, who bring skills, technology, training, capital, purchasing relationships and other benefits to assist business expansion and job creation.

The Initiative creates a new model of corporate philanthropy that goes well beyond donating money to social services. It takes advantage of corporations giving what they do best, which is their business knowledge, contacts and an ongoing business relationship. Through Corporate Partners, inner-city companies gain expertise in improving their strategic plans, improving operating practices, upgrading management, accessing capital, improving information systems, and professionalizing financial management and organizational structure. Corporate Partners also provide links between inner-city companies to trade groups and industry associations.

While inner-city companies benefit from this relationship, Corporate Partners also can create and expand business activity for themselves through opportunities for franchising and retailing, treating the inner city as a distinct market, tailoring their operating practices and developing strong ties with the local communities. They can establish new relationships with the inner-city companies as supplier, preferred customer and partner in new ventures. They can also develop new inner-city borrowers. Participation in the *Corporate Partners Network* represents a marketing opportunity with an underserved community as well as locally and nationally. There is also value to the Corporate Partners in expanding business relationships with other members of the *Network.*

The *Corporate Partners Network* is being formalized and expanded. Results from the pilot effort in Boston have been very encouraging. The Vault, a group of the most senior private sector leaders in Boston, has agreed to embrace the Initiative as a flagship program and become our partner. An expanding group of partners is providing services. Goodwin, Procter & Hoar has provided legal expertise enabling two inner-city clients to finalize expansion and renovation plans, Lotus Development Corporation has offered access to its management training programs to our clients and Coopers & Lybrand has offered financial and management expertise to our Boston clients. The Boston Consulting Group has recently completed a significant study of the inner-city economy that will be shared with Boston's leadership, and J. Robert Scott, the Boston-based international executive search firm, is conducting several searches. Several Corporate Partners have begun working with inner-city clients in Oakland and Baltimore.

While Corporate Partners have so far been involved in a single city, several have the potential to become involved in a number of cities or even nationally. The Initiative will pursue vigorously the expansion of the *Corporate Partners Network,* consisting of both single city and national Partners. We believe this new type of corporate philanthropy will set an example that has the potential to expand far beyond the Initiative itself.

The Equity Capital Network

The *Equity Capital Network* is still in development. The aim is to design and capitalize one or more for-profit equity capital vehicles focused exclusively on funding inner-city based companies around the country. We have found the greatest constraint in inner cities is equity capital, not debt, and that existing venture capital sources overlook the inner city and are not well structured for the types of businesses most likely to be located there. We have been working on the design of three prototypes—a targeted Equity Fund, a tailored Angel Network, and a Business Development Competition which would be highly publicized and aimed at increasing the supply of entrepreneurial inner-city companies.

There is one private equity fund in the Midwest that has successfully funded inner-city companies, and we are working with its principals as well as with many other sophisticated investors to develop our model. One of our convictions is that our ability to leverage the presence of *Inner City Advisors, Corporate Partners* and *Business Schools* to assist portfolio companies will set a new fund apart from others.

Organization

The Initiative is currently a nonprofit organization that aims to migrate toward self-sufficiency through establishing fee relationships with capital providers, providing training to public, nonprofit and community leaders, and generating other sources of fee income. Currently the senior management of the Initiative consists of two full-time executive directors, who are MBA graduates, and a director of development. The team all have significant work experience and possess strong leadership capabilities.

A small support staff is also in place. Three of the four currently budgeted managing directors of the *Advisors* have been hired, and we are interviewing for the fourth position. These positions are financed locally in Boston, Baltimore and Oakland. In addition, the Initiative has been fortunate to benefit from many individuals and organizations who have worked part-time on various parts of our agenda as well as numerous students and volunteers involved in projects.

This small organization is overwhelmed for encouraging reasons. There is enormous interest and demand for information about our research and our programs, and an insatiable appetite for speeches, interviews, advice and assistance in bringing our programs to new cities. Such cities as Atlanta, Cleveland, Philadelphia, Denver and Miami have been gearing up, and local champions are anxious to establish the ICIC model in their community. Many more cities have called, but we have lacked time to develop them.

At this stage, the Initiative needs an infusion of patient capital, new staff, board leadership, and outside partners to allow us to develop the national organization to meet these demands. We are searching for a full-time director of research and communication, and ultimately a research associate, to coordinate the writing of more articles and position papers and to deal with the press and the many interested groups across the country. We are also searching for a full-time director of the *National Business School Network* to do missionary work in top business schools and enhance the value we can deliver to already participating schools. We also need to hire and develop one or more senior people, who could take responsibility for initiating and supervising the Initiative's programs in additional cities. Finally, we need senior CEO-level leadership, who could act as chairs to complement Professor Porter's personal efforts. (Professor Porter is spending more than 20 percent of his time on the Initiative.) It is our intention to keep the central organization small because of the huge leverage we can get by enlisting volunteers, getting corporate participation and stimulating self-financing efforts.

The Initiative is aggressively expanding its Board of Directors. Since its inception the Initiative has been governed by a small Board, but recognizes the necessity of enhancing and formalizing the role of the Board. National leaders are being invited to join the Board from corporations, professional service firms, foundations, academia and organizations involved in inner-city development. This Board will ensure the mission of the Initiative is achieved by assisting in establishing policies and programs, providing management oversight and providing assistance in fundraising. The Board will also help communicate the ICIC model to business and community leaders across the country.

Local advisory boards are established in each participating city and will be comprised of local leaders who represent similar constituencies. These local boards will also include clients of the Initiative and public sector representatives.

Funding

To date, the Initiative has raised about $1 million at the national and local levels. Raising money for city-dedicated efforts has proven easier than financing the national organization. Yet the national organization is what codifies and disseminates the ideas, designs and manages the programs and mobilizes organizations and communities.

Funding for the central organization has come from Professor Porter, a cadre of CEOs, and a few pioneering companies, such as Textron, Lotus, Bankers Trust and Citicorp, and recently, our first large grant from a major foundation, the Kauffman Foundation. What we need at this stage is a more substantial, organized, and longer-term effort to raise $500,000 to $750,000 per year for the next two or three years to allow us to scale up the effort. It is critical to respond to the interests from the many cities in a timely fashion before the opportunity is lost. With time, we are confident that support from major foundations will be forthcoming, as will fee income.

In addition to funding the Initiative itself, we will be seeking capital for the *Equity Capital Network* vehicles as they are developed. The

Business Development Competition will require only $150,000–200,000 annually for expenses and prizes. An Equity Fund would require from a few million to tens of millions of dollars, depending on the number of cities in which it will operate.

Summary

The Initiative for a Competitive Inner City has made considerable progress during the past two years in disseminating a new model of inner-city competitive advantages and opportunities. It has also implemented several programs and established pilot rollouts in three cities, while reaching the advanced stages of adding two additional cities. The Initiative is at a critical stage of development, because the demands for its services from many cities, corporations and business schools are far greater than can be currently met.

Over the next five years the Initiative plans to expand its research and communication efforts and bring its model of inner-city economic development to many more cities. This will require significant fundraising and a growing organizational sophistication and maturity. It will also require ongoing analysis and review of ICIC's approach to ensure it is achieving its mission *to foster healthy economies in America's inner cities that create jobs and economic opportunity for local residents.* During the next five years, we are certain to learn much more about ways to improve the economic health of inner cities. This learning will undoubtedly result in new approaches, programs and partnerships. The underlying mission of the Initiative for a Competitive Inner City, however, will remain constant.

16

MAKING COMPARATIVE ADVANTAGE WORK FOR ECONOMIC OPPORTUNITY

William Schweke, Corporation for Enterprise Development*

Michael Porter's "The Competitive Advantage of the Inner City" is one of the most important articles in the fields of economic and community development authored in the last ten years. All development policymakers and professionals should look closely at the piece (as well as the longer paper that it is drawn from), reflect on its message and decide how best to respond to its many recommendations.

In summary, I believe that the article provides a needed correction to the prevailing emphases in the field of economic and community development. But it is not a complete and holistic framework for inner-city development. It stresses the significance of identifying and sustaining comparative advantage, but it insufficiently addresses the challenge of ensuring that investments in clusters, economic sectors, and anchors (e.g., ports, airports, downtowns) work for greater economic empowerment and opportunity.

This response to Porter's work is organized into three main sections: (1) where we agree; (2) where we differ; and (3) where we go from here.

WHERE WE AGREE

Michael Porter of Harvard University has authored a provocative report and magazine article that contends that "a sustained economic base in inner cities will only come about through private, for-profit initiatives and investment based on economic self-interest and true competitive advantages, not through artificial inducements, charity, or government mandates."

A central element in Porter's model is that "building viable businesses must be based on an understanding of an economic value of an inner-city location." Although the inner city is fraught with disadvantages, "there are excellent opportunities to build profitable businesses . . . by capitalizing on the competitive advantages it offers such as location, demand conditions, linkages to regional clusters, and human resources." Porter concludes by outlining the steps business, government, and the nonprofit sector must take to develop a community strategy that will create the market conditions to attract economic investment and activity to the inner city.

There is tremendous value in Porter's critique, policy framework, and specific recommendations. In the rest of this section, I will note several of his work's strengths.

Recognition of the "Economic Problem"

While recognizing that there is no single, simplistic answer to the problems facing inner-city areas and their residents, the best starting place is the one that Porter focuses on: the problem of jobs. He recognizes that the essential prerequisite for generating more, and better, employment opportunities is the creation of a sustainable, export-oriented, economic base.

A Sense of Importance

Porter's work is animated by an appropriate sense of urgency. Many residents of these cities are suffering—the majority of the poor live in metro areas.

Close to one-third of the nation's population still resides in central cities. We should care about those living there—their job opportunities, their quality of life and their future.

These areas still perform crucial social and economic functions, and the futures of cities and suburbs are closely tied. Crime and pollution can spill over urban boundaries. Inadequate school systems will not produce the competent workers required by suburban business owners, wherever they operate.

Indeed, the basic message underlying his logic, analysis, and recommendations is simple. You either pay now or pay more later. Escaping to suburbia is no solution. The costs and problems will head there as jobs continue to move from the central core and inner-ring suburbs begin to look like inner-city ghettos. Thus, there is a sound "business" reason for aiding individuals and communities in battling poverty and decline: it can improve economic prospects for all areas, not just low-income neighborhoods, and build the necessary foundations, such as a well-educated workforce, for tomorrow's economy.

The Need for New Directions

Porter also asks tough questions about the effectiveness of past approaches. Obviously, our society has spent a lot on past anti-poverty efforts. And if they had worked, wouldn't our problems be less, rather than more? What makes us think that doing more of the same would not just accomplish more of the same. And what makes us think that today's "program flavor of the month" is any more likely to revitalize cities and combat urban poverty than our past failed attempts?

Not only must we explore new approaches, we must also be much more cautious in our claims about what is possible and what is not (especially in the short-run). We must be much more frugal in our use of public resources. Our efforts to promote urban revitalization and to combat urban poverty must be more effective in terms of both impact and costs. In short, our initiatives must, indeed, pass much tougher tests if the citizenry is to support them. And this is the daunting policy design, implementation, and citizen education challenge facing all urban revitalization advocates.

Many of Porter's recommendations and critiques are on-the-mark. Although he does not adopt a "laissez-faire" approach to urban revitalization, he is very aware of countless ways that "government failure," not just "market failure" weakens the economic engines of central cities. He, appropriately, points out the limits of community-based organizations in playing more direct roles in business ownership and direct entrepreneurial ventures. For example, Porter admits that CBOs have "expertise in the development and implementation of housing and social programs. CBOs, however, lack the skills, experience, or appropriate incentives to develop, fund, or operate businesses. Recently, there has been a movement among CBOs to become directly involved in business development. While there have been a few isolated and qualified successes, our research suggests that this is a misdirected strategy and a poor use of government and community resources." Instead, they

> Should work to change community and workforce attitudes, help improve public services, and act as a liaison with residents to quell unfounded opposition to new businesses . . . CBOs can also leverage

their expertise in real estate and act as a catalyst to facilitate environmental cleanup and development of commercial and industrial property . . . CBOs can also play an active role in screening and referring employees to local businesses.[1]

However, in these remarks Porter tends to treat community-based development organizations as a "monolith" and misses the tremendous variety of practice and organization. Many of these groups already do what he suggests. Others have embarked on other successful and unsuccessful approaches that he does not discuss.

Porter contrasts his model, based on harnessing the unique economic advantages of the inner city, against a backdrop of six marginally successful or failed socially oriented models that have dominated past efforts to revitalize the inner city. In doing so, he criticizes a great deal of past CBO practice. His criticisms are as follows:

1. *The Real Estate Model* sees the development of real estate projects in the inner city as driving economic development. *Flaw in the model*: Real estate projects are the outcome, not the driver, of economic development.

2. *The Location Incentive Model* uses financial inducements to attract industry to the inner city. *Flaw in the model*: Companies will stay for only as long as they receive subsidies.

3. *The Social Conscience/Philanthropy Model* is based on exhorting firms and individuals to support the inner-city economy out of good will. *Flaw in the model*: Charitable giving cannot be guaranteed to last indefinitely and creates a system of dependency.

4. *The Mandate Model* is based on the use of set-asides and other minority preferences to foster inner-city development. *Flaw in the model*: Although mandates and preferences are necessary to eliminate bias and to jump-start minority companies, preferences can be abused, and companies that grow up with mandates and preferences rarely move beyond them.

5. *The Community Entrepreneurship Model* envisions the creation of many small businesses by inner-city residents as the driver of economic development. *Flaw in the model*: As a sole strategy for job creation, microenterprises are too small to create the large number of well-paying jobs or to achieve the quality or cost to compete on a regional or national level.

6. *The Migration Model* assumes the failure of the mentioned models and posits that jobs will never be created in sufficient numbers in the inner city but are plentiful in the suburbs. Therefore, transportation mechanisms are essential to connect inner-city residents to suburban jobs. *Flaw in the model*: Connecting inner-city residents to suburban jobs can be only part of the solution. Inner-city residents are at extreme disadvantage in competing for suburban jobs as a result of poor information about employment opportunities and their lack of informal ties to employers in the suburbs.

Although these criticisms over-simplify some of the issues involved and overlook a number of the virtues of these approaches, Porter's critique also helps to clarify some of the limits of these policy "workhorses."

Identifying and Sustaining Comparative Advantage

Porter's starting point is the need to promote a self-sustaining development dynamic in our troubled inner cities. He emphasizes, appropriately, that this process of wealth generation must be built on real comparative advantage—building competitive businesses by capitalizing on existing strengths, new trends of change, knowledge of competitors, and special market niches.

I would contend that four questions should drive most development efforts. They are: What policy directions and actions should we take to keep our business climate healthy as locations outside the city become increasingly accessible and available? What partnerships and infrastructure should we emphasize to ensure sustainable regional growth? What strategies and investments will keep the city competitive with other cities (both national and global) into the next century? And what roles could inner-city commercial and industrial districts and neighborhoods play in this overarching strategy?

The typical recipes for city (and regional) development that Porter touches on hold considerable promise:

- Develop a custom-fit strategic plan—the development agenda must be guided by a thoughtful and practical plan, which is feasible in economic, political and managerial terms.
- Start with location, such as access to resources and inputs, prox-

imity to markets, the role of corridors and ports, clusters of firms, etc.

- Build off "anchors," such as downtowns, convention centers, and universities, as well as focus on "traffic."
- Look for "complementarity" among local economies in a region (e.g., manufacturing center, tourism center, education center, etc.) and develop ways to make the whole greater than the sum of the parts.
- Find clusters of related or similar, but profitable, firms and encourage their growth.
- Build from you've got (e.g., can existing firms be expanded and modernized? What are the opportunities for forward and backward linkages?)
- Audit your development "building blocks"—education, infrastructure, amenities, financial capital sources—and see if anything can be responsibly done.
- Lower your regulatory costs and administrative hassles for businesses, without undermining the necessary purposes of these regulations.
- Improve city services that significantly affect businesses.
- Assist with land assembly problems for companies that wish to expand, start up, or relocate to your community.

Thus, to succeed at either combating poverty or increasing local business viability, city economies must be positioned to win in the marketplace, and local development professionals in the public, private and nonprofit sectors should heed many of these suggestions. In addition, the customized development action plan must seek to build development institutions and programs that are "sustainable." Federal, state, county, local, private sector, and foundation investments must build lasting partnerships that work for the long haul. (Economic development is an evolutionary and incremental process and not just a matter of doing deals.)

WHERE WE DIFFER

Despite the wisdom of much of Michael Porter's work on this subject, there are some errors of judgment, of emphasis and of omission, that should be pointed out. At first look, Porter's approach appears to provide a coherent theory of action that potentially ties all the actors together, but there are a number of missing pieces. To start, it does not go far enough in spelling out the role of the public and nonprofit sectors. Instead, his private sector orientation tends to sound like a new "panacea," rather than a very significant piece of the puzzle. Second, its analysis is based on a limited history of the field. More has been tried, both successfully and unsuccessfully, than Porter's article suggests, and we must draw additional lessons from this multidecade experience with urban revitalization and complementary social and educational investments. Third, his critique of traditional approaches is somewhat oversimplified and, occasionally, there is more polemical heat, rather than light. Lastly, his work tends to leave out some important issues: the reinvent government agenda, the limits of trickledown development approaches, the role of governance in urban decline, the challenges of working in today's fiscal environment, the importance of investing in good jobs and good businesses (not just any jobs and any businesses), and the continued value of pursuing conflict as well as collaborative approaches to development.

The "Silver Bullet"

There are no "silver bullets" or 100 percent solutions. Although Porter's argument does not imply that he regards his approach as a new panacea, it is being taken as one. Likewise, rather than using his ideas as a means of complementing what was right about earlier antipoverty and urban revitalization efforts, it could be regarded as a substitute. The article, at times, seems to suggest that it is the solution, rather than an important *piece* of the solution.

The entire economic and community development field is plagued by too many false debates and choices—business attraction versus community development, social versus economic interventions, investing in people as opposed to investing in places, competitiveness versus opportunity strategies, and so forth. All are important. All have their place. Some will be more relevant depending on circumstances. Indeed, "best practices" are whatever works in a given context. And this is why the good, hard-headed strategic planning that Porter calls for is so desperately needed in every community.

The Limited History

Although the article and the longer paper reflected an intelligent mind that has done some homework at looking at the problems and opportunities facing inner-city development today, it is based a lot on fieldwork in the Boston area and a few other communities. Therefore, it does not fully appreciate the rich history of success and failure of urban revitalization during the last twenty-plus years. Many of the solutions that Porter advocates have been tried, at least in part. We need to study more closely these efforts, ranging from urban renewal to model cities, from UDAGs to CDBG, from Carter's urban policy to Reagan's benign neglect, from enterprise zones to CDCs. This history does not profoundly change many of Porter's recommendations, but they put them into a larger context, lower our expectations some about their potential benefits, underscore the political and managerial difficulties of running big city service delivery, highlight the challenges provided by both professional and financial resource constraints in our most troubled cities, underscore the largely negative impacts of class and race on urban policy and city spatial structure, and emphasize the importance of social investments.

Watch Out for "Strawmen"

Porter's account of the flaws in traditional approaches are a bit "one-sided," and over-simplified.

- *Real Estate.* Although he is right in noting that real estate is not the real driver, he misses the importance of how real estate investment can be linked to business development. It can open up opportunities for local entrepreneurship, as it also improves amenities. It can reduce a firm's operating costs, lower investment risks, create "anchors" for leveraging additional investment and business development, and expand markets by attracting or holding onto middle class residents. It may have been overemphasized in the past, but it is a powerful engine for development and for changing the atmosphere of an entire community.
- *Location Incentives.* Porter rightly emphasizes that businesses should choose locations principally on their real comparative advantages and that subsidy approaches will keep such companies around only as long as the incentives last. There is also another aspect of this issue that I will refer to as the "arms race" regarding incentives for new and old employers to relocate or stay put. This inflationary spiral of subsidy dollars is wasting scarce public resources. Finding a way to slow down this competition and make these tax incentives and governmental investments more publicly accountable and fiscally responsible are critical challenges facing

all cites across America. In addition, troubled central cities also face even tougher business incentive dilemmas. These areas often possess locational disadvantages as compared to their more well-heeled competitors. Their tax bases are smaller, and social service demands are higher. Yet, because of underutilized infrastructure, many business incentives meet a cost-benefit test more easily than fast-growing suburban regions. How might these tough issues be wrestled with?

- *Social Conscience/Philanthropy.* Foundation and corporate responsibility dollars are still very important. If wisely invested in more high-leverage approaches, these dollars help cover costs that other traditional private sector funds would never touch. Porter argues that corporate leadership and funding should target those development initiatives and social investments that are most related to business bottomlines. This is a point well taken if we want to develop more sustainable development partnerships and tap business expertise where it is most helpful. Many communities are also discovering that corporations are increasingly mobile and are loosening their ties and loyalties to the communities in which they do business and as a result decreasing their level of public involvement. Fewer middle-managers either spend enough time to know an area or have the latitude and encouragement from headquarters to really get involved in civic business. In many cities, this is creating new barriers to forging necessary strategic alliances for urban revitalization and reform.
- *Mandate.* Many programs have been hindered by their terrible technical assistance and their lack of attention to building networks and personal relationships between white and minority entrepreneurs. Yet, there are a number of good examples of how "affirmative action" efforts have provided financing, mentoring, and technical assistance, thereby strengthening local minority businesses.
- *Community Entrepreneurship.* Obviously, microenterprise is not going to create enough good jobs to have a lasting effect on poverty in the surrounding community. But such programs are very important in creating role models for local communities to copy and in enhancing the human capital and workplace skills of the microentrepreneurs.
- *Migration.* Porter is right about the difficulties that inner-city residents face in accessing jobs in the suburbs. But, given the rate

of job creation in these areas, providing new transportation options, information about job opportunities, appropriate education and training services, participant and employer recruitment must be tackled. And there are numerous successful models, like Project Quest in San Antonio, that point to how these problems might be effectively addressed.

An "Imbalanced" Approach

Porter's advocacy of the importance of creating the conditions for profitable inner-city businesses is irrefutable. He may be justified in pushing hard on his points in order to make sure that the concerns of businesses are really addressed and that appropriate policy reforms are not held back by corrupt politicians, poorly run governmental bureaucracies, and noisy political constituencies.

But we need to be guided by a more holistic concept of the development process and practice than is implied in some of Porter's analysis and strategy. Development is much more than location incentives and business support: it must include educational and social services, and other means of engaging and enhancing underused human assets to address national and global competition.

Development means more than what the local firm and the area chamber of commerce do to enhance the business climate. Development is increasingly "everybody's business," ranging from the school district to the port authority.

In many respects, his article recognizes that each of the players—governmental, private sector, and nonprofits—have important roles to play and that each are necessary to a successful effort. But there is a tendency in Porter's article to suggest that the private sector is "the" savior and not just an extremely critical partner.

Indeed, sorting out the respective roles is as important as creating a more profitable environment for the private sector. Unless we get the "how" of development right, the "what" will never succeed.

Reinvent Government

This is a related theme with which Porter sympathizes, but is underdeveloped in his article. He probably agrees with the proposition that the concept of government-as-usual is bankrupt. New attention to organizing development program delivery for greater quality and impact is essential (also sorting out the appropriate actors—sometimes it's the public, but other times it's the private or nonprofit sectors). Development initiatives, like all other areas of government, must meet higher standards of accountability, for cost-effectiveness, and for customer-friendliness. And in most cases, they must seek to do "more" with "less." Those that deny these trends, that do not innovate and that do little to either educate constituencies and political leadership about the rationale and benefits of their programs will only face inevitable budget cuts and possible elimination. "Reinvent government" is not a fad: it is now an imperative, for both political and management reasons, and a standard operating procedure.

Furthermore, Porter's agenda will not succeed unless Americans truly embrace the idea that neither a smaller government nor a bigger one will work unless we really deal with what Brookings' Center for Public Management calls the administrative "fine print." Just denouncing governmental stupidities or arguing that the public sector's only role is to "get out of the way" does not help develop systems that can effectively deliver direct services or professionally oversee their contracting-out.

The Limits of Trickledown

Without a strong economy, exporting goods and services beyond its boundaries, inner cities are doomed. Likewise, there is a strong connection between poverty and economic growth. In a growing economy, there is steadier employment and less joblessness, higher wages and more money accruing to all income classes. These gains will accrue to the poor and lift some of them out of poverty.

But the normal process of growth does not help all individuals equally. A rising tide does not lift all boats: many of the poor are not in the workforce and others are stuck in dead-end jobs where they are unlikely to benefit from economic growth.

If mainstream programs like Porter's are going to provide benefits to more of the economically disadvantaged, they must be complemented with more effective social investments and improved job brokering initiatives.

In my view, social and economic progress are inextricably linked. As Porter contends, it is becoming increasingly clear that we cannot solve social problems like crime, drug abuse, family breakup, malnutrition, and homelessness without solving the economic problems that contribute to them. But the converse is also true: economic progress depends on social progress. Without serious and efficient investments in developmental childcare, early education, a better school-to-work transition, dropout prevention, and adult retraining, a large proportion of today's and tomorrow's workforce will be unable to contribute to the economy.

There is a danger posed by an over-reliance on export-based approaches, which, at times, Porter's work seems to extol. Such approaches can create "gentrified islands" of business vitality that do not expand opportunities to the city's poorer residents. Furthermore, without successful efforts in addressing crime, affordable housing, and education, middle class and young families will continue to flee these areas. (Research has confirmed that such population shifts are one of the strongest correlates of city decline and inviability.)

Is Governance Destiny?

Porter's work also makes too strong a claim for the importance of economic engines in turning around central cities. Many metropolitan areas are imperiled by their lack of coherent governance, planning and service delivery. Although governance may not be "destiny," inappropriate governmental arrangements can make it next to impossible to deal effectively with issues like jobs, poverty, welfare, crime, housing, fiscal viability, transportation, infrastructure, and growth management. For instance, the research and thinking of former Albuquerque mayor David Rusk is very important here. Rusk contends that "elasticity," the ability to expand geographic borders, is the key to success for the modern city. Cities that are free to grow—usually by annexation—and follow the movement of the middle class to the suburbs—are uniquely equipped to encompass these population and employment shifts into their own economic and political base. Those that cannot are doomed to follow in the steps of Detroit, where only 7 percent of the assessed property value of the Detroit metro area now lies within the city limits.

Rusk has even calculated a "point of no return." When a city's population has declined by 20 percent from its peak, when the minority population has topped 30 percent and when per capita income has fallen below 70 percent of that in the suburbs, the city is no longer able to recover on its own. Historically, he says, no city in that category has been able to close the income gap with its suburb by even one percent from one decade to the next. Lastly, Rusk concludes that new economic recruitment and other such development gimmicks will not cure what ails these cities and turn them around—only a fundamental change in governance, along with building more affordable housing in the suburbs (in order to deconcentrate the urban poor), discouraging sprawl development, making increased investments in the maintenance and modernization of existing infrastructure (where it is cost-effective), developing tax base sharing mechanisms, and so forth will cure these cities.

This failure to deal with creating more effective regional actions and structures will diminish the benefits of strategies like Porter's, because they will not mobilize action at the appropriate level, they will not amass the necessary resources, they will not address the "real" economy (which is more regional, than city or neighborhood), and they will not tackle the inextricable connections between increased employment and income disparities and unplanned suburban growth.

True, Porter's research and recommendations do advocate the need to "think and act regionally," but they do so, disconnected from a larger policy debate and the larger demographic, political, and economic trends that are making central cities increasingly enviable as economies and as tax-generating jurisdictions.

Generating Additional Resources

Porter admits there is a need for public investment as part of this comparative advantage approach. Wise expenditures for modem infrastructure, for cleaning up brownfields, and for providing good education and workplace preparation are all mentioned in his writings. But his work does not reflect the new fiscal environment to follow from the new federal budget. All cities and states will face substantial cuts in their development and social services expenditures. And this is the new environment in which urban revitalization policymakers, practitioners, and advocates must shape their strategies.

Cities have been steady losers in terms of fiscal federalism, at least since the Reagan era. The latest federal budget proposals will only cut back resources further. (Many states will be losing close to one-quarter of their combined state taxes and user fees. A state like Maryland will lose close to $6.5 billion during the next seven years.) What many critics of the federal government do not see is that much of the development activities carried on by state and local governments and grassroots nonprofit development organizations are financed with federal dollars. How do inner cities deal with this megaproblem? And how do they do so at a time when many business and taxpayer groups want to cut state and local taxes as well? Furthermore, what should policymakers do to address the fiscal hemorrhage caused by today's business incentive "arms race" where hundreds of billions are being squandered in new tax incentives and customized development packages to attract the latest business "plum?" Implementing Porter's vision will have to take place on this terrain.

As one approach to dealing with these difficulties, I suggest that cities try to "generate" additional resources by tackling the following:

- *Eliminate anti-urban city policies and practices at the federal, state, regional and local levels.* This is a tough order, given the current political climate in Congress. But this approach recognizes that many expenditure, tax and regulatory approaches have powerful, unintended locational biases that hurt inner cities. Removing or lessening these should be the first order of business.

- *Create non-place targeted, pro-urban policies and programs, especially in the education and training fields (education reform, school-to-work, adult literacy and occupation retraining, employment brokering, etc.).* Given the waning political power of central cities, urban advocates should seek to support and establish policies and programs that, although not focused explicitly on urban areas, differentially aid them, because of the needs of their particular populations. (It also allows policymakers to avoid the political challenges of developing programs solely targeted on the poor and minorities.)

- *Create new regional alliances for mounting metro-wide development and employment strategies, for sharing resources, and for planning key transportation and infrastructure investments.* Not all problems can be solved at "home." Instead, today's urban policy should recognize that local economies cross city, town, and county boundaries, and therefore also seek creative solutions in new inter-local and regional alliances. Furthermore, this is probably one of the few practical ways that central cities can attract additional outside resources, as well as explore methods of removing some of the negative effects of jurisdictional fragmentation.

- *Redirect existing city funds to better uses.* Little new resources will be forthcoming to central cities. To cope with this reality and given the complex nature of many urban problems, innovative city leaders will have to break with "government-as-usual" and discover ways to do more—and to do it better—with less. This will mean creating new partnerships with the private and nonprofit sectors, involving "customers" more in program design and delivery, building local capacity, leveraging other development efforts, and linking more creatively social and economic strategies. And high on this agenda is for city and regional policymakers to find a way to slow down "bidding for business" and make incentive programs more strategic, cost-effective, and synergistic (with other development programs).

Since no federal urban policy will be forthcoming, cities with their state and regional government, foundation, and private sector allies will have to create a new "virtual urban policy" from the grassroots up.

INVESTING IN GOOD JOBS AND GOOD BUSINESSES

Porter also lets the business community off the hook. The difficult challenge for advocates for urban revitalization is that the private sector is both the problem and the solution.

For example, the vast majority of the economics community admits that the U.S. economic pie has been sliced much more unevenly during the last decade-plus—family and individual income is becoming more unequal, the gap between educated and less educated workers is growing, and the decline of trade unions and the failure of the government to raise the minimum wage have also increased wage inequality. In addition, the loss of blue collar jobs is not being replaced by alternatives that provide equivalent wages. This changing composition of employment, along with its shift to the suburbs, has especially undermined the fortunes of black males.

The reasons for these changes are complicated and somewhat disputed, but economists Richard Murnane and Frank Levy point out that American companies have responded to today's increased global competition in one of three ways. A minority of companies invested in improving product quality and reducing costs by redesigning production processes and upgrading the skills of the workforce, and in so doing, paying higher wages. More companies introduced new technology, which allowed them to both reduce the number of employees and to replace higher priced labor by relatively low priced labor. By far the most common response, however, was to cut costs while retaining the same technology and work experience organization, to demand wage and benefit concessions from workers, speed up production lines, and to transfer production to lower wage economies. This led to a reduction in semi-skilled jobs but did nothing to change the skill requirements of existing workers.

Thus, how are we to tackle these challenges? How do we encourage more companies to choose the "high road" (higher skills and higher pay)? What advice does Porter's work offer beyond upgrading workforce skills? How do we get more companies to adopt high performance workplaces that deliver real pay, fringe benefits, and employee involvement to their workers? How can productivity gains benefit workers and not just upper management? How might organized labor help create a new "social contract" that fosters increased competitiveness and good jobs? How do we set up a better "pipeline" into such jobs for the economically disadvantaged? How do we help new workers to advance in a time that internal career ladders are being eliminated from many companies? How do we help individuals "job-hop" their way to upward mobility, rather than joining one company and rising in the ranks over time? How do we invest in good jobs and good companies in a world of increasing international competition? How can the new economic functions of today's cities create opportunities for the urban poor and not just urban professionals? Although creating an economic development policy does not allow us to follow a blueprint like an architect's drawing, it should still allow us to target resources on where we get the best return. So, how do we promote more good jobs and good businesses, without substituting governmental judgments for private sector ones?

Tackling these problems successfully will determine whether our evolving city economy and its suburbanizing structure continue to create the conditions of an American apartheid and whether our society has a robust middle class for the poor, the working class, and new immigrants to aspire to.

THE GOOD COP AND THE BAD COP

Michael Porter is also very critical of the conflict-oriented tactics of many community groups vis-à-vis business. Up to a point, his arguments are persuasive. In many cases, community organizations have failed to understand the importance of a viable private sector and what it takes to create the conditions for profitable enterprise. And likewise, they have often placed inordinate hopes in the roles of government and community development corporations as means of job creation.

It should be emphasized as well that development is ultimately transactional and that you cannot create jobs and promote entrepreneurial initiative by solely resorting to dragging the private sector, kicking and screaming, to the table. There must be mutual advantage linking both the business community and the local populace.

In addition, the entire field of "collaborative problem solving," "mediation," "getting to yes" negotiation, and so forth have a lot to teach grassroots community organizations. If we are to lower the transaction costs of doing civic business and reaching a consensus about where we go from here, developing such skills and techniques are very important for all leadership segments, from the poorest to the most affluent.

Yet, the road to urban revitalization is not a "love-in." Just because we should constantly seek more "win-win" solutions does not mean that Alinsky-style, conflict-oriented, community organizing and advocacy has gone the way of the "dodo." Indeed, our experience with Community Reinvestment Act organizing demonstrates the need for both "good cops and bad cops." We need mobilized constituencies and effective advocates for the poor to turn up the heat. But we also need sophisticated deal makers, who know the technicalities of development and who can identify the solutions, policies, and projects that better meet both the citizenry's and the private sector's respective self-interests.

WHERE WE GO FROM HERE

Urban revitalization advocates face some very large obstacles in making good development policy happen in central cities. In addition to the countless barriers posed by their economies, local governments, tax bases, and demographics, we are operating within shrinking political parameters. The body politic is reluctant to approve new or increased taxes. And a growing cynicism among the electorate toward politics and politicians, combined with growing distrust of government, are setting a higher standard of accountability and effectiveness for public sector spending when it comes to dealing with cities' looming social and economic problems.

These new realities suggest the following twin challenges for today's urban reformers: First, how do we progress on creating real working models for urban development policy and practice that foster *viable* city economies and provide increased opportunities for *all* citizens? Second, how do we accomplish this agenda in a time of shrinking resources and dwindling political capital?

This will not be easy. We cannot oversell our programs. We must better leverage scarce government sources. We need to select our most high priority partnerships, projects, and investments. And we must discover new ways to use our social investments to foster entrepreneurship, higher workforce skills, and savings and asset development among the poor.

Lastly, in agreement with Michael Porter, we must speed the development of businesses and industries that will strengthen our comparative advantage in the global economy. Moreover, to emphasize my major point, we must ensure that the people currently being left behind by economic change who are held back by poverty's snares are capable of obtaining and accessing jobs in these new and growing urban firms.

ACKNOWLEDGMENT

* I would like to acknowledge the many conversations with my colleagues at the Corporation for Enterprise Development, which have helped to improve this article. In particular, I would like to single out: Brian Dabson, Bob Friedman, Carl Rist, Puchka Sahay, and Cicero Wilson. Cicero is currently working on an article about Michael Porter's work, and I have drawn liberally from some of his criticisms of Porter's analysis of the weaknesses of traditional models of urban revitalization. And the thinking on comparative advantage was aided by earlier work with Graham Toft on regional strategies in a CFED contract with the state of Oregon. Work on this article was supported by a grant on rethinking urban policy provided by the MacArthur Foundation.

NOTE

1. M. Porter, "The Competitive Advantage of the Inner City." *Harvard Business Review*, May–June 1995, p. 70.

17

ECONOMIC DEVELOPMENT OR SOCIAL DEVELOPMENT? A STRATEGY FOR REBUILDING INNER CITIES

Arnold Graf, Industrial Areas Foundation

Every Monday morning John leaves the rooming house where he rents a room and walks four and a half miles to the newly constructed *Baltimore Sun* plant that was partially subsidized by Baltimore City. Each week he hopes that he will be selected to stuff the newly printed newspapers with the various supplements of the day. Some weeks he works, and some weeks he doesn't. When he gets selected to work he earns $4.25 per hour.

When the Baltimore Orioles are in town, Sam, who lives in a homeless shelter and works for a cleaning contractor, catches a bus to the wholly publicly subsidized Camden Yards baseball park to begin his $4.25 per hour janitorial job. Sam's night is made particularly long because he is required to arrive at the stadium two hours prior to game time. This is so even though he is not paid for these two hours.

Each day, Mary arrives to work at the downtown office building where she has been working for three and a half years. She has been a reliable, trustworthy janitor who has been praised regularly by the tenants whose offices she cleans. Mary, who still earns $4.25 per hour at her job, marvels at the downtown renaissance that has taken place over the past thirty years. This nationally acclaimed renaissance has taken, to date, over two billion dollars of city, state, and federal public dollars.

For the past three years, the BUILD (Baltimoreans United In Leadership Development) organization, an affiliate of the Industrial Areas Foundation and AFSCME (American Federation of State, County, and Municipal Employees Union) have partnered to birth a new organization of low-wage workers—The Solidarity Sponsoring Committee.

For over thirty years cities and states across the country have lifted up the notion of economic development as the answer to their diminished well-being. For cities this has usually meant a strategy built on heavily subsidized renovated downtowns that are aimed at developing the tourist, entertainment, and service industries.

For states this has often meant patching together a quilt of incentives, e.g., tax abatements, low-interest loans, grants, free infrastructure work, etc., in order to outbid competing states for new businesses or to retain current businesses.

The primary justification for this strategy, i.e., pouring billions of public dollars into private sector hands, is done in the name of job creation. As the argument goes, only through this means will we be able to end poverty and rebuild our inner cities.

For this to happen, cities and states need to create a "good business climate" to retain and attract new enterprises. What a "good business climate" usually translates into is low taxes, limited regulations, no unions and/or low wages, public sector financial resources, good quality of life, and a skilled work force. Politics and social programs have failed. We must turn to economics and the free market.

Although the ironies in this argument abound, not the least of which is that the strongest proponents of less government and more free enterprise are the same people who argue for heavy public subsidies to wealthy entrepreneurs, this argument is carrying the day.

This argument has become so widely accepted that you can hear it resonate not only in city halls and state legislatures across the country, but it echoes in the editorial pages in many university urban studies departments, in many African-American churches, and in neighborhood organizations throughout the country.

Economics is in. Politics is out. Somehow, in this way of thinking, economics has become unfastened from politics and has ascended in importance beyond social development.

A common argument heard in many communities today is that political strategies worked for the '60s and '70s, but those strategies have gone as far as they can go. What is needed for the '90s and beyond are economic strategies. The first phase of the civil rights movement was political development; the next phase needs to be economic development.

This article is not an argument against economic development, or the free market system, even though there is in reality no such thing as free markets. Capital formation is essential for the health and well-being of any community. The problem is with who benefits from the fruits of the development and the idea that economics is somehow divorced from politics and more important than social development.

For over fifty years the Industrial Areas Foundation (IAF) has been assisting local communities in developing citizen organizations. These organizations, mainly comprised of local churches, have built their success around the strength and talents of thousands of clergy and lay leaders.

The IAF organizations work on a wide range of issues—from getting cities to replace stop signs to getting states to restructure and refinance their school systems; from pressuring to get a drug den demolished to rebuilding entire neighborhoods with new affordable homes; from reducing exorbitant water rates to figuring out the financing for a new water and sewage system; from pressuring local banks to make more mortgage money available to low-income communities to getting legislation passed that ensures thousands of low-wage workers a living wage.

At the very heart of this is the belief that it is the sector of voluntary associations—family, congregations, and other institutions—that gives the market its meaning, not the other way around.

Economics untied to a meaningful political and social vision winds up feathering very few nests. This too often has been the case as cities and states have developed and implemented their economic development strategies. It has led to a multibillion dollar Marshall Plan for the nation's downtowns, but has done little for the working poor and the inner-city neighborhoods in which they reside.

Unfortunately, as is the case in many other cities, while the two billion dollar-plus public dollars has helped to remake downtown Baltimore into a tourist industry, the neighborhoods of the city have experienced a precipitous decline.

The problem here is that economic development is not synonymous with job and wage development. The tourist industry, while it takes large amounts of public dollars to build and maintain, pays paltry wages.

After thirty years of an economic development strategy that has stressed heavy public investments, thousands of hard-working African-American Baltimoreans have been left in the position of having to work for their poverty.

This became a stark reality to the leadership of the BUILD organization after they completed a series of visits with the growing number of people who were being fed at their soup kitchens. To everyone's surprise, the leadership found that 40 percent of the people they were feeding were working people, and to their further surprise, they learned that many of the people they talked with were working in the downtown area.

Not only were the church members subsidizing the new developments in downtown Baltimore with their tax money, but they were also subsidizing some of the work force with food.

Since 1977 the BUILD organization has worked diligently to form a powerful ecumenical broad-based organization. Over its eighteen-year history, BUILD has become known for its success in building hundreds of affordable homes for low- and moderate-income people, for conceiving of a very successful multimillion dollar scholarship program for high school graduates, for registering and turning out to the polls thousands of new voters, for introducing the concept of community policing to the city, and for successfully working on a host of other quality-of-life issues.

Notwithstanding BUILD's track record, which has been written about locally and nationally, the leadership was faced with rapidly declining and violent neighborhoods and schools and, worst of all, a growing number of despairing people who were losing all sense of hope.

What is needed then? What kinds of strategies should be employed to rebuild our central cities?

While there is no one strategy that will act like a magic bullet, there is one strategy that is at the heart of a holistic rebirthing.

If what we mean by economic development is the development of "living wage" jobs that enable a person to raise a family, then we are on the right track. If what we mean by economic development are thoughtful strategies that target business development in our central cities, then we again are on the right track.

There is something, however, that precedes this "right" kind of economic development or at least encompasses it; and that is the development of social organizations. By social organizations, I mean mediating institutions, voluntary associations that are nongovernmental in their genesis and support. These are organizations that stand sometimes outside of and sometimes in between the public and private sectors. Sometimes they ally with one or both of these sectors, and sometimes they attack one or both of them.

These social organizations, i.e., congregation, neighborhood, union, extended family, etc., are what make up the fabric of a healthy civic life—a life that must be healthy and vibrant in order for us to develop political and economic strategies that are universal in their application and reward.

Without a powerful civic sector, there is nothing to keep politics from becoming narrow, mean, and self-serving. Without a powerful civic sector there is no way to control the destructive excesses of the market sector.

A healthy society revolves around keeping a healthy balance between the competing interests of the market sector and the civic sector. Today, the balance is way out of line. This is the case because, for one, our politics is dominated by the market sector; and second, so many of our once-vibrant mediating associations have lost their vision and strength.

The challenge is to build a network of new social institutions. For the past twenty-five years the IAF has built fifty such organizations in twenty states based on some of the following principles:

1. *Pluralism.* The organization should be multiracial and include a broad range of interests. It should be comprised of many denominations, different neighborhood groups, homeowners and renters, low-income and moderate-income people, etc. Organizations built on this principle include a mix of goals and interests and avoid a parochial narrow focus.

2. *Power.* Power means the ability to act. Power evolves from organized money and/or organized people who come together around a common focus. IAF organizations vigorously pursue power, not to dominate but to seek just and reciprocal relationships with the political and market sectors.

3. *"Iron Rule."* "Never do for people what they can do for themselves." This rule, while difficult to adhere to, is central to our understanding of education, leadership, and effective organization building. The iron rule implies that the most valuable and enduring forms of development—intellectual, social, political—are those that people freely choose and fully own.

4. *Leadership.* Most leaders are made, not born. The birthing of meaningful social organizations depends upon the development of the vast array of talented but untrained people who live in our cities.

5. *Public Relationships.* With the collapse of our voluntary associations, people are becoming increasingly unknown to each other. The stranger is no longer just the person from out of town, he/she is also the person down the street. A vision of development cannot be produced by a roomful of strangers. A vision for the common good can only be developed by leaders who have built a level of trust that frees them to share, argue, and compromise.

These types of relationships take time and nurturing. They start with a commitment on the part of leaders to systematically conduct individual face-to-face meetings. Here is where people share their interests, anger, and visions for themselves and their community. It is out of these encounters that people discover the common interests on which they are willing to act.

6. *Action.* Effective organizations work in the public arena. They engage large numbers of people to act on their values and vision. These actions can be to challenge an unjust situation, to create new allies, or to challenge the leadership of the organization to a greater degree of accountability. Whatever the reason of the action is, the purpose is to elicit a reaction so that space for new possibilities can be created.

7. *Money.* The civic sector, to effectively engage the political and market forces, must be comprised of social organizations that pay their own way. IAF organizations do not accept government money for their core budgets. They raise their own money from dues and from participating denominations and private foundations. Without meaningful dues, people do not own their own organization and development.

The leadership and vision is there. They are resident in the thousands of hard-working people who live and raise their families in the central cities throughout the country. They need to be nurtured, developed, aimed, and systematically acted upon.

Three years ago John, Sam, and Mary did not know each other. Each lived out their lives in quiet despair and growing hopelessness.

Today, they are not only known to the people with whom they work, but they have formed relationships with people who live across town, with clergy and lay leaders of the BUILD organization, and with leaders and organizers of AFSCME.

They belong to the Solidarity Sponsoring Committee, an organization of low-wage inner-city residents. In SSC's brief two-year history, they conceived of and helped pass the first "living wage" ordinances in the country. This bill means that as of today, approximately 4,000 low-wage workers now earn $6.60 per hour instead of $4.25 per hour. They and hundreds of others are part of an organization that is challenging the city and the state on the way they spend millions of dollars in the name of an economic development strategy that neglects workers' lives and their neighborhoods, and they are challenging private employers who receive public subsidies to pay a living wage.

The leadership of SSC sits on city and state economic and wage task forces. They are exploring the possibilities of forming a worker-owned co-op temporary agency for which a business plan has just been completed.

From the outside, SSC looks like an organization where economic interests are paramount. From the inside SSC looks like an effort to build a new institution for low-wage inner-city residents.

From the inside, you see new relationships; you go to picnics where you meet fellow members and their families; you have a Thanksgiving meal together; you go to a worship service together; you see people dreaming about how to start their own co-op "temp" agency; you see people hungry for knowledge and training; you see people who have a great deal to teach their fellow leaders and organizers; and you see people, who never before spoke in public, address hundreds of fellow members, politicians, and the media with strength, dignity, and eloquence.

While the majority of SSC's efforts are aimed at economic betterment, SSC is at its core a social organization . . . a fledgling mediating institution; an organization that knows that without a social vision and the power to implement that vision, they will forever be the victims of the market instead of its co-creators.

18

MR. PORTER'S "COMPETITIVE ADVANTAGE" FOR INNER-CITY REVITALIZATION: EXPLOITATION OR EMPOWERMENT?

James H. Johnson, Jr., Walter C. Farrell, Jr.,
and Geraldine R. Henderson,
Urban Investment Strategies Center

INTRODUCTION

Michael Porter, a distinguished Harvard business professor, has advanced an interesting and provocative strategy for revitalizing the American inner city. Noting the increasing economic distress and the crushing cycle of poverty therein, he rightfully concludes that the crippling social problems of the inner city—drug abuse, crime, and other associated ills—may be the most pressing issues facing our nation.[1] He also has determined that " . . . the efforts of the past few decades to revitalize the inner cities have failed,"[2] largely because these efforts have been guided by a government-facilitated, social service model. To continue in this vein, he reasons, will serve to undermine economic development and to worsen social problems. Thus, what is needed for the creation of a sustainable economic base in the inner city, in his view, is "private, for-profit initiatives and investment based on economic self-interest and genuine competitive advantage" and that "increasing social investment and hoping for economic activity to follow" will not cure the inner city's problems.[3]

Our primary observation, consistent with that of the *Black Enterprise* Board of Economists, is that Porter tends to oversimplify the approach to successful economic development in the inner city.[4] He paints a picture of a world in which absolutely nothing has been done to address its severe social and economic problems, although both public and private sector leaders are toiling away with some success on a daily basis.[5] As observed by others, not only is his framework not tested, but he has dismissed numerous inner-city initiatives currently underway.[6] We have two sets of concerns about Porter's competitive initiative for the American inner city.

First, where is he getting his data? Porter employs quite a few numbers to make his points, but he does not cite sources to allow for their confirmation or refutation, or at least an understanding of their original and intended context. Were they the result of primary data collection? If so, will these data be made available to others? If not, what secondary sources were employed? He also restricts "inner-city" inhabitants to certain ethnic groups; however, not all ethnic minorities live in inner cities, and many inner cities contain more than just ethnic minorities.

More specific concerns with Porter's view of inner-city redevelopment are listed below:

- Porter posits that Alpha Electronics, a company that was induced, with local government tax breaks, to move to the South Bronx, never should have moved to the inner city because it did not have the competitive factors to sustain its success. If this view were generalized to all inner-city communities, which one of them would possibly have what it takes? Would all fall short of the necessary ingredients, thereby ruling out the possibility of ever having such a firm in an inner city? Is Porter suggesting that inner-city communities should stay out of the rapidly growing high technology sector of the overall economy?

- Porter also uses a retail business, Goldblatt Brothers in Chicago, as an example of a firm that has successfully reentered the inner city. Whereas his observations have merit, he fails to recognize the potential costs that this locational decision posed for inner-city residents. When this large retailer moved in, many smaller retail establishments were forced out of business, giving Goldblatt monopoly power. Thus, although Goldblatt adapted its product configurations to the social and economic needs of the inner city, consumers were exploited—in terms of price—because the retailer held a monopoly. Would the residents of inner-city Chicago have been better off with several smaller stores which would have stimulated greater price competition for these same retail products?

- Porter also uses several minority-owned companies as examples of firms that have "drawn their advantages from serving inner-city residents' cultural and ethnic needs," but he fails to include the demographic indexing data to support such a claim. In several cases, however, he misrepresents the facts. For example, Brooks Sausage, which has only recently become minority-owned again, is a monopsony whose only client has been and remains the McDonalds Corporation. And although McDonalds has done an excellent job in penetrating the inner-city market, its reach extends to a significantly diverse customer base—both socioeconomically and geographically.

- Another example is Parks Sausage, a company that Porter, himself, acknowledges is a nationally viable brand that competes favorably with its majority-owned counterpart, Jimmy Dean Sausage. In other words, none of these companies has focused solely on the cultural and ethnic needs of inner-city residents. Porter makes similar arguments for *Essence, Black Enterprise,* and *Ebony,* but the indexing data reveal that these three African American-oriented magazines serve principally an upscale clientele, with a limited number of subscribers in the inner city.

- A distinct pattern emerges when Porter discusses the types of firms that would be best suited for the inner city. The best businesses would be those in which the clients and employees are not afraid to visit the business or come to work (unlike Alpha Electronics) or firms that do not have a need for client visits (e.g., Be Our Guest or Matrix Exhibits.) From this perspective, it appears that there may be a focus on those entrepreneurs and workers who are not residents of inner cities. In articulating his competitive strategy, Porter seems to equivocate between luring businesses from outside the inner city to *exploit* inner-city resources and *empowering* inner-city residents to take advantage of business and employment opportunities.

- Porter highlights an important topic when he mentions the potential market demand located within inner cities. However, he does not attempt to quantify the magnitude of that demand, citing only the high population densities that exist. He neglects to mention that inner-city residents are more likely to spend on personal items (e.g., hair and skin care products) and household electronics (e.g., radios, televisions, etc.) than their suburban counterparts. As a consequence, inner-city residents are attractive to manufacturers for reasons other than family size.[7]

- Furthermore, in his eagerness to identify black hair care firms as examples of businesses that respond to the "unique cultural and ethnic" demands of the inner city, Porter did not acknowledge the historical tendency of such firms to be integrated in regional clusters. On the southside of Chicago, for example, a cluster of minority-owned black hair care firms (Soft Sheen, Luster Products Johnson Products) existed long before Porter turned his research attention to the inner city.

- Porter treats much too superficially the disadvantages of the inner city as a place to do business. After pointing out the problems and challenges confronting minority business owners, he suggests that the private sector be given the responsibility for "making things right." Moreover, he asks inner-city residents to be more trusting of the private sector—without presenting a strategy for firms to change their exploitative and discriminatory ways of doing business in the inner city.

- While increasing numbers of business schools (Northwestern University, University of North Carolina at Chapel Hill, Duke University, University of Chicago, etc.) and other organizations (e.g., the National Black MBA Association and the National Society of Hispanic MBAs Association) have initiated technical assistance programs for inner-city business owners, Porter is unaware of or intentionally ignores their existence. These entities have focused their energies on inner-city economic development over an extended time period.[8]

- Porter states that "direct subsidies to businesses do not work," but he offers no documentation to support this conclusion. One only needs to consider large-scale tobacco and peanut farmers, who have received massive federal subsidies, and those majority-owned businesses that have received tax breaks and other locational incentives from state and local governments to realize the hypocrisy of this assertion.

Earlier evidence from the 1980s, when both the Reagan and Bush administrations tried to deregulate business in order to facilitate the competitiveness of U.S. companies in the global marketplace,[9] points to the potential pitfalls of Porter's economic model. During those administrations, the federal government aggressively relaxed environmental regulations and reduced the budgets and slashed the staffs of governmental agencies that were charged with enforcing laws governing workplace health, safety, and compensation, as well as hiring, retention and promotion practices.[10]

The types of companies that Porter presents as examples of competitive inner-city business enterprises—mainly hospitality services and craft specialty industries—were, interestingly enough, the primary beneficiaries of the federal government's efforts to foster competitiveness during the 1980s. Research indicates that such organizations were able to remain in the inner city and make a profit by hiring newly arrived illegal immigrants rather than native workers, by creating a work environment reminiscent of nineteenth-century sweatshops, and by paying employees the minimum wage at best.[11]

Furthermore, the evidence indicates that, while generating substantial profits for the owner, these so-called competitive-sector companies typically did little to improve the quality of life of inner-city workers and their communities. In fact, a recent study suggests that competition between Latino immigrants and native blacks for jobs in these types of companies was one of the triggers of the Los Angeles civil unrest of 1992.[12] Given the negative outcomes of prior efforts to foster competitiveness, it is not at all clear that the private sector should take the lead role in revitalization initiatives. Resolving the seemingly intractable problems of the inner city will require the mobilization of a broader range of the nation's assets, in collaboration with corporate America.[13]

Moreover, there must be an equality of status and responsibility across those institutions. No single entity should be allowed to set the agenda for revitalizing the economic base of the inner city. Rather, the private sector, philanthropic organizations, and the government must all work collaboratively to direct their resources to economically viable projects; community-based organizations and institutions of higher learning, especially business schools, must be actively engaged in designing and implementing these initiatives. Otherwise, we run the risk of advancing the notion that a knight in shining armor from the outside can initiate an economic turnaround without the support of inner-city residents. The launching of Rebuild LA in the aftermath of the 1992 civil unrest in Los Angeles cautions us against such an approach. After much fanfare and media hype, it was found that the corporate sector, alone, could not gentrify the economically depressed South Central Los Angeles community.[14]

REVIVING THE INNER CITY: AN ALTERNATIVE STRATEGY

If the United States is to compete effectively in the twenty-first century world economy, strategies must be developed to reverse economic decay, rebuild human capital, and reduce the debilitating social problems (poverty, crime, drug abuse, school failure, etc.) in our inner cities. To effectively address these challenges, it is imperative, in our view, that the following strategies be implemented.

First, and foremost is private-sector job creation. There is an urgent need to pursue inner-city employment anchors or job generators which are linked to the growth sectors of the economy. In contrast to Porter's model and the enterprise-zone concept of attracting companies back to central cities, however, these employment anchors must be fostered from within the community. Aspiring entrepreneurs must be encouraged and assisted in the development of businesses that employ substantial numbers of inner-city workers and that pay decent wages. Without such employment anchors, the general retail and low-level service establishments that remain in depressed urban neighborhoods will likely continue as marginal enterprises. On the other hand, with a stable supply of better-paying jobs generated by anchor businesses, these retail and other establishments are more likely to prosper and grow as workers will have more discretionary income to purchase nonbasic items.

Second, recruitment and training of workers must be tied directly to specific job opportunities. Research shows that generic education and training programs—that is, those not connected to specific job placement—have not succeeded in the past, especially for the inner-city poor, and they are unlikely to succeed in the future.[15] Customized training programs, on the other hand, have proven to be a highly effective economic development tool. Studies show that such programs are most effective when they are offered at no cost to prospective employers as part of a locational incentive package. As Rosabeth Moss Kanter points out in her new book, *World Class: Thriving Locally in the Global Economy*, customized training programs have been instrumental in luring major job generators to selected, formerly economically depressed areas of the South. The BMW plant in Spartanburg, South Carolina, and the Mercedes Benz plant in Vance, Alabama, are recent examples. And for individuals participating in these programs, the job placement rates are phenomenal—reportedly as high as 99%.[16]

Third, if we are to revitalize our central cities, the foregoing economic development strategies must be undertaken in conjunction with efforts to mend the social fabric of these communities. In recent public policy debates regarding the steadily deteriorating social conditions of economically distressed communities, one perspective has held sway: that a decline in individual responsibility and family values and morals has contributed to rising rates of poverty, joblessness, family disruption, out-of-wedlock births, and gang- and drug-related violence in our cities and throughout the nation.[17] Based on this interpretation of the underlying causes of the problems plaguing inner cities, policymakers have instituted what some consider paternalistic and punitive policies, to reduce the level of violence, and to foster normative behavior among the disadvantaged. But there is growing evidence that these policies may not yield the desired results. It is clear, for example, that the "get tough on crime" policies enacted by a number of states during the 1980s have not significantly reduced the incidence of illegal and violent criminal activities in economically distressed communities.[18]

An emerging school of thought posits that providing greater access to individual and community-based social resources is the key to resolving these and related problems of distressed urban neighborhoods.[19] In earlier decades, community-based institutions such as the boys and girls clubs, the YMCA/YWCA, and churches played a "mediating" role in disadvantaged communities, encouraging poor youth to pursue mainstream avenues of mobility and discouraging them from engaging in antisocial behavior. However, such institutions lost much of their financial support during the 1980s and thus became less effective precisely at the time that the problems confronting the disadvantaged were worsening.[20] Churches also became less central to the lives of inner-city residents. In order to reverse the trend of increasing antisocial behavior among inner-city youth and increasingly punitive solutions to their problems, a new generation of social resource programs designed to mend the social fabric of inner-city communities must be devised.

Finally, all of the nation's assets, including the resources of government, community-based organizations, the business sector, the philanthropic community, and especially our colleges and universities, must be mobilized if we are to successfully revitalize inner-city communities. What is needed are institutions capable of designing and implementing cooperative, collaborative, and coordinated strategies that draw upon and fully utilize the complete range of community assets to deal with heretofore intractable problems of the inner city.[21]

THE URBAN INVESTMENT STRATEGIES CENTER

At the University of North Carolina at Chapel Hill (UNC-CH), such an institution, the Urban Investment Strategies Center (UISC), has been established (Figure 1); it is designed to facilitate UNC's broad-based capacity to engage in comprehensive community revitalization that is consistent with the approaches noted.[22] Within the university, the UISC plays a major coordinating and integrating role, strategically drawing upon and focusing the substantial faculty expertise and resources in the

FIGURE 1
University of North Carolina at Chapel Hill Urban Investment Strategies Center

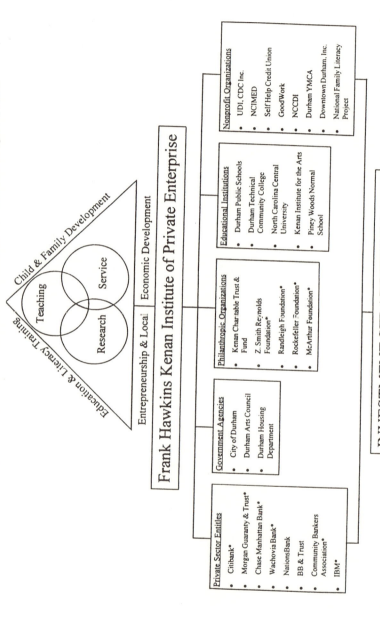

Child & Family Development

Teaching   Service

Research

Education & Literacy Training

Entrepreneurship & Local Economic Development

Frank Hawkins Kenan Institute of Private Enterprise

Private Sector Entities
- Citibank*
- Morgan Guaranty & Trust*
- Chase Manhattan Bank*
- Wachovia Bank*
- NationsBank
- BB & Trust
- Community Bankers Association*
- IBM*

Government Agencies
- City of Durham
- Durham Arts Council
- Durham Housing Department

Philanthropic Organizations
- Kenan Charitable Trust & Fund
- Z. Smith Reynolds Foundation*
- Randleigh Foundation*
- Rockefeller Foundation*
- McArthur Foundation*

Educational Institutions
- Durham Public Schools
- Durham Technical Community College
- North Carolina Central University
- Kenan Institute for the Arts
- Piney Woods Normal School

Nonprofit Organizations
- UDI, CDC Inc.
- NCIMED
- Self Help Credit Union
- GoodWork
- NCCDI
- Durham YMCA
- Downtown Durham, Inc.
- National Family Literacy Project

INVESTMENT STRATEGIES BOARD

*Contributing Partners

social sciences (economics, geography, sociology, and political science), in the professional schools (business, city and regional planning, social work, education, and public health), and in selected research centers and institutes on the problems confronting economically distressed urban communities. Outside the university, the UISC forges the types of strategic alliances that are necessary to successfully revitalize inner-city communities. It builds capacity in community development to sustain, on a long-term basis, the partnerships forged within and outside the university through a two-pronged approach of training programs and community outreach (Figure 2).

The UISC's core activities are organized around three substantive themes that are central to the revitalization of the inner city: entrepreneurship and community economic development, child and family development, and education and literacy training. Why these three areas? Simply put, because businesses are unlikely to survive and communities are unlikely to prosper if the local population is poorly educated, if families are unstable, and if drugs and crime are major problems.

Training and Technical Assistance Programs

The UISC's training and technical assistance programs are designed to achieve three objectives: (1) to upgrade the technical and managerial skills of existing community development specialists, including the employees of community development corporations, other nonprofit, community-based organizations, and government agencies; (2) to provide aspiring inner-city entrepreneurs with assistance in the "nuts and bolts" of sound business practices; and (3) to recruit and train the next generation of community development practitioners. The UISC supports a variety of innovative technical assistance/training programs, both for the personnel of local community economic development agencies and for minority entrepreneurs. The primary vehicle for managerial assistance and knowledge transfer is the Urban Enterprise Corps (UEC), which provides staff and technical expertise and establishes linkages among the various UISC training/technical assistance initiatives.

The Urban Enterprise Corps

Launched on a pilot basis in June 1994, with support from two foundations and three New York area banks, the UEC promotes entrepreneurship and local economic development by linking new or underperforming

FIGURE 2
Organization of UISC Programs

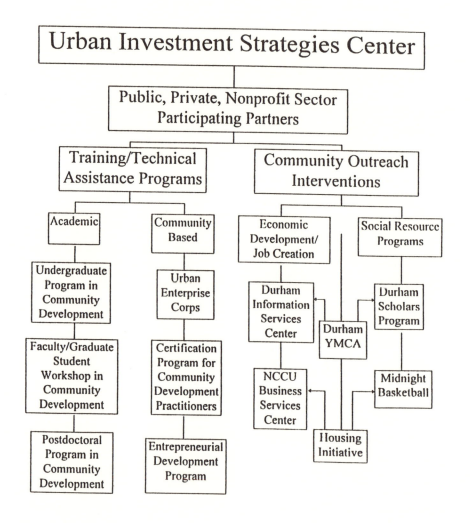

minority businesses with emerging market opportunities in the growth sectors of the local, national, and global economy.[23] To achieve this goal, the UEC recruits and trains talented graduates of the nation's leading MBA programs to provide technical and managerial assistance to inner-city businesses, community-based economic development institutions—including minority-owned banks, credit unions, and savings and loan associations—and other distressed community economic revitalization initiatives. In launching the UEC, the goal was to empower these entities to control their own destinies and to become self-sufficient, thereby shaping the nature and trajectory of change in their communities. Through a steady supply of committed, and well-trained MBA talent, the UEC transfers knowledge of sound business principles and practices to help foster minority enterprise success.

During the UEC's first year of operation, six recently graduated MBAs were placed in six economic development organizations with histories of working with minority business enterprises in distressed communities. In their placements, Corps members utilize their considerable formal business training and expertise in a variety of ways, including:

- assisting placement organizations and religious organizations with a range of micro-enterprise, shopping centers, and affordable housing development projects;
- training both minority entrepreneurs and economic development practitioners in the managerial basics, from business plan development to implementing effective cost-accounting procedures;
- matching aspiring minority entrepreneurs with business opportunities in the growth sectors of the domestic economy and with export opportunities in the global marketplace (e.g., with emerging markets in South Africa and Southeast Asia);
- designing custom-training programs that link residents of economically distressed communities with real job prospects in emerging business ventures; and
- working with community development corporations, other economic development organizations, churches and other religious organizations, as well as with aspiring minority entrepreneurs, to raise and/or secure capital to support business start-ups and expansions.

Currently, nine MBAs are participating in the UEC—five from the inaugural year of the program and four who joined the program in June of 1995. In addition to continuing to work with community development corporations and other community economic development organizations in the inner city, the Corps also is working directly with a series of new business start-ups and a set of existing businesses which have enormous job creation potential (see Tables 1 and 2). The Corps is being aided in its effort to provide technical and managerial assistance to these businesses by a cadre of twenty-eight second-year MBAs from the Kenan-Flagler Business School at UNC and the Fuqua Business School at Duke University. The second year MBAs are enrolled in a Kenan-Flagler Business School elective course, "Entrepreneurship and Local Economic Development," which requires that they undertake a practicum in a minority business enterprise. This course is used to recruit future interns for the UEC.

Our evaluations of the UEC, involving interviews with the executive directors of the placement sites, revealed the following:

- There has been a significant transfer of knowledge, skills, and expertise to existing personnel in the CDCs in which the Corps members have been placed.
- The UEC has afforded the existing staff members of the CDCs the opportunity to pursue additional education and training, which, in turn, will enhance their expertise in business development.
- The energy, enthusiasm, and skills that the recent MBA graduates have brought to the six CDCs in which they were placed have substantially heightened interest in the UEC among both MBA students and executive directors of CDCs throughout the state of North Carolina and the country. We received requests for application materials from more than 100 MBAs who graduated this past spring, and requests for Corps members from a dozen of the state's CDCs. In addition, once word got out to the minority small business community in the state that the UEC had commenced activities, we received numerous requests to have Corps members assigned to their businesses. The interest in the UEC, needless to say, far exceeds the resources that we currently have at our disposal.

In addition, data provided by three of the businesses we have been working with since the fall of 1994 indicate that these companies experienced substantial growth over the last three years—both in terms of gross receipts and the number of employees. As Table 3 shows, these compa-

TABLE 1
Urban Enterprise Corps
Managerial and Technical Assistance Program 1995–1996
New Business Start-Ups

Company	Type of Business	Location
Carolina Health Group, Inc.	HMO	Greenville, North Carolina
Car World	Auto Parts Store	Durham, North Carolina
Lewis Barbecue	Food Service/Catering	Durham, North Carolina
Med Trans	Medical Transcription Services	Durham, North Carolina
McNeil Enterprises	Limo Service/Parking Lots	Charlotte, North Carolina
Roland Dedicated Logistics	Truck Driver Training School With Ryder and Global Transpark	Kinston, North Carolina

nies, collectively, expanded their workforces by 79 percent (from 52 in 1993 to 93 in 1995), and their gross receipts increased by 145 percent (from $2.7 million to $6.8 million in 1995). The CEOs of these firms attribute this growth and expansion directly to the technical assistance and network opportunities afforded them as a result of their relationship with the UEC and the Kenan Institute of Private Enterprise at the University of North Carolina at Chapel Hill.

Training Services for Community Development Practitioners

The UISC, utilizing the skills of the UEC members, is spearheading a new initiative inspired by interviews with Community Reinvestment Act (CRA) officers, in both small and large banks in North Carolina, regarding their experiences, especially difficulties, in working with CDCs to foster local economic development. Through these interviews, it became clear that CDCs in North Carolina are confronted with two interrelated problems. The first is an image problem. Because the CDC movement emerged out of the War on Poverty Programs of the 1960s, CDCs are often viewed in the banking and corporate communities primarily as extensions of the social welfare bureaucracy, as Porter notes. The second

TABLE 2
Urban Enterprise Corps
Managerial and Technical Assistance Program 1995–1996
Minority Businesses

Company	Type of Business	Location
American Safety Products	Lab equipment, disposal, clothing, gloves, respirators, ergonomic furniture	Raleigh, North Carolina
Blackwell and Associates	Health services	Burlington, North Carolina
C & C Enterprises	Residential construction	Henderson, North Carolina
Golden Enterprises	Contract assembly of electric mechanical material/inventory management	Greensboro, North Carolina
I-Supply	Business forms, printing services, hot melt adhesives, film	Charlotte, North Carolina
Monarch Temporary Services	Temporary employees	Durham, North Carolina
Roland Dedicated Logistics	Ground transportation, warehousing, and inventory management	Morrisville, North Carolina
RBI Precision Manufacturing	Precision machining and manufacturing	Rocky Mount, North Carolina

is the inability of most CDC practitioners to speak the same language as their corporate and banking counterparts. That is, they often lack the business skills and acumen needed to develop viable business plans and to convince the corporate and banking communities that their proposed projects merit financial support.

As federal resources for urban areas become scarce, CDCs will play an increasingly important role in urban revitalization efforts. If CDCs are to be successful in the future in their efforts to secure capital from the corporate and banking communities, and from financial intermediaries such as the Local Initiatives Support Corporation (LISC), they must be-

TABLE 3
Contract & Employment Expansion Statistics for Three Firms Assisted by the Urban Enterprise Corps for 1993–1995

Industry	Contract Expansion			Employment Expansion*		
	1993	1995	% Change	1993	1995	% Change
Metal Fabrication Firm	$960,000	$3,100,000	222.9	13	36	176.9
Electronic Mechanical Assembler	$1,800,000	$2,800,000	55.5	19	23	21. 1
Logistical Transportation Service Firm	$29,000	$934,000	3120.7	20	34	79
Total	$2,789,090	$6,834,000	145	52	93	78.8

* Full-time Employment Opportunities

gin to operate less like social service agencies and more like business enterprises. The business skills of CDC personnel will need to be upgraded substantially in order to foster this new image, and this is one of the principal objectives of the community development practitioners training program.

Modeled after business school executive education programs, the UISC's CDC Professional Certification Program is designed to assist CDC practitioners in obtaining the knowledge, understanding, and training in the "nuts and bolts" of sound business development. The program offers three levels of education and training: a program for entry-level practitioners, one for mid-career CDC professionals, and an advanced program for executive directors of CDCs (Table 4). As Table 4 shows, the program provides courses in general management, accounting, marketing, strategic and long-range planning, organizational development, real estate and commercial development, finance, business demography, entrepreneurship and local economic development, and human resource management (including diversity training). The courses are taught by leading UNC Kenan-Flagler Business School and North Carolina Central University (NCCU) Business School faculty as well as by recently graduated MBAs participating in the UEC.

TABLE 4
CDC Professional Certification Program Curriculum (tentative)

Tier I (Entry level)	Tier II (Mid-level)	Tier III (Executive level)
Community Economic Development Process	Economic/Community Development Strategies	Long-Range Strategic Planning
Basic Financial Management/Accounting	Advanced Financial Management	Financial Planning: Strategies for the Long-Term
Developing Affordable Housing or Microenterprise Programs	Commercial Real Estate Development	Entrepreneurship for Non-profits and Community Groups
Coalition-Building	Developing Community Partnerships	Creating Constituencies and Furthering Partnerships
Proposal and Grant Writing Skills	Fundraising/Development	Organizational Leadership/Development
Public Speaking/ Communications	Legal Issues for Non-profits and CDCs	Negotiation and Dispute Resolution
Public Relations Strategies	Organizational Marketing	
Diversity Training	Human Resources Management	Cultivating Boards of Directors

Training Services for Local Entrepreneurs

Research shows that most inner-city African-American residents who aspire to entrepreneurship and micro-business development as an avenue of upward mobility and financial security are less likely to have the requisite education and training, business skills, knowledge of the banking system, and access to the social capital resources (i.e., family, friends, and role models with expertise in these areas) to form and maintain a successful business.[24] As a consequence, the failure rate of these businesses tends to be very high. In an effort to improve the survival rate of minority business enterprises, the UISC has launched the Entrepreneurial Development Program (EDP), which is organized around the life stages of business development (Table 5).

Tier I: **Classes for start-ups or businesses in the feasibility stage**. Courses concentrate on the development of a strong business plan, the exploration of funding options, and the development of initial marketing and financial management plans.

TABLE 5
UISC Entrepreneurial Development Program Curriculum

Tier I (Entry level)	Tier II (Mid-level)	Tier III (Executive)
Developing a Business Plan	Marketing Strategy	Strategic Planning: Five Years Out
Legal Business Structures/ Start-up Checklists	Entering the Competitive Bidding Process	Financial Planning: Strategies for Growth
Start-up, Direct & Indirect Costing	Insurance, Taxes and Business Reporting Requirements	Negotiation and Dispute Resolution
Introduction to Financial Statements	Business Accounting	Advanced Accounting/ Recordkeeping
Pricing (Products and Services)	Customer Relations/Quality Control	Managerial Competencies
Developing a Marketing Plan	Market Assessment/Distribution Channels/Advertising	Export Opportunities
Common Causes of Business Failure	Capital Financing/Working Capital	Business Demography and Advanced Marketing Strategy
Sales Forecasting and Business Budgeting	Personal Policies	Using Technology for Business

Tier II: **Classes for existing yet unstable businesses**. This level of instruction focuses on growing a business (i.e., from home-based to a commercial location), time management skills, and expanded finance and marketing skills.

Tier III: **Classes for more mature businesses**. Instruction focuses on expansion techniques (e.g., how to find export opportunities) and how to deal with "graduating" from an active generator in one's own company to a full-time manager of a growing staff.

The Entrepreneurial Development Program (EDP) also includes a formal mentoring component. UISC links participants in the program, especially those enrolling in Tier I and Tier II training, with successful entrepreneurs from similar businesses and industries. The goal is to strengthen program participants' connections to the wider business community and to additional sources of technical know-how, guidance, and inspiration.

By counseling younger businesses, successful entrepreneurs will foster economic development in distressed communities and may themselves benefit from networking opportunities and other collaborative ventures.

Academic Training Program

To attract new minority talent to the field, the UISC, in collaboration with the North Carolina Central University (NCCU) Public Administration Program, offers formal research and training programs in community economic development. Building upon the concept of an educational pipeline, the UISC recruits promising undergraduate, pre-doctoral, and post-doctoral scholars with applied research interests and expertise in the social sciences and related professions to participate in its programs. It would be ideal if students would enter as freshmen and then matriculate through the "pipeline" of education and training programs described below. In reality, it is most likely that students will enter at later stages of their academic careers. Irrespective of when they enter and exit the programs, the goal is to equip participants with the requisite interdisciplinary practical skills that will enable them to contribute as entrepreneurs, service providers, or policy analysts in the revitalization and redevelopment of the social, economic, and physical infrastructure of inner-city communities.

The UISC's academic activities are organized around a set of formal training initiatives: (1) *Undergraduate Program in Community Development,* (2) *Faculty-Graduate Student Workshop in Community Development,* and (3) *Postdoctoral Research and Training Program in Community Development.*

The *Undergraduate Program in Community Development* is designed to equip college students with the requisite interdisciplinary research and technical skills that will allow them to have a significant impact on the future vitality and livability of inner cities. To achieve this goal, the program is structured as follows (Figure 3): Students initially enroll in an interdisciplinary lecture course, "School and Economic Processes in the City," designed to broaden their knowledge and understanding of the forces that have contributed to the decline of U.S. cities. Following successful completion of this course, students are offered specialized training, depending on their substantive interest, in one of the UISC's "core" areas: child and family development, entrepreneurship and community economic development, or education and literacy training.

After successfully completing the sequence of courses that comprise

FIGURE 3
Program in Community Development

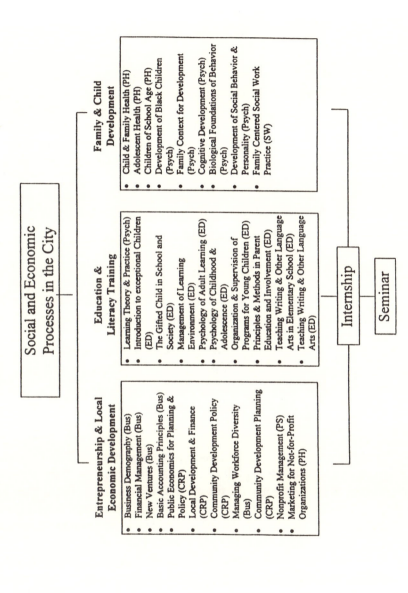

Social and Economic
Processes in the City

**Entrepreneurship & Local
Economic Development**

- Business Demography (Bus)
- Financial Management (Bus)
- New Ventures (Bus)
- Basic Accounting Principles (Bus)
- Public Economics for Planning &
  Policy (CRP)
- Local Development & Finance
  (CRP)
- Community Development Policy
  (CRP)
- Managing Workforce Diversity
  (Bus)
- Community Development Planning
  (CRP)
- Nonprofit Management (PS)
- Marketing for Not-for-Profit
  Organizations (PH)

**Education &
Literacy Training**

- Learning Theory & Practice (Psych)
- Introduction to exceptional Children
  (ED)
- The Gifted Child in School and
  Society (ED)
- Management of Learning
  Environment (ED)
- Psychology of Adult Learning (ED)
- Psychology of Childhood &
  Adolescence (ED)
- Organization & Supervision of
  Programs for Young Children (ED)
- Principles & Methods in Parent
  Education and Involvement (ED)
- Teaching Writing & Other Language
  Arts in Elementary School (ED)
- Teaching Writing & Other Language
  Arts (ED)

**Family & Child
Development**

- Child & Family Health (PH)
- Adolescent Health (PH)
- Children of School Age (PH)
- Development of Black Children
  (Psych)
- Family Context for Development
  (Psych)
- Cognitive Development (Psych)
- Biological Foundations of Behavior
  (Psych)
- Development of Social Behavior &
  Personality (Psych)
- Family Centered Social Work
  Practice (SW)

Internship

Seminar

each of these specializations, students are required to undertake an internship in a business, community-based organization, governmental agency, or the Urban Enterprise Corps (UEC). The purpose of the internship is twofold: to provide the students with practical experience in a community setting and to provide fledgling inner-city institutions with needed technical assistance. The *Undergraduate Program in Community Development* concludes with an undergraduate research seminar in which each program participant is required to complete a senior thesis.

The goal of the *Faculty-Graduate Student Workshop in Community Development* is to facilitate the formulation of public policies to revitalize inner-city communities and to increase their economic competitiveness in the global marketplace. The workshop focuses on cutting-edge issues in the substantive areas of child and family development, entrepreneurship and community economic development, and education and literacy training. In addition to being exposed to guest lectures by experts from other universities, policy think-tanks, and governmental agencies, students are afforded the opportunity to work directly with distinguished faculty on a range of policy-relevant projects in the substantive areas mentioned above. Students who successfully complete this program are eligible to pursue advanced training in the Center's *Post-doctoral Research and Training Program in Community Development* or to join the UISC's Urban Enterprise Corps. Post-doctoral scholars completing one to two years of supervised research in the UISC are expected to compete for tenure-track faculty positions in major universities, research positions in national policy think-tanks, and/or top administrative positions in community development institutions. In short, the academic research and training programs are designed to:

(1) generate interdisciplinary and policy-relevant research that contributes to strategies to rebuild the physical infrastructure, improve the quality of the workforce, and create jobs in the inner city;

(2) create a real link between the University and poor inner-city communities, resulting in a two-way flow of talented students from the communities to the University and of talented students from the University to work in economically distressed communities;

(3) develop a cadre of talented undergraduate, graduate, and postdoctoral scholars who have chosen to devote at least some

part of their professional careers to the provision of sorely-needed technical assistance in inner-city institutions; and

(4) produce the next generation of minority and women scholars for faculty positions in research universities and research positions in policy think-tanks.

SOCIAL RESOURCES PROGRAMS

In addition to the training programs described previously, the UISC also works with existing government and community-based organizations to expand, develop, and implement new programs to address the educational and social needs of inner-city communities. Two such projects, launched under the auspices of the UEC, are currently underway.

Durham Scholars Program

The Durham Scholars Program seeks to foster and facilitate college access and matriculation among at-risk youth in Durham's most economically distressed communities. The program is comprised of two components: a College Outreach and Retention Program for Eleventh and Twelfth Graders and a College Preparatory Academy for Sixth Graders. Total funds committed thus far exceed $3.6 million.

The College Outreach and Retention Program is designed to have an immediate impact on college attendance and matriculation rates of at-risk minority youth in Durham. Beginning in the 1995–96 academic year and each year thereafter, through the year 2001, eight (8) need-based college scholarships (up to $10,000 annually) will be offered on a competitive basis to disadvantaged youth who graduate from high school and who qualify for admission to any Durham area college or university or other post-secondary educational/ skills training institution (i.e., Durham Technical Community College, area trade schools/programs, North Carolina Central University, the University of North Carolina at Chapel Hill, Duke University, and other designated area educational institutions). During their junior and senior years of high school, those selected for program participation will be provided with a number of academic and social supports aimed at improving academic performance and enhancing those skills necessary for the successful completion of a post-secondary education program.

The College Preparatory Academy for Sixth Graders is a long-term strategy for promoting post-secondary education graduation among at-risk youth. This program builds upon recent research findings which indicate that efforts to promote college attendance among at-risk, inner-city youth have a higher probability of success if the recruitment efforts begin in the middle school years (preferably by grade six) and, at the very latest, upon entrance to high school. Over the next six years, beginning in academic year 1995–96 and continuing through academic year 2000–01, a cohort of 30 sixth-graders from Durham's economically distressed communities will be selected annually to participate in the College Preparatory Academy.

Beginning in grade six and continuing through high school graduation, students selected for participation in this program will be required to take a set of extracurricular college preparatory classes designed to develop or sharpen their communication skills (reading, writing and public speaking), their personal skills (problem solving, note-taking, time-management, decision making and critical thinking), and their technical skills (math, science, and computer usage). In addition, the young people are linked with college-level tutors (including both students and retired college professors) who will assist them with both their normal school work and their college preparatory courses. Also, throughout the year, the students have the opportunity to participate in program-specific and community-based activities, including field trips, designed to broaden their intellectual and sociocultural horizons.

Both the College Preparatory Academy for Sixth Graders and the College Outreach and Retention Program are augmented with a Parental Involvement Program and a Crisis Intervention and Counseling Program. Previous research indicates that programs which seek to foster college attendance and matriculation among at-risk students are far more likely to succeed when their parents or guardians are actively involved in the educational process. Thus, in an effort to ensure successful outcomes, acceptance into the program is contingent upon the mandatory participation of the at-risk students' parents or guardians in a parallel set of educational activities. To cope with distractions, problems, and challenges that arise in their personal, family and community environments, the participating students and their parents and/or guardians will have access to two licensed clinical social workers and social work graduate student interns from UNC at Chapel Hill. The goal here is to assist students in resolving issues that hinder them from focusing on their academic and personal development.

Several major corporations have approached us about using the Durham

Scholars Program to increase employment opportunities for inner-city youth and to diversify their workforces. For example, we have entered a partnership with the Harris-Teeter Corporation, a North Carolina-based grocery store chain, to offer DSP program participants the opportunity to enter the field of retail management. Under the partnership, Harris-Teeter will provide four-year college scholarships, annually, to up to fifteen DSP program participants, and the UISC, in collaboration with the Kenan-Flagler Business School, will offer a formal training program that will prepare the scholarship winners for management positions in the Harris-Teeter Corporation upon graduation from the University of North Carolina at Chapel Hill. In addition to the guarantee of a full-time management position with the grocery store chain upon successful completion of the undergraduate program in retail management, all scholarship recipients will be offered a part-time job in one of the Triangle Area Harris-Teeter grocery stores during their undergraduate years at UNC.

Through similar UISC-corporate partnerships, we are in the process of developing, as part of the UNC undergraduate curriculum, customized training programs to increase minority youth access to business and employment opportunities in other growth sectors of the economy, including construction management, agile manufacturing and global logistics, and international trade. These areas were selected in an effort to strategically position DSP participants (and other minority youth) for emerging business and employment opportunities associated with the North Carolina Global Transpark (GTP) and the U.S. Department of Commerce's Big Emerging Markets (BEMs) initiative.[25]

Touted as North Carolina's next Research Triangle Park, the GTP is a high-technology industrial and transportation complex that is designed to provide logistical infrastructure and value-added services essential for successful twenty-first century manufacturing. Currently under construction on a 20,000 acre site in Kinston, N.C., roughly 90 miles east of the Research Triangle in the economically depressed Coastal Plain region of the state, the GTP is designed to link North Carolina with rapidly emerging commercial opportunities in the most dynamic markets in the world, especially in Southeast Asia, where a sister facility is under construction.[26]

Fostered by the Clinton Administration as part of its National Export Strategy, the BEMs project seeks to encourage commercial cooperation with ten markets (the Chinese Economic Area [China, Hong Kong, and Taiwan], India, ASEAN [Indonesia, Malaysia, the Philippines, Singapore, Thailand, Brunei, and Vietnam], South Korea, Mexico, Brazil, Argentina, South Africa, Poland, and Turkey) in which market opportunities for American businesses are particularly great, and to help U.S. firms seize the opportunities these markets offer.[27] By linking with these two initiatives—the GTP and the BEMs—the goal is to ensure greater minority participation in export-related economic development and job creation. The utility of this strategy is supported by recent research which shows "that the share of total U.S. employment depending on exports for jobs reached 10.0 percent in 1992—up from 6.7 million jobs in 1986."[28]

Triangle Area Midnight Basketball League

Midnight Basketball Leagues are another example of a new generation of social resource programs designed to encourage personal responsibility and career aspirations among young male residents of inner cities. A recent evaluation of the first year of the Midnight Basketball League in Milwaukee, Wisconsin, revealed that the program: (1) created a safe haven in which the participants and the fans could engage in positive social activities, (2) channeled the energy of gang members in a positive direction, and (3) significantly improved the educational and career aspirations of program participants. According to Milwaukee Police Department statistics, crime rates in the target area decreased by 30 percent during the program's first year of operation. Moreover, the program achieved these outcomes with a modest investment of $70,000—roughly the same amount required to maintain two inner-city minority males in prison for one year.[29]

In view of the success of the Milwaukee program, the UISC has teamed with Research Triangle area YMCAs (in Raleigh, Durham, and Chapel Hill, NC) to launch a pilot Midnight Basketball League in an effort to provide a safe, positive, and exciting forum for late-night recreation and education/career development of disadvantaged youth. Players come from the 18- to 25-year-old minority male population in the Triangle's distressed communities. The league is organized around a specified number of regular season games and a series of playoff games, much like the NBA. During the regular season, games are scheduled several nights a week. Personal responsibility/mentoring sessions and team practice sessions are held on alternate nights. Mentors are recruited from the corporations sponsoring the teams and from other private-and-public sector organizations, including area colleges and universities.

A Youth Entrepreneurs component, using local youth groups in Durham, Raleigh, and Chapel Hill, provides concession services at the games. The

Urban Enterprise Corps, in partnership with REAL Enterprises (a Durham-based high school business development program), recruits and trains the youth entrepreneurs and provides management assistance. Profits from the concessions are directed toward educational assistance programs and scholarships. As the program grows and matures, the entrepreneurial component will be expanded to include league memorabilia (i.e., caps, shirts, etc.).

The league commissioner works with local law enforcement agencies to establish a community policing program in the Triangle area communities in which the games are played. The safety of both players and spectators is ensured at league events, and law enforcement agencies are able to increase their outreach into communities frequently distrustful of any police presence. Finally, many players are eligible for the successful Youth Build program, which is one example of the "funnel" to training programs and employment opportunities that the League provides. One of the commissioner's duties is to forge additional job- and skills-training linkages appropriate for this group.

ANTICIPATED OUTCOMES OF UISC INTERVENTIONS

There are many different organizations working in the field of community development, but few are able to analyze and devise comprehensive investment strategies for the economically distressed areas of our cities. The UISC is designed to guide targeted intervention programs based on a comprehensive strategy because: (1) it taps into resources of the Kenan Institute of Private Enterprise, the Kenan-Flagler Business School, other UNC departments, and departments and professional schools of partner universities; (2) it builds on good relationships with community-based and local government organizations formed by its Urban Enterprise Corps; (3) it has good relations with the local business community; and (4) the "community practitioner track" provides important research and analysis to benchmark programs directed at core aspects of urban investment.

By assigning MBA graduates to provide technical expertise and business acumen at minimal cost to the mostly underfunded community and economic development organizations, the Urban Enterprise Corps will greatly expand the capacity of these organizations to improve economic conditions and opportunities in the inner city. The Professional Certification Program for Community Development Practitioners addresses a critical issue that many people within the community development field consider vitally important and necessary—improving the business skills of the community development practitioners. The impact of this program will be seen in the improved management of community-based organization and in more effective communication between such organizations and the business and banking communities. As the non-profit sector becomes more involved in community development efforts, business acumen will become essential to its survival. By creating the certification program, the UISC fills a badly needed niche in the community development structure and thereby helps build capacity among community-based and local government organizations.

The Entrepreneurial Development Program (EDP) builds upon existing structures to form a more coordinated and expanded training program for local entrepreneurs than is currently available in most economically distressed communities. The three-tiered program graduates entrepreneurs who will be able to open and grow their own businesses by understanding the market, assessing their financial needs, providing solid business plans when applying for loans, and otherwise taking advantage of the resources available. In addition, the EDP, over the long run, will ensure expanded access to capital for local start-ups as entrepreneurs learn to develop "bankable" business plans and as banks become more comfortable in making small CRA loans.

The Durham Scholars Program (DSP) provides a unique opportunity for a cadre of at-risk youth to increase their probability of graduating from high school, of being accepted to college or other postsecondary institutions, and of being able to meet the financial obligations once accepted. By providing both long-term academic and financial support, the DSP will create a pool of minority high school and college graduates from the inner city who will be the next generation of community leaders. Midnight Basketball provides an avenue for both positive recreational activity and learning through league competition, personal responsibility training, and educational assistance for prime working-age minority males who are neither at work nor in school, that is, they are idle. Moreover, the youth entrepreneurial aspects of the program serve to capture the interest of teenagers not able or willing to compete, but who are interested in acquiring business skills and experience.

In sum, a number of direct benefits will accrue to economically distressed communities from the training/technical assistance and community outreach programs of the UISC: more and better employment opportunities; increased self-sufficiency and business savvy among CDCs and other community-based organizations; and positive, future-oriented activities for at-risk youth. Beyond these obviously significant benefits, the

UISC also serves, we believe, as a model for the types of university-urban community-private sector partnerships that are necessary to spark the process of reinvestment in and revitalization of the nation's inner cities.

CONCLUSIONS

Porter has devoted minimal direct and detailed attention to the role of the business community, including the nation's business schools, in revitalizing the inner city. It is assumed that businesses will locate in inner-city communities if the capital gains tax is eliminated and if environmental, health, and workplace regulations are reduced or eliminated. There is no history, however, of success of such strategies in inner-city communities. Research indicates that the major priorities for businesses when making locational decisions are access to markets, access to a quality labor force (often code words for no blacks), infrastructure, and crime rates. These business factors are considered much more important in site selection than tax rates.[30] Although Porter discusses these factors in his overall development strategy, it is not entirely clear as to who is to be the primary beneficiary—inner-city ethnic minority entrepreneurs and workers or private sector entrepreneurs from the outside.

In view of these problems, some policy analysts advocate the promotion of entrepreneurship and micro-business development among the residents of poor communities as a more viable revitalization and job creation strategy.[31] Data from the most recent survey of minority-owned business enterprises (MBEs) suggest that this is a potentially more realistic policy option to pursue. Between 1982 and 1987, MBEs grew by more than four times the rate for all businesses (64 percent vs. 14 percent). In 1987, minorities owned about 9 percent of all U.S. firms, up from 6 percent in 1982.[32] Morover, these gains have occurred not in the traditional areas of minority business development (i.e., retail and personal service, with secondary concentration in "other services" and construction); rather, they have occurred in the so-called emerging areas of minority entrepreneurship: business services; finance, insurance, and real estate, transportation and communication; and wholesale trade. According to Bates and Dunham,

> The emerging area firms are most commonly started by better educated owners, many of whom have attended four or more years of college. Financial capital investments are higher than in traditional

lines of business. Consequently, emerging firms tend to be larger scale, have lower failure rates and generate more jobs relative to their traditional cohorts.[25]

They note further that the growth of these emerging firms has been facilitated by "opportunities offered by government minority business preferential procurement and set-aside programs,"[34] programs which Porter would recommend for elimination.

Despite the recent rapid growth in economically more viable minority business establishments, major obstacles remain for minority business development. This is especially the case for blacks who aspire to pursue entrepreneurship in central city communities. In fact, recent reports suggest that many of the minority entrepreneurship gains made during the 1980s may have been reversed as a result of the Supreme Court decision in *City of Richmond v. J.A. Croson Co.* in January 1989.[35]

The *Croson* decision imposed strict limits on programs aimed at encouraging government to do business with minority concerns. Thirty-two states and 200 cities and counties had minority set-asides prior to the *Croson* decision. By 1991, according to Hinds, many of the states, including New York, New Jersey, and California, and at least two dozen of the cities had suspended their set-aside programs. In most of the other jurisdictions, Hinds notes that the programs were either challenged in court or were under administrative review.[36] This situation has been exacerbated even further in the wake of the more recent *Adarand Constructors v. Pena* decision in 1995, holding that federal affirmative action programs must be subjected to the most searching constitutional scrutiny. Affirmative action initiatives in both the public and private sectors have been dealt a crushing blow. Many experts have concluded that the shift in Washington could prompt companies to return to their old habits whereby minorities were rarely afforded meaningful business opportunities.[37]

In addition to the deleterious effects of the *Croson* and *Adarand* decisions, there are also other institutional and procedural barriers to the formation, survival, growth, and continued diversification of actual and potential minority business enterprises in inner-city communities.[38] The institutional barriers include the inadequate flow of capital for minority business development, growth, and diversification from commercial banks, savings and loans, and other financial institutions,[39] the hesitancy or outright refusal of commercial insurance companies to grant coverage to business enterprises in inner-city areas,[40] and inadequate attention to management and technical training by governmental agencies that have been established to support and encourage minority business development.[41] Porter would have us believe that the private sector—in exchange for a more "business friendly environment"—would step in to fill these gaps, although it never did so before, when there was no government coercion.

The procedural impediments also include the failure of school counselors to advise prospective graduates of career and business opportunities in the skilled trades; the operation of the "good old boy network" in all phases of the government procurement process, including certification, notification, and contract letting; and the refusal of federal procurement officials to downsize government contracts to facilitate the participation of small minority businesses.[42] These constraints are likely to be especially problematic for poor inner-city residents who aspire to pursue entrepreneurship and micro-business development as an avenue of upward mobility and financial security. They are least likely to have the requisite education and training, business skills, knowledge of the banking system, and access to the social capital resources (i.e., family, friends, and role models with expertise in these areas) to form and maintain a successful business.

Michael Porter has offered a useful perspective that has encouraged many scholars and practitioners, alike, to refocus on the trenchant problems of the American inner city. We believe that he has stimulated a necessary debate on "where we should go from here" in fostering a competitive advantage for disadvantaged urban communities. However, we are convinced that the principles developed in his earlier work, *The Competitive Advantage of Nations*,[43] will not work in the inner city. It is imperative that the "competitive advantage" be designed for the *empowerment* of inner-city workers and entrepreneurs rather than for the *exploitation* of inner-city resources by outside majority-owned businesses.

NOTES

1. Michael E. Porter, "The Competitive Advantage of the Inner City," *Harvard Business Review* (May-June, 1995): 55–71.

2. Ibid, p. 55.

3. Ibid, p. 56.

4. Mark Lowery, "Revitalizing Inner Cities," *Black Enterprise* 26 (Board of Economists Report) (January 1996): 64–67.

5. Committee for Economic Development, *Rebuilding Inner City Communities: A New Approach to the Nation's Urban Crisis* (New York: Committee for Economic Development, 1995); Arthur B. Shostak, ed., "Impacts of Changing Employment: If the Good Jobs Go Away," *The Annals of the American Academy of Political and*

Social Science 544 (March 1996).

6. Mark Lowery, "Revitalizing Inner Cities."

7. Marcus Alexis and Geraldine Henderson, "The Economic Base of African American Communities: A Study of Consumption Patterns," in *The State of Black America 1994,* edited by Billy Tidwell (New York: National Urban League), pp. 51–84.

8. Walter C. Farrell, Jr. and James H. Johnson, Jr., "Five Keys to Business Success," *The Milwaukee Courier* (July 16, 1994): 4.

9. David Grant and James H. Johnson, Jr., "Conservative Policy Making and Growing Urban Inequality in the 1980s," *Research in Politics and Society* (1995): 127–159.

10. James H. Johnson, Jr. and Walter C. Farrell, Jr., "The Fire This Time: The Genesis of the Los Angeles Rebellion of 1992," *North Carolina Law Review* 71(June 1993): 1403–1420; Grant and Johnson, "Conservative Policy Making and Growing Urban Inequality."

11. James H. Johnson, Jr. and Melvin L. Oliver, "Structural Changes in the Economy and Black Male Joblessness: A Reassessment" in *Urban Labor Markets and Job Opportunity*, edited by George E Peterson and Wayne Vroman (Washington, D C: Urban Institute, 1992), pp. 113–147.

12. James H. Johnson, Jr. and Walter C. Farrell, Jr., "The Fire This Time . . . ," pp. 1412–1413.

13. James H. Johnson, Jr., "The Clinton Presidency and the Future of US Cities," *Kenan-Flagler Business School Magazine* 5 (Special Postelection Issue) (1993): 8.

14. James H. Johnson, Jr., and Walter C. Farrell, Jr., "The Fire This Time . . . , pp. 1418–1419.

15. James Fitzgerald and William Patton, "Race, Job Training and Economic Development: Barriers to Racial Equality in Program Planning," *Review of Black Political Economy* 23(1994): 93–112.

16. Rosabeth Moss Kanter, *World Class: Thriving Locally in the Global Economy* (New York: Simon and Schuster, 1995).

17. Ed Gillespie and Bob Shellhaus, eds, *Contract With America: The Bold Plan By Rep. Newt Gingrich, Rep. Dick Armey, and the House Republicans to Change the Nation* (New York: Random House, 1994).

18. Joan Petersilia, "Crime and Punishment in California: Full Cells, Empty Pockets, and Questionable Benefits," in *Policy Choices for Los Angeles and the Nation,* edited by James Steinberg, David Lyon, and Michael Valana (Santa Monica, CA: Rand Corporation, 1992), pp. 175–206.

19. Walter C. Farrell, Jr. and James H. Johnson, Jr., "Access to Social Resources is Key to Problems in the Inner City," *The Wisconsin Review* (October 1994): 24.

20. David Grant and James H. Johnson, Jr., "Conservative Policy Making and Growing Urban Inequality."

21. James H. Johnson, Jr., "The Clinton Presidency and the Future of US Cities."

22. James H. Johnson, Jr. and John D. Kasarda, *A Proposal to Establish An Urban Investment Strategies Center at the University of North Carolina at Chapel Hill* (Chapel Hill, NC: Frank Hawkins Kenan Institute of Private Enterprise, 1993).

23. Ibid.

24. Timothy Bates, *The Major Studies of Minority Business: A Bibliography Review* (Washington, D.C.: Joint Center for Political and Economic Studies, 1991).

25. Noel P. Greis, John D. Kasarda, and Gyula Vastag, *Agile Logistics and Global Strategy: The Global Transpark* (Chapel Hill, NC: Publications Series of the Frank Hawkins Kenan Institute of Private Enterprise, January 1995); Carol McGiflert,

"The Big Emerging Markets Initiative," *Business America* 116(August, 1995): 4–17.

26. Noel P. Gries, John D. Kasarda, and Gyula Vastag, *Agile Logistics and Global Strategy: The Global Transpark.*

27. Carol McGiffert, "The Big Emerging Markets Initiative," pp. 4–17.

28. Lester A. Davis, "U.S. Exports of Goods and Services Support Rising Share of U.S. Jobs," *Business America* 116(August, 1995): 23.

29. Walter C. Farrell, Jr., James H. Johnson, Jr., Marty Sapp, Roger M. Pumphrey, and Shirley Freeman, "Redirecting the Lives of Urban Black Males: An Assessment of Milwaukee's Midnight Basketball League," *Journal of Community Practice* 2 (1996): 91–107.

30. David Osborne, "The Kemp Cure-All," *New Republic* (April 3, 1989): 21–25; Neil Pierce "Kemp's Enterprise Zones: Breakthrough or Chimera?" *Nation's Cities Weekly* (June 5, 1989): 4, Robert Cole and Donald Deskins, "Racial Factors in Site Location and Employment Patterns of Japanese Auto Firms in America," *California Management Review* 31 (1988): 9–22.

31. Ray Lopez, "Micro Means Business," *City Times* (*Los Angeles Times Weekly*), (September 20, 1992): 8–21.

32. William O'Hare, "Reaching for the Dream," *American Demographics* 14(January 1992): 32–36.

33. Timothy Bates and Constance Dunham, "Facilitating Upward Mobility Through Small Business Ownership," in *Urban Labor Markets and Job Opportunity*, edited by George Peterson and Wayne Vroman (Washington, D.C.: Urban Institute, 1992), pp. 239–281.

34. Ibid., p. 244.

35. Michael Hinds, "Minority Businesses Set Back Sharply by Court's Ruling," *New York Times* (December 23, 1991): A1.

36. Ibid.

37. James H. Johnson, Jr. and Walter C. Farrell, Jr., "Affirmative Efforts: Common Ground for the Common Good," *Alliance* (Kenan-Flagler Business School, University of North Carolina at Chapel Hill), (Fall 1995): 7.

38. Timothy Bates, *The Major Studies of Minority Business: A Bibliography Review.*

39. Paul Lee, "Recession Strikes Minority Business With Extra Fury," *Los Angeles Times* (May 29, 1992): Al.

40. James Peterson, "Private Sector is Crucial to the Rejuvenation Effort," *Los Angeles Times* (June 8, 1992): D1 & D4.

41. Timothy Bates, *The Major Studies of Minority Business: A Bibliography Review*; Richard Vartabedian, "U S. Program to Help Minority Firms Plagued by Failures," *Los Angeles Times* (July 7, 1991): D1, D7, & D8.

42. Timothy Bates, *The Major Studies of Minority Business: A Bibliography Review*; Harold Rose and Walter Farrell, "Need Exists for Set-Asides Based on Race, Gender," *The Business Journal* (May 20, 1991): 5.

43. Michael E. Porter, *The Competitive Advantage of Nations* (New York: Free Press, 1990).

19

A DIALOGUE ON THE ATLANTA PROJECT WITH
JANE SMITH, EXECUTIVE DIRECTOR

BOSTON: Would you give us an overview of The Atlanta Project?

SMITH: In 1991, President Jimmy Carter became energized about doing something in the Atlanta environment that might be used as a learning tool and as an example for the rest of the country while we benefited from it here. So for several months, he spent time on an idea that would eventually be called The Atlanta Project (TAP). He assembled, as only former presidents can, the CEOs of all the major corporations, all the CEOs of academic institutions, and the CEOs of service-provider institutions, for a series of meetings at The Carter Center. During subsequent months he also invited local residents. These efforts gave birth to The Atlanta Project. The ideas that would guide it came from an enormously diverse group of people using their best thinking from all disciplines. Some had worked on inner-city issues and others were completely disconnected from the community. Some people had worked in integrated environments and others had not. They included Republicans, Democrats, and Clergy.

TAP's emphasis was on urban revitalization, with a focus on poverty. Its scope included a population of 500,000 people and encompassed the cities of Atlanta, Decatur, Forest Park, College Park, East Point, and Clayton, Fulton, and DeKalb Counties. It was thought that the vast geography and enormous population could be serviced because there were so many corporations, academic institutions and service providers that could come together and work in this area. It was decided that TAP would be neighborhood-based and resident-driven—that it would be residents who would say what the needs were and that the residents would be involved in the discussion about the identification and use of resources. Assembling and facilitating this was going to be the special niche that the Carter Center identified for TAP. TAP was to bring people together, to facilitate and construct the discussion based on everybody's best thinking.

The city was excited that a former president was taking this initiative. I read the speeches carefully. He never said that TAP was going to decrease teenage pregnancy, build affordable housing, and get rid of drug lords. But the inspirational talks left the community believing this to be the case. It was felt that TAP would take care of all the things that nobody else would fix. But, if you read the literature, what's there are the words facilitation, collaboration, resident involvement: Bottom up, it's a process discussion.

BOSTON: TAP's goal then is to identify the problems and then to facilitate a coalition between residents and service providers?

SMITH: Yes, and the people who deliver the services at the county, city, and state levels as well as churches, boys and girls clubs, and the Red Cross. So our job is to bring all of the service delivery people together with the residents. But soon the community began asking what we were doing. And we responded by engaging in certain "quick fix," short-term "feel good" strategies. We used public relations and marketing strategies so that people could see us doing something and feel better about us, because as the months passed the public's perception was becoming negative. The "quick fixes" were a necessary move strategically, but in retrospect, it was unfortunate that we were not able to better communicate what business we were in. Had that occurred, we could have spent the time doing more of what we were supposed to be doing.

BOSTON: The heightened expectation was that TAP would march in dutifully and solve poverty. Do you view it as a failure on your part to communicate the essence of what TAP's mission was, or do you view it as a misinterpretation of what your mission was?

SMITH: Rather than a failure, I would have to say it was a poor or less than desirable attempt at communicating our objectives. We should have been able, in a short period of time, to have people understand what TAP does, just as the Urban League, United Way or the Boy Scouts are able to communicate. We know that United Way gives money to agencies. We may not know anything else, but we know that. We know that the Boy Scouts builds leaders. We know the Urban League is involved in civil rights and similar issues. We should have been able to hit the landscape with an understanding of our one or two main objectives. About the only common understanding we had was that Jimmy Carter was intimately involved, and he was a good man who worked to give everybody a fair opportunity.

While all of this was going on we set up twenty-one neighborhood sites to work out of and a headquarters, The Carter Collaboration Center (CCC). The offices in the neighborhoods were called cluster offices, because they each represented neighborhood clusters that they serviced. A cluster has from seven to fourteen well-established neighborhoods in it; each has an identifiable history. The clusters were to provide residents with a place to come, talk, plan, and gain access to resources. Different corporations supported them. For example, TBS (Turner Broadcasting System) supported the Douglas cluster. Georgia Tech supported the Tri-Cities cluster. These two clusters have done a miraculous job; I am proud of them. As a sociologist, I understand the significance of the kinds of community organizations that have been established in these areas over a two- to four-year-period. Neighborhood associations are working together in these clusters and they are maximizing resources and eliminating duplications and filling in places where voids exist.

BOSTON: How are the clusters organized administratively? What is the relationship between the cluster coordinator, the Carter Collaboration Center and the community?

SMITH: The cluster has a coordinator who lives in the community. Ninety percent of our cluster coordinators have lived in the clusters as adults, some even as children. Coordinators are very well known, and they have a civic history—some through PTAs, some through neighborhood planning units, some just because their families are well known. The few coordinators who did not live in the cluster have moved in because it is required that the coordinator live in the community. This is unlike teachers and police officers, who work in the community but may live elsewhere. We feel it is important that they be able to feel the life of the cluster. The coordinator is the liaison between the residents and the resources—the corporations, academic institutions, state and federal governments—as well as the CCC. At the CCC, there are people who have experience in different areas who work with the cluster. We didn't look for experts. These people are available to and work with the cluster staff. Clusters also have an assistant cluster coordinator, a full-time clerical person, interns from colleges and universities and a full-time corporate advisor.

BOSTON: What are the issues and how are they identified?

SMITH: During the planning period, we decided that each cluster would work on economic development, housing, education, children and youth, health, arts, and public safety. Each cluster had to have committees to identify the needs and begin the process of acquiring resources for those needs. Each cluster then had a steering committee, which was like an advisory council, made up of chairs of the various committees. So there was an advisory committee of chairs working with the cluster staff on a variety of jobs. We did that for three years. The first year was dismal—very elementary because the residents weren't used to planning. The second year was much better, and the third year has just been great. For example, the Brown Village has produced a strategic plan that has a statement of conditions of the cluster, the needs outlined by the residents, and potential resources that have been identified for the fiscal year. We believe these kinds of comprehensive neighborhood plans are unique in the country. Now, given that we're going to have a few more years to operate, we are really going to be able to get the resources to implement these plans. These things take a long time. Originally, we thought that we would be in business for only five years. That is, from the day of the announcement of the president's intention, we planned for four operational years. We now will go forward. But we don't know if it will be for three, four, or five more years. Eventually, we will go out of business because The Carter Center's strategy is to go in, set up an agreement, and then come out.

BOSTON: In addition to the cluster, what do you identify as some of your most tangible achievements in terms of the fulfillment of TAP's mission?

SMITH: We have identified about forty or fifty issues where we state the problems or needs and bring the collaborators together for the mission. Sometimes The Carter Center process ends with the identification of the solution because we don't do the work. One example is the Common Access Form, and it's my favorite story of The Atlanta project. When former President Carter went to see President Clinton to discuss TAP (during the 1992 campaign), President Clinton said one of the things he wanted to do was downsize the bureaucracy around human and social services. He stated that if there was anything TAP could do, to please do it. We came back from those conversations and then asked our residents about their interactions with the federal government. They said it was a pain to

work with the feds, that you have to go to so many different buildings and fill out so many different forms to get benefits. So we
collected the forms that working class and poor people had to fill
out. We found eight forms with a total of sixty-four pages. Often
people had to go to three or as many as eight different offices to get
placed into the system. We worked with federal representatives in
the Federal Executive Board and state representatives in Governor
Miller's office on those eight forms. We reduced them to one form
with eight pages (rather than eight forms with sixty-four pages).
This form is now being used for veteran benefits, social security
benefits, and welfare benefits. It's being tried in two of our clusters
and eight other states. The president and vice president have promoted its use around the country. This worked because we included
the residents in the discussion.

A second example is that the City of Atlanta has had an incredible backlog on property tax liens. The residents in our Brown
cluster were living in houses with absentee landowners, and they
believed they were going to be evicted. Our housing staff found that
the city was going to sell these tax liens to Fulton County. The
bottom line was that some properties were going to be taken away.
But the people living in those houses were not a part of those
discussions. Many elderly people had lived there for twenty to
twenty-five years and did not even know who owned the properties.
TAP provided classes for the residents to learn what was going on,
and brought in its bank partners so that those who did own property
could get loans to pay their taxes.

We really have about twenty extraordinary stories like this.

BOSTON: A lot of people are familiar with TAP's immunization program.

SMITH: But immunization is only now beginning. It took four years. The
goal of the immunization program was to implement a computerized tracking system so that the county governments (which deliver
the services) could keep up with a three-year-old Person X, for
example. Person X could move anywhere in the state, and we could
type in his number and have his entire immunization record. At the
time, this could not be done in the state of Georgia. Four years ago,
we went door to door to identify children in each family. It has
taken three years of incredible work by a newly formed organization called MATCH. Our health coordinator works along with other
members from the State, federal government, and the Carter Center.
They have put together a computerized system for Georgia based

on our immunization drive three years ago. This took three years to accomplish. If we are going to be criticized for systemic things, I don't like to be applauded for "feel good" things. This community remembers when we went door to door, which is a "feel good." We have to take them to the MATCH project which is systemic. The door to door drive was simply to seed. We turned all the paperwork over to MATCH. This immunization/MATCH work is only one of many TAP collaborations.

BOSTON: What are the key issues for urban revitalization?

SMITH: We believe that an accelerated inner-city revitalization effort rests in individual homes. In TAP, family means a lot. But the family has endured profound changes over the last twenty-five years in both function and value. We believe after four years of work, we have to take a holistic approach to the human service process around young families. That means prenatal, parenting training, and preschool for kids. We've been saying in this country for so many years that we have to start at the beginning, but we have been spending a lot of money in other places. Now you can do the holistic thing all you want but it's not going to make a difference without a job. Adults must have jobs. We want to do economic development so that the landscape is right for that family and for small businesses to begin in those neighborhoods. Code enforcement is another area with which we have had successes. This has to do with clearing off lots, removing dilapidated cars, getting rid of rats and rodents, eliminating drug exchanges, prostitution, and gang behavior in vacant homes. Code enforcement plus affordable housing is part of the landscape of economic development. Another part of this landscape is technology, the super highway in the inner city. We believe that we cannot be left behind. If we don't address this, we can do all the entrepreneurial development we want, all the job placement we want. But we will be left behind. So this is the holistic approach—you need the family, plus these other basic items.

BOSTON: Do you see the objectives of TAP as being at odds with the ideas that Michael Porter proposes, or do you see commonalities with Porter's approach?

SMITH: I see both, and when I don't represent him accurately, please correct me. Two things: One is that I think the holistic approach that is taken by a city has to reflect the history and the needs of that city. And so I do not think that a market analysis, a market-driven

economic development strategy should necessarily be the lead focus for any and every city.

BOSTON: I think that is a significant difference between your approach
and Porter's approach. Porter raises the entrepreneurial approach as
being the engine that drives everything, regardless of history or
location.

SMITH: When I was reading his work, I was amazed at his shortsighted-
ness in understanding the talent, skills and resources in the inner
city. You have to have people with the skills and the education to
be the entrepreneurs. People who do not live in the neighborhoods
that TAP has worked in are not coming to start businesses with a
population base that has a poor education and often nonmainstream
values. We've been begging folks, particularly food chains, to locate in TAP communities. Less and less, do we find people who can
sustain those kinds of activities living in those communities, and
less and less, do we find people who are willing to come in and
remain there. When you go into one of these communities and see a
closed restaurant on the corner, it may have been owned by an
African American who lived outside that neighborhood, and who
after six or seven years of work decided the cost wasn't worth it,
the insurance wasn't worth it, the turnover of the employees wasn't
worth it. I don't mean to be critical of the people I love and with
whom I work. It's just a characteristic of hopelessness that causes
certain kinds of behavior. When I read Porter I wonder how he is
going to get started, how he is going to kick that off when others
have tried in different ways. I fall right back into a simultaneous
holistic approach that would have at least equal emphasis on education and human resources and for some cities, for some period of
time, lead in on the education or the human services aspect before
the economic development even hits.

BOSTON: In your opinion, is there still a role for the government, in terms
of employee training programs, in terms of supporting community-
based organizations, in terms of affirmative action for businesses in
inner cities? Porter's position is that the market process must be
allowed a greater latitude to resolve the problems that the government has not or cannot.

SMITH: I speak from personal as well as TAP experience. I am a person
who believes there is a role for government in the personal affairs
of many, and I think that role is one that is constructive in the sense
that it creates opportunities for individuals and makes amends for

opportunities lost. So, therefore, I believe in affirmative action and other things like that. I look back at what has happened and know that people in my family and families like mine have benefited from government set-aside programs. But I wish that we could make these programs more targeted. What I'm saying is that I'm not sure the effort was as focused and as sustained as it could have been. I'm wondering how many poor people really received the benefits of our very special efforts in the 1960s, '70s and '80s that I was able to enjoy. In summary, I think there's a role for the government. It is about positive, constructive things, whether it is making up for lost opportunities or creating new ones. I just think that it has to be targeted.

BOSTON: Is the inner city in Atlanta better off for TAP having been there?

SMITH: TAP made a decision recently to continue its operations. Had TAP ceased to exist, our efforts would have been lost. Had we closed our doors on August 31, the root would not have taken. This would have been bad, not just for residents, but for the companies that have put in so much money for the well-intentioned service providers. Now we are going to be able to sustain those roots for a little bit longer. Because we are going to have a few extra years, we will be able to enrich what we have done and watch the growth in programs like immunization, for example. Some of our clusters are just two years old. These four years were about root development—planting a seed, covering it up and watching that root sprout. Had we ceased to exist past August 31, 1996, I would have had to say "no" to you, because I think all of the roots would have just rotted. And, oh, what a loss for this city. Talking nationally, for a minute, people have been in awe of TAP. When we first started, there was a little bit of envy because we had a former president who could go to the White House. As we matured, the other cities watched us and applauded us, and said, "Wow." We've never seen such corporate and academic support. For example, Georgia Tech has changed the landscape of public housing facilities in clusters where it is working, bringing students in and designing playthings for kids. Thank goodness we are going to have a few more years to better clarify what business we're in, how we run it and make sure that the roots can get above ground so that we can have some outcomes and changes.

BOSTON: There was a presumption, rightly or wrongly, that TAP would start in Atlanta and spread nationally.

SMITH: That was wrong. The literature says that we would share our
stories so that others could benefit in designing their own. It was
never about replication. Nationally, people have watched us and
applauded us for what we have been able to do.

During the next phase, which will be targeted towards children,
youth, and families, we really want to elevate the expert input and
academic discussion around what we're doing. The people who are
working with us now are good facilitators and have good networks,
but they often are not experts in the fields in which they are working. I'd like to do more of that, because that will assist us in being
more targeted. We also have to get involved with the Georgia legislature. There is a lot that has to be changed around work, family,
and health policies. So, hopefully, we can begin to work with the
legislature around some of these issues.

Part III:
Responses from Michael Porter
and the Editors

AN ECONOMIC STRATEGY FOR AMERICA'S INNER CITIES: ADDRESSING THE CONTROVERSY

Michael E. Porter

The economic distress of America's inner cities is one of the most pressing issues facing the nation. The lack of businesses, investment, and most importantly, jobs in these disadvantaged urban areas not only perpetuates a crushing cycle of poverty, but fuels other social problems such as crime and drug abuse.

The time has come to recognize that revitalizing our nation's inner cities requires a radically different approach. We must stop trying to cure the problems of these distressed urban areas by perpetually expanding social programs and hoping that economic activity will follow. Our nation's urban policies and programs have fallen into the trap of only redistributing wealth. The necessity and the real opportunity is to create income and wealth, by harnessing the power of market forces rather than trying to defy them. The private sector must play a leading role, and in many ways, is already beginning to do so.

I am honored by the willingness of *The Review of Black Political Economy* to devote an entire issue to ideas put forward in my article, "The Competitive Advantage of the Inner City."[1] The many scholars who reviewed the article all share with me a strong conviction about the importance of revitalizing inner-city neighborhoods. I welcome the by-and-large constructive commentary which mirrors the range of perspectives and criticism that I have encountered since my article was first circulated. I support many of the recommendations made by the authors, and am pleased to see many areas of agreement.

We all agree that more, better jobs are desperately needed in the inner city and that improvements must be made in infrastructure, job training, and school systems. We all agree that building social capital is important. And we all agree that inner-city residents, community-based organizations, government, and the private sector must all work together to revitalize inner cities and build healthy communities and a growing, sustainable economic base. In my response, I would like to first briefly summarize the core of my argument, and then respond to some of the important issues that have been raised.

A STRATEGY FOR INNER-CITY ECONOMIC DEVELOPMENT

My article, first and foremost, was a call for an economic strategy for inner cities as a complement to (not a substitute for) the many programs designed to increase human capital and meet the basic human needs of disadvantaged populations. An economic strategy is needed to build viable businesses that can provide the employment opportunities sorely needed in or near distressed inner-city neighborhoods—neighborhoods in which, in most cases, African Americans and other people of color represent the majority of the population.

While efforts to provide education, housing, healthcare, and other needed services are essential and must continue, these must be balanced with a genuine and realistic economic strategy focused on business and job development. Today, the great majority of efforts and resources are targeted toward meeting residents' immediate needs rather than generating jobs and economic opportunity that will mitigate the need for social programs in the long run.

My research was based on studies of nine major inner cities,[2] hundreds of interviews nationwide with inner-city-based companies, community-based organizations, bankers, government officials, and others, an extensive survey of the literature, and close advisory relationships with more than a dozen inner-city companies in Boston. Given the paucity of attention to inner-city business development, there is little or no comprehensive data yet available on inner-city companies, even in individual cities. While we have begun to compile such data, this represents an important priority for future research.

My article begins with the premise that a sustainable economic base can be created in the inner city only as it has been elsewhere: through private, for-profit initiatives and investments based on economic self-interest and genuine competitive advantage instead of artificial inducements, government mandates, or charity. An economic strategy must focus on the position of the inner-city economy in the regional economy, rather than treating inner cities as separate. Otherwise, economic activity there will not be sustainable. While the changing economy, with its dual challenges of global competition and technological advances, has adversely affected inner cites, it has also created new opportunities. The future inner-city economy will not look like the urban economy of many decades ago but will consist of a different array of businesses.

Instead of starting with the premise that inner cities are devoid of business and cannot compete, my strategy begins with the premise that inner cities must compete. There are many businesses present today in inner cities, a surprise to many who assume that little economic activity exists because of these communities' well-known problems. Inner-city businesses are concentrated in sectors such as food processing and distribution; printing and publishing; light manufacturing; recycling and remanufacturing; business support services for corporations; and entertainment and tourist attractions. These are all areas where genuine competitive advantages of an inner city lie.

Economic development in inner cities will come only from enhancing the advantages of an inner-city location and building on the base of existing companies, while dealing frontally with the present disadvantages of the inner city as a business location (many inflicted by poor government policies). There is genuine economic potential in inner cities that has been largely unrecognized and untapped.

The Competitive Advantages of Inner Cities

Our analysis of major cities nationwide has found that often-discussed advantages such as low-cost labor and real estate are largely illusory. Inner cities have available workers, but wages are not less than in rural areas or in other countries. Real estate costs may be lower than nearby high-rent downtown areas, but cheaper real estate is available in the suburbs and elsewhere. The changing nature of the world economy means that inner cities will not be able to compete if low cost labor and cheap real estate are the only advantages. Instead, we must recognize the genuine competitive advantages of inner cities, which fall into four areas:

Strategic location. Inner cities occupy what should be some of the most valuable locations in their respective regions, near congested high-rent areas, major business centers, entertainment complexes, and transportation and communications nodes. As a result, inner cities can offer a competitive edge to logistically sensitive businesses that benefit from proximity to downtown, proximity to transportation infrastructure, and a central location amid concentrations of companies. The just-in-time, service-intensive modern economy is only heightening the time and space advantages of such a location. This powerful advantage, which has not been fully developed or utilized, explains the continued existence and growth of the many food processing, printing, business support services, warehousing and distribution, and light manufacturing companies in most inner-city areas.

Unmet local demand. The consumer market of inner-city residents represents the most immediate opportunity for inner-city-based entrepreneurs and businesses. Despite low average incomes, high population density translates into an immense local market with substantial purchasing power. Making the market even more attractive is the fact that there tend to be few competitors serving it. At a time when suburban markets are saturated, inner-city markets remain poorly served—especially in many types of retailing, financial services, and personal services (see Figure 1). While the median household income in inner-city Baltimore is 39% lower than the rest of the city, the aggregate spending power is nearly the same, and the estimated retail spending per establishment is *two-thirds greater* in the inner city than in the rest of the city.[3] Inner-city-based businesses which serve this demand, especially those focused on meeting its unique needs, will have an advantage over more distantly located establishments.

Integration with regional clusters. Longer-term opportunities for inner cities lie in capitalizing on nearby regional clusters of firms and industries—unique concentrations of competitive companies in related fields. The ability to access competitive clusters is much more far reaching in its economic implications than simple proximity to the city. Building on local clusters involves tapping powerful external economies and leveraging private and public investments in skills, technology, and infrastructure. An effective economic strategy for inner cities must focus on better linking them to nearby clusters. For example, Boston is home to a world-class healthcare cluster that abuts the inner city. There are opportunities to link inner-city companies to this cluster as well as to develop focused programs for training and the development of job opportunities for inner-city residents.

Human resources. While inner-city populations present many workforce readiness challenges (discussed in greater detail later in this article), inner-city residents can be an attractive labor pool for businesses that rely on a loyal, modestly skilled workforce. There is the potential to build on this resource, with new approaches to education, job placement, and training. However, this requires debunking deeply entrenched myths about the nature of inner-city residents. The first is that inner-city residents do not want to work and opt for welfare over gainful employment.

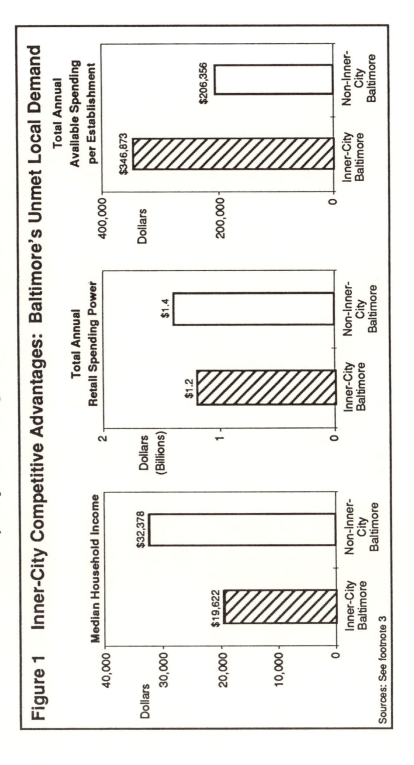

Figure 1   Inner-City Competitive Advantages: Baltimore's Unmet Local Demand

Sources: See footnote 3

Although there is a pressing need to deal with inner-city residents who are unprepared for work, our survey of businesses in inner cities nationwide shows that many inner-city residents are industrious, loyal employees.

Furthermore, contrary to popular perception, inner-city residents sometimes possess unique skills that are not found in significant concentrations elsewhere. In Kansas City, American Echo, a manufacturer of hospital beds and mattresses, finds an inner-city workforce with excellent stitching skills. Similarly, Eaves & Brooks Costume Company in New York reports that, "we're getting first-class cutters and tailors."[4] And the CEO of Harlem's largest private employer, the Alexander Doll Company, reports "We're very devoted to our workforce [primarily immigrants from the Dominican Republic, who learned sewing in factories there]. At the present time, it is the single advantage to this location."[5]

A second myth is that the inner city lacks entrepreneurs. In fact, there is a demonstrated capacity for entrepreneurship among inner-city residents, most of which has been channeled into microenterprises and the provision of social services. For instance, inner cities have a plethora of social service providers as well as social, fraternal, and religious organizations. Behind the creation and building of those organizations is a whole cadre of local entrepreneurs who have responded to intense local demand for social services and to funding opportunities provided by government, foundations, and private sector sponsors. The challenge is to create a climate whereby other inner-city residents, with similar talent and energy, build for-profit businesses that become meaningful employers, and create wealth.

The third myth is that skilled minorities, many of whom grew up in or near inner cities, look for businesses and employment only in more affluent areas. Today's large and growing pool of talented minority managers represents a new generation of potential inner-city entrepreneurs. Many of these managers have developed the skills, networks, capital, and confidence to join or start entrepreneurial companies in the inner city. We know of some—including former students of mine—who are doing so. As the awareness of the economic opportunities in inner cities grows, more will follow.

The Business Environment in the Inner City

As business locations, inner cities suffer from many disadvantages: discrimination, high taxes and business costs in areas such as utilities and insurance, crime, poorly maintained logistical infrastructure, burdensome regulations and permitting requirements, environmental pollution, and a weak education and training system. I will discuss some of these disadvantages in my response to the commentators' criticisms. However, a few general principles about improving the business environment in inner cities should be highlighted.

First, the inner city's disadvantages as a business location must be seen as an economic problem and must be addressed as part of an economic strategy. Too often, addressing weaknesses such as a poorly trained workforce or deficient logistical infrastructure are approached with only the social welfare of residents, not the needs of business, in mind. For example, inner-city training programs often fail to screen applicants— and even give priority to the least prepared residents in the name of fairness. Employers are then disappointed with the graduates.

Second, attempting to offset disadvantages with operating subsidies to businesses is futile. A more effective approach is to address the impediments to doing business directly. We must reduce unneeded regulatory hurdles, simplify permitting, reorient environmental cleanup requirements, and so on. There is simply no other solution.

Third, our research indicates that many of the inner city's disadvantages are not inherent, but the result of poor strategies and obsolete public policies. There are many best practices nationwide that could be adopted in every inner city. For example, New York City and a handful of other cities are adopting highly successful police force management and crime-fighting techniques that disproportionately benefit high-crime inner-city areas. The results have been dramatic: while major crime has fallen slightly across the country, in New York City it has fallen dramatically in the past few years (17.5% in 1995 alone), to levels not seen since the early 1970s.[6]

RESPONSE TO THE COMMENTATORS

The critiques of my article reflect, in many respects, the national debate over the issue of how to revitalize our nation's inner cities. Unfortunately, many of the responses indicate a misunderstanding of our arguments. Some focus on the question of assigning blame for past problems, while others appear to long for economic conditions which no longer exist. There is also a preoccupation with process—who should be consulted, etc.—rather than content, and there is a strong bias toward relying on government and not-for-profit institutions for solutions.

Part of the reason for the vigorous debate surrounding inner-city economic development is the definition of the term economic development. The American Economic Development Council (AEDC) says economic development is "the process of creating wealth through the mobilization of human, financial, capital, physical and natural resources to generate marketable goods and services."[7] But as John Blair notes, "economic development concerns reach into numerous aspects of community life. . . . In practice, distinctions between social, political, and economic development concerns are fuzzy."[8] This has led to a tendency to widen the definition of economic development to include virtually everything, and for different definitions to emerge. The result has been both confusion in communication and unnecessary controversy. Individuals and organizations have also tended to focus on one or a few specific elements of economic development which they care deeply about, and assert their primacy.[9]

For the purposes of our research, we focus on the creation of jobs and sustainable business activity that benefits disadvantaged inner-city residents. This does not deny the importance of improved housing, healthcare, and schools to the overall revitalization of inner cities. These topics are simply outside the scope of our primary focus.

Our approach to inner-city economic development, rooted in a business and competitiveness perspective, is fundamentally different from most existing efforts, and reflects the new realities of the inner city and of the national and international economy. It has not yet been implemented comprehensively at the inner-city level, although the core principles have been proven many times in states and countries.

The specific critiques of our argument fall into five broad categories: the role of the private sector, the role of community-based organizations, the role of government, appropriate types of job creation, and barriers to change.

THE ROLE OF THE PRIVATE SECTOR

Underlying many of the critiques is deep skepticism that the private sector is best suited, willing, or able to play a leading role in inner-city economic revitalization. Many skeptics have pointed to the ugly scars left by the private sector in inner cities—departures of companies, poor treatment of workers, and damage to the environment. They argue that the private sector is the problem and not the solution. Professors Blakely and Johnson, for example, both argue, in effect, that inner-city economic development efforts must be controlled by individuals and organizations within the inner city.

Given the track record of outsiders, both in government and the private sector, the desire for local control is understandable. I agree that there should be local input, but empowerment alone is not enough. True empowerment will come only through increased economic activity and opportunity. An isolationist, statist approach will guarantee the continued decline of inner cities, just as it doomed the economies of so many developing nations around the world. Conversely, the evidence is overwhelming that there is a strong tie between economic openness and economic progress in developing countries.[10]

We can state unequivocally, based on our research in inner cities and in many countries, that inner-city economic development efforts will continue to fail until businesses (both in the inner city and in the surrounding economy) are seen as the cornerstone and get involved. Inner cities will succeed only when they are connected to the surrounding economy, welcome new investment and entrepreneurs with minimal demands, and are satisfied with the degree of autonomy and control characteristic in other communities.

The notion that government and nonprofit organizations can or should be the driving force behind creating for-profit businesses in inner cities strains credibility. Government, community organizations, and inner-city residents cannot realistically and economically revitalize inner cities alone—they lack the management skills, technology, capital, and appropriate incentives.

Will the private sector step forward? Yes, it will, not because it is forced to, but because the inner city can offer an attractive market, an advantageous location, and good employees. We see evidence that the private sector is already investing in inner cities, and that the trend is accelerating, although much remains to be accomplished.

Supermarkets, for example, facing market saturation in the suburbs, are launching successful stores in inner cities.[11] The chief development officer of Vons, where 25% of new supermarkets in the 1990s will be urban, versus none in the 1960s, said, "There are 1.7 milllon people within reach of our advertising, warehouses and manufacturing who can't shop at a Vons, while the suburbs are over-stored."[12] The CEO of Lucky concurs, saying, "This isn't a philanthropic exercise. There are good food customers who come out in large numbers to buy high-margin items like meat and produce that offset higher urban costs."[13] At Finast, one-third of total 1992 sales in Ohio were generated by the eleven urban stores (out of 41 total).[14]

In Harlem, Fairway has opened a large, thriving supermarket that employs 170 people, 120 of whom are neighborhood residents. Pathmark has committed to open another supermarket in Harlem, in conjunction with the Local Initiatives Support Corporation's Retail Initiative program. A Pathmark company spokesman said city stores are "disproportionately profitable. Last year, they accounted for only 22% of the chain's 147 stores, but contributed 25% of its profits. In the 1990s, 50% of the chain's new stores will be urban, compared to 25% in the 1980s."[15]

Other retail, service, and franchise companies are also undertaking profitable ventures in inner cities.[16] In the Bronx, Caldor opened two stores which are already two of the five top-grossing stores in the country, and Rite-Aid announced that it will expand from eleven to more than fifty stores in the Bronx in the next few years.[17] Rite-Aid also reports that its Harlem store, opened in 1994, fills more prescriptions than any other store in the city.[18] In South-Central Los Angeles, the Magic Johnson Movie Theaters consistently rank in the top five theaters among the 21,800 surveyed nationwide, and plans are underway to open similar complexes in Atlanta, Houston and Harlem.[19] In Boston, the stores in the new South Bay mall include the highest volume Stop & Shop in the four-state region, Kmart in Massachusetts, and Toys 'R' Us in New England.[20]

Initially driven by the requirements of the Community Reinvestment Act but increasingly motivated by self-interest, banks are making major investments in inner cities in new branches and in the area of home mortgages. Bank of America, for example, now makes half of its home mortgages in California through a successful program launched in 1990 called Neighborhood Advantage. The program has generated $6 billion in home loans since its inception. This program evaluates credit-worthiness using nontraditional methods and requires lower down payments, yet the delinquency and foreclosure rate is two-thirds lower than Bank of America's conventional portfolio.[21]

Why aren't market forces working better? Many skeptics have asked, "If the inner city truly has important competitive advantages, why isn't the market working?" There are a number of answers.

First, there are many misperceptions and biases about the inner city and its opportunities—what economists call information imperfections. Fed by media coverage, inner cities are seen by many as combat zones devoid of economic activity, and populated by people with no ambition, skills, or resources. These perceptions have severely retarded investment and business development in areas with obvious market opportunity.

Second, many of the inner city's advantages have been diluted, while the disadvantages remain. For example, the strategic location advantage of many inner cities has often been dissipated by inadequate infrastructure investments and maintenance. The many disadvantages of the inner city as a business environment can and must be addressed. Until this happens, the disadvantages will continue to outweigh the advantages for many companies.

Finally, there is exceedingly limited and garbled communication between entrepreneurs and companies, on the one hand, and advocates for inner cities (e.g., community-based organizations, foundations and government) on the other hand. The fundamental source of the problem is different, and sometimes contradictory, objectives. Advocates for the inner city, wary of further exploitation, often position themselves as gatekeepers, making demands of companies, for example, to hire only locally, donate profits to various initiatives, and cede some degree of control or ownership to local entities. For example, when Pathmark sought to open a much-needed supermarket in Queens, it was forced to donate more than $400,000 to other merchants and to youth groups in the area.[22] Businesspeople are taken aback when they encounter, or even read about, such demands. They expect a welcoming local community and insist on full control of their businesses.

The result of these different agendas is often tension, if not outright hostility. Advocates for inner cities often feel that companies are not doing enough for their communities, while businesspeople feel victimized by what they perceive to be unreasonable demands and expectations.

Inner cities must compete for investment and jobs. Yet their advocates too often inadvertently get in the way, and then blame companies for being irresponsible. The best and only way to develop the economies of inner cities is to make them attractive places in which to invest and do business, both for residents and nonresidents. We see some hopeful signs that attitudes about business in inner cities are improving.

How can the private sector become more involved? While there are many organized, successful efforts to involve corporations in inner-city issues such as housing and education, it is ironic that few initiatives exist to engage the private sector through business-to-business activity. Nor is this due to lack of interest on the part of the private sector for programs that make economic sense. In fact, we believe so strongly in the need for better linkages between the private sector and the inner-city economy that we have created a new organization, the Initiative for a Competitive Inner City. The Initiative is developing programs to engage companies, professional service firms and business school students, faculty, and alumni in assisting and creating inner-city companies. The response from the private sector has been extremely heartening.

The Initiative is also working to address the barriers to inner-city business development through dispelling the myths about inner cities that hold back investment, developing strategies to enhance the competitive advantages and ameliorate the present disadvantages of inner cities, and improving communication between the private sector and advocates for the inner city. Many companies—among them Bank of America, Citibank, John Hancock, Lotus Development Corporation, Pacific Gas & Electric, and Textron—are actively involved. Additionally, more than thirty of the nation's leading graduate business schools have joined us to create or expand programs linking students and faculty with inner-city companies. The response gives us confidence that the business community is ready to try new approaches based on sound, economically driven strategies.

In Boston, beginning in early 1994, the Initiative organized a program to marshal in-depth consulting support from experienced MBA students and faculty to help inner-city-based companies realize their competitive advantages. The two- to four-person teams addressed a range of managerial issues and produced concrete benefits for client companies. Over the past three years, 69 students working on 20 teams have provided consulting services worth an estimated $350,000.[23] In addition, the principals of the Initiative and I have provided further assistance to client companies, and established relationships with legal, accounting, information technology and financial partners in the region to provide pro bono services to clients. Overall, since the program began, our clients have created nearly 200 new jobs for inner-city residents, representing over $3,000,000 per year in wage income.[24] The Initiative is now expanding this program to other cities and business schools.

THE ROLE OF COMMUNITY-BASED ORGANIZATIONS

My article clearly struck a nerve with a number of authors with its discussion of the appropriate role for community-based organizations (CBOs), especially community development corporations (CDCs). Great effort and funding has been rightly directed at creating and building

CDCs, and many have been remarkably successful in building and managing low-income housing, stabilizing neighborhoods, and recreating local market demand. They deserve much credit for helping to create the conditions under which the private sector would consider investing.

Now, however, inner cities are ready to move to the next stage, which will require new strategies from CBOs of all types. Our model, with its focus on private, for-profit initiatives, seems threatening to the CBOs, who see themselves as advising, financing, and owning inner-city companies. It should not be. CBOs can, and must, play a role in inner-city economic development efforts. But choosing the proper strategy is critical, and many CBOs will have to refocus their activities. CBOs, like every other player, must identify their capabilities, resources, and limitations, and participate in economic development with the right strategy.

In the area of true business development, the record of CBOs is mixed. While there are a number of noteworthy successes—for example, New Communities Corporation has a majority equity stake in a Pathmark supermarket in Newark's Central Ward with sales per square foot twice the national average[25]—the strategy of advising, lending to, or operating businesses is a questionable one for most CBOs. In general, they are not equipped to provide much of the specialized input businesses need, and their efforts often end in failure. Moreover, CBOs can and must reach out to the private sector institutions and entities that will be essential to the ongoing growth and development of their local communities. In the modern, complex economy, it makes little sense to attempt to recreate the expertise and resources that already exist.

While it is difficult to generalize about such a diverse group of organizations, we believe that CBOs' economic development efforts should be guided by a business-based model. They should seek to build networks with mainstream business institutions (e.g., business schools, banks, corporations, chambers of commerce) instead of attempting to duplicate them. In many cases, CBOs already have strong relationships with the mainstream business community through, for example, efforts to develop affordable housing. These relationships can be leveraged to broker valuable business-to-business connections and resources. Thus, instead of advising businesses directly, CBOs should connect local companies with high-quality existing resources. Instead of setting up a new loan program, they should facilitate access by businesses to financing, first through banks and, failing that, through the myriad of public and quasi-public financing sources already present in most cities.

Within this framework, CBOs are uniquely positioned to change community attitudes. As discussed earlier, inner-city residents and advocates often dissuade interested businesses from locating in their communities by, for example, making demands on companies to meet their community's social needs, hampering company expansion efforts, and opposing the start-up of new businesses that compete with existing ones. CBOs, through their knowledge of and influence within inner-city communities, can play a crucial role in altering these and other community attitudes. They can act as a liaison with residents to quell unfounded opposition to new businesses, while at the same time serving as a forum for addressing legitimate concerns and ensuring that past problems are not repeated.

With their networks both in the community and in the private sector, some CBOs already are or could become effective job training providers. The Bidwell Training Center in Pittsburgh,[26] Project: HOPE in Detroit,[27] and Boston's One With One are all doing an outstanding job training and placing inner-city residents in good jobs in nearby clusters.

Many CBOs are also well positioned to address the vexing problem: inner-city-based businesses do not always hire many inner-city residents.[28] CBOs have, on occasion, responded by demanding that new inner-city companies hire a certain percentage of their employees from the local area, or criticizing and ostracizing existing companies that do not hire a sufficient number of local residents. This approach has backfired in the long run by driving companies away and contributing to the general perception of a hostile business environment. A more productive approach is to understand the needs and perceptions of local businesses, and develop programs to address them.

The roots of this problem often go beyond poor work ethic, training, and work readiness to issues such as lack of informal networks and employer bias. CBOs can play an important role in helping overcome these barriers and connecting inner-city residents to nearby jobs. To expand on a case study I cited in my *Harvard Business Review* article, the South Brooklyn Local Development Corporation (SBLDC) played an important role in connecting local residents to jobs in the Red Hook industrial area by developing relationships with nearby businesses and screening and referring employees to them. For example, to meet the needs of the large number of local trucking and bus companies, SBLDC created a customized, intensive training program to help carefully screened local residents of the projects get their commercial driver's licenses, and then hired two women to walk around the neighborhood, knocking on the doors of employers, to create the kind of personal referral networks the people in the project didn't have. The result was that of 32 people who entered the program, 28 completed it, 25 got their licenses, and 18 got good jobs. At \$185,000/year, the program's cost is modest, given its results.[29]

Finally, CBOs with relevant experience can facilitate site improvement, development, and expansion. We have found that many businesses seeking to expand or locate in the inner city have difficulty finding suitable sites or navigating the approval and permitting process. CBOs often have significant expertise in real estate which could be applied to the development of commercial and industrial property (including site assembly, demolition, and environmental cleanup), identifying appropriate sites for expansion, and assisting companies in the permitting and approval process.

There are many examples of CBOs that are successfully collaborating with businesses. In Boston, the Dorchester Bay EDC was responsible for rehabilitating a building which was then occupied by one of our clients, Americas' Food Basket supermarket. The supermarket has operated successfully there and has helped revitalize the entire Uphams Corner shopping district. Another example of collaboration is cited by the CEO of First National, a leading supermarket chain:

> Cultivating close ties to community groups is the place to start. They can help identify and train local residents who will be reliable workers. Nonprofit community groups may also have development expertise and access to government financing and tax breaks. . . . It creates trust that dispels the view that outside chains come in to take advantage—a problem that Korean grocers had in Los Angeles and the Arabs in Cleveland.[30]

These examples do not involve CBOs owning and operating supermarkets, but rather helping to create the conditions whereby private investors and entrepreneurs will invest.

THE ROLE OF GOVERNMENT

Our critics seem to think we advocate that government at all levels should simply abandon the inner city and allow private initiatives to take over. This is puzzling because the *Harvard Business Review* article clearly states otherwise. The issue is not the importance of a continuing government role, but exactly what that role should be. My article is indeed highly critical of past and present government programs because they have, in general, defied economic logic, distorted incentives and failed to ease racial tensions. Local governments bear significant responsibility for the disinvestment by the private sector in inner cities by failing to maintain schools, infrastructure, and public safety, raising taxes excessively, and creating a morass of costly regulations.

Professors Henry, Dymski, Goldsmith and others want to use government spending as a substitute for developing an economy through competitive advantage. In contrast, we see a continued, vital role for government in inner-city economic development, but a role focused not on direct intervention but on creating a favorable environment for business (e.g., improving the public school system, training workers, upgrading infrastructure, streamlining regulation).

Government as a marketer. In the area of economic development, a critical role of government is to act as a marketer—courting, welcoming, and assisting companies. Based on hundreds of interviews with businesses, government officials and others across the country, we have unfortunately found that government rarely plays this role in inner cities. For example, the CEO of a major Oakland corporation that was deciding whether to expand its plant in Oakland or open a new one in Houston said that in Houston, he was met at the airport by city officials, shown appropriate parcels of land, and given all required permits and waivers on the spot. In contrast, he was frustrated that neighborhood groups and city government in Oakland had stymied his attempts to win approval to expand his existing plant because of concerns over more traffic.[31]

Contrast this with Tupelo, Mississippi. With a population of 30,000 people in an impoverished rural area, Tupelo illustrates a business-friendly city government. While there are many factors in Tupelo's progress, a critical one is that the city government bends over backwards to be welcoming and hospitable toward businesspeople. One CEO said, "They really know how to push the right buttons. In New York, just to get someone to talk to me, I had to make three phone calls. With Tupelo, six guys met me at the airport. They had five different sites ready for me to look at."

The results have been astounding: More than eighteen Fortune 500 companies and a range of international and smaller companies have set up production in Tupelo, the unemployment rate is significantly lower than the state average (and for blacks, is half the state average), racial tensions are low, the schools are well-funded, student test scores are above the state and national averages, and per capita income is the second-highest in the state.[32] And all of this without millions of dollars in business subsidies.

Can economic progress be made while discrimination remains a serious problem? It is clear that discrimination has precluded African Americans and other people of color from the educational and economic opportunities that have been afforded many other groups in American society. The current economic weakness of inner-city communities, and the human capital deficits that plague them, in many ways reflect the legacy of discrimination, and it is clear from our research that discrimination remains a serious problem.

However, the problems of inner cities go beyond discrimination to many factors that magnify its effects. While continuing to work to eliminate discrimination, we must move forward with a positive strategy to address other parts of the inner-city problem based on sound economic principles and building competitive companies. Our experience has been that such an economic strategy emphasizes mutual benefits and brings people together.

The role of affirmative action and government set-aside programs for minority businesses. A central tool employed to counter discrimination has been affirmative action, which has created opportunities for minorities in a number of occupational and educational fields. In the area of business-related affirmative action programs such as minority preferences for government contracts, further steps must be taken to better link these programs to businesses that will employ or create wealth for residents of distressed communities instead of targeting minority entrepreneurs regardless of income levels and whom they employ. While minority-owned firms are more likely to hire inner-city residents,[33] we have seen many nonminority-owned businesses in or near inner cities that are providing thousands of good jobs to inner-city residents. They should qualify for assistance as well. To quote President Clinton, "We need to do more to help disadvantaged people in distressed communities, no matter what their race or gender."[34]

These programs also need to be refined to promote sustainable businesses, not just guarantee companies a market, and in so doing dull motivation and retard cost and quality improvements. These pitfalls are not just true for minority set-asides—we have seen them in all parts of this country and the world. It is not surprising, therefore, to see that a 1988 General Accounting Office report found that within six months of graduating from the Small Business Association's purchasing preference program, 30% of the companies had gone out of business. An additional 58% of the remaining companies claimed that the withdrawal of the SBA's support had had a devastating impact on business. We believe that companies benefiting from set-asides must demonstrate movement toward self-sufficiency in order to retain them, so that incentives are more aligned with creating sustainable, profitable businesses. With modifications we have suggested, we are confident that the current attacks against preference programs would diminish significantly.

The role of subsidies. Some critics have falsely claimed we believe there should be no subsidies, where subsidies refer to the use of public resources. My point is not about the need for public resources, but what form the subsidies should take. Public funds (subsidies) will be necessary to economically revitalize inner cities, but they must be spent in support of an economic strategy based on competitive advantage instead of distorting business incentives with futile attempts to lure to inner cities businesses that lack an economic reason for locating there. It is appropriate for government funds to be used to prepare a site for business by assembling parcels of land, improving infrastructure, doing environmental remediation, and providing better public safety. However, the businesses that then locate there should not receive ongoing operating subsidies or they are unlikely to become sustainable in the long run.

Professor Fainstein cites the Hunt's Point Food Distribution Center in the South Bronx as a critique of our model. Instead, it strongly supports it. In this case, the government *created the conditions where the private sector could thrive* by buying and developing 329 acres. It did not try to invest in or operate the businesses, which now employ 20,000 people and handle the bulk of the meat, fruit and vegetables that enter the New York City metro area. Hunt's Point also illustrates the leverage of clusters to create competitive advantages to support exports regionally. Another approach to site development, which is being implemented by Mayor Bret Schundler in Jersey City, is to bundle unattractive parcels of city-owned land with desirable ones and auction them off to private developers who must clean up all the parcels as part of the deal.

The proper use of tax incentives. Both at the federal and state levels, various tax incentives have been used over the years to support economic development in designated depressed areas, often called enterprise zones. While we support measures that make inner cities more competitive—and higher taxes than the surrounding region are often a significant disadvantage[35]—the record of enterprise zones is not encouraging. As we have seen again and again, businesses that locate in an area because of tax breaks or other artificial inducements, rather than genuine competitive advantages, are not sustainable. Research is accumulating from around the world that few businesses make location decisions based on tax incentives, especially the modest ones commonly associated with enterprise zones.[36] Thus, the bulk of the tax break goes to businesses that would have been operating in the enterprise zone anyway. Enterprise zone incentives are perverse in a number of other ways as well. They often fail to encourage hiring residents of the depressed area, but only encourage locating there, nor do they appear to promote entrepreneurship by residents.[37] The tax breaks are also generally not based on successfully turning a profit, which should be at the root of all incentives.

The Clinton Administration's Empowerment Zone approach—a comprehensive plan in which tax breaks are only one part of the overall effort—is a half-step in the right direction. It required cities to develop comprehensive development plans that went far beyond tax breaks and sought to encompass not only business development, but also other critical areas such as job training, housing, and social services. Yet in actual practice, true business development is only a small part of Empowerment Zone efforts. The rush to take advantage of government funds has caused the process to become highly contentious and politicized, further drawing attention away from economic development.[38] Indeed, the well-intentioned Empowerment Zone initiative illustrates the powerful forces that are working against an economic approach to the inner-city problem.

Do inner-city residents genuinely want to work, and do they make good employees? There is little doubt that inner cities as a whole have an undereducated, underskilled population with a disproportionate number of people who are ill-equipped for work for a variety of reasons. Despite this, many employers report great satisfaction with their inner-city workforce. The following quotations are from our interviews with employers in inner-city Boston and Oakland.[39]

I have no problem finding people. They come to me. I hand out 2-4 applications every day. . . . I have no problem getting them up to speed. . . . There are a lot of nice people here. . . . I've never had crime problems or seen drug problems.

We're very devoted to our workforce. At the present time, it is the single advantage to this location.

The people are experienced, and the company is able to retain a lot of the workforce.

Turnover is very low; people just don't quit.

There is a great pool of blue collar workers in the inner city.

I have no problem finding willing and able workers. . . . I get two or three applications per day.

A lot of our workers are second-generation and are very loyal.

These perspectives are reinforced by a study in central Harlem, which concluded that, "The ratio of job seekers to successful hires in the fast food restaurants studied. . . . is approximately 14 to 1."[40]
However, there is certainly evidence that the work ethic and qualifications of some residents of inner cities is sorely lacking. The following three quotations reflect all-too-common comments we have heard from inner-city employers[41]:

I am dying for qualified labor but I can't afford to hire someone who can just show up for work. . . . There are a lot of unskilled people available, but they don't meet our needs. Of the inner-city residents we try to hire for semi-skilled welding jobs, more than half flunk a drug test and few make it through the internship period.

The vast majority [of the inner-city workers I hired] lacked basic attitudes rather than skills. It was very difficult to find individuals who consistently arrived at work on time, followed directions, worked as a team, or showed even a modest degree of enthusiasm or ambition. It was necessary to frequently test for drug use to control this problem as well as exercise careful supervision to prevent crime in the workplace. Despite the fact that our wages and promotion opportunities were the best in each area, it was often difficult even to find willing candidates.

Even when I hire through families or personal recommendations, I have found that 50% of the African Americans I hire don't work out. In contrast, 95% of Vietnamese I hire work out, as do 90-95% of Peruvians. Immigrants—at least certain groups of them—appreciate the job, are very reliable, and come to work every day. If you ask them to do something, they do it and don't give you any problems.

These quotations raise a number of important issues. First, they underscore the reality that the inner-city workforce has a disproportionate number of people who are problematic employees. Thus, to hire from the inner city, companies must have effective strategies for identifying good employees. Cultivating personal networks in the community, and building relationships with CBOs (as discussed earlier), are essential.

Second, employers widely report much higher satisfaction with immigrant workers, many of whom are black or Latino and live in inner cities. Thus, perhaps a more relevant distinction than inner-city versus non-inner-city employees, or blacks and Latinos versus other ethnic groups, is long-resident poor versus poor recent immigrants. The former tend to have greater problems entering the workforce, whether they are blacks in the inner city or, for example, whites in the Ozarks. Immigrants, on the other hand, tend to be a self-selecting group who find a low income in the United States far better than the situation in their home country. They tend to work harder than everyone.

Finally, these quotations and our other interviews illustrate that some white inner-city business owners and managers are often quick to unfairly judge entire groups of people based on only a few experiences. This is one of the most important areas in which faulty perceptions are working against economic progress.

It is clear that the inner-city workforce is diverse and complex and cannot easily be summarized. While there are many problems with the workforce, our research reveals that there is a meaningful proportion of unemployed or underemployed inner-city residents that are ready and able to be good employees. The challenge is to create more accessible jobs and better connect these people to them.

Improving the training system. A critical part of the solution to the human resource problems discussed above is the job training system.[42] Unfortunately, the existing system in the United States is ineffective. Training programs are fragmented, overhead intensive, and disconnected from the needs of industry and recipients. Many programs provide poor training for nonexistent jobs in industries with no projected growth. For example, a study of the Job Training Partnership Act showed that young men who had dropped out of school and enrolled in the program earned 8% *less* than those who were given no training.[43]

Inner-city job training programs have an especially difficult challenge because they must overcome many inner-city residents' low education levels, poor work skills, and attitudes. Outlined in my *Harvard Business Review* article were a number of strategies both to engage the private sector to create and certify training programs, which could be built around industry clusters in the inner city and in the nearby regional economy, and also to tap into existing private sector training programs, especially corporate ones. Below are three illustrations of important principles and strategies that should be widely adopted.

Two case studies highlight the strong potential benefits of corporate involvement. In 1968, Polaroid Corporation launched Inner City, a wholly owned subsidiary set up "to provide Boston's unemployed and underemployed residents with an entry into meaningful employment."[44] Inner City receives no public funding. It is a genuine business that packages film for Polaroid and offers a range of printing, copying, remanufacturing, product assembly and packaging fulfillment services. The more than 2,500 inner-city residents who have gone through the eight-month program received on-the-job training from the beginning and, after placement, "over 70% are still with the same company after one year of employment—the highest retention rate of any job training program of this type in the country."[45]

Another interesting new corporate endeavor is e.villages, a for-profit computerized data processing service and job training provider founded by Hamilton Securities, a national real estate investment banking firm, and Adelson Entertainment, a Los Angeles-based film and television producer. e.villages has created a pilot program in inner-city Washington DC. Nine previously unemployed or underemployed residents were given advanced computer training and are now part-owners of the resulting business, located in the housing project where the employees live. The new business performs database services for Hamilton Securities and other corporate clients. e.villages seeks to expand this concept nationwide.

A third example highlights a serious flaw in the current job training system: the lack of proper incentives for training providers. Because success is difficult to define and evaluate, training providers are rarely held accountable for their results. This leads to a situation where funding is doled out based on political connections or the number of people who graduate from a program, rather than desired outputs (long-term employment and increased earnings). A small for-profit company, America Works, is pioneering a new system, and offers an exciting new model that is active in New York City, Albany, and Indianapolis. America Works trains, places, and supports welfare recipients in private-sector jobs that pay an average of $9/hour and offer full medical benefits. Of those placed, 70% are hired permanently after a four-month probationary period; of these, 90% are still working after one year. This documented success, resulting in the placement of over 3,000 permanent workers, is far better than that of any other inner-city job training provider we have encountered.[46]

What is unique about America Works, and which helps explain its success, is the incentive system under which it is compensated. America Works receives payment (generally from state welfare agencies) only when a welfare recipient is successfully placed in a full-time job and has completed the probationary period. The $5,000-$6,000 cost to the state is far outweighed by the welfare savings, which can exceed $20,000 in the first year alone. Sadly, because its model is so threatening to established providers, America Works has encountered fierce criticism and resistance.

The appropriate role of government in improving access to capital. The issue of access to capital provides an especially illuminating example of appropriate versus inappropriate government intervention. Most government efforts have focused on the creation of government loan pools and quasi-public financing entities that have produced fragmentation, market confusion, and excessive overhead costs, and have made many uneconomic investments. Even while Professor Dymski proposes more of the same, he admits that some will be loss generators.

The only viable solution is to harness market forces and the resources of the private capital markets. In the area of debt financing, we argue that mainstream financial institutions must be engaged through direct incentives such as transaction fees to cover high overhead costs associated with small transactions and partial loan guarantees that mitigate some—though not all—of the risk. Additionally, increased disclosure of inner-city business lending would motivate progress.

Regarding equity capital, our proposal is to *eliminate* the tax on capital gains and dividends from long-term equity investment in inner-city-based businesses (or subsidiaries) that employ a minimum percentage of inner-city residents. This proposal would, we believe, maintain a focus on genuine profit and result in a flow of new equity capital from a wide range of sources flowing into inner cities. The cost, which is likely to be modest, would be decisively outweighed by tax revenues from higher employment of inner-city residents.

Given the history of exploitation in inner cities, is less regulation risky? While I argue forcefully against needless, inefficient, and destructive government regulation, I do not, as Dr. Johnson charges, favor scrapping laws that govern ".... workplace health, safety, and compensation. ... " Instead, my primary focus is on the astounding number of rules, permits, and regulations that have accumulated at the federal, state, and especially, city government levels over many years. It is truly ironic that the areas in the United States that are most in need of business development are the most over-regulated. The laws that Dr. Johnson seems to uncritically support not only deter businesses needlessly, but slow down progress on environmental clean-up and workplace safety.

Merely registering and legally operating a small business in an inner city is daunting. For example, according to Steve Mariotti, the founder of National Foundation for Teaching Entrepreneurship, which teaches entrepreneurship to "at-risk" inner-city youth, "The minority entrepreneur usually ends up being his own lawyer and accountant. . . . The paperwork, cost, and confusion. . . . drive would-be entrepreneurs away from certainty and down a slippery slope. They develop contempt for the government because they no longer see it as their ally. That drives people into the underground economy, where there are no contracts. Matters of dispute are settled with gun or a beating. . . . Once an entrepreneur moves into the balkanized—and chaotic—underground economy, growing the business is not a viable option."[47]

Absurd laws and regulated monopolies also plague inner-city entrepreneurs. According to a leading magazine for entrepreneurs, "about 10% of all jobs in this country require some sort of license, and many of those are low-skill, entry-level occupations such as taxicab driving, working as a street vendor, cosmetology, trash hauling, and recycling. The licensing process in these fields is often onerous and . . . preserves existing monopolies at the expense of those least able to defend themselves."[48] For example, in Washington, DC, the city shut down a nascent hair braiding business because of a 1938 law that mandated that employees have extensive schooling in hair treatments using chemicals and techniques that had not been used for at least 30 years.[49] Additionally, many cities strictly limit the number of peddlers' licenses, often a first entrepreneurial endeavor.

Taxicabs are an especially visible and depressing case study. The taxicab industry is regulated in 87% of large U.S. cities, at an added cost to U.S. consumers of $800 million per year.[50] In New York City, there are fewer medallions today than there were in 1935. In Denver, no new medallions have been issued since 1947. The result is windfall profits for medallion owners (generally a few large companies), a huge barrier to entry for aspiring inner-city entrepreneurs who wish to operate van and livery services, and poor service for the cities' residents, especially in inner-city areas, where poor transportation hampers residents' efforts to find and keep jobs in other parts of the region. Mayor Stephen Goldsmith of Indianapolis deregulated the taxicab industry a few years ago, and the result has been lower prices, better service, and a flourishing of new entrants, many of whom are inner-city-based entrepreneurs.

Regulation also affects larger businesses and community-based organizations. Alan Hershkowitz, a senior scientist with the National Resources Defense Council, who is working with the Banana Kelly CDC to develop a proposed paper recycling project in the South Bronx, speaks for a large number of developers and businesspeople we have interviewed: "There is usually a lengthy, labyrinthine permitting process in cities. In rural areas, you do not even have to file an environmental impact statement."[51] When Harlem's famed Sylvia's soul food restaurant sought to open a new restaurant in Camden, NJ, creating 50-75 jobs, it expected approval within two weeks. Instead, "after a frustrating year of unsuccessfully trying to secure the various approvals from city boards, the restaurant has put off its plans to move to Camden."[52] A final example shows that for-profit businesses are not the only victims. Rev. Calvin Butts of the Abyssinian Development Corporation in Harlem laments, "If we could sit down with the city and have an ordinary negotiation, we could easily build twice the number of [housing] units, and I assure you it would cost a lot less."[53]

The permitting process can be streamlined, as the case of Indianapolis again illustrates. There, Mayor Goldsmith formed a panel comprised of ten local business leaders and entrepreneurs as well as 150 volunteers and charged it with examining all of the city's permitting and regulatory requirements. For each requirement, the panel asked, "Is there something unique about Indianapolis that would justify additional regulation above and beyond what is already required by the state and federal government?" The result was that entire volumes of antiquated regulations and permits were eliminated.[54]

In the area of zoning, antiquated laws reflecting an economy that has not existed for decades are another major problem in many cities. For example, large swaths of land in New York City remain zoned for manufacturing and industrial usage, despite the fact that few if any of these businesses remain. This land should be rezoned to allow residential and retail development.

In the area of environmental policy, it is ironic that current legislation (especially the Federal Superfund law), intended to foster clean-up of the nation's estimated 200,000 to 500,000 vacant urban industrial sites, has instead hampered these efforts.[55] According to Henry L. Henderson, Chicago's environmental commissioner, "The shadow of crushing liability and the fear of lenders made it impossible for small businessmen to get loans to develop urban properties." The result, according to Mr. Henderson, "was an unintended effect of a law designed to protect the environment: the abandonment of urban areas by businesses that built factories, warehouses and commercial centers on unspoiled greenfields in rural areas, draining badly needed jobs from inner cities."[56]

Liability and cleanup laws must be modified so that lenders, developers, and businesses will return to the inner city. We are pleased to see that more than half the states have passed legislation or developed policies to reduce the liability threat inherent in such properties and ease cleanup requirements. Congress is considering a host of similar proposals. Similarly, the Clinton Administration initiated a $10 million grant program last year to fund cleanup, and has modestly relaxed the Superfund law that governs hazardous-waste cleanups.[57]

APPROPRIATE TYPES OF JOB CREATION

Dead-end jobs. Professors Blakely, Schweke, and Johnson all take me to task for supposedly advocating only low-wage, dead-end jobs. This is not what my article states or implies, and I am in complete agreement that an inner-city economic development strategy should focus on growing companies and industries that offer decent jobs. However, my article stressed the need for realism about the inner city's competitive advantages and disadvantages and the capacity of the workforce. For the present, any job that offers a foundation for economic self-sufficiency and advancement is a good job. Over time, market forces and improving skills (hopefully due in part to an improving public school system) will raise the quality of inner-city employment opportunities.

Advocates for the inner city who denounce low-skill jobs as "dead-end jobs" are in fact denying many inner-city residents the entry-level opportunities they need. What is most important is to get people onto the economic ladder, even if it is at the lowest rung. While the poorest 20% of households are, on average, faring worse and worse, there is tremendous economic mobility among individual households. For example, an ongoing University of Michigan study examined those who were in the bottom 20% of all earners in 1975 and found that by 1991, only 5% were still in the bottom 20%, while 80% had made it into the top 60% of earners (i.e., the middle class), and the average annual income for the entire group had increased by $25,322.[58] Michael Cox, vice president of the Federal Reserve Bank of Dallas, concludes that "the evidence suggests that holding low income jobs is largely a transitory stage for people with little work experience. . . . If people get into the workforce—at any level—and stay there, they will likely be rewarded. There is a permanent underclass, but it consists for the most part of people who have dropped out of the workforce entirely."[59]

Unfortunately, some inner-city residents are unwilling to take these entry-level jobs. In a study by Harvard economist Richard Freeman of out-of-work inner-city black youth, over 70% in 1980—and nearly 75% in 1989—said they could easily find a job, but generally rejected the readily available hamburger flipper or checkout clerk jobs as low-paid or leading nowhere.[60] As Myron Magnet argues:

> Most families don't rise from poverty to neurosurgery or mergers and acquisitions in one generation. It goes by stages, it takes time, and it often starts humbly. But if cleaning houses, making up hotel rooms, cutting meat, or cooking french fries is being a sap—if it makes the person doing it feel himself in a demeaning, false position, earning "chump change" in a "dead-end job," rather than being decent and honest—then it is that much harder to put a foot on the bottom of the ladder.[61]

The importance of retailing. The concept of dead-end jobs also often manifests itself in the debate over whether retailing should be an important part of an inner-city economic development strategy. Our model identifies many business opportunities in inner cities, and emphasizes the importance of building businesses that "export" goods and services outside the inner city. It is by no means restricted to retailing. However, there is great opportunity for new retailing that should not be ignored. The solution is twofold: increase the inflows of money (primarily by improving employment opportunities and building "export" businesses) *and* increase the quality and number of retail and service businesses within inner cities. The net result, if both of these strategies were implemented, would be many more jobs and greater accumulation of capital in these communities.

Critics say that new retailers merely drive out existing neighborhood businesses, provide only dead-end jobs, and result in the transfer of wealth out of the community when businesses owned by outside entities take their profits out. We strongly disagree, and support the expansion of new, high quality retailing in inner cities, including national chains, for many reasons.

First, profit as a percentage of sales for retail businesses is typically low, even for the best performers, so that any profits "taken out" of the community are dwarfed by the wages paid to employees. Wages are easily ten times or more the size of profits.

Second, unlike many other types of industries, most retail jobs are held by local residents. Although we do not argue that all such jobs provide a full "living wage," they help employees learn basic work skills. Also, many of these jobs are filled by youth, who are statistically much more likely to be unemployed and get into trouble with the law, and have an especially great need to learn basic work skills.

Third, not all retail and service jobs are as dead-end as they appear. Many retailers promote heavily from within. For example, at McDonald's, which employs 12% of all teenagers working in formal jobs, 67% of restaurant managers, 60% of senior management, and 33% of franchise owners began as crew workers.[62]

Fourth, it is well documented that the circulation of money within inner-city communities—the so-called money multiplier—is extremely low. For example, in the neighborhoods of Marshall Heights, Columbia Heights, and Anacostia in Washington DC, the leakage of grocery dollars ranges from 65% to 79%.[63] This means that the neighborhood's income creates few local jobs. More and better retailing, resulting in more local spending, would begin to improve this situation.

Fifth, local residents in almost every inner city pay more for basic goods than nearby urban and suburban residents—from 8 to 27% in the studies we have seen[64]—meaning that "a poor family of three that should spend about $2,700 a year on food would. . . . spend $700 a year more."[65] How tragic that our society's poorest citizens, who spend 34% of their after-tax income on food, pay more—and get worse selection and quality—than everyone else.[66] Rather than tolerate an inferior shopping experience, inner-city residents often suffer great inconvenience to travel outside their communities to shop—thereby exacerbating the outflow of jobs and capital. New, high quality retailing in inner cities can ameliorate these problems and help make a neighborhood attractive to existing and prospective residents. This, in turn, helps retain a strong middle class in these communities.

Sixth, retailers can act as anchor tenants and create a climate whereby other investment will occur. For example,

There hadn't been a single large-scale investment in Glenville, Ohio since the mid-1960s before Finast opened a superstore. At the same time, 32 condominiums ($75,000 each) opened next door. A 50-unit housing development is under construction nearby. Fifth World Bancorp opened a branch in the Finast store. Rite Aid set up a drugstore across the street. A few blocks away, a corporate partnership is restarting a shuttered factory.

"Finast," says the Rev. E.T. Caviness, president of Cleveland's Baptist Minister's Conference and director of Ohio's Civil Right Commission, "is the best thing that could have happened to us."[67]

It is a mistake to hold back competitive businesses to protect uncompetitive ones. While some local businesses will be hurt by the new competition—which has resulted in pitched battles in many cities[68]—many of them will adapt and even prosper. Other retailers (old and new) will benefit from the increased foot traffic that a major anchor tenant can generate. For example, the 14,000 people that Americas' Food Basket attracts to Boston's Uphams Corner neighborhood every week has contributed to the renaissance of the entire business district.

Finally, some retailers can be "export" businesses. For example, look at Boston's South Bay Mall, which draws customers from all over Boston and the suburbs because of its easy access to the adjacent expressway, or the recently opened Fairway supermarket in Harlem, which runs a shuttle bus to the Upper West Side of Manhattan and draws suburban commuters from the nearby West Side Highway. Or consider one of our clients, Americas' Food Basket supermarket, which recently opened a food wholesaling business focusing on Latino-oriented products that serves the greater Boston area.

BARRIERS TO CHANGE

Any effort to move more toward a market-based economic strategy for inner cities engenders suspicion and even outright resistance from some important constituencies. We have found little resistance from businesspeople—quite to the contrary. The barriers to change are most likely to appear in some (not all) community organizations and sometimes in government.

The concentration of poverty in inner cities has led to many programs to serve the poor, which not only attract more poor families but also result in a network of institutions that depend on the existence of poverty for their survival. These numerous institutions are major employers in inner cities, and can be resistant to changes in the status quo.

In recognizing this reality, we want to emphasize that we have immense and growing respect for the many people and organizations who courageously provide much-needed, effective assistance to disadvantaged inner-city residents. What we object to are the politicized, ineffective organizations that are concerned not with the genuine needs of their communities, but with their own survival. We are hopeful that further education and dialogue revolving around the principles of economic strategies will lead to their widespread adoption.

The relationship between welfare reform and an economic strategy. As welfare reform becomes more likely, the need for more jobs for inner-city residents becomes even more pressing. Forcing welfare recipients to enter the workforce is futile if there are no jobs available.

An important component of any welfare reform measure should be the elimination of disincentives to enter the workforce. Currently, if someone is motivated and fortunate enough to find a job, the welfare safety net disappears quickly, which greatly reduces the fruits of one's labor, especially if the job does not pay well. In many states, a welfare recipient loses medical benefits if income exceeds a meager $150 per week. A six-year study of single mothers on welfare found that "in order to leave the welfare rolls without lowering their living standards, the mothers studied would need an extra $190 a month for work-related costs (including transportation, child care, and clothing), plus $128 for higher rents (lower housing subsidies)."[69] The perverse incentives also afflict those trying to escape welfare via entrepreneurship. For example, if a person on welfare accumulates liquid assets exceeding $1,000, he or she loses eligibility, and a welfare recipient can only own a car (an essential requirement of most entrepreneurs) up to a value of $1,500.

The solution is not to drop the safety net, but rather to phase it out as someone's income rises. To quote Leonard M. Greene, Director of the Institute for Socioeconomic Studies, "While welfare may 'pay' better than work in the short term, work nearly always pays better over the long haul. So we should offer the poor assistance without penalizing them for earning their own money."[70] Similarly, the maligned Earned Income Tax Credit should be enhanced, with appropriate modifications to minimize abuses, not eliminated. Finally, while early attempts have had a mixed record, we endorse the principle of requiring work from welfare recipients who are able to do so.

CONCLUSION

Inner cities must compete, and can compete. Developing a new strategy will require an understanding of what is unique about each inner city, how to build on its advantages, and a plan to eliminate or reduce the many disadvantages to conducting business. This process will require the commitment and involvement of business, government, and the nonprofit sector.

As funding for traditional urban programs comes under increasing attack, those of us concerned with inner cities should not be defending failed past approaches. Instead, we need new, market-oriented strategies that will build on strengths and engage the private sector. Despite popular perceptions, there is genuine economic opportunity in inner cities. Working together, we can unlock it.

ACKNOWLEDGMENT

This article has benefited from extensive research and assistance by Whitney R. Tilson, Executive Director of the Initiative for a Competitive Inner City. I would also like to thank Barbara J. Paige and Ronald A. Homer for their invaluable comments, and many other students and individuals whose research over the last several years made this article possible.

NOTES

1. *Harvard Business Review* (May-June, 1995): 55–71.

2. Atlanta, Baltimore, Boston, Chicago, Los Angeles, Newark, New York City, Oakland, and Washington DC. We define inner-city areas as census tracts where the median household income is no more than 80% of the median for the SMSA and where the unemployment rate is more than 25% greater than the state average.

3. From "The Competitive Advantages of Inner City Baltimore," by Mercer Management Consulting and the Initiative for a Competitive Inner City, unpublished, 1995. Sources of data: 1990 Census, Dun & Bradstreet data, Mercer analysis.

4. *New York Times,* 9/4/95.

5. *New York Times,* 10/2/94. p. 5.

6. "One Good Apple," *Time* (January 15, 1996); "How to Run a Police Department," George Kelling, *City Journal* (Autumn 1995).

7. Richard D. Bingham and Robert Mier (Eds.), *Theories of Local Economic Development: Perspectives from Across the Disciplines*, (SAGE Publications, 1993), p. i.

8. John P. Blair, *Local Economic Development*, (SAGE Publications, 1995), p.22.

9. See analysis of literature of inner-city economic development in "Benchmarking Theory and Best Practices of Inner City Economic Development," by Dwight Hutchins and Kate Moriarty. Harvard Business School and Kennedy School of Government, unpublished, May, 1996.

10. See Jeffrey D. Sachs and Andrew M. Warner, "Economic Reform and the Process of Global Integration." Brookings Papers on Economic Activity, 1995:1,1–118.

11. For example, a study by the New York City Department of Consumer Affairs showed one supermarket for every 5,700–7,000 residents of the Upper East Side, Brooklyn Heights, and Upper West Side, but only one supermarket for every 63,818 residents of parts of Williamsburg and Bedford-Stuyvesant. Cited in *New York Times,* 6/6/92.

12. *New York Times,* 6/27/93, p. 5.

13. *Wall Street Journal,* 6/8/92, p. 1.

14. Ibid.

15. *New York Times* op. cit.

16. For further information on inner-city retailing, see "Inner City Retailing" by Jon Patricof and Willy Walker. Harvard College and Harvard Business School, unpublished, May 1995. For information on franchising, see "Inner City Franchising Opportunities" by Paul Singh, unpublished, 1996.

17. *New York* magazine, 11/21/94.

18. *Wall Street Journal,* 7/25/96, p. B1.

19. *New York Times,* 1/8/96.

20. *Boston Globe,* 12/3/95.

21. "Banking on the New America: The Business Case for Investing in the Inner City." Speech by Richard M. Rosenberg, Chairman and CEO of BankAmerica Corporation to 17th Annual Real Estate and Economics Symposium, UC Berkeley Center for Real Estate and Urban Economics, San Francisco, December 14, 1994.

22. *New York Times,* 8/18/ 95.

23. 69 students * $42.50/hour * 120 hours/student = $351,900. Hourly wages based on $1,700 weekly salaries paid by Boston area consulting firms to summer MBA student interns.

24. Number of new jobs at each client * average wage rate for each client * 1,800 hours per employee per year. According to clients, almost all new jobs have gone to inner-city residents.

25. *New York Times,* 4/28/95.

26. See Harvard Business School case study, *Bidwell Training Center,* 9-693-087, 1993.

27. See *New York Times,* 4/21/96.

28. See study of the Red Hook area of Brooklyn by Philip Kasinitz and Jan Rosenberg, "Why Enterprise Zones Will Not Work: Lessons from a Brooklyn Neighborhood." *City Journal* (Autumn 1993): 63–9. Also, see their latest unpublished work, cited in *The Washington Post National Weekly Edition,* March 25–31, 1996, p. 34. Also, see study by Shorebank Corporation that shows that of the nearly 46,000 light manufacturing jobs in the Austin neighborhood of Chicago, fewer than 10% go to local inner city residents (interviews with Shorebank senior management, 2/12/96). Finally, see various enterprise zone studies cited in a footnote below.

29. See unpublished study by Philip Kasinitz cited in *The Washington Post National Weekly Edition,* March 25–31, 1996, p. 34.

30. John A. Shields, CEO, First National Supermarkets, *New York Times,* 6/27/93, p. 5.

31. Comments made by the CEO of Dreyers Ice Cream at the Holy Names College Business Symposium in October, 1995.

32. *Wall Street Journal,* 3/3/94, p. 1.

33. See survey led by Margaret Simms conducted by the Joint Center for Politi-

cal and Economic Studies (in conjunction with *Black Enterprise* magazine and the National Minority Supplier Development Council) published in *Black Enterprise* June 1996. Also, see various studies by Prof. Timothy Bates, Wayne State University.

34. *Business Week,* 7/31/95.

35. For example, "the citizens of Detroit must contend with a total tax burden that is about *seven times* higher than the average Michigan municipality." Stephen Moore, Director of Fiscal Policy Studies, Cato Institute, cited in *The Detroit News,* 12/19/93.

36. A General Accounting Office study found that fewer than 30% of employers cited "financial inducements" as an important location decision factor. Eleven other factors were more important.

37. "Academic studies have found that as little as 15% of the workers in some enterprise zones actually live there." *New York Times,* 1/26/96; in a Louisville, KY enterprise zone, only 14% of the jobs created by companies that received tax breaks were filled by people who were unemployed or on welfare, *New York Times,* 10/31/90, p. A18; in Indiana, only 6.35% of manufacturing jobs and 30% of retail jobs went to enterprise zone residents; "a survey of 155 zones in 28 states by the National Center for Enterprise Zone Research found that only 5.3% of zone businesses were minority-owned," *Financial World,* 9/1/92, p. 23.

38. For example, in New York City, the federal government is threatening to withdraw its $100 million contribution unless a political impasse between the city and state governments is resolved. See *New York Times,* 5/18/96, p. B1.

39. Quotations from interviews in Spring 1995.

40. "Finding Work in the Inner City: How Hard is it Now? How Hard will it be for AFDC Recipients?," Katherine Newman & Chauncy LeMon, Working Paper, October 1995.

41. Quotations from inner-city Baltimore manufacturer, interviewed April 1996; inner-city manufacturing and distribution businesses in New Jersey and Louisiana, interviewed June 1995; and manufacturer in Harrison, NJ, letter dated March, 1995.

42. For further background and analysis, see "A Survey and Analysis of the Inner City Job Training System" by Chelli Devadutt and Julie Fletcher. Harvard University Kennedy School of Government, unpublished, May, 1995.

43. *New York Times,* 11/7/93.

44. 1992 annual report.

45. 1991 Inner City annual report.

46. Interview with America Works, 2/21/95; company materials.

47. *Inc.* magazine, May 1994, p. 85.

48. Ibid, p. 86.

49. Ibid, p. 86.

50. "An Economic Analysis of Taxicab Regulation," Federal Trade Commission, 1984. Department of Transportation study, 1992.

51. Quoted in *New York Times,* 12/4/95.

52. *New York Times,* 5/19/96

53. *The Death of Common Sense,* Philip K. Howard, 1994, p. 106.

54. *City Journal* (Spring 1994): 54.

55. *Business Week,* 5/27/96, p. 80.

56. Quoted in *New York Times,* 12/4/95.

57. *Business Week,* 5/27/96, p. 80.

58. Frank Stafford and Sandra Hofferth, Panel Study of Income Dynamics, University of Michigan Institute for Social Research, ongoing study.

59. "It's Not a Wage Gap But an Age Gap," *New York Times*, 4/21/96.

60. Richard B. Freeman, "Help Wanted: Disadvantaged Youths in a Labor Shortage Economy," unpublished manuscript, 1989. Cited in Myron Magnet, *The Dream and the Nightmare*, 1993, p. 47.

61. Magnet, pp. 143–44.

62. Interview with McDonald's corporate communications department, 7/25/96.

63. "Action Plan for Community Retail and Economic Development in Washington D.C." Public Voice for Food and Health Policy, 1995, cited in *Washington Post*, 3/7/96.

64. 13-25% more than suburbanites and 27% more than New York's Lower East Side, New York's Community Food Resource Center, cited in *New York Times*, 6/27/93, p. 5 and *Wall Street Journal*, 7/25/96, p. B1; 8.8% more than suburbanites in a 1991 study by the New York City Department of Consumer Affairs, cited in "The Ghetto's Hidden Wealth," *Fortune*, 7/29/91.

65. *New York Times*, 6/27/93, p. 5.

66. Department of Labor study, cited in *The Economist* 10/10/92.

67. *Wall Street Journal*, 6/8/92, p. A5.

68. See LISC and Pathmark's efforts to gain approval for a new supermarket in Harlem.

69. Study by Katheryn J. Edin, Rutgers University, and Laura Lein, University of Texas at Austin, to be published by the Russell Sage Foundation, cited in *Business Week*, 5/20/96, p. 26.

70. *New York Times*, 6/24/96.

LOCATION PREFERENCES OF SUCCESSFUL AFRICAN AMERICAN-OWNED BUSINESSES IN ATLANTA

Thomas D. Boston and Catherine L. Ross

Revitalizing inner cities is one of the nation's most challenging problems. The failure to meet this challenge has led to an enormous waste in human and economic resources. The distress of the inner city is not fundamentally about dilapidated buildings and worn out infrastructures. It is about conditions that deprive individuals of the capacity to fulfill their human potential. Dilapidated buildings are important mainly because they house the broken spirits of those who have lost all hope of attaining a better life.

The core element of revitalizing inner cities is the restoration of human potential. This means creating communities where individuals have the opportunity and capacity to play an important role in determining their future. It also means reintegrating these communities, as equal partners, in the economic, political and cultural life of surrounding metropolitan areas.

As editors of this special issue of *The Review*, we have had the unique privilege of reading each of the splendid articles that precede this one. With this in mind, we will present information on a case study of successful African American-owned businesses in Atlanta, Georgia. In doing so, we will try to shed further light on the ideas that Michael Porter and others propose regarding the revitalization of the inner city. In particular, we will address four questions: (1) Where do successful African American-owned businesses locate in Atlanta? (2) Why do they locate there? (3) Whom do they employ? and (4) What are their business-related attributes?

Inner-city residents and society as a whole must develop a sense of optimism that the problems of these areas, though challenging, can be resolved. One reason that Michael Porter's ideas are refreshing is because they reflect a measure of optimism about the inner city that has not been seen for decades.

These areas are in desperate need of visionaries, creative thinkers, leaders and above all, entrepreneurs. They need individuals who can mobilize resources, both economic and human. Along with this, there are several conditions that are critical for success. First, there needs to be a plan that is comprehensive enough to allow progress to be diffused throughout the entire community, rather than being concentrated among a privileged few.

Second, there must be political support for critical improvements in infrastructure. Third, the opportunity cost of developing the inner city must be brought in line with the costs associated with competing alternatives. Finally, a balance must be maintained between individual profitability and the welfare of the community. This means that the process of tapping the "competitive advantages of the inner city" must contribute to improving its human potential rather than stifling it. In communities where genuine economic development is occurring, these conditions exist.

It is painfully clear that there is a difference between community revitalization and the accelerated growth of a few businesses or industrial districts. The benefits from the growth of industrial districts do not necessarily "trickle down" to the inner cities where they are located.

Economic growth is the process of creating wealth. Economic development on the other hand is the process of creating a balance between wealth generation and the improvement of the human condition. In communities that are experiencing development, this balance is usually achieved through resolving the competing interests of stakeholders. Too often however, the inner city does not have active stakeholders. Seldom do we see vigilant community associations or neighborhood business organizations in these areas. As a result, the equation becomes unbalanced in favor of interests that are outside of the community. Businesses and politicians either engage in benign neglect of the inner city, or exercise eminent domain to control it.

Porter is quite right in emphasizing the key role that businesses must play in revitalizing inner cities. But his critics are also correct to keep in focus the importance of maintaining a balance between profitability and the welfare of the whole community.

BACKGROUND

By now, the explosive growth of African American-owned businesses in the Atlanta Metropolitan area is well known. One figure best states this fact. The most recent Census Bureau *Survey of Black-Owned Business Enterprises*[1] reveals that between 1987 and 1992 the nation's African American-owned businesses increased by 46%, from 424,165 to 620,912. At the same time, all small businesses increased by 26%. But during this five-year-period, African American-owned businesses in the Atlanta Metropolitan area nearly doubled, increasing from 11,804 to 23,488.

Our research indicates that nationally, only about one-third of black business growth can be attributed to the growth in income in local areas. In Atlanta at least, minority business affirmative action programs have provided a tremendous stimulus to this growth. Over the last fifteen years, these programs have operated in the city, the county, the school system, the transit authority, the stadium authority, the hospital authority, and the olympic committee.

In 1994, we documented 1,451 minority and women-owned firms that are registered in these programs. Interestingly, the industries they represent are highly diversified, relatively fast growing, and very non-traditional. These businesses have nothing in common with the old "mom and pop" enterprises that formerly dominated the African American business landscape. For example, among these 1,451 firms, the top ten industries, ranked in order of the percent of firms in each, are: general building contractors (8.7%), computer and data processing (5.7%), engineering and architectural services (5%), services to buildings (4.8%), business services (4.6%), management and public relations (4.6%), special trades contractors (4%), machinery and equipment wholesalers (3.8%), commercial printing (3.3%), and electrical goods wholesale (3.1%).

What is happening in Atlanta is also occurring in metropolitan areas across the country especially in locations where minority set-aside programs have been effective. In Atlanta, a new African American entrepreneur has emerged. This new entrepreneur is young, well educated, operates increasingly in non-traditional industries, has significant management, administrative and business-related experience, and is an aggressive risk taker. This new entrepreneur thrives on "opportunity," and Atlanta has provided the vehicles for this.

THE NEW AFRICAN AMERICAN ENTREPRENEUR

A snapshot of the newly successful black entrepreneurs in Atlanta looks like this:[2] They are very well educated; in fact two-thirds have college degrees, one-fourth have graduate degrees; 80% are between the ages of 35 years and 54 years old; their preferred form of business organization is the corporation; they are heavily concentrated in providing business services; only two-thirds of them are married; 80% are first generation business owners; one-fourth of them operate businesses in neighborhoods where the annual family income is less than $25,000; 80% of them feel that they have a special responsibility to assist black communities; 85% believe that minority business affirmative action programs are beneficial to black business development; 50% of these business owners derive 15% or less of their revenue from the public sector; 80% of their employees are African American; 62% of their customers or clients are non-African American; 21% of their employees are from low income inner-city neighborhoods; and their average gross revenue is $606,208.

In this research, we will explore the locational attributes and business characteristics of the newly successful entrepreneurs of Atlanta in a degree of detail that has never before been undertaken. Who are they, what are their backgrounds, where are they located, who do they employ, how successful are they, and most importantly, how important are they in the struggle for inner-city revitalization?

For years, Tim Bates, the nation's leading researcher on African American-owned businesses, has sought answers to two important questions: (1) Do African American owned firms make a difference in generating employment opportunities for African Americans? (2) Do they make a difference in revitalizing low-income communities? Until recently, data limitations made these two questions very difficult to answer with any precision. But new studies are providing convincing evidence that African American firms are about eight times more likely to employ African Americans than are firms owned by non-African Americans.

Bates's recent book is devoted to this topic. Published in 1993, the book is entitled *Banking on Black Enterprise: The Potential of Emerging Firms for Revitalizing Urban Economies*.[3] He pioneers the use of the Census Bureau's Characteristics of Business Owners (CBO) data to examine the employment and community development potential of black-owned firms.

CBO data, first compiled in 1987, surveys 125,000 self-employed individuals and oversamples Blacks, Hispanics and other minorities and women. The data are unique because they are the only government source that provides a profile of the human capital characteristics of business owners along with a profile of the establishments they operate.

Using this information, Bates concludes that black business development is important to generating inner-city jobs and reversing urban decline. He advocates supporting newly emerging black-owned businesses in nontraditional industries. The rationale is that these businesses are not only experiencing a significant growth in financial and employment capacity, but they also employ a predominantly black workforce.

The rapid growth of newly emerging black businesses is due in large part to the changing human capital characteristics of black business owners, their more ethnically diverse consumer market, greater access to debt and equity capital, their geographic dispersions throughout metropolitan areas, and the new market opportunities made available to minority-owned firms by set-aside programs at the federal, state and local levels.

Because of the growing employment capacity of black-owned businesses, Bates argues for public policies targeted at supporting them. He suggests that such policies will stimulate community development because emerging black businesses, even when not located physically within the urban poverty areas, still employ workers that are predominantly black. By contrast, he finds that black workers are a distinct minority in white-owned firms, even when such firms are located in distressed urban areas that are predominantly black.[4]

WHY SOME POLICYMAKERS OVERLOOK BLACK-OWNED BUSINESSES

There is no question that black-owned businesses must play an important role in community revitalization. But usually these businesses are not given serious consideration as a solution to urban distress. A part of this problem is due to the lingering perception that virtually all black businesses are still marginal enterprises that operate in traditional industries such as personal service and retail. But these aggregate statistics, reported in Census Bureau surveys, mask an important underlying dynamic that is taking place among newly emerging black businesses.

One limitation of CBO data used by Bates is that it cannot provide information on the location of emerging black-owned businesses. It is true that such businesses employ predominantly black workforces. But the workers and firms may be located in middle-class suburban communities. If this is the case, there may not be an association between promoting black businesses and reducing urban unemployment and poverty. But by examining primary data on Atlanta, we will show that there is indeed an association between the two and the notion that successful black-owned businesses have abandoned the city for the suburbs is incorrect.

Studies have also demonstrated that the Census Bureau's *Survey of Minority-Owned Business Enterprises, Black*, the most frequently used data for information on African American businesses, has a critical omission. That is, by omitting subchapter C corporations from its survey universe, census data understates the employment and financial capacity of African American-owned businesses by perhaps as much as 50% or more.[5] The Census Bureau has acknowledged this omission.[6] It is important to keep this limitation in mind when attempting to gauge the progress of African American business growth. In particular, this limitation contributes greatly to the perception that these businesses are still marginal enterprises. Yet, the most significant growth is taking place among businesses that are not included in the Census Bureau's survey.

Another reason why black businesses are overlooked is because there is a growing "misperception" that virtually all successful black-owned businesses are moving to the suburbs.[7]

The Main Argument

In Atlanta, the most successful African American entrepreneurs have significant financial and employment capacities, employ mainly African American workers, locate mainly in African American neighborhoods and recruit heavily from low income neighborhoods. If African American-owned businesses are about eight times more likely to employ African American workers than are all firms, and if these same firms are located mainly in African American neighborhoods and recruit a large percentage of their workforce from inner-city neighborhoods, what should we conclude about their importance to the revitalization effort?

We have to conclude that an important element of any strategy to revitalize inner cities, at least where African Americans reside, must be a focus on the promotion of African American-owned businesses. Hence, policies that promote the formation of African American businesses are likely to contribute positively to the revitalization effort, while policies that adversely affect this process are likely to have a negative effect. But the key to business promotion is opportunity. For black entrepreneurs, opportunity matters, and strategies must be designed to enhance it. By contrast, strategies that deny or short circuit opportunity, will also short circuit the revitalization effort.

It is important to note that we are not claiming that black-owned businesses are revitalizing Atlanta's inner cities. But we *are* claiming that were they to exist in sufficient numbers, they would have a greater impact than perhaps any other strategy.

Data

Data for this study are derived from two sources. First, we were allowed exclusive access to the City of Atlanta's and Fulton County's Office of Contract Compliance certification records on minority-owned firms. These records include a complete financial profile of firms as well as resumes of business owners. We examined records on 876 firms owned by minorities and white women, of which 722 are owned by African Americans. These firms were certified either in 1992 or 1993; therefore financial information reflects these years. Additionally, we mailed a survey instrument to all 1,451 minority-owned and white women-owned firms certified with various public agencies in the Atlanta Metropolitan area. Excluding surveys returned for bad addresses, the response rate was 28%. This includes 233 firms owned by African Americans. Compliance data collection was completed in the Spring of 1994. The survey was completed in January of 1995.

WHERE DO SUCCESSFUL AFRICAN AMERICAN-OWNED FIRMS LOCATE?: RESULTS FROM COMPLIANCE DATA

Table 1 provides information on the financial and employment characteristics of firms in the compliance data. The results indicate that 57.9% of these firms are corporations and their mean revenue is $855,548. Nationally, only 4 percent of African American firms are corporations and their mean gross revenue is $555,545. While the mean revenue of all African American-owned firms was $52,000 in 1992, the mean revenue of the firms in our compliance data set is $606,208. Clearly, this is a very select group. The table indicates that these corporations employ 5,080 workers; thus 79.3% of all employment is concentrated in corporations. Likewise, Table 4 indicates that all firms employ 6,410 workers of whom 4,944 are African American workers.

Table 2 provides information on the educational attainment of these

TABLE 1
Ownership and Revenue Characteristics of African American-Owned Firms, Atlanta Metropolitan Area, 1993

Legal Form of Ownership	Number of Firms	Percentage of Total	Mean Revenue of Firms	Number of Employees	Percentage of Total	Mean Number of Employees
Proprietorship	278	38.5%	$153,209	1,132	17.7%	4.39
Partnership	26	3.6%	$527,049	198	3.1%	7.92
Corporation	418	57.9%	$855,548	5,080	79.3%	12.86
Total	722	100.0%	$606,208	6,410	100.0%	9.45

Source: Office of Contract Compliance, City of Atlanta and Fulton County.

business owners. It reveals that 83% have attended college, 62% hold college degrees, 29.8% have attended graduate school and 22.2% hold graduate degrees. Finally, Table 3 provides information on the industry distribution, income and racial characteristics of the neighborhoods where these firms are located. These firms are most heavily concentrated in construction (26.3%), business services (24.4%), engineering and management services (14.4%), and wholesale services (11.6%). The table also gives the mean revenue of the zip code where the firms are located. This information was derived by using a geographic information system to cross-reference the income and racial characteristics of three counties in the Atlanta MSA to the zip codes of firms in the compliance data. These counties are Fulton (where the City of Atlanta is located), Cobb and Dekalb. A small portion of the City of Atlanta extends eastward into Dekalb County.

The data reveal that, except for agriculture and mining (which are not inner-city enterprises and therefore not of interest in this study) firms located in the highest income areas tend to be concentrated in the following industries: business services ($40,577), communications, ($38,644), other retail ($37,383), other transportation services ($36,996), engineering and management services ($36,935), and wholesale ($34,812). By contrast, firms in the lowest income neighborhoods tend to be concentrated in food and eating establishments ($19,333; however there is only one observation), real estate ($24,959), light manufacturing ($26,705), other services ($27,597) and personal services ($29,163). The percent of the population that is black residing in these neighborhoods is provided in the last column of the table.

TABLE 2
Educational Attainment of African American Business Owners
Atlanta Metropolitan Area, 1993

Highest Educational Level Attained	Number of Principal Owners	Percentage of Total
High School Degree	24	4.6%
Technical or Vocational Degree	64	12.4%
Some College or Associate Degree	107	20.7%
College Graduate	184	35.5%
Some Graduate School	24	4.6%
Graduate or Professional Degree	115	22.2%
Total	722	100.0%

Source: Office of Contract Compliance, City of Atlanta and Fulton County

This column provides insight into the kinds of industries that tend to be located in neighborhoods of particular racial composition. For example, personal services are concentrated in neighborhoods that are 83% black. This is exactly what one would expect. Other industries that are found in predominately black neighborhoods are; other services (74%), health services (69%), light manufacturing (67%), real estate (66%), and construction (64%). Also, we expect retail food service to be located in such neighborhoods, but our data contains only one observation on such establishments.

Michael Porter uses a very liberal working definition of the inner city. He defines it as census tracts where "the median household income is no more than 80% of the median for the MSA and where the unemployment rate is more than 25% greater than the average for the State."[8] By this definition, virtually all of Fulton County, which encompasses the City of Atlanta, would qualify as an inner city. Specifically, the 1990 median family income of the Atlanta MSA was $36,051 while the median income of Fulton County was $29,978 (or 83% of the former). As such, Porter's very broad definition is counter-intuitive. That is, when we think of the inner city, we have in mind certain distinct geographical areas with specific socioeconomic attributes, not vast regions of the county. Of course, we sympathize with his attempt to reduce the concept to a quantifiable standard, and perhaps if we were not analyzing one city we would be forced to do likewise. However, the limitations of doing so should be recognized.

TABLE 3

Industry Distribution of African American Business by Neighborhood Characteristics, Atlanta Metropolitan Area, 1993

Standard Industrial Classification	Number of Firms	Percentage of Total	Income of Zip Code Where Firm is Located[1]	Mean Percent of the Population in Zip Code that is Black[2]
Agriculture and Mining	3	0.4%	$53,981	41.0%
Business Services	176	24.4%	$40,577	46.0%
Communications	4	0.6%	$38,644	45.0%
Other Retail	25	3.5%	$37,383	45.0%
Other Transportation	6	0.8%	$36,996	38.0%
Engineering and Management Services	104	14.4%	$36,935	51.0%
Wholesale	84	11.6%	$34,812	57.0%
Construction	190	26.3%	$33,612	64.0%
Health Services	12	1.7%	$33,148	69.0%
Finance and Insurance	13	1.8%	$32,755	53.0%
Local Transportation and Trucking	15	2.1%	$31,763	59.0%
Personal Services	6	0.8%	$29,163	83.0%
Other Services	56	7.8%	$27,597	74.0%
Light Manufacturing	20	2.8%	$26,705	67.0%
Real Estate	7	1.0%	$24,959	66.0%
Retail (Food and Eating)	1	0.1%	$19,333	75.0%
Total	722	100.0%	$35,291	57.0%

Source: Office of Contract Compliance, City of Atlanta and Fulton County
Note:
1. This value is derived for each industry by taking the average of the median income of zip codes where firms are located.
2. This value is derived for each industry by taking the average of the percent blacks in each zip code where firms are located.

Rather than offering a definition of the inner city, we will simply disaggregate communities by income thresholds and examine the outcome based on this. Realistically speaking, a precise definition of the inner city is very elusive. Attempts to do so are somewhat reminiscent of earlier attempts by development economists to define the "Third World." Intuitively, researchers understood clearly the phenomena associated with Third World economies. But attempts to define it created contradictions. It was variously defined as countries in the Southern Hemisphere, countries below a certain per capita income threshold, former colonial countries, and even countries of color. In the end, the definition was not as important as the collective consciousness about its common attributes. We believe the same thing is true for the inner city.

Table 4 indicates that in the highest poverty neighborhoods, that is, neighborhoods where the median family income is $15,000 or less, we find only 3% of these successful black owned businesses. Such neighborhoods account for 14% of all families in the three county Atlanta MSA, or 58,425 out of 417,618 families. In zip codes where the median family income is between $15,000 and $25,000 (where $25,000 is 69% of the median income of the Atlanta MSA), we find 23.7% of all African American businesses and 98,488 families or 15.4% of all families. Combined, we find that 26.6% of all black-owned businesses examined in our data are located in neighborhoods where the median family income is $25,000 or less.

Except for the very poorest neighborhoods, we find successful African American-owned businesses, examined in our data, well represented in lower-income communities. Table 4 also reveals that the most successful black-owned businesses, as measured by gross revenue, are located in the lowest income neighborhoods. That is, the mean revenue of businesses in neighborhoods where income is $15,000 or less is $2,089,239. Similarly, the median revenue of these firms is also higher than that of firms in other neighborhoods. The same is true for businesses in neighborhoods where family income varies between $15,000 and $25,000.

Consider the employment characteristics of these firms. On average, they employ 9.4 workers, but in the two lowest income areas, they employ 11 workers. Therefore, the conclusion is inescapable that African American-owned firms represented in our data, having the highest revenue and employment capacities, tend to be located in lower income neighborhoods of Atlanta. The penultimate column of the table reports black employment within firms by income characteristics of neighborhoods. It reveals that 82% of the employees in black-owned firms in the lowest income neighborhood are black, while 75% of the employees of firms located in the highest income neighborhoods are black. While African American-owned firms tend to employ African American workers, this tendency is stronger among firms in the lowest income neighborhoods.

Finally, we attempted to determine the profitability of firms based on the places they chose to locate. Profitability in this case is measured by net profits before taxes divided by gross revenue. The last column of

TABLE 4
Distribution of African American Businesses by Income Characteristics of Zip Codes Where They are Located

Income Class of Zip Code Based on 1990 Census	Number of Firms	Percent of Total	Mean Revenue of Businesses in Income Class	Median Revenue of Businesses in Income Class	Total Employment in Zip Code	Mean Employment per Firm	Total Black Employment	Black Employment as a Percent of Total Employment	Median of Net Profits Divided by Gross Revenue for Firms in Income Class
$0 to $14,999	20	2.9%	$2,089,239	$412,283	187	11.69	153	81.8%	0.02
$15,000 to $24,999	161	23.7%	$707,021	$140,151	1,724	11.34	1,323	76.7%	0.03
$25,000 to $39,999	255	37.5%	$263,719	$110,148	1,568	6.56	1,277	81.4%	0.066
$40,000 to $59,000	182	26.8%	$723,485	$53,357	1,267	7.28	926	73.1%	0.036
$60,000 and Greater	62	9.1%	$576,181	$145,289	476	8.07	355	74.6%	0.022
Total/mean/median	722	100.0%	$606,208	$108,168	6,410	9.45	4,944	77.1%	0.039

Source: Office of Contract Compliance, City of Atlanta and Fulton County

Table 4 reports the median profitability for firms in various neighborhoods. Median profit rate for all companies is 3.9%. It is highest for
firms in neighborhoods with incomes between $25,000 and $39,999
(6.6%). It is lowest in· the highest income neighborhoods (2.2%), followed by the poorest neighborhoods (2.6%).

Charts 1 through 3 present this information on the spatial location of
black-owned firms visually. Chart 1 shows the distribution of the black
population by zip code. The highest concentration of blacks is found in
the central portion of Fulton County. This central region is almost coinci-
dent with the City of Atlanta. The clear, unshaded zip code located at the
center of the dark concentration, representing a 0% to 9% black population, is Fort McPherson Army base. The lighter shaded zip codes that are
north-north east of Fort McPherson comprise the central business district.
Chart 2 plots zip codes by median family income. Income is highest in
northern neighborhoods of the MSA, where African Americans are not
heavily concentrated. Finally, Chart 3 shows the location of the 722
successful black-owned firms. The largest number of firms are in areas
where blacks are most heavily concentrated.

WHY DO SUCCESSFUL BLACK-OWNED FIRMS CHOOSE SPECIFIC LOCATIONS?

In the survey, an open-ended question was asked of respondents in an
attempt to determine why they chose their current location. Responses
were then coded to derive the categories listed in Table 5. The results
indicate that the top six reasons are: To be close to customers and clients
(19.2%); Cost Considerations (19.2%); Because the location is convenient and accessible (16.3%); Because they operate out of a home office
(12.3%); To be close to home (9.4%); To be close to the central business
district (4.9%); and, To be close to the interstate (3.4%). All other reasons were insignificant.

The top three reasons account for 54.7% of all responses. These explanations are also compatible with Porter's idea of developing business
clusters as a way of attracting commerce to the inner city. Further, they
are consistent with several other strategies. These explanations can be
restated as follows: to attract businesses, we need to provide lower cost
office space in convenient locations that are close to nearby markets.

CHART 1
Black Percentage of Total Population by Zip Code, 1990
Cobb, Dekalb, & Fulton Counties

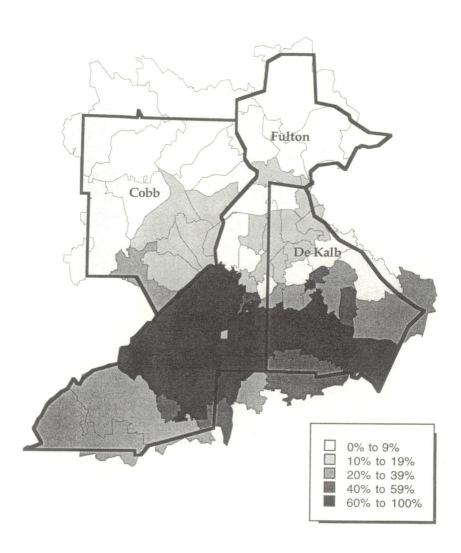

Source: STF3A, Bureau of the Census, U.S. Department of Commerce, 1992

CHART 2
Median Family Income, All Persons, by Zip Code, 1989
Cobb, Dekalb, & Fulton Counties

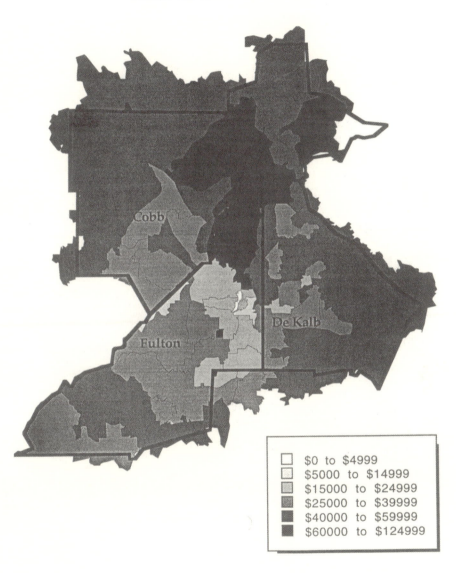

Source: STF3A, Bureau of the Census, U.S. Department of Commerce, 1992

CHART 3
Location of Black-Owned Businesses Examined, by Zip Code
Cobb, Dekalb, & Fulton Counties

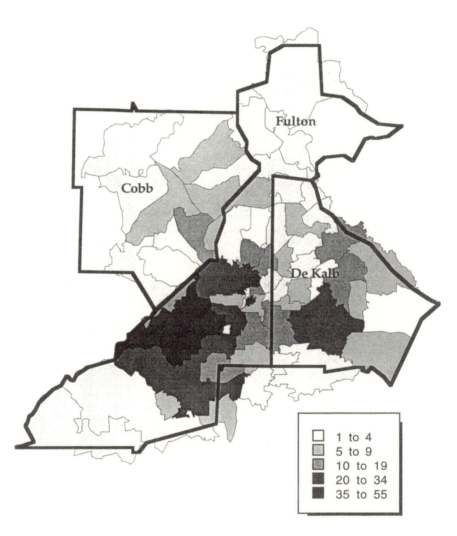

TABLE 5

Reason Given for Present Business Location, Atlanta African American Business Owners, 1994 Survey

Reason	Number of Responses	Percent of Total
Close to Customers/Clients	39	17.5%
Cost Effective	39	17.5%
Convenient and Accessible	33	14.8%
Home Office	25	11.2%
Close to Home	19	8.5%
Close to the CBD	10	4.5%
Close to Interstate	7	3.1%
For Employee's Convenience	5	2.2%
Transit Accessible	4	1.8%
Prestige and Visibility	3	1.3%
Market Demographics	3	1.3%
Unique Facilities	3	1.3%
Close to Suppliers	2	0.9%
Acquired Existing Business	2	0.9%
Own the Property	2	0.9%
Political Correctness	2	0.9%
Close to Airport	2	0.9%
Availability of Parking	1	0.4%
To avoid Close Competitors	1	0.4%
Other	1	0.4%
Total	223	100.0%

Source: Authors' survey of minority-owned businesses

Table 6 provides information on where these firms recruit the majority of their workforce. The City of Atlanta is encircled by Interstate 285, which is commonly referred to as the perimeter. The city itself is located at about the center of this quasi-circle. With this in mind, our survey finds that 34.5% of firms report that most of their employees reside outside of the perimeter but within the five-county MSA. Further, 25.6% of the firms report that their employees reside close to the central business district. Additionally, 18.8% indicate that most of their employees live outside of the CBD but within the City of Atlanta. Table 7 provides additional information on the residential patterns of employees in these firms. It shows that for firms located in the poorest neighborhoods, 23.3% of their employees are from inner-city neighborhoods. Firms in neighbor-

TABLE 6
Place of Residence of Most Employees. Atlanta African American Business Owners, 1994 Survey

Category	Number of Owners Responding	Percent of Total
Close to CBD	57	25.6%
Outside of CBD but Within City	42	18.8%
Outside of City, Within Perimeter	39	17.5%
Outside Perimeter (Within 5-County MSA)	77	34.5%
Outside 5-County MSA	4	1.8%
Missing Values	4	1.8%
Total	233	100.0%

Source: Authors' survey of minority-owned businesses

TABLE 7
Percent of Workforce Hired from Inner-City Neighborhoods Based on Where Firm is Located. Atlanta African American Business Owners, 1994 Survey

Median Income of Zip Code	Mean Percent of Employees From Inner City	Number of Owners Responding	Percent of All Respondents
$0 to $14,999	23.3%	10	4.5%
$15,000 to $24,999	29.8%	59	26.5%
$25,000 to $39,999	22.7%	66	29.6%
$40,000 to $59,000	14.7%	55	24.7%
$60,000 and Greater	11.9%	21	9.4%
Missing Values	17.4%	12	5.4%
Total	21.4%	223	100.0%

Source: Authors' survey of minority-owned businesses

hoods with incomes between $15,000 and $24,999 recruit 29.8% of their employees from the inner city. The lowest percentage of recruitment of inner-city residents occurs in firms located in neighborhoods where the median income is $60,000 or greater. They recruit 11.9% of their employees from the inner city. Overall, 21.4% of all employees in these firms are recruited from the inner city.

TABLE 8
Educational Requirement of Nonmanagement Employees for Firms, by Locations. Atlanta African American Business Owners, 1994 Survey

Category	Firms in Neighborhoods Where Median Imcome is Less than $25,000		Firms Located in Neighborhoods Where Median Income is Greater than $25,000	
	Percent of Total	Number Responding	Percent of Total	Number Responding
At Least High School	43.5%	30	40.3%	62
At Least Some College	18.8%	13	16.2%	25
At Least College Degree	14.5%	10	9.7%	15
Graduate Education	—	—	1.3%	2
No Educational Requirement	20.3%	14	26.0%	40
Missing Values	2.9%	2	6.5%	10
Total	100.0%	69	100.0%	154

Source: Authors' survey of minority-owned businesses

TABLE 9
Survey Question: Do You Feel that Black Entrepreneurs Have a Special Responsibility to Assist in Developing Black Communities?

Category	Firms in Neighborhoods Where Median Imcome is Less than $25,000		Firms Located in Neighborhoods Where Median Income is Greater than $25,000	
	Percent of Total	Number Responding	Percent of Total	Number Responding
Strongly Agree	47.8%	33	46.1%	71
Agree	36.2%	25	32.5%	50
Neither Agree nor Disagree	11.6%	8	11.7%	18
Disagree	1.4%	1	1.3%	2
Strongly Disagree	—	—	0.6%	1
Not Applicable	1.4%	1	3.9%	6
Missing Values	1.4%	1	3.9%	6
Total	100.0%	69	100.0%	154

Source: Authors' survey of minority-owned businesses

We also asked these respondents to indicate the level of educational attainment required of their nonmanagement employees. This question is designed to try to assess the quality of jobs offered by these firms. Table 8 indicates that 43.5% of firms residing in neighborhoods where the median income is $25,000 or less require at least a high school degree, while 20% of firms have no educational requirement. Similarly, 33% of firms require some college or a college degree. It is interesting that the educational requirement of black firms in lower income neighborhoods is slightly higher than that of firms in higher income neighborhoods. In particular, 26% of firms, in neighborhoods where income is greater than $25,000, indicate they have no educational requirement, 25.9% require some college or a college degree and 40.3% require at least a high school degree.

Finally, the survey attempts to assess the sense of responsibility that these black entrepreneurs have for developing black communities. The results are reported in Table 9 for black-owned firms located in higher income and lower income neighborhoods. For firms in higher income neighborhoods (that is, $25,000 and above), 76.8% either strongly agree or agree that black entrepreneurs have a special responsibility to develop black communities. Among firms located in lower income neighborhoods, 84% strongly agree or agree that blacks have a special responsibility in this regard.

CONCLUSIONS

This article provides quantitative information on the location patterns and financial characteristics of some of Atlanta's most successful black-owned firms. In the process, we have demonstrated that a crucial element of inner-city revitalization must be the promotion of African American-owned businesses. We have shown that the most successful of these firms tend to locate in lower income neighborhoods, they employ African American workers and they recruit a significant portion of their workforce from the inner city. Therefore, it is wrong to neglect these firms in favor of strategies designed to attract outside businesses into industrial districts of the inner city. These strategies have simply perpetuated the poverty of the inner city. Yet, we do not call for the wholesale abandonment of this strategy. Clearly, in the short-run, African American businesses do not have the capacity to absorb the labor supply in these communities. But their employment capacity is not only growing, it is much greater than is commonly recognized. It is not unreasonable to believe that with the right kind of public policies, within a period of ten years enough capacity can be built within these firms to reduce black unemployment to levels that are equal to unemployment in the surrounding areas. Although this is not a revolutionary objective, it would be a revolutionary accomplishment. Imagine a policy that would equalize racial disparities in unemployment. Nothing like this has existed thus far. Yet, the ingredients are clearly in place to achieve it. Our fear, however, is that policy analysts will continue to overlook the obvious in order to find more grandiose schemes to revitalize inner cities.

Our results suggest that a key component of the solution is to create "clusters" of African American-owned firms alongside, or in place of, the industrial clusters that Porter has so clearly described.

NOTES

1. U.S. Department of Commerce, Bureau of the Census, *1992 Economic Census: Survey of Minority-Owned Business Enterprises, Black* (Washington, D.C.: U.S. Government Printing Office, 1996).

2. Thomas D. Boston, *Strict Scrutiny: The Challenge to Minority Set-asides* (New York: Routledge, forthcoming, 1997).

3. Timothy Bates, *Banking on Black Enterprise: The Potential of Emerging Firms for Revitalizing Urban Economies* (Washington, D.C.: The Joint Center for Political and Economic Studies, 1993).

4. Ibid.

5. Thomas D. Boston, "Characteristics of Black-Owned Corporations in Atlanta: With Comments on the SMOBE Undercount." *The Review of Black Political Economy* Vol. 23, No. 4 (Spring, 1995); Margaret C. Simms, "Employment Potential Within Minority Businesses," Research in Progress (Washington, D.C.: Joint Center for Political and Economic Studies).

6. Nancy Feigenbaum, "Black Businesses Prosper: A Recent Census Bureau Study Undercounted Blacks' Success." *The Orlando Sentinel* (May 3, 1996): B1, B6.

7. Jeanne Saddler, "Young Risk-Takers Push the Business Envelope." *The Wall Street Journal* (May 12, 1994): B1–B2.

8. Michael Porter, "An Economic Strategy for America's Inner Cities: Addressing the Controversy" *The Review of Black Political Economy*, This issue, note 2, p. 333.